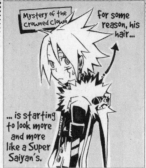

Mystery of the Crowned Clown

For some reason, his hair...

... is starting to look more and more like a Super Saiyan's.

I used to really like meat dishes, but lately they've lost their appeal. Is this what people mean when they say your tastes change when you grow up? But then I hated milk, miso soup, and bananas as a child, and I still do.

—Katsura Hoshino

Shiga Prefecture native Katsura Hoshino's hit manga series *D.Gray-man* has been serialized in *Weekly Shonen Jump* since 2004. Katsura's debut manga, "Continue," appeared for the first time in *Weekly Shonen Jump* in 2003.

Katsura adores cats.

D.GRAY-MAN
VOL. 11
The SHONEN JUMP ADVANCED
Manga Edition

STORY AND ART BY
KATSURA HOSHINO

English Adaptation/Lance Caselman
Translation/Toshifumi Yoshida
Touch-up Art & Lettering/Kelle Han
Design/Matt Hinrichs
Editor/Gary Leach

Editor in Chief, Books/Alvin Lu
Editor in Chief, Magazines/Marc Weidenbaum
VP, Publishing Licensing/Rika Inouye
VP, Sales & Product Marketing/Gonzalo Ferreyra
VP, Creative/Linda Espinosa
Publisher/Hyoe Narita

Printed in the U.S.A.

Published by VIZ Media, LLC
P.O. Box 77010
San Francisco, CA 94107

SHONEN JUMP ADVANCED Manga Edition
10 9 8 7 6 5 4 3 2 1
First printing, November 2008

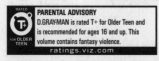

www.viz.com

www.shonenjump.com

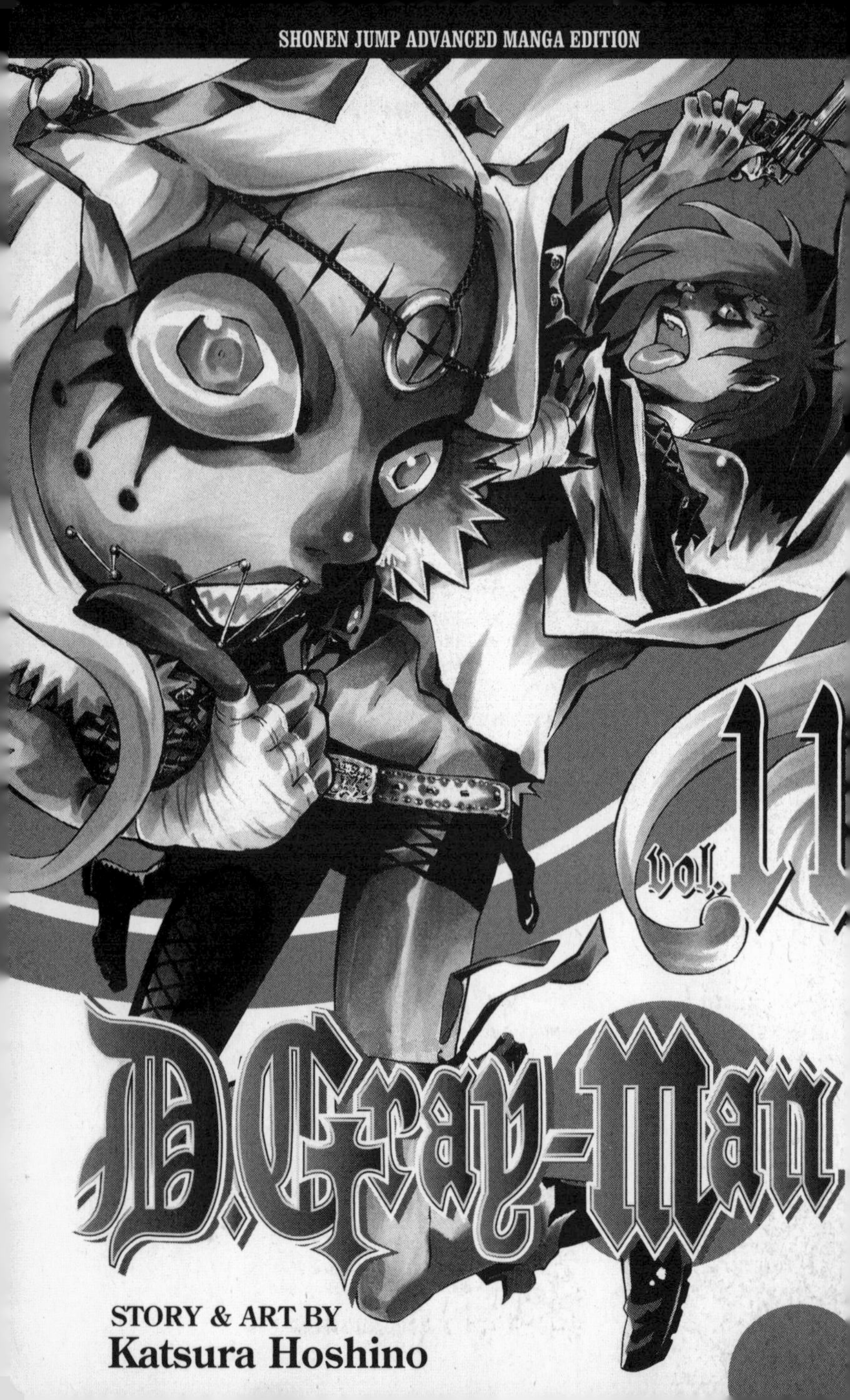
SHONEN JUMP ADVANCED MANGA EDITION
vol. 11
D.Gray-man
STORY & ART BY
Katsura Hoshino

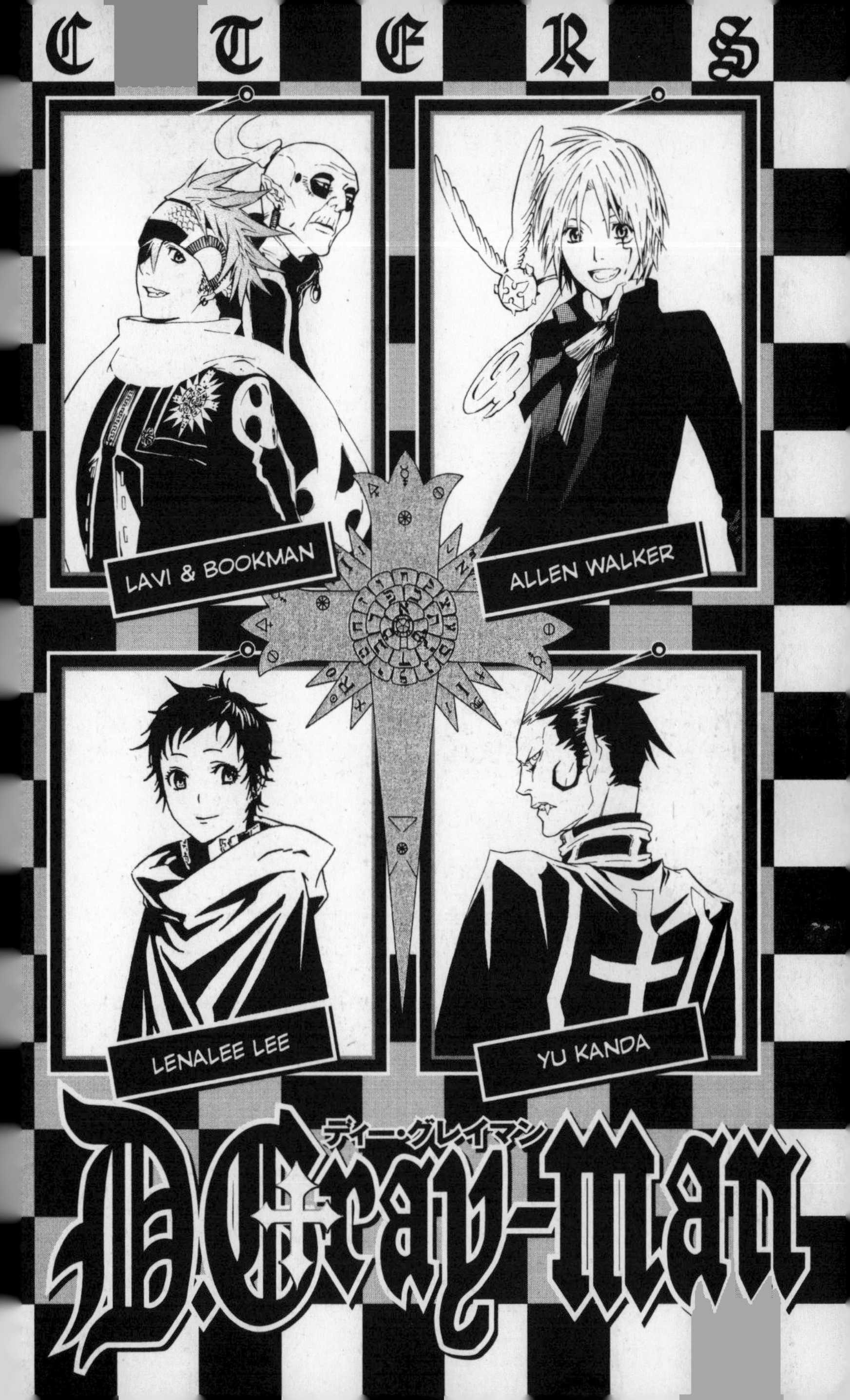
C T E R S
ALLEN WALKER
LAVI & BOOKMAN
YU KANDA
LENALEE LEE
D.Gray-man
ディー・グレイマン

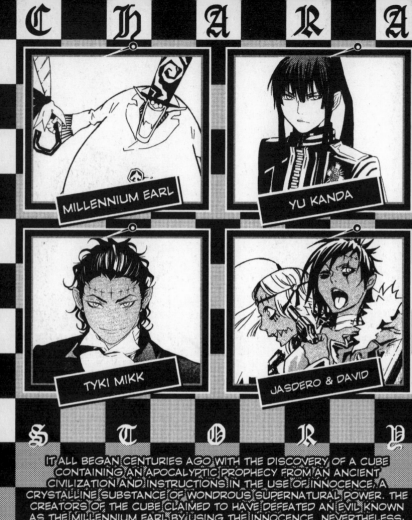

C H A R A

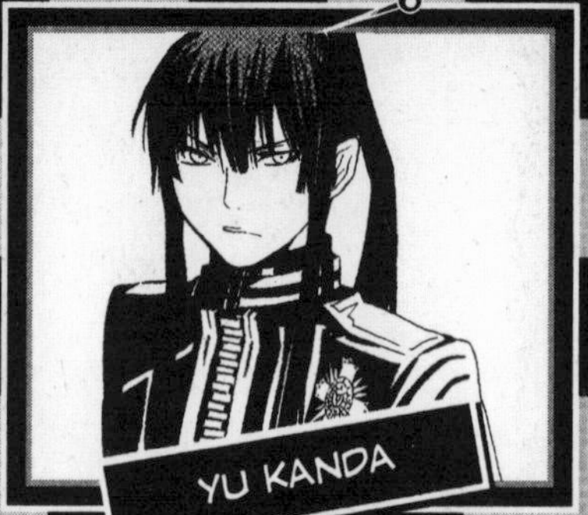
YU KANDA

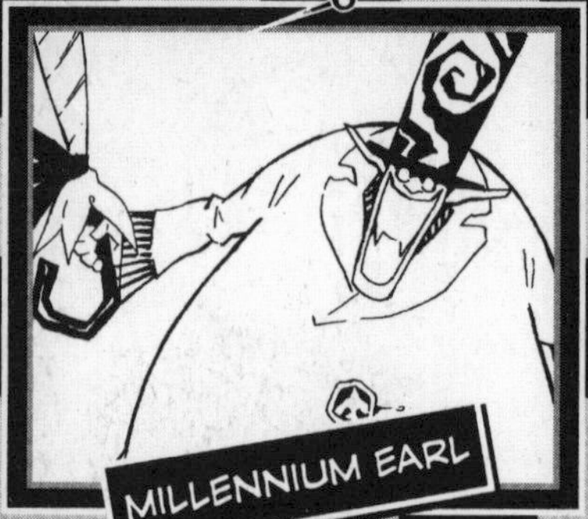
MILLENNIUM EARL

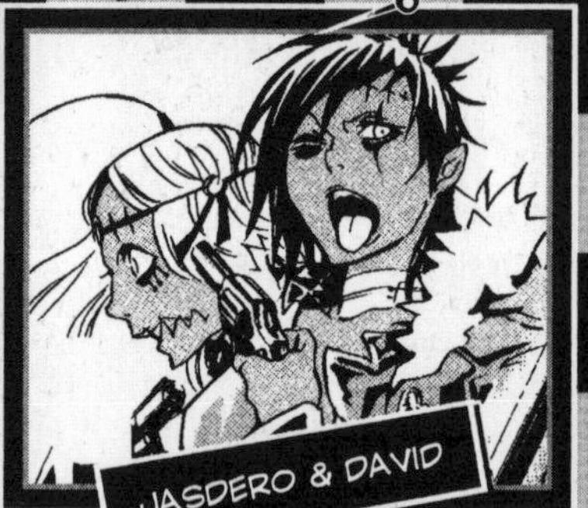
JASDERO & DAVID

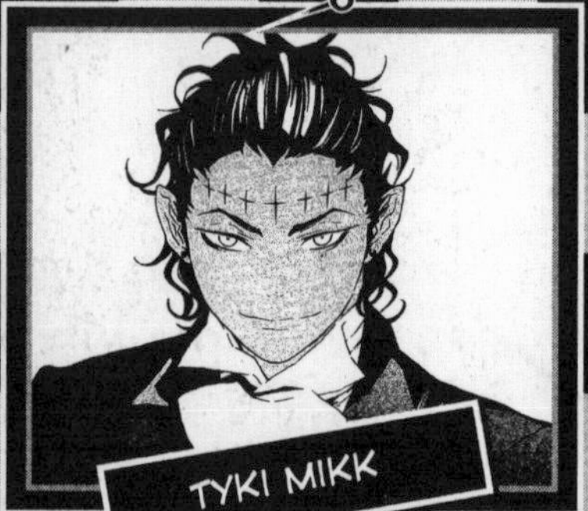
TYKI MIKK

S T O R Y

IT ALL BEGAN CENTURIES AGO WITH THE DISCOVERY OF A CUBE CONTAINING AN APOCALYPTIC PROPHECY FROM AN ANCIENT CIVILIZATION AND INSTRUCTIONS IN THE USE OF INNOCENCE, A CRYSTALLINE SUBSTANCE OF WONDROUS SUPERNATURAL POWER. THE CREATORS OF THE CUBE CLAIMED TO HAVE DEFEATED AN EVIL KNOWN AS THE MILLENNIUM EARL BY USING THE INNOCENCE. NEVERTHELESS, THE WORLD WAS DESTROYED BY THE GREAT FLOOD OF THE OLD TESTAMENT. NOW, TO AVERT A SECOND END OF THE WORLD, A GROUP OF EXORCISTS WIELDING WEAPONS MADE OF INNOCENCE MUST BATTLE THE MILLENNIUM EARL AND HIS TERRIBLE MINIONS, THE AKUMA.

ALLEN ARRIVES IN JAPAN TO JOIN HIS FELLOW EXORCISTS. THEY SOON FIND THEMSELVES TRAPPED INSIDE AN OBSOLETE ARK THAT HAS BEGUN TO DISINTEGRATE. WHILE TRYING TO REACH THE ONLY MEANS OF ESCAPE, THEY ENCOUNTER SKIN BORIC OF THE CLAN OF NOAH. KANDA FORCES THE OTHERS TO GO ON WITHOUT HIM, BUT HE AND BORIC BOTH PERISH IN THE BATTLE THAT FOLLOWS. NOW ALLEN AND THE OTHERS MUST MAKE THEIR WAY OUT OF THE ARK OR BE DESTROYED WITH IT. BUT THE FORCES OF THE EARL HAVE OTHER PLANS.

D.GRAY-MAN
Vol. 11

CONTENTS

THE 98TH NIGHT: TWIN'S ROOM

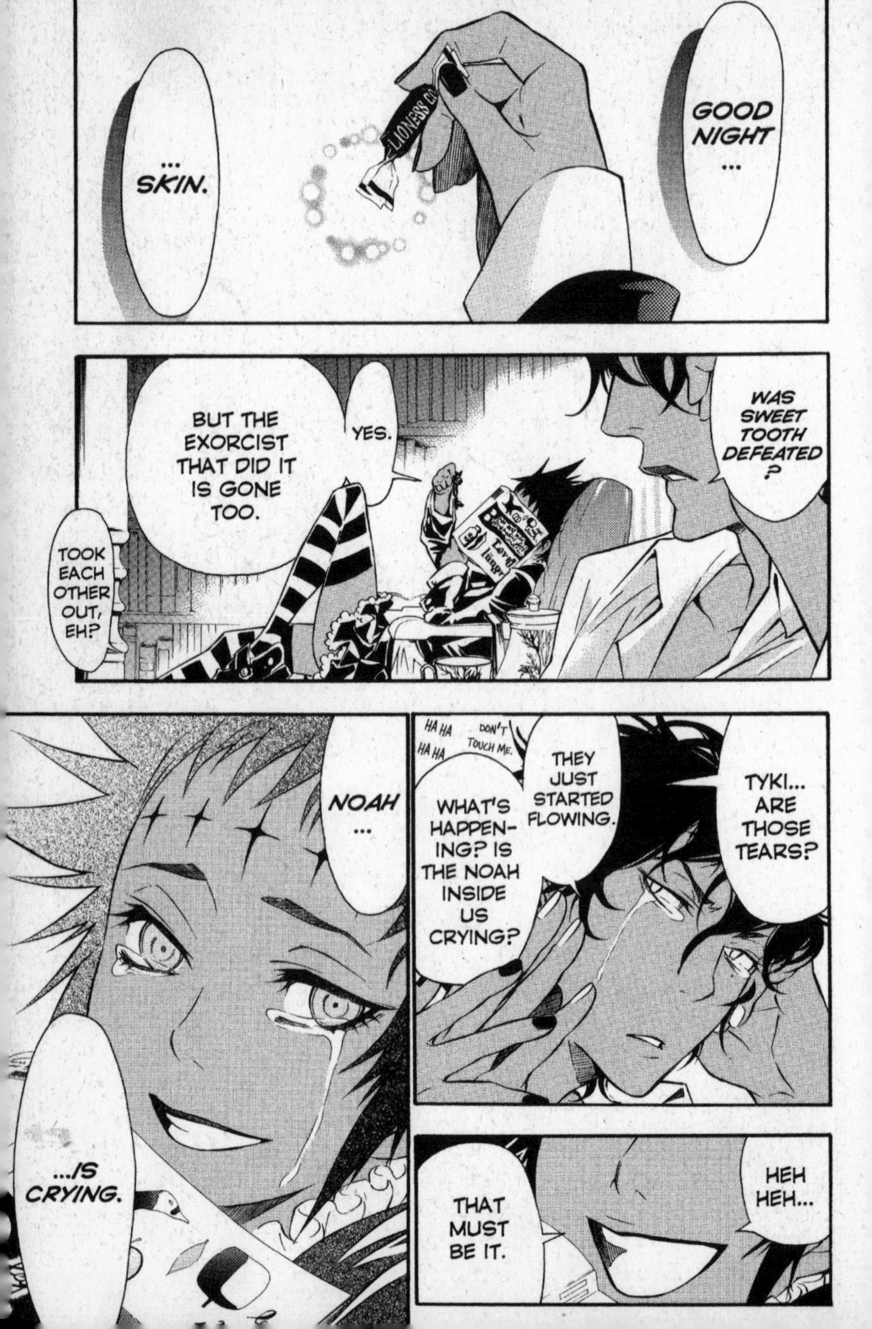
GOOD NIGHT...
...SKIN.
WAS SWEET TOOTH DEFEATED?
YES.
BUT THE EXORCIST THAT DID IT IS GONE TOO.
TOOK EACH OTHER OUT, EH?
TYKI... ARE THOSE TEARS?
THEY JUST STARTED FLOWING.
DON'T TOUCH ME.
HA HA HA HA
WHAT'S HAPPEN-ING? IS THE NOAH INSIDE US CRYING?
HEH HEH...
THAT MUST BE IT.
NOAH...
...IS CRYING.

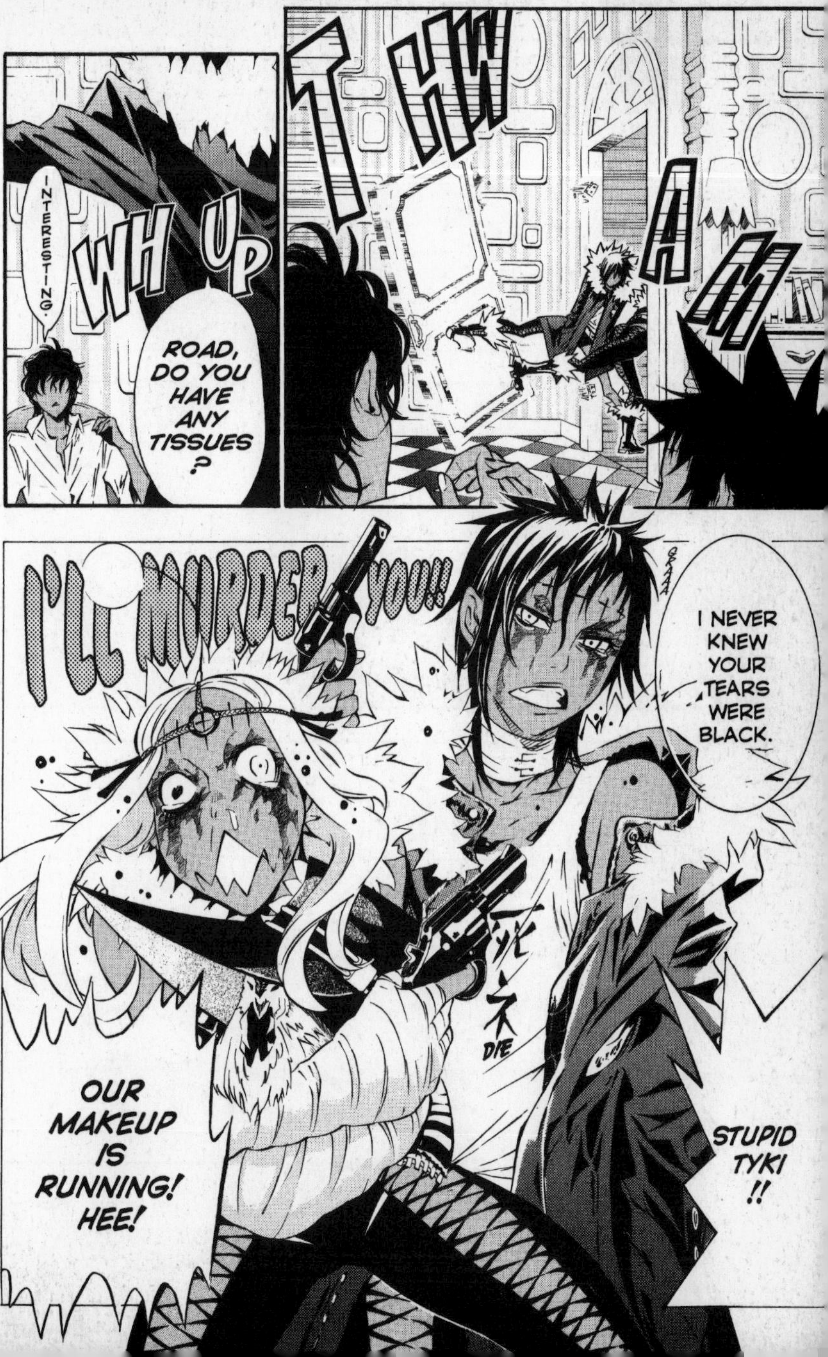
THWAM
WHUP
ROAD, DO YOU HAVE ANY TISSUES?
INTERESTING.
I NEVER KNEW YOUR TEARS WERE BLACK.
I'LL MURDER YOU!!
死ネ
DIE
STUPID TYKI!!
OUR MAKEUP IS RUNNING! HEE!

THE 98TH NIGHT: TWIN'S ROOM

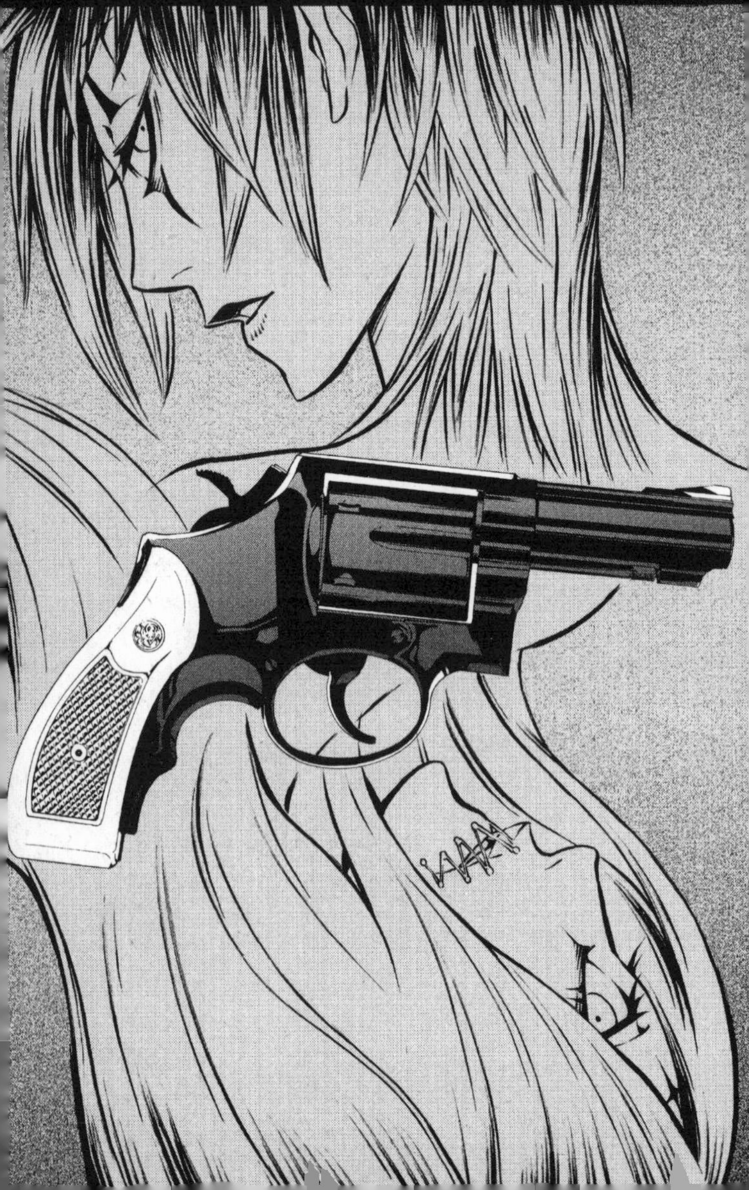

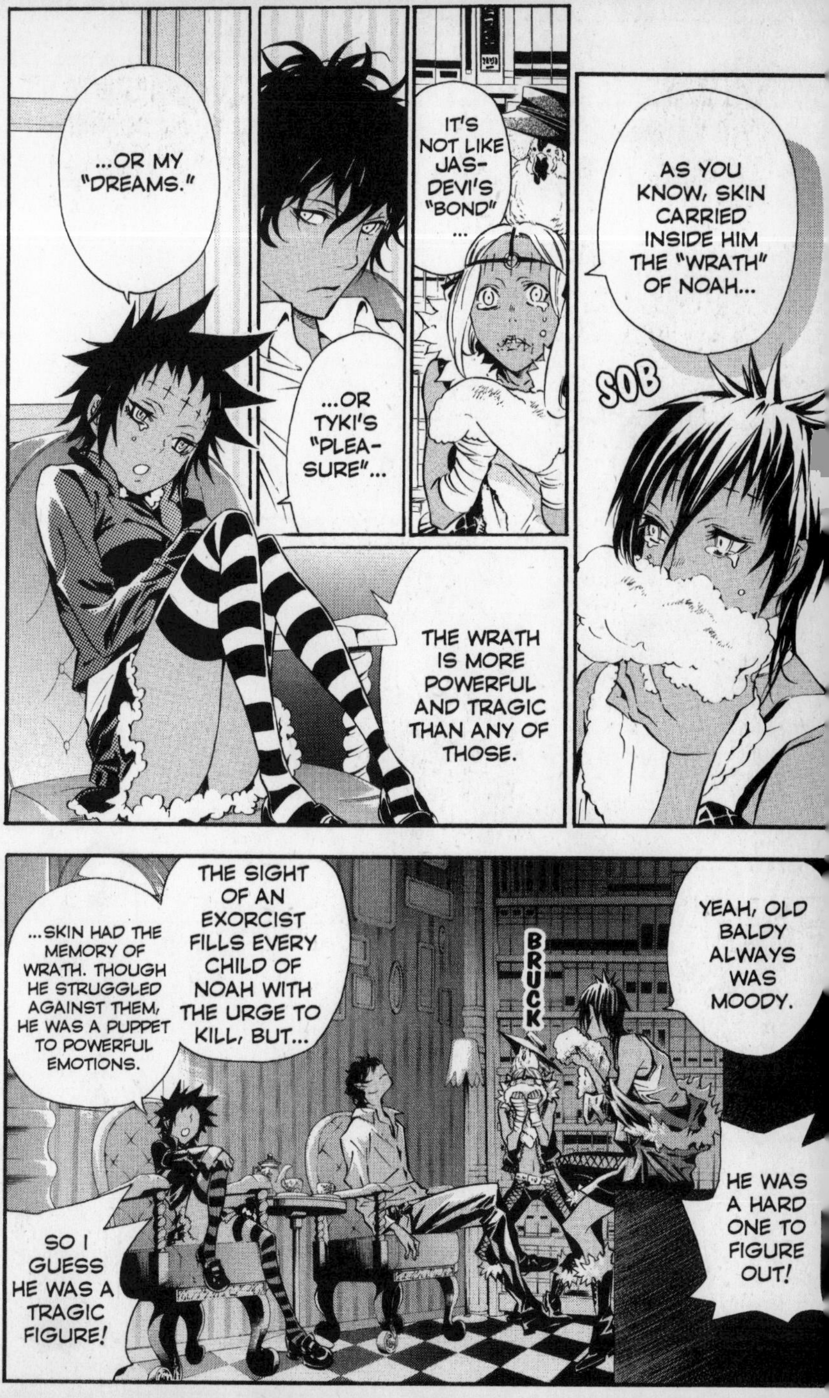
AS YOU KNOW, SKIN CARRIED INSIDE HIM THE "WRATH" OF NOAH...
SOB
IT'S NOT LIKE JAS-DEVI'S "BOND"...
...OR TYKI'S "PLEA-SURE"...
...OR MY "DREAMS."
THE WRATH IS MORE POWERFUL AND TRAGIC THAN ANY OF THOSE.
YEAH, OLD BALDY ALWAYS WAS MOODY.
HE WAS A HARD ONE TO FIGURE OUT!
BRUCK
THE SIGHT OF AN EXORCIST FILLS EVERY CHILD OF NOAH WITH THE URGE TO KILL, BUT...
...SKIN HAD THE MEMORY OF WRATH. THOUGH HE STRUGGLED AGAINST THEM, HE WAS A PUPPET TO POWERFUL EMOTIONS.
SO I GUESS HE WAS A TRAGIC FIGURE!

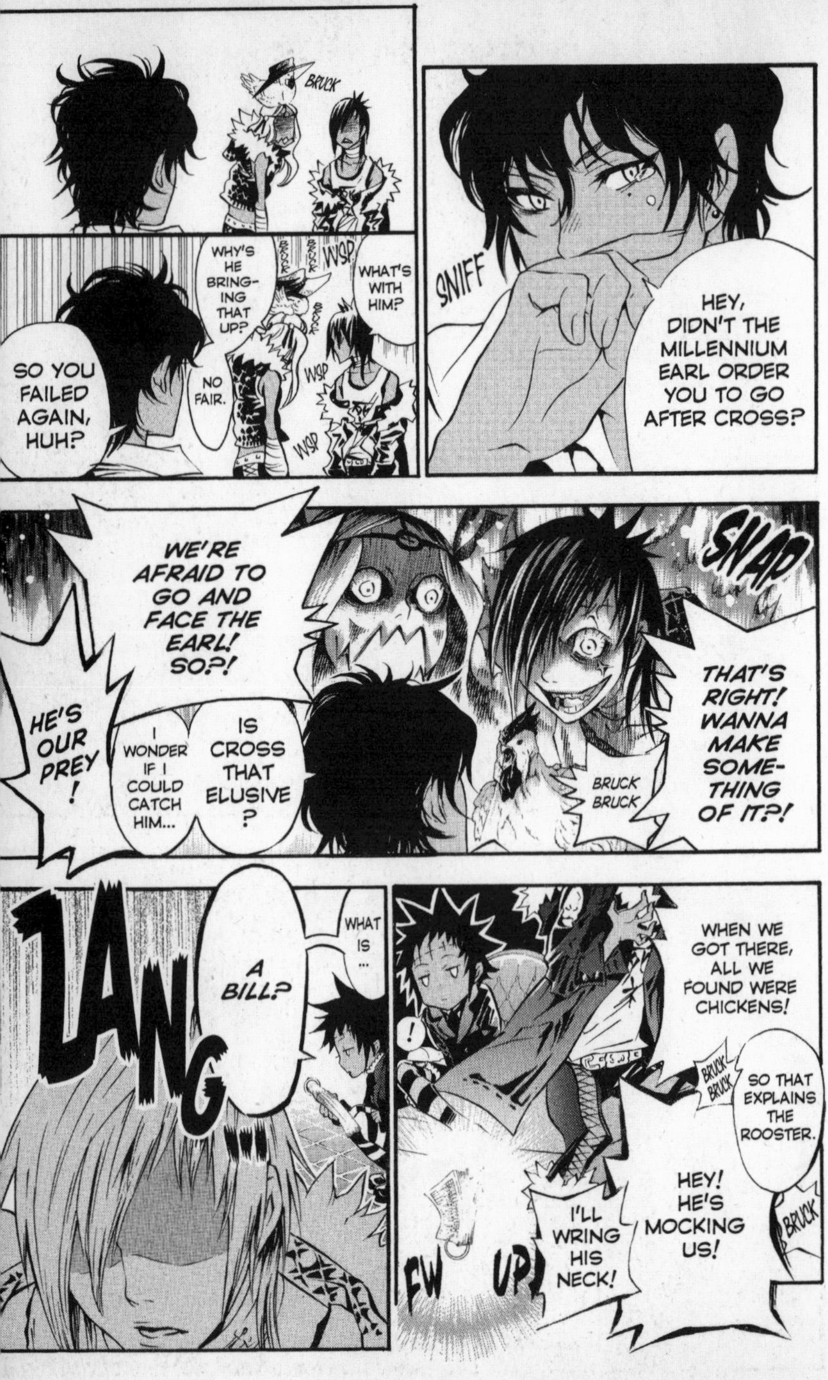

SNIFF
HEY, DIDN'T THE MILLENNIUM EARL ORDER YOU TO GO AFTER CROSS?
BRUCK
WHAT'S WITH HIM?
WHY'S HE BRING-ING THAT UP?
BRUCK BRUCK
BRUCK
WSP
NO FAIR.
WSP
WSP
SO YOU FAILED AGAIN, HUH?
SNAP
THAT'S RIGHT! WANNA MAKE SOME-THING OF IT?!
BRUCK BRUCK
IS CROSS THAT ELUSIVE?
I WONDER IF I COULD CATCH HIM...
WE'RE AFRAID TO GO AND FACE THE EARL! SO?!
HE'S OUR PREY!
WHEN WE GOT THERE, ALL WE FOUND WERE CHICKENS!
!
BRUCK BRUCK
SO THAT EXPLAINS THE ROOSTER.
BRUCK
HEY! HE'S MOCKING US!
I'LL WRING HIS NECK!
FW UP!
WHAT IS...
A BILL?
ZANG

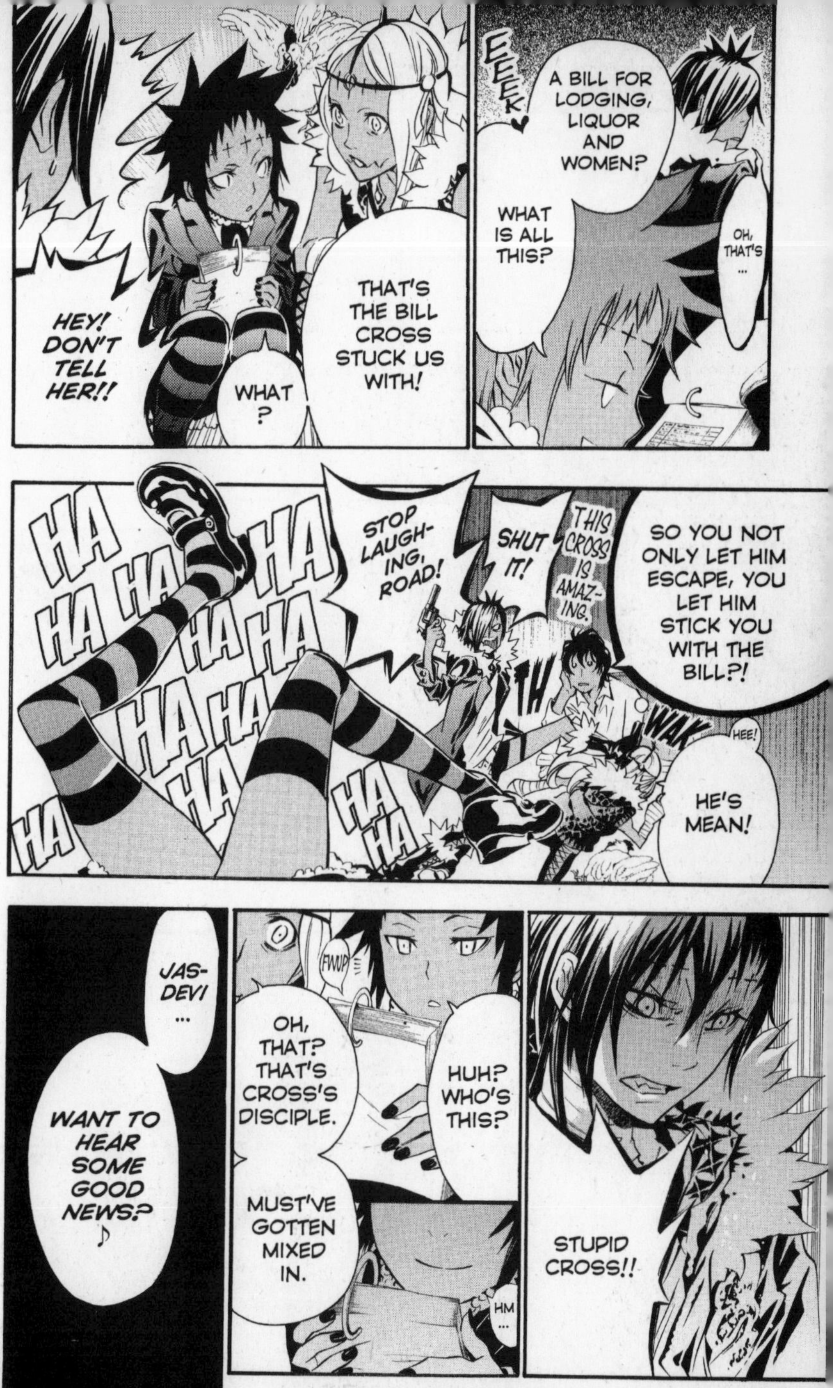
A BILL FOR LODGING, LIQUOR AND WOMEN?
EEEK ♥
OH, THAT'S ...
WHAT IS ALL THIS?
THAT'S THE BILL CROSS STUCK US WITH!
WHAT ?
HEY! DON'T TELL HER!!
SO YOU NOT ONLY LET HIM ESCAPE, YOU LET HIM STICK YOU WITH THE BILL?!
THIS CROSS IS AMAZ-ING.
SHUT IT!
STOP LAUGH-ING, ROAD!
HEE!
HE'S MEAN!
WAK
TH
HA HA HA HA HA HA HA HA HA HA HA HA HA HA HA
STUPID CROSS!!
HUH? WHO'S THIS?
FWUP
OH, THAT? THAT'S CROSS'S DISCIPLE.
MUST'VE GOTTEN MIXED IN.
HM ...
JAS-DEVI ...
WANT TO HEAR SOME GOOD NEWS? ♪

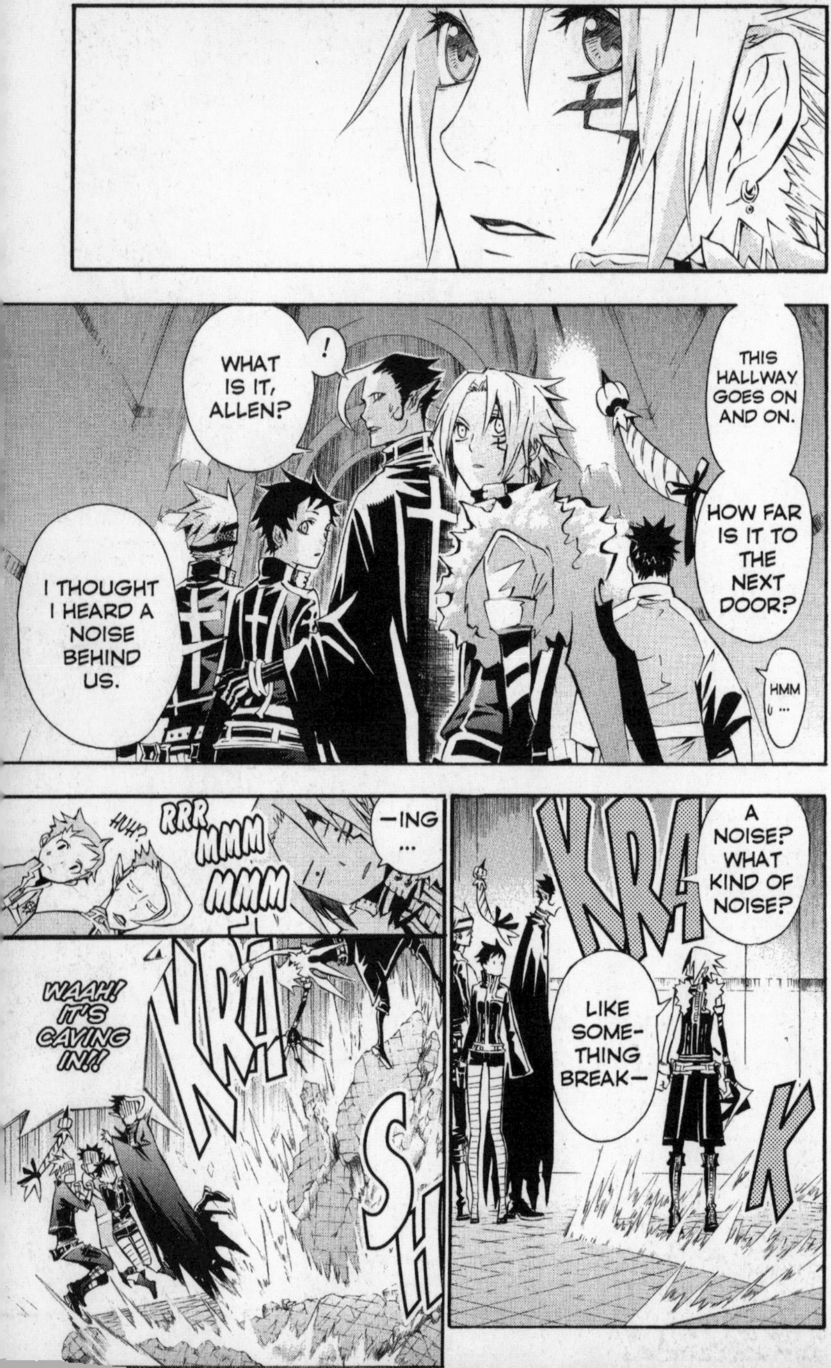
THIS HALLWAY GOES ON AND ON.
HOW FAR IS IT TO THE NEXT DOOR?
HMM...
!
WHAT IS IT, ALLEN?
I THOUGHT I HEARD A NOISE BEHIND US.
A NOISE? WHAT KIND OF NOISE?
KRAK
LIKE SOME-THING BREAK—
—ING...
RRRMMMMMM
HUH?
KRASH
WAAH! IT'S CAVING IN!!

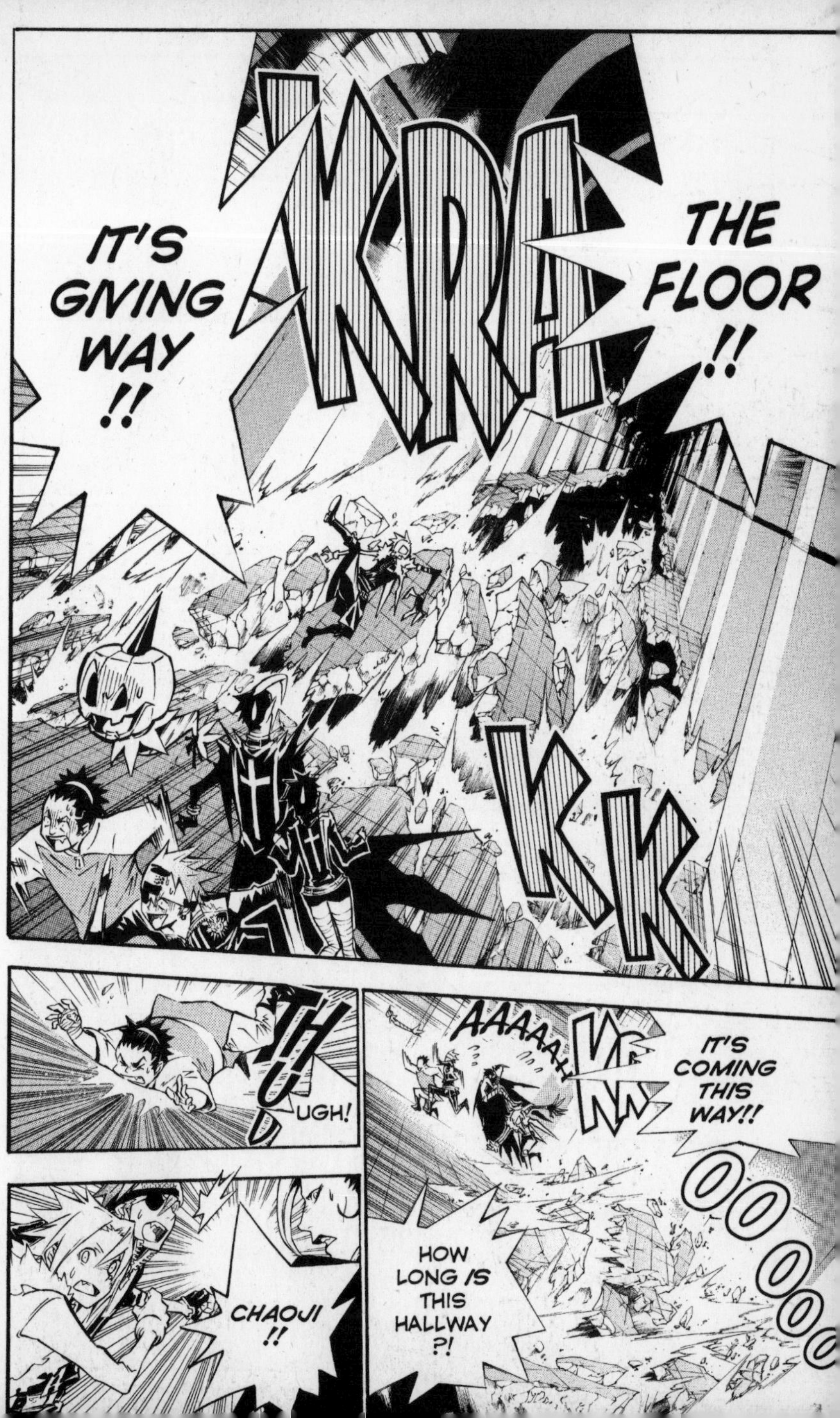
THE FLOOR !!
KRA
IT'S GIVING WAY !!
KK
AAAAAAH
KK
IT'S COMING THIS WAY!!
OOOOOO
HOW LONG IS THIS HALLWAY ?!
THUD
UGH!
CHAOJI !!

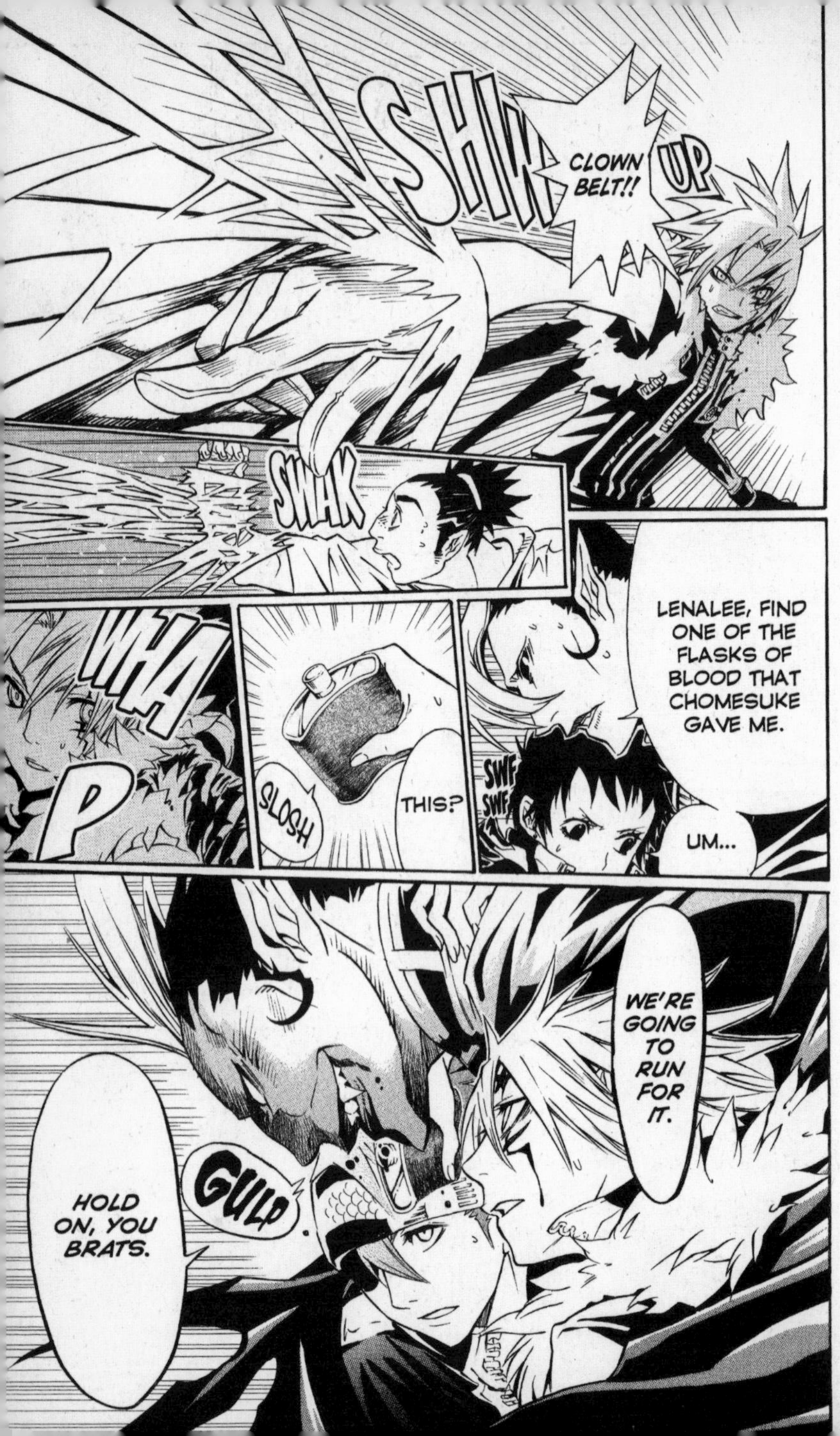

SHI
CLOWN BELT!!
UP
SWAK
LENALEE, FIND ONE OF THE FLASKS OF BLOOD THAT CHOMESUKE GAVE ME.
SWF SWF
UM...
THIS?
SLOSH
WHAP
WE'RE GOING TO RUN FOR IT.
GULP
HOLD ON, YOU BRATS.

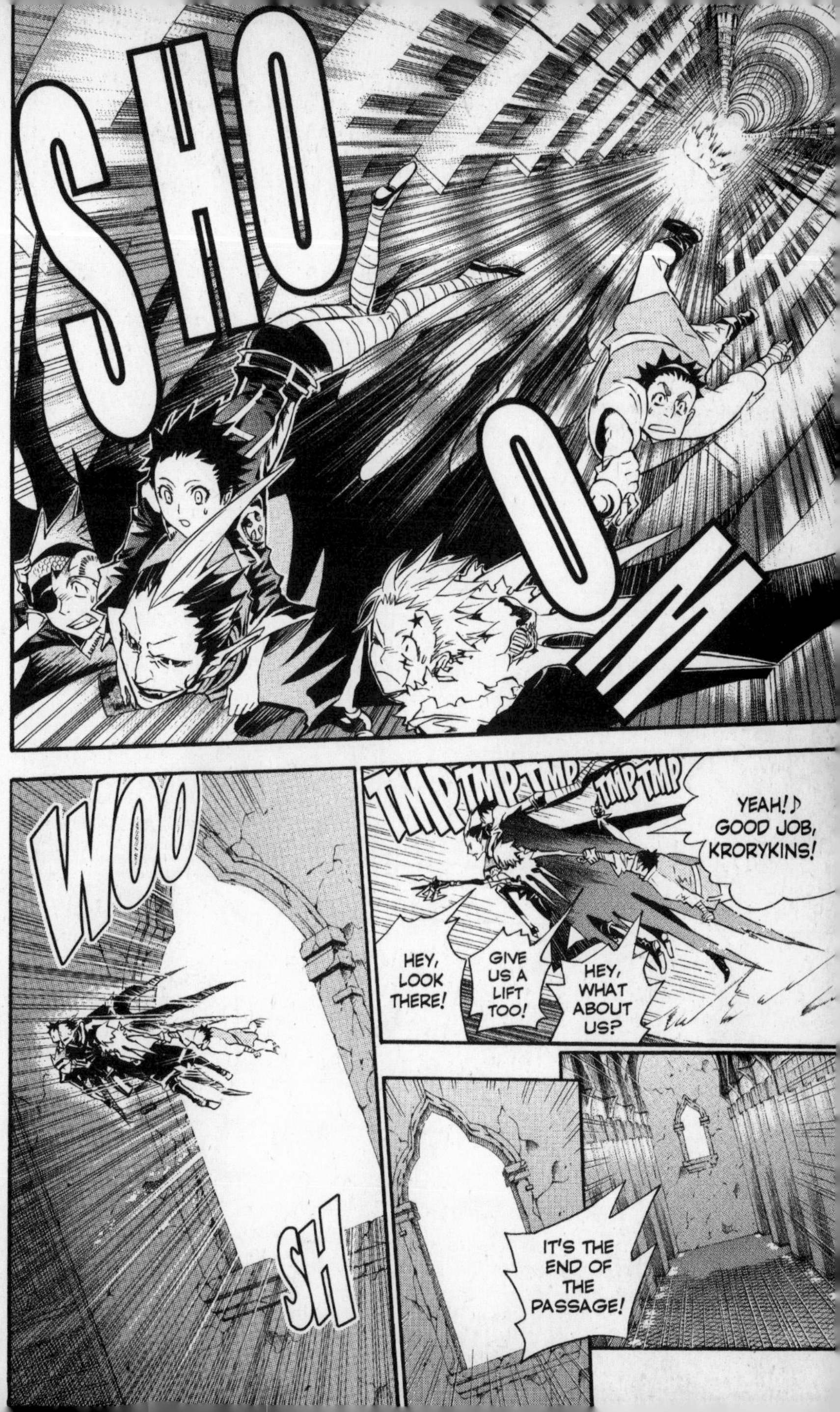
SHO
OOM
TMP TMP TMP TMP TMP
YEAH!♪ GOOD JOB, KRORYKINS!
HEY, WHAT ABOUT US?
GIVE US A LIFT TOO!
HEY, LOOK THERE!
IT'S THE END OF THE PASSAGE!
WOO
SH

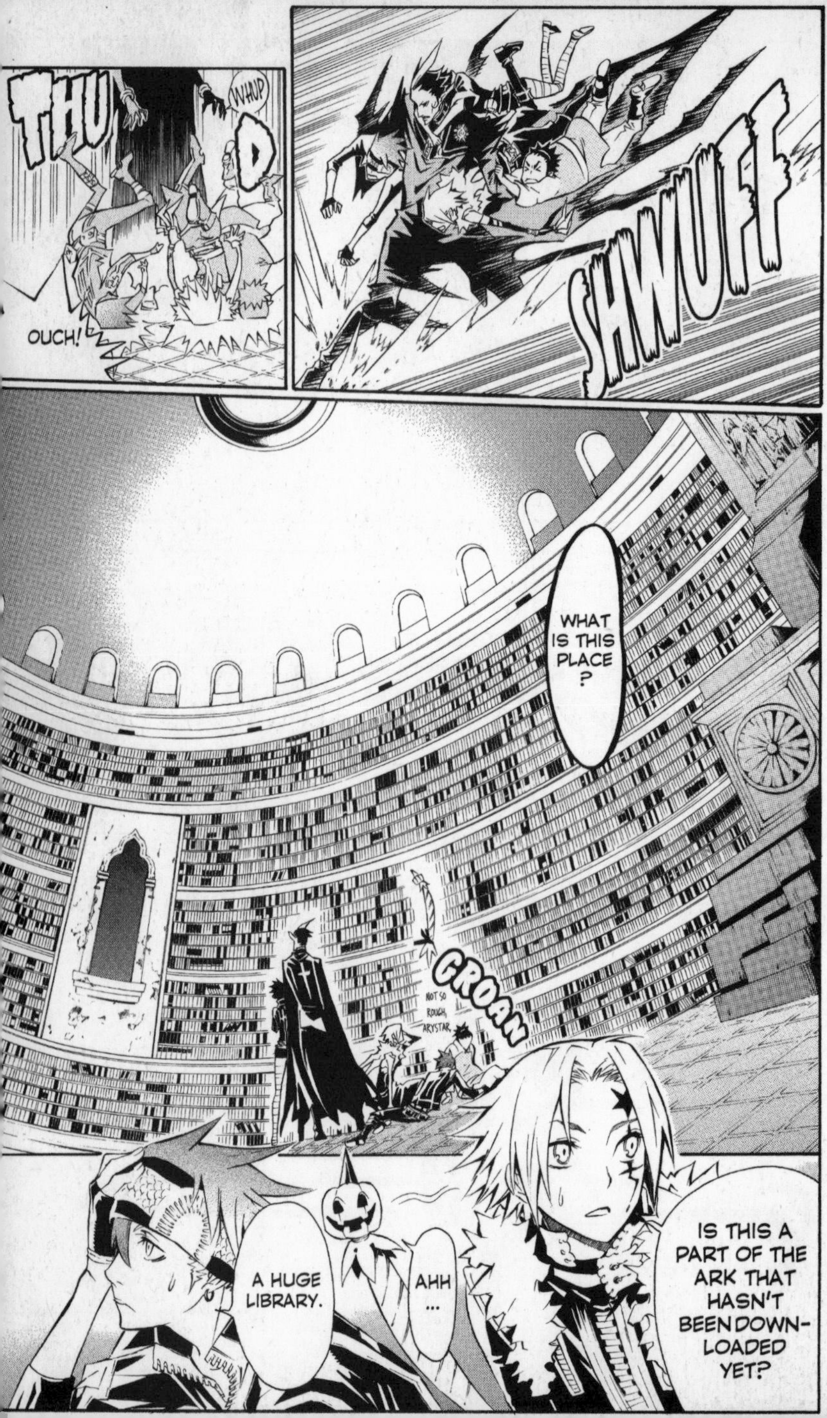
SHWUFF
THUD
WHUP
OUCH!
WHAT IS THIS PLACE?
GROAN
NOT SO ROUGH, ARYSTAR.
IS THIS A PART OF THE ARK THAT HASN'T BEEN DOWN-LOADED YET?
AHH...
A HUGE LIBRARY.

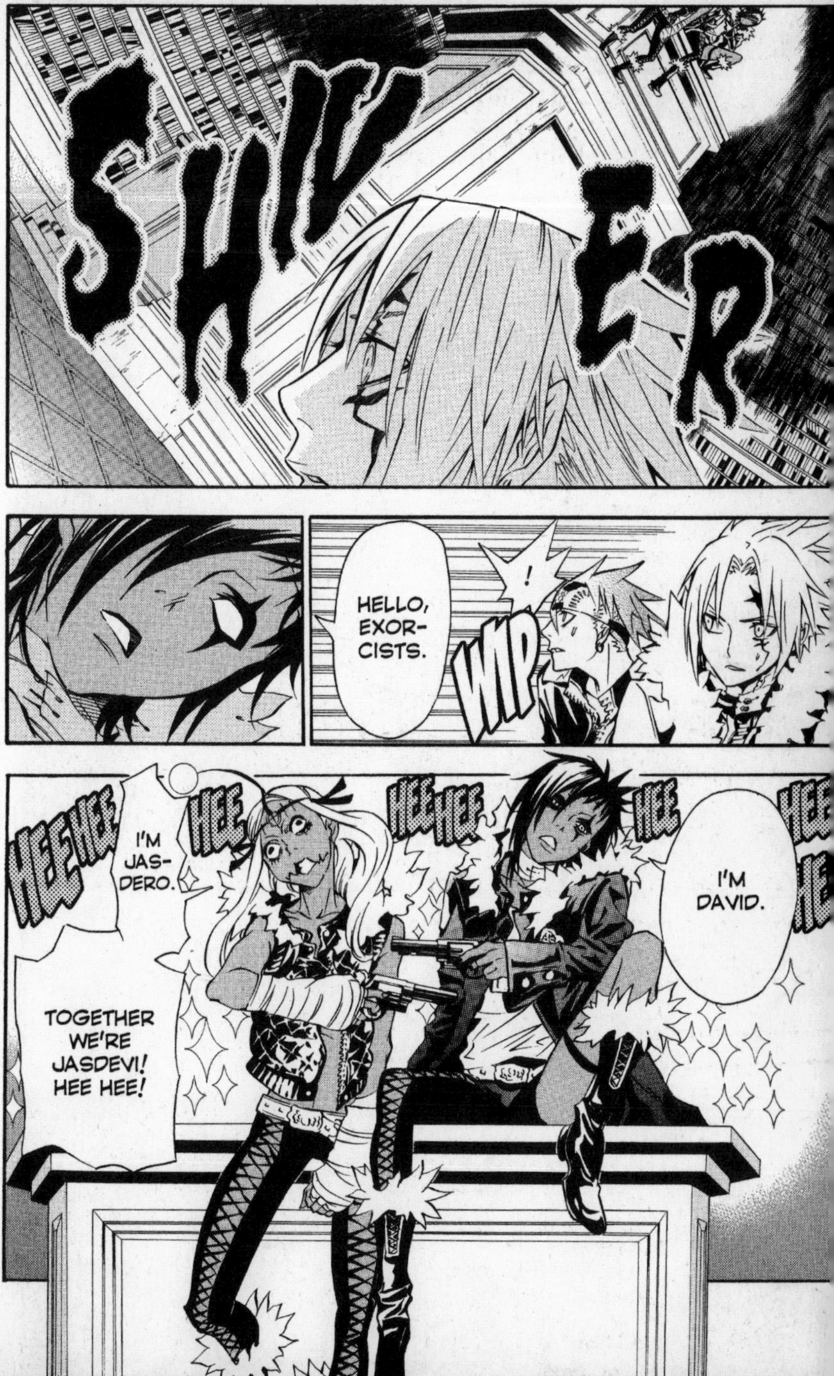
SHIVER
!
WIP
HELLO, EXORCISTS.
HEE HE
I'M DAVID.
HEE
HEE HEE
HEE
I'M JASDERO.
HEE HEE
TOGETHER WE'RE JASDEVI! HEE HEE!

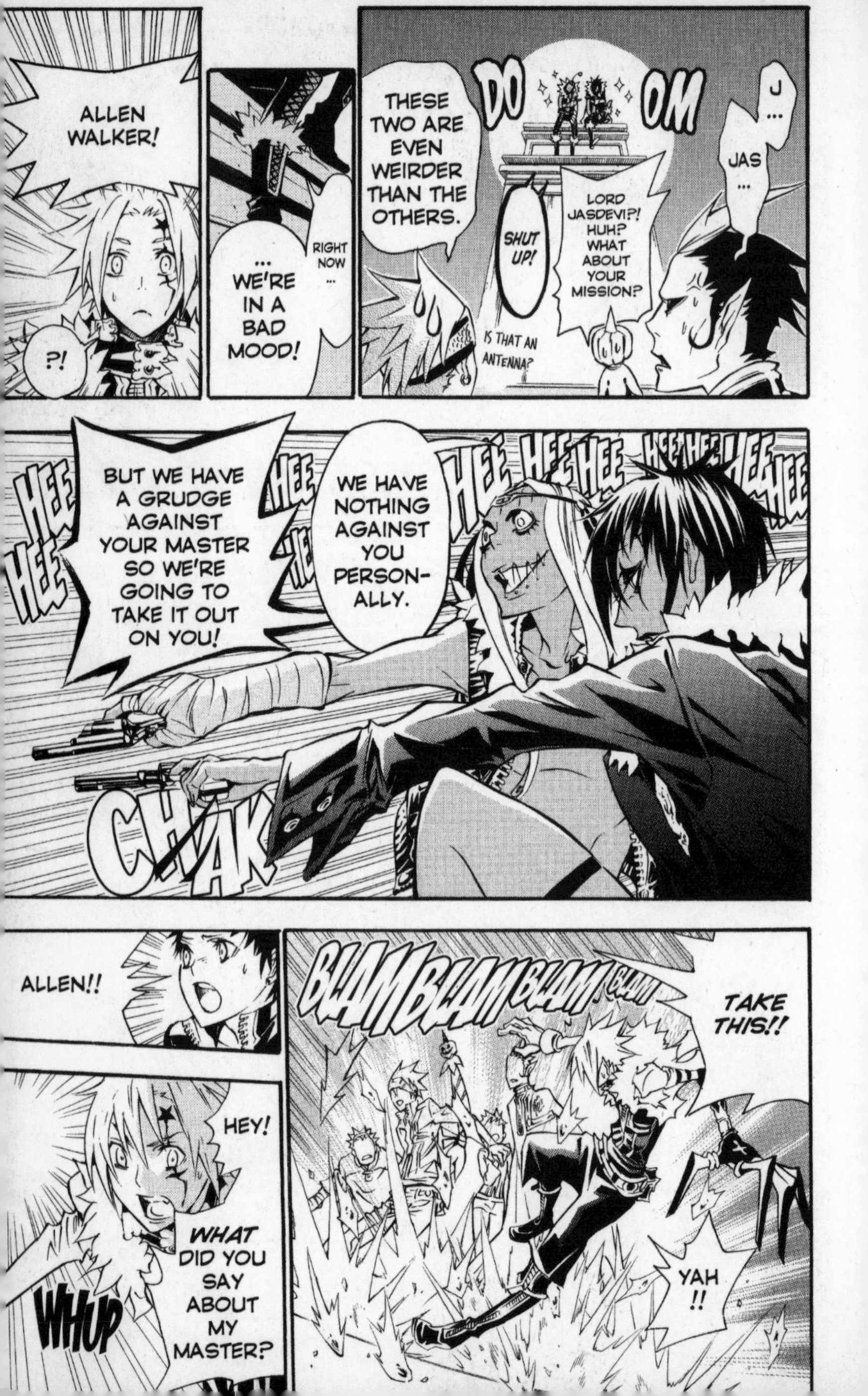
J ... JAS ...
LORD JASDEVI?! HUH? WHAT ABOUT YOUR MISSION?
DO OM
SHUT UP!
IS THAT AN ANTENNA?
THESE TWO ARE EVEN WEIRDER THAN THE OTHERS.
RIGHT NOW ...
... WE'RE IN A BAD MOOD!
ALLEN WALKER!
?!
HEE HEE HEE HEE HEE HEE HEE HEE
WE HAVE NOTHING AGAINST YOU PERSON-ALLY.
BUT WE HAVE A GRUDGE AGAINST YOUR MASTER SO WE'RE GOING TO TAKE IT OUT ON YOU!
HEE HEE HEE HEE
CHAK
TAKE THIS!!
BLAM BLAM BLAM BLAM BLAM
YAH !!
ALLEN!!
HEY!
WHAT DID YOU SAY ABOUT MY MASTER?
WHUP

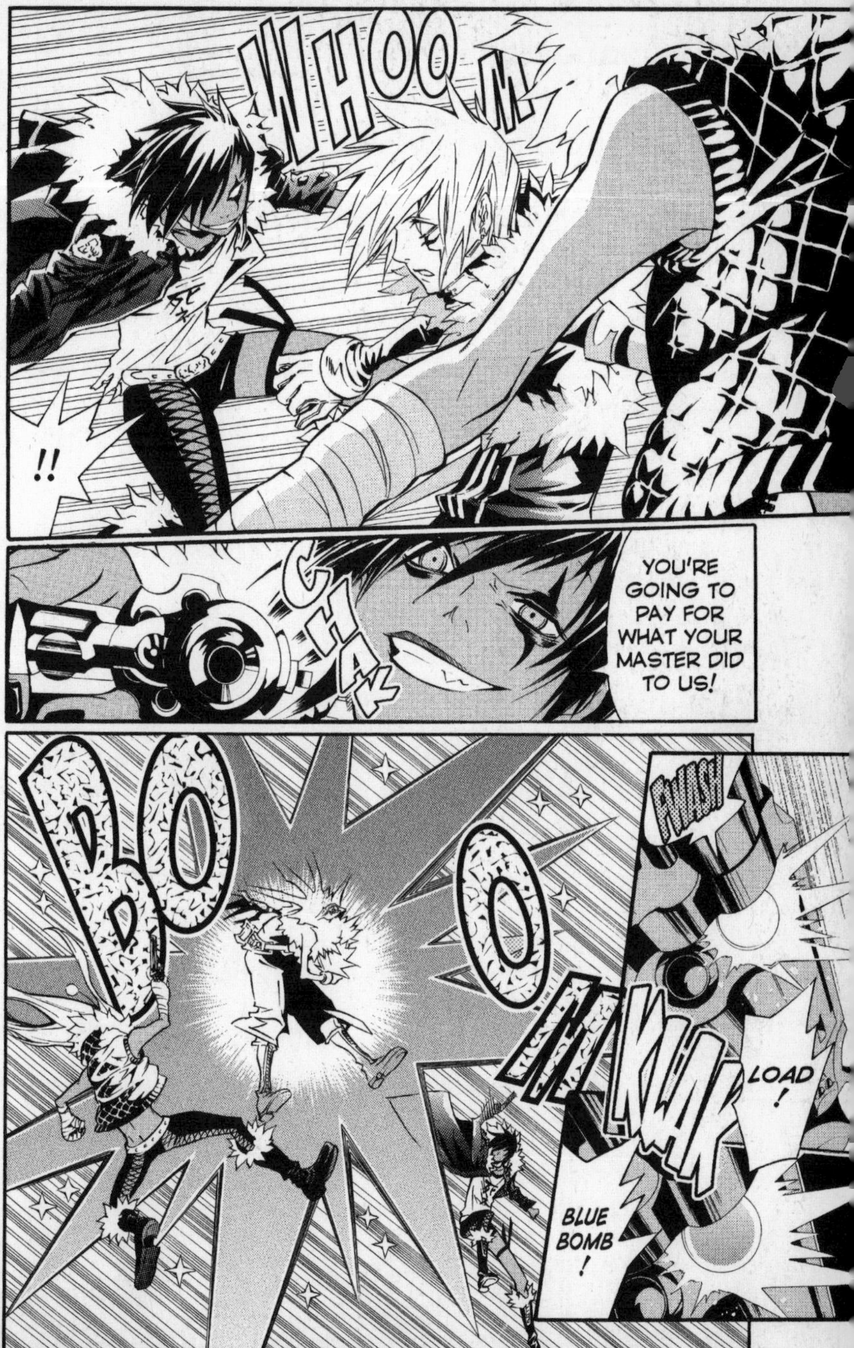
WHOOM
!!
GCHAK
YOU'RE GOING TO PAY FOR WHAT YOUR MASTER DID TO US!
PWASH
LOAD!
BLUE BOMB!
KWAK
BOOM

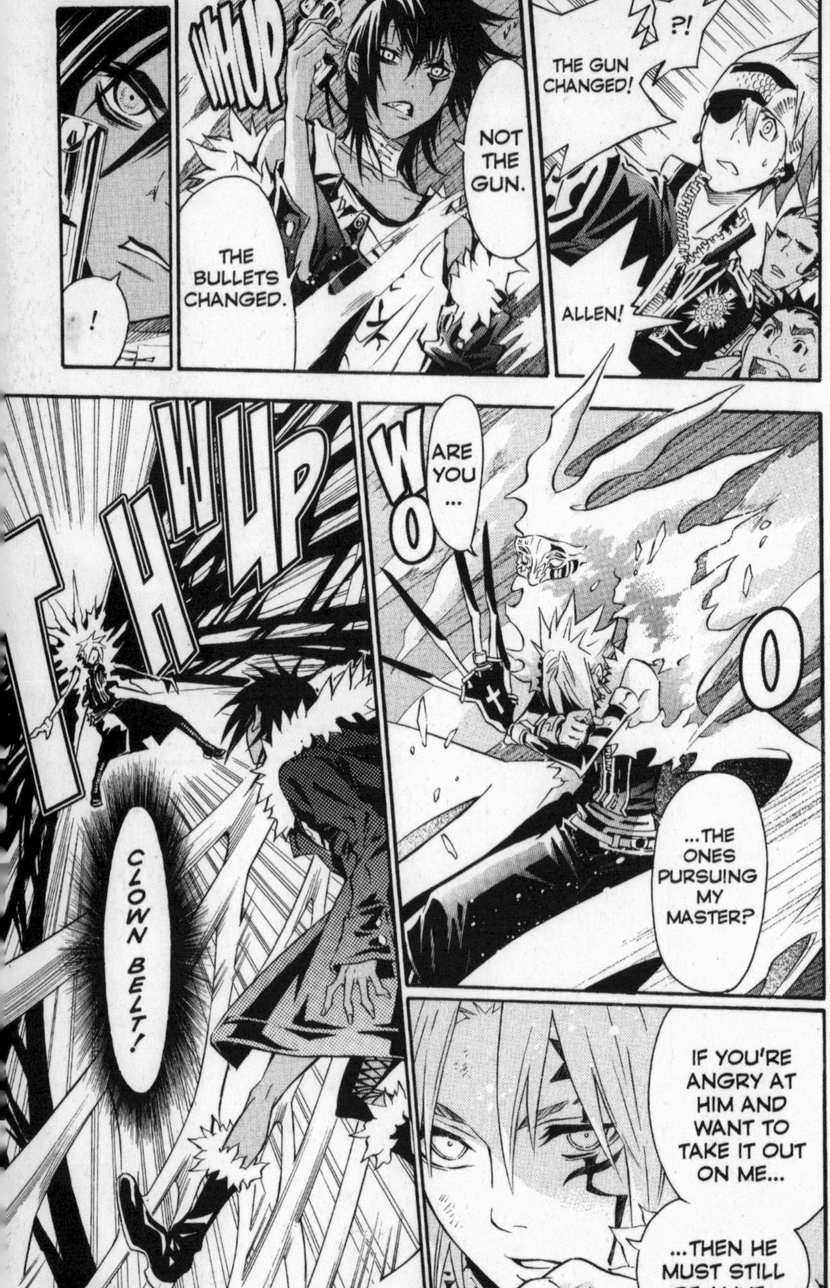
?!
THE GUN CHANGED!
ALLEN!
WHUP
NOT THE GUN.
THE BULLETS CHANGED.
!
WOOO
ARE YOU ...
...THE ONES PURSUING MY MASTER?
IF YOU'RE ANGRY AT HIM AND WANT TO TAKE IT OUT ON ME...
...THEN HE MUST STILL BE ALIVE.
THWHUP
CLOWN BELT!

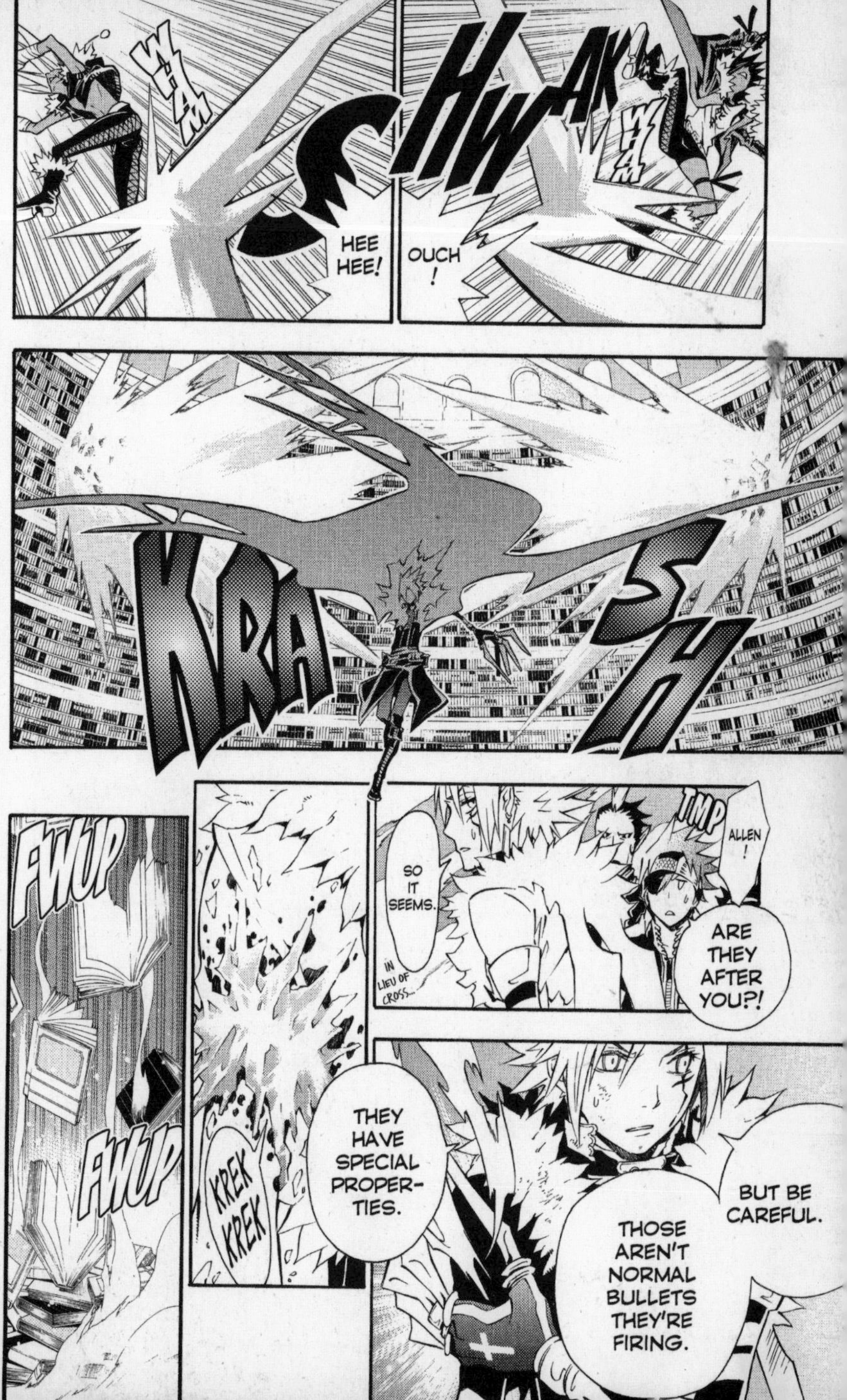
SCHWAK
WHAM
OUCH!
WHAM
HEE HEE!
KRASH
TMP
ALLEN!
ARE THEY AFTER YOU?!
SO IT SEEMS.
IN LIEU OF CROSS...
BUT BE CAREFUL.
THOSE AREN'T NORMAL BULLETS THEY'RE FIRING.
THEY HAVE SPECIAL PROPER-TIES.
KREK KREK
FWUP
FWUP

READ THIS WAY

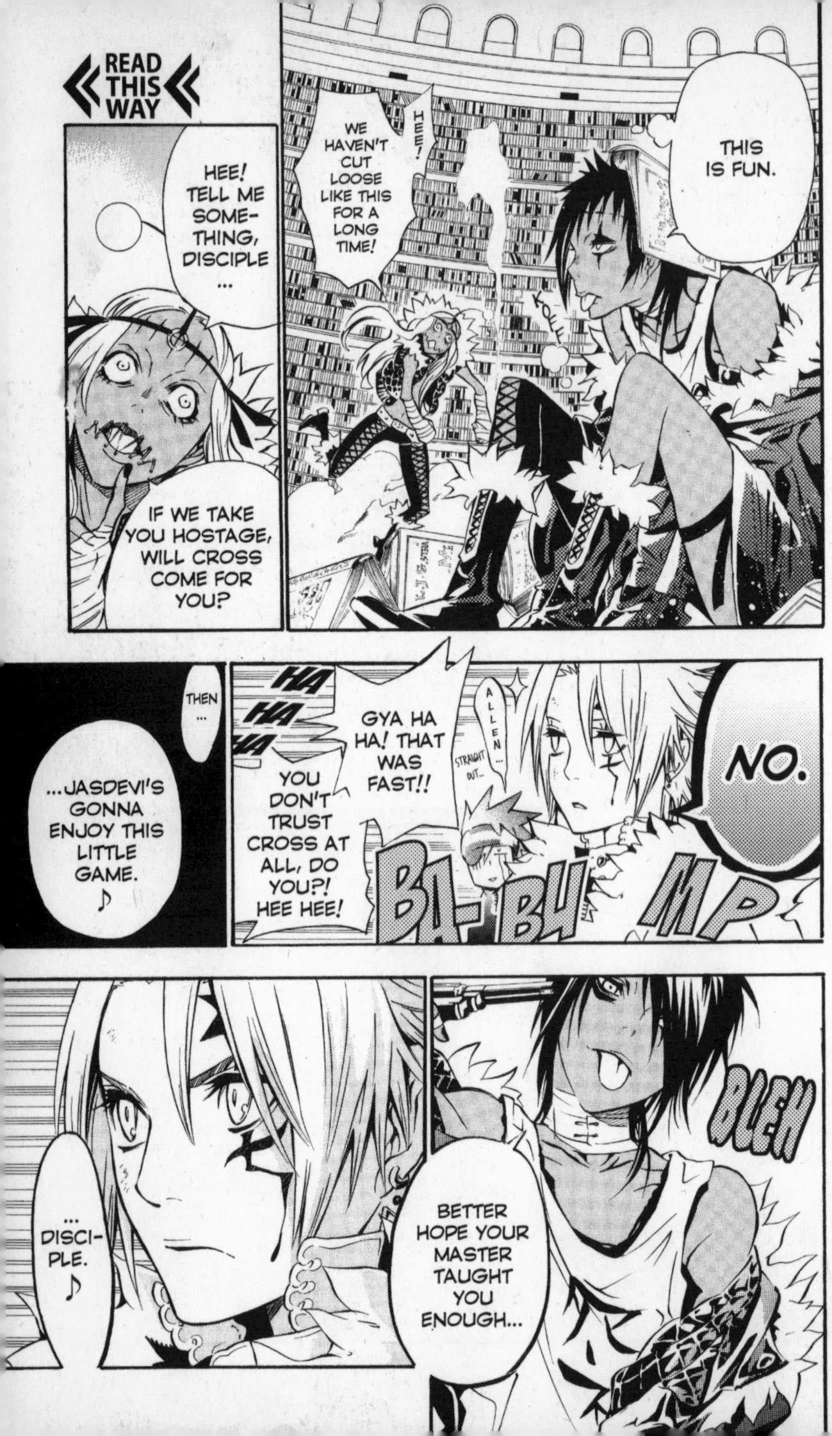
THIS IS FUN.
WE HAVEN'T CUT LOOSE LIKE THIS FOR A LONG TIME!
HEE!
HEE! TELL ME SOMETHING, DISCIPLE ...
IF WE TAKE YOU HOSTAGE, WILL CROSS COME FOR YOU?
NO.
BA-BUMP
ALLEN ...
STRAIGHT OUT...
GYA HA HA! THAT WAS FAST!!
HA HA HA
YOU DON'T TRUST CROSS AT ALL, DO YOU?! HEE HEE!
THEN ...
...JASDEVI'S GONNA ENJOY THIS LITTLE GAME. ♪
BLEH
BETTER HOPE YOUR MASTER TAUGHT YOU ENOUGH...
... DISCIPLE. ♪

Q: DOES THE CLAN OF NOAH CELEBRATE CHRISTMAS AND NEW YEAR'S?

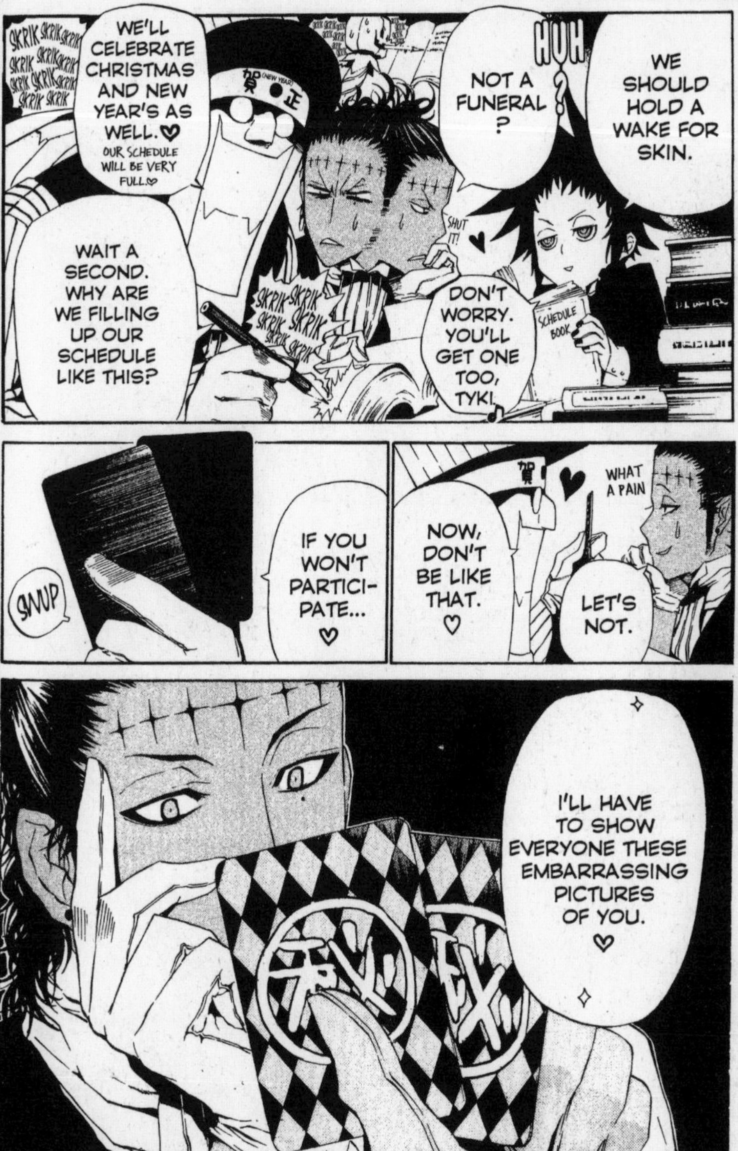
WE SHOULD HOLD A WAKE FOR SKIN.
HUH
NOT A FUNERAL?
WE'LL CELEBRATE CHRISTMAS AND NEW YEAR'S AS WELL. ♡ OUR SCHEDULE WILL BE VERY FULL. ♡
(NEW YEAR)
SKRIK SKRIK SKRIK SKRIK SKRIK SKRIK SKRIK SKRIK SKRIK SKRIK SKRIK
SHUT IT!
DON'T WORRY. YOU'LL GET ONE TOO, TYKI. ♪
SCHEDULE BOOK
SKRIK SKRIK SKRIK SKRIK SKRIK SKRIK
WAIT A SECOND. WHY ARE WE FILLING UP OUR SCHEDULE LIKE THIS?
WHAT A PAIN
NOW, DON'T BE LIKE THAT. ♡
LET'S NOT.
IF YOU WON'T PARTICIPATE... ♡
SNUP
I'LL HAVE TO SHOW EVERYONE THESE EMBARRASSING PICTURES OF YOU. ♡

THE 99TH NIGHT: DEBT CRISIS

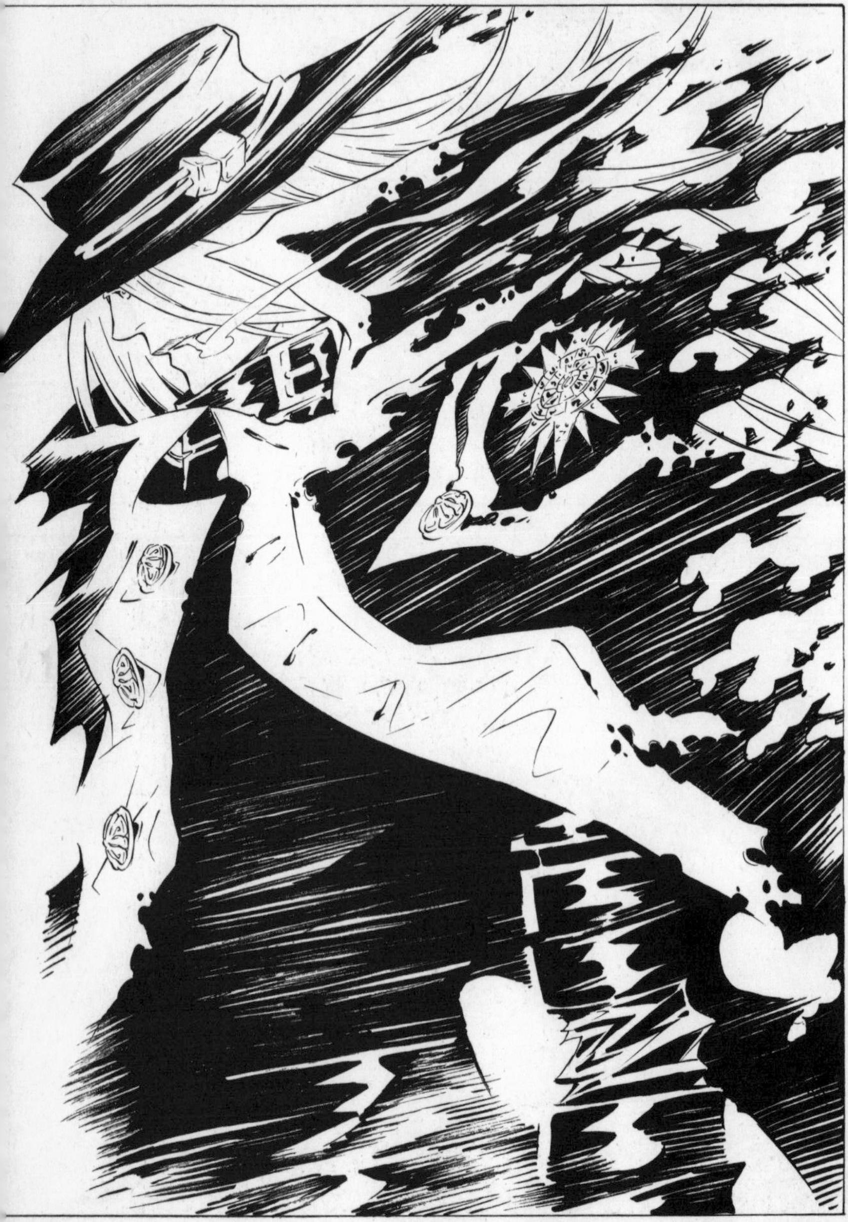

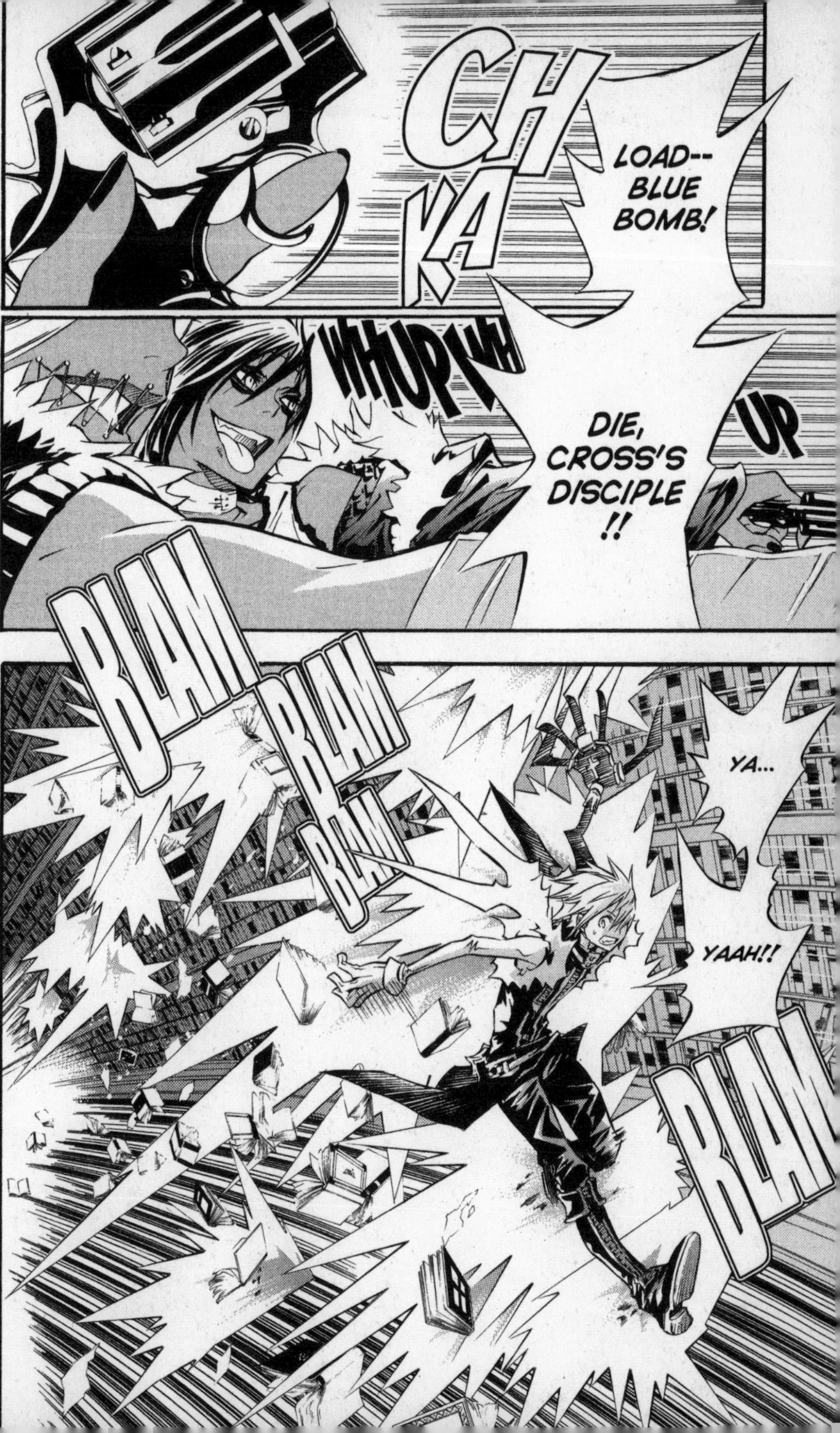
CHKA
LOAD-- BLUE BOMB!
WHUP
UP
DIE, CROSS'S DISCIPLE !!
BLAM
BLAM
BLAM
YA...
YAAH!!
BLAM

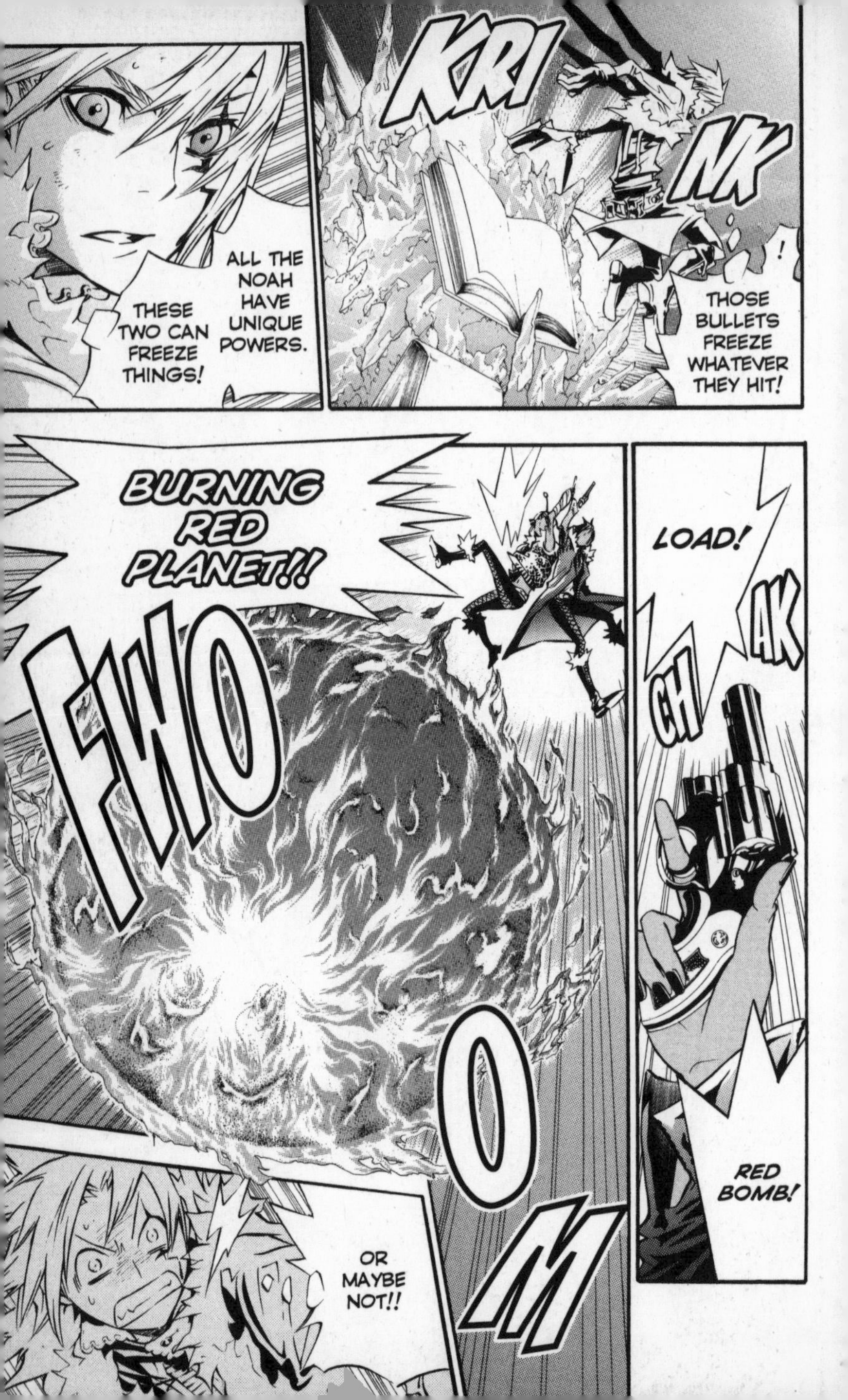
KRI
NK
THOSE BULLETS FREEZE WHATEVER THEY HIT!
ALL THE NOAH HAVE UNIQUE POWERS.
THESE TWO CAN FREEZE THINGS!
LOAD!
CH
AK
RED BOMB!
BURNING RED PLANET!!
FWO
O
M
OR MAYBE NOT!!

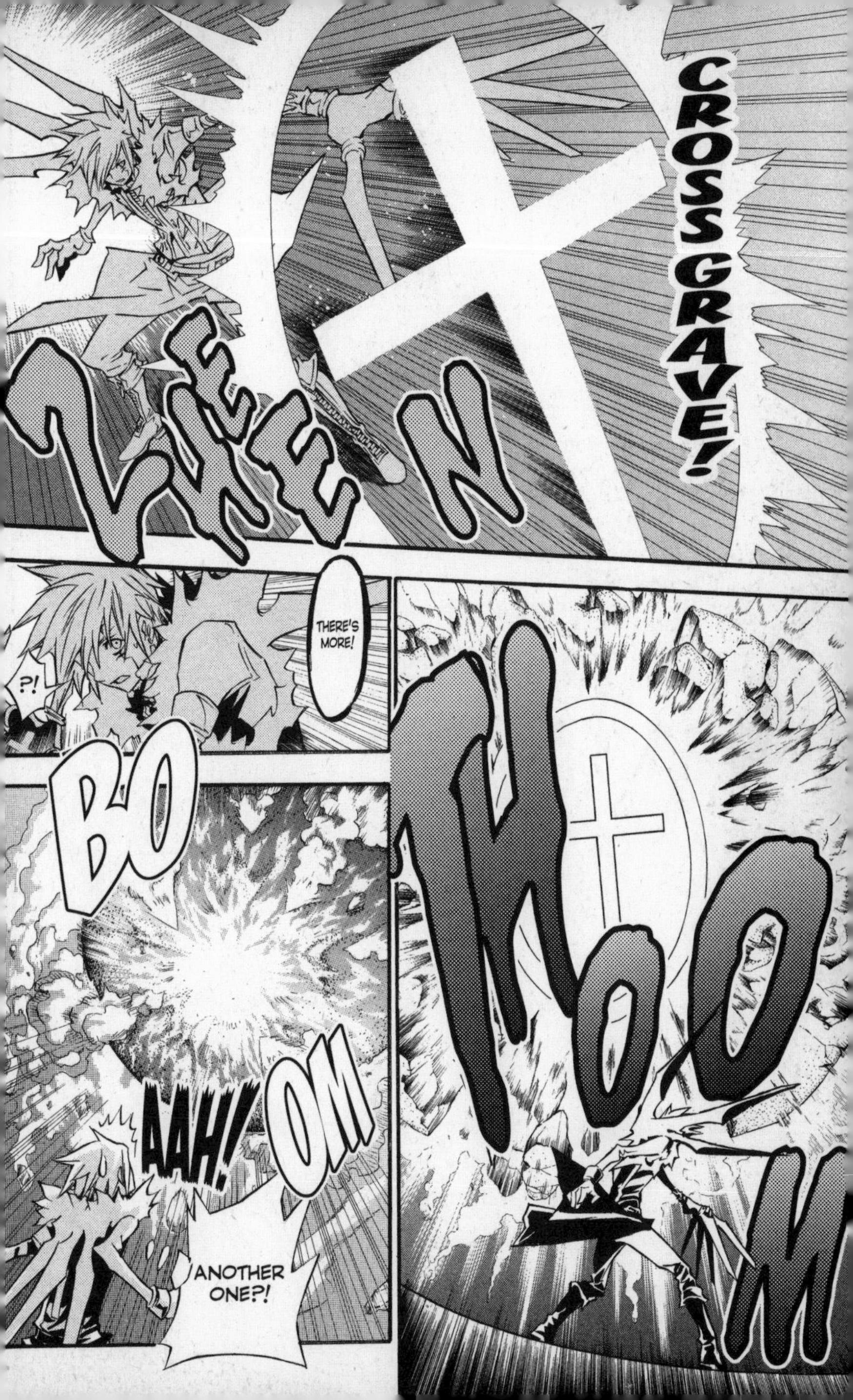
CROSS GRAVE!
ZHEEN
WHOOM
THERE'S MORE!
?!
BOOM
AAH!
ANOTHER ONE?!

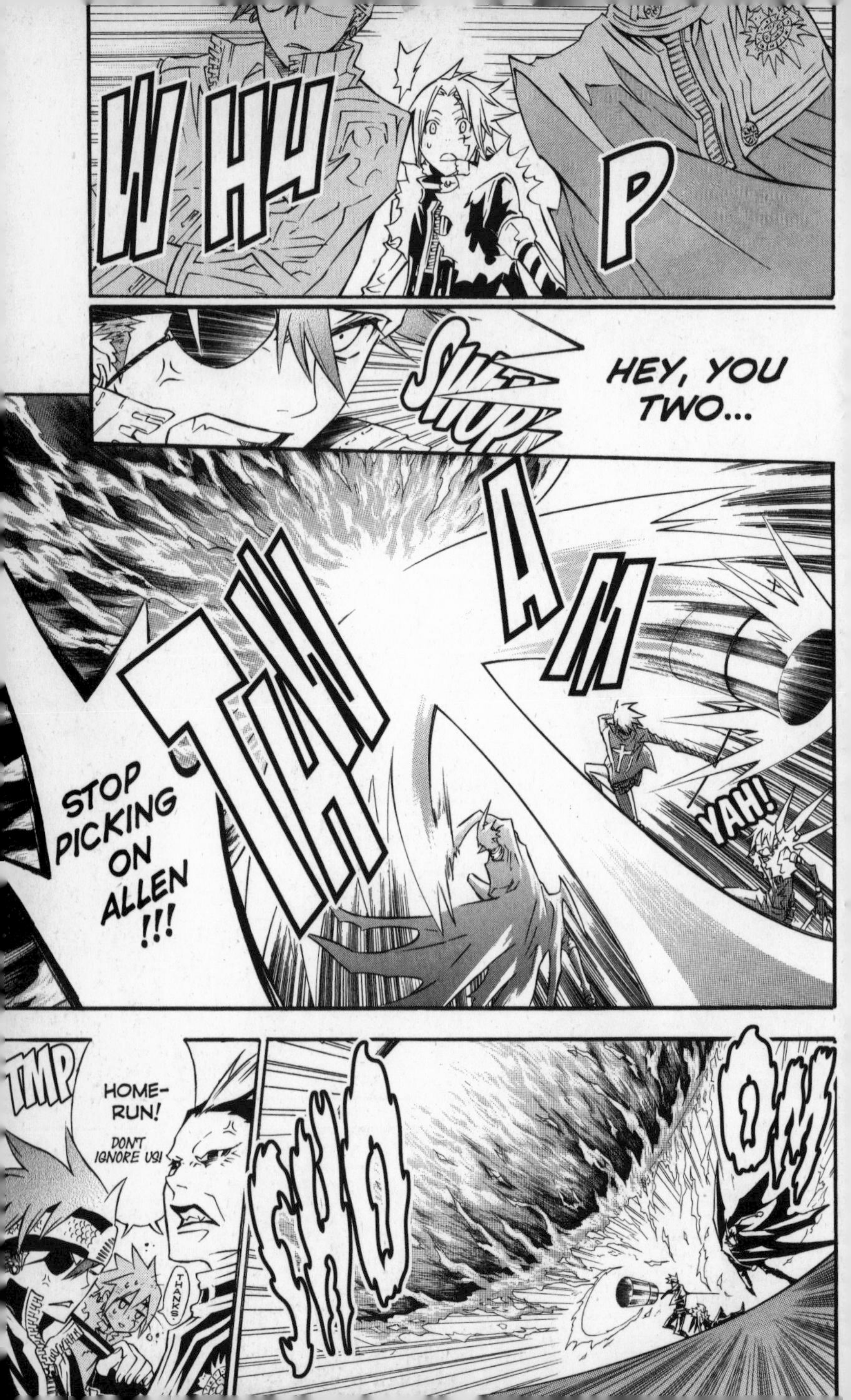
P
WHY
HEY, YOU TWO...
SHUP
YAH!
STOP PICKING ON ALLEN !!!
TMP
HOME-RUN!
DON'T IGNORE US!
THANKS.

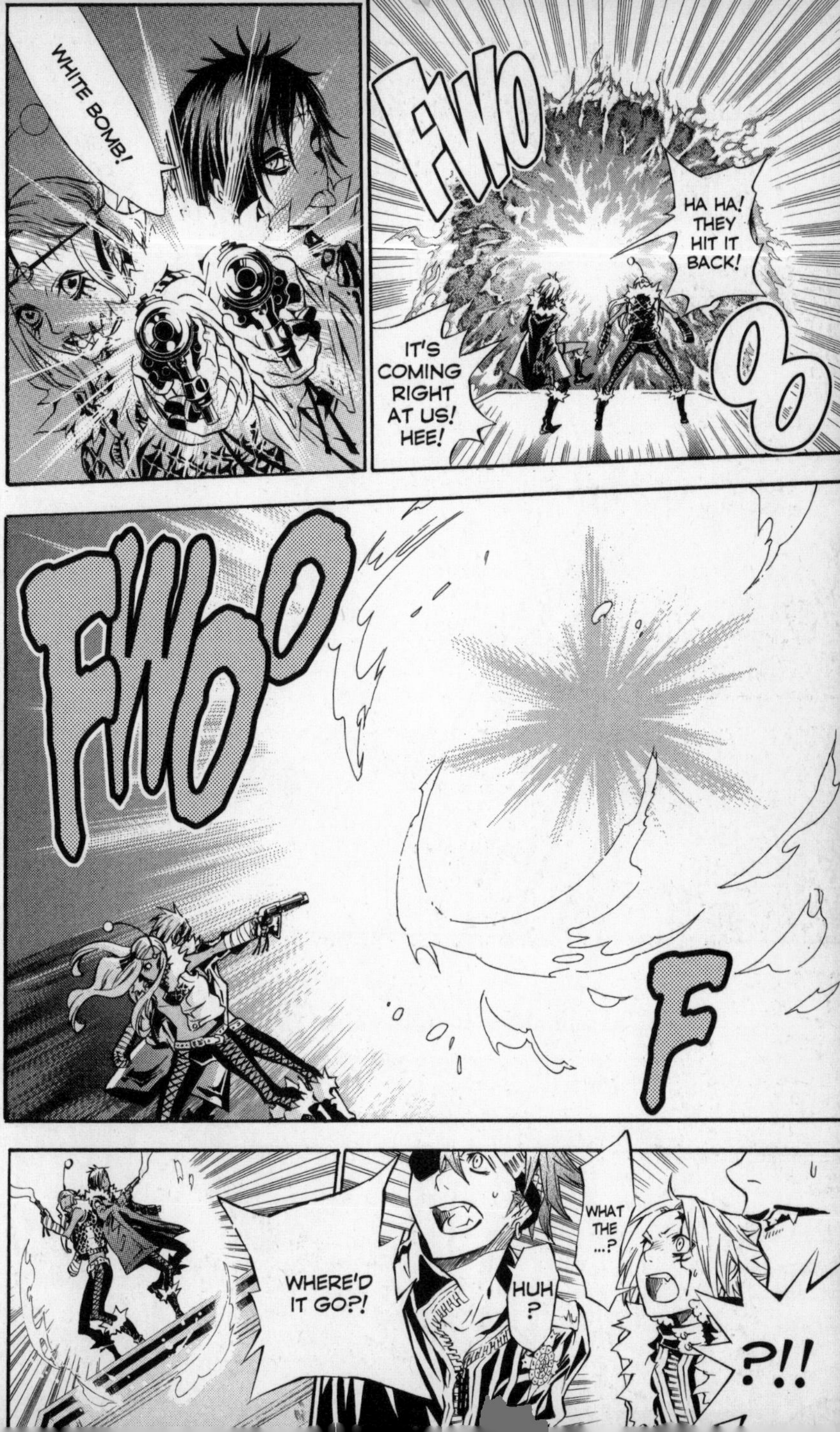
FWO
HA HA! THEY HIT IT BACK!
IT'S COMING RIGHT AT US! HEE!
WHITE BOMB!
FWOO
F
WHAT THE ...?
?!!
HUH ?
WHERE'D IT GO?!

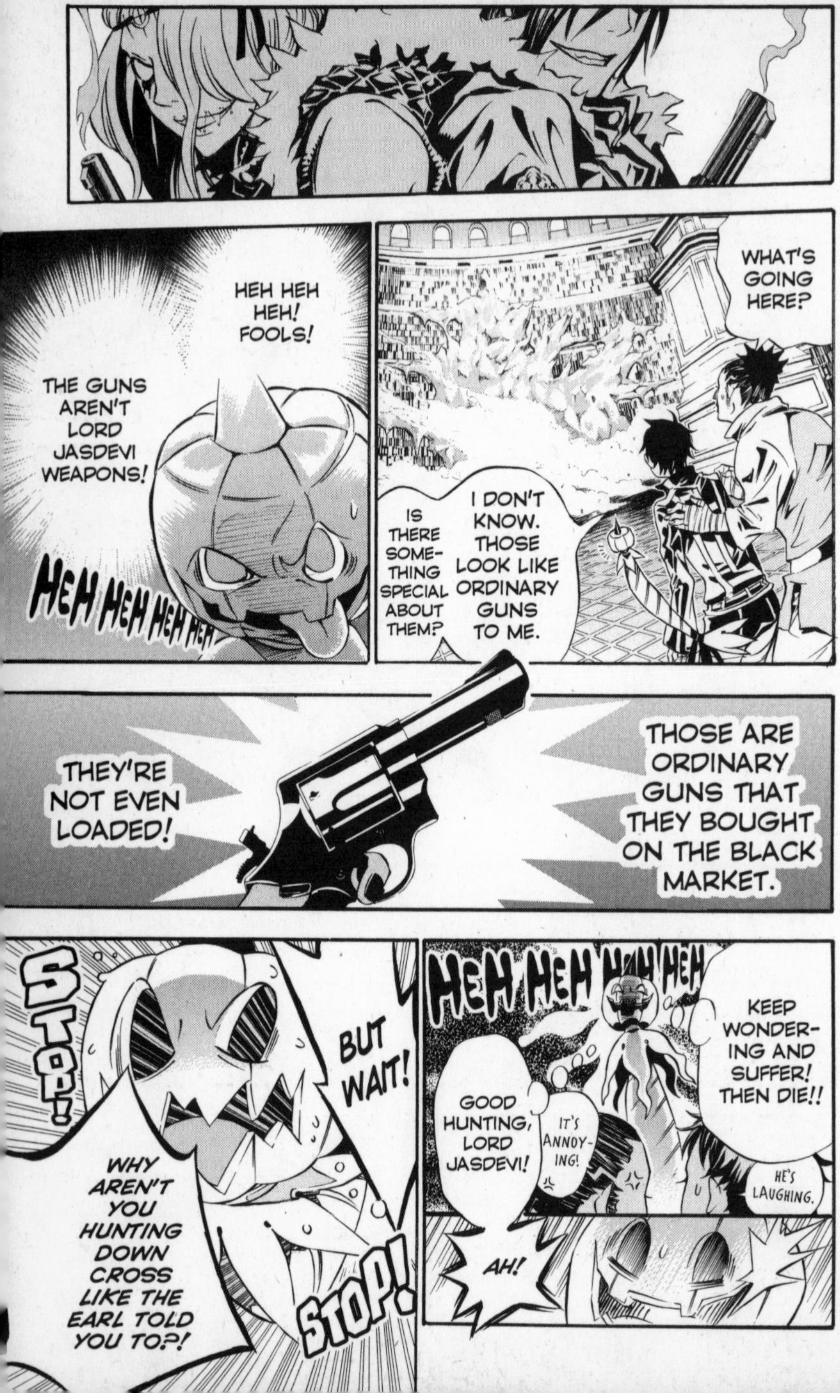
WHAT'S GOING HERE?
I DON'T KNOW. THOSE LOOK LIKE ORDINARY GUNS TO ME.
IS THERE SOMETHING SPECIAL ABOUT THEM?
HEH HEH HEH! FOOLS!
THE GUNS AREN'T LORD JASDEVI WEAPONS!
HEH HEH HEH HEH
THOSE ARE ORDINARY GUNS THAT THEY BOUGHT ON THE BLACK MARKET.
THEY'RE NOT EVEN LOADED!
HEH HEH HEH HEH
KEEP WONDERING AND SUFFER! THEN DIE!!
HE'S LAUGHING.
IT'S ANNOYING!
GOOD HUNTING, LORD JASDEVI!
AH!
BUT WAIT!
STOP!
WHY AREN'T YOU HUNTING DOWN CROSS LIKE THE EARL TOLD YOU TO?!
STOP!

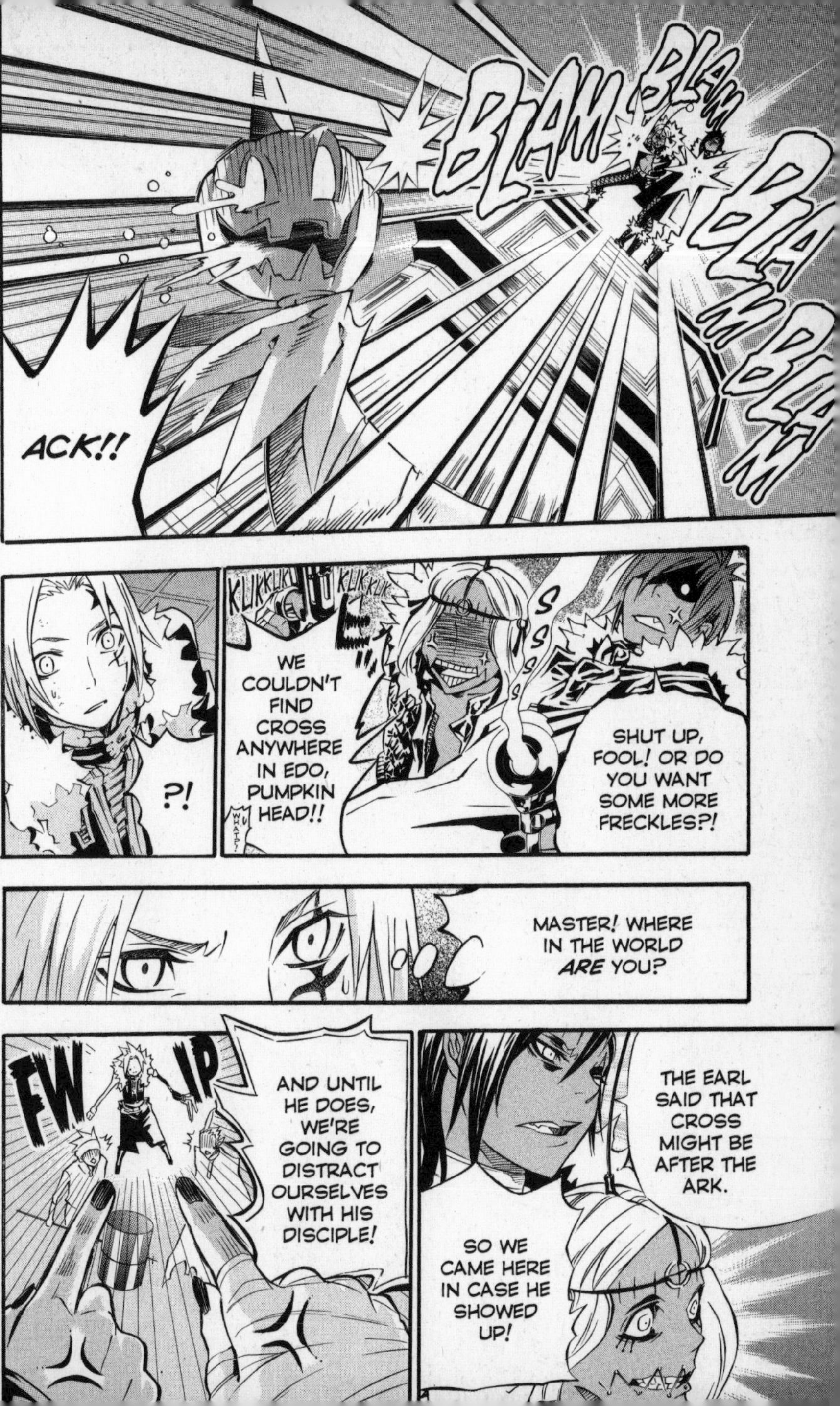
BLAM BLAM BLAM BLAM
ACK!!
KLIKKLIK KLIKKLIK
SSSS
SHUT UP, FOOL! OR DO YOU WANT SOME MORE FRECKLES?!
WE COULDN'T FIND CROSS ANYWHERE IN EDO, PUMPKIN HEAD!!
WHAT?!
?!
MASTER! WHERE IN THE WORLD *ARE* YOU?
THE EARL SAID THAT CROSS MIGHT BE AFTER THE ARK.
SO WE CAME HERE IN CASE HE SHOWED UP!
AND UNTIL HE DOES, WE'RE GOING TO DISTRACT OURSELVES WITH HIS DISCIPLE!
FWIP

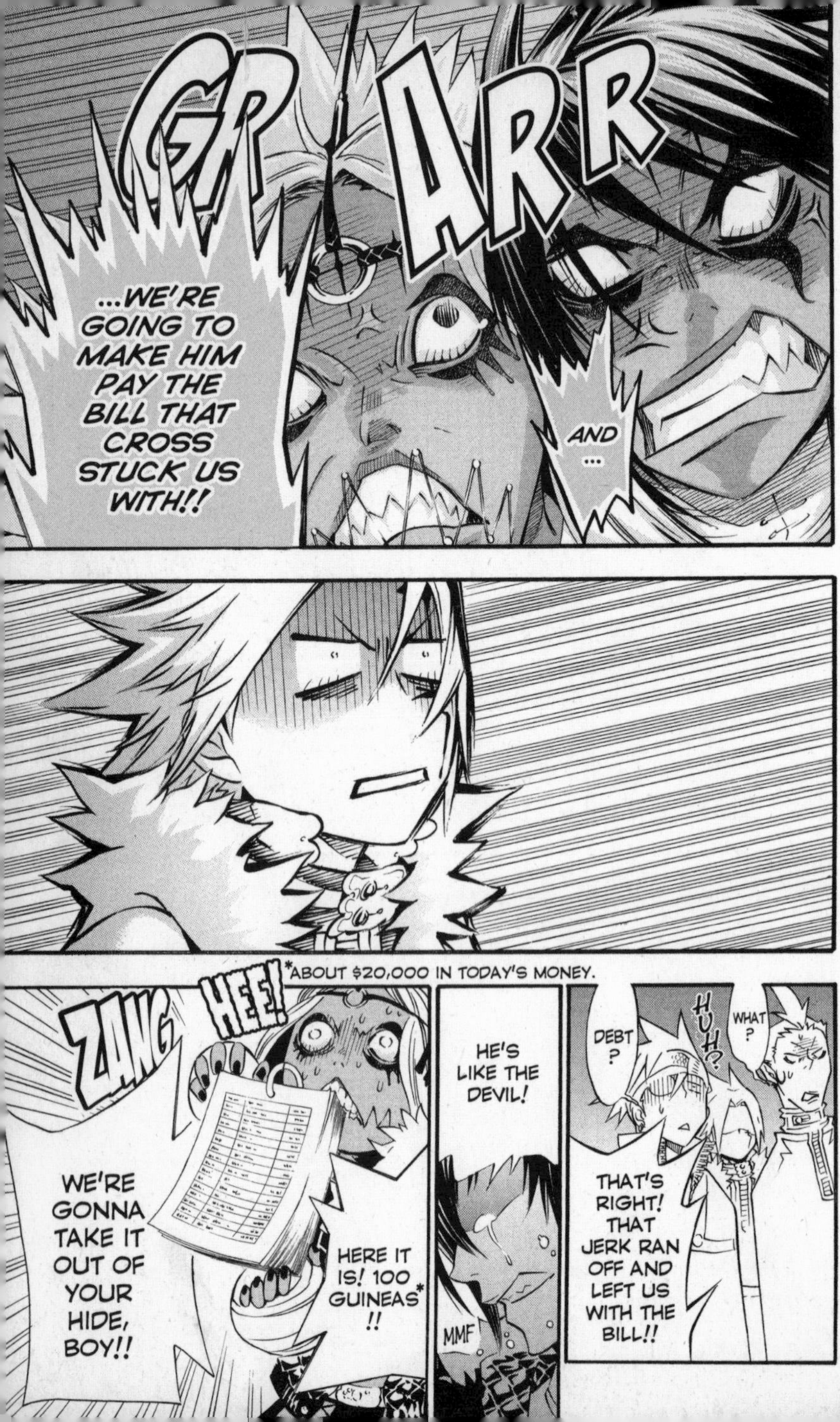
GRARR
AND ...
...WE'RE GOING TO MAKE HIM PAY THE BILL THAT CROSS STUCK US WITH!!
*ABOUT $20,000 IN TODAY'S MONEY.
WHAT ?
HUH?
DEBT ?
THAT'S RIGHT! THAT JERK RAN OFF AND LEFT US WITH THE BILL!!
HE'S LIKE THE DEVIL!
MMF
ZANG HEE!
HERE IT IS! 100 GUINEAS* !!
WE'RE GONNA TAKE IT OUT OF YOUR HIDE, BOY!!

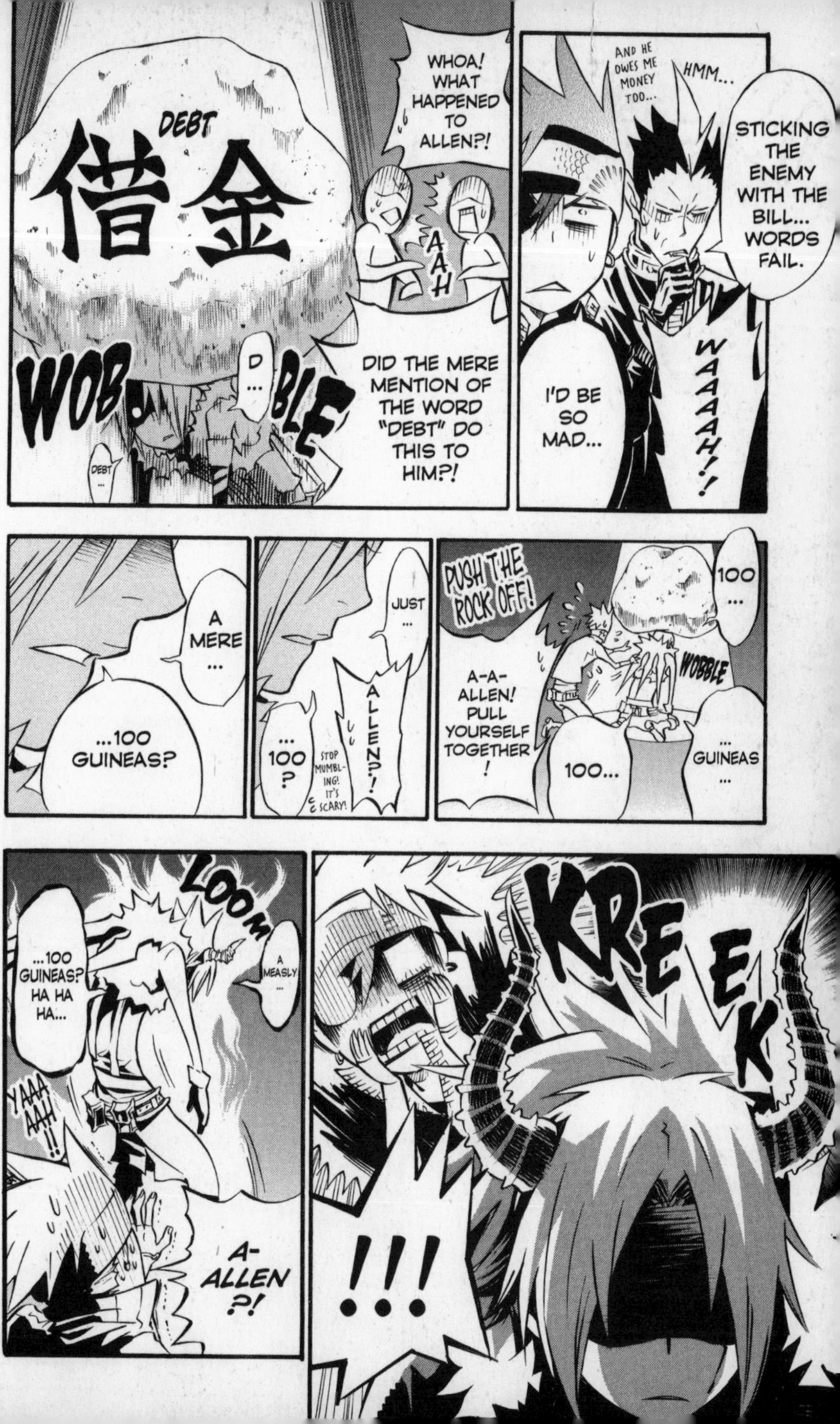
HMM...
AND HE OWES ME MONEY TOO...
STICKING THE ENEMY WITH THE BILL... WORDS FAIL.
I'D BE SO MAD...
WAAAAAH!!
WHOA! WHAT HAPPENED TO ALLEN?!
AAH
DID THE MERE MENTION OF THE WORD "DEBT" DO THIS TO HIM?!
DEBT
借金
WOBBLE
D...
DEBT...
100...
PUSH THE ROCK OFF!
WOBBLE
A-A-ALLEN! PULL YOURSELF TOGETHER!
...GUINEAS...
100...
JUST...
ALLEN?!
...100?
STOP MUMBLING! IT'S SCARY!
A MERE...
...100 GUINEAS?
KREEK
!!!
LOOM
A MEASLY...
...100 GUINEAS? HA HA HA...
YAAAAAH!!
A-ALLEN?!

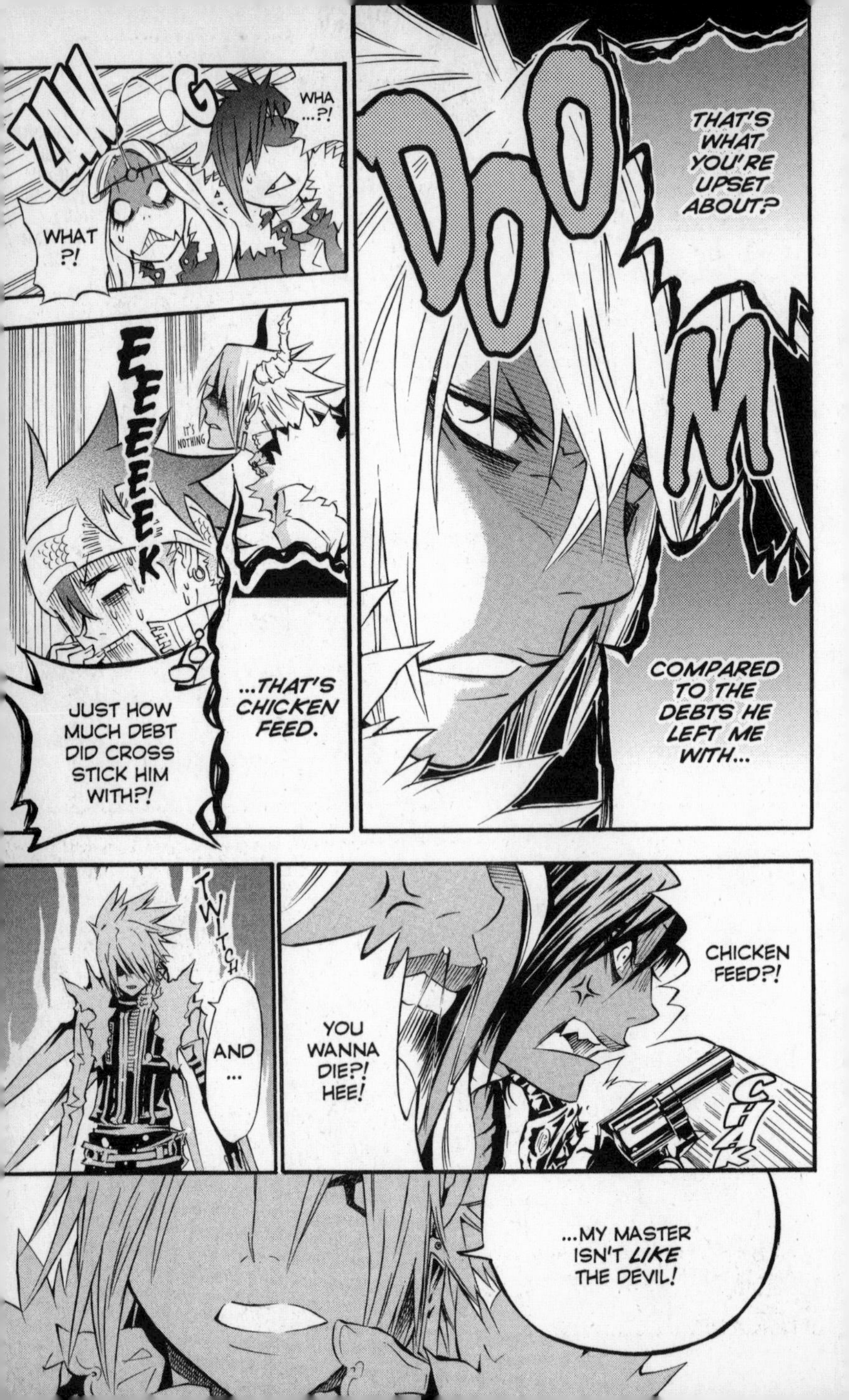
DOOOM
THAT'S WHAT YOU'RE UPSET ABOUT?
COMPARED TO THE DEBTS HE LEFT ME WITH...
WHA ...?!
ZAWG
WHAT ?!
IT'S NOTHING
EEEEEEK
...THAT'S CHICKEN FEED.
JUST HOW MUCH DEBT DID CROSS STICK HIM WITH?!
CHICKEN FEED?!
CHAK
YOU WANNA DIE?! HEE!
TWITCH
AND ...
...MY MASTER ISN'T *LIKE* THE DEVIL!

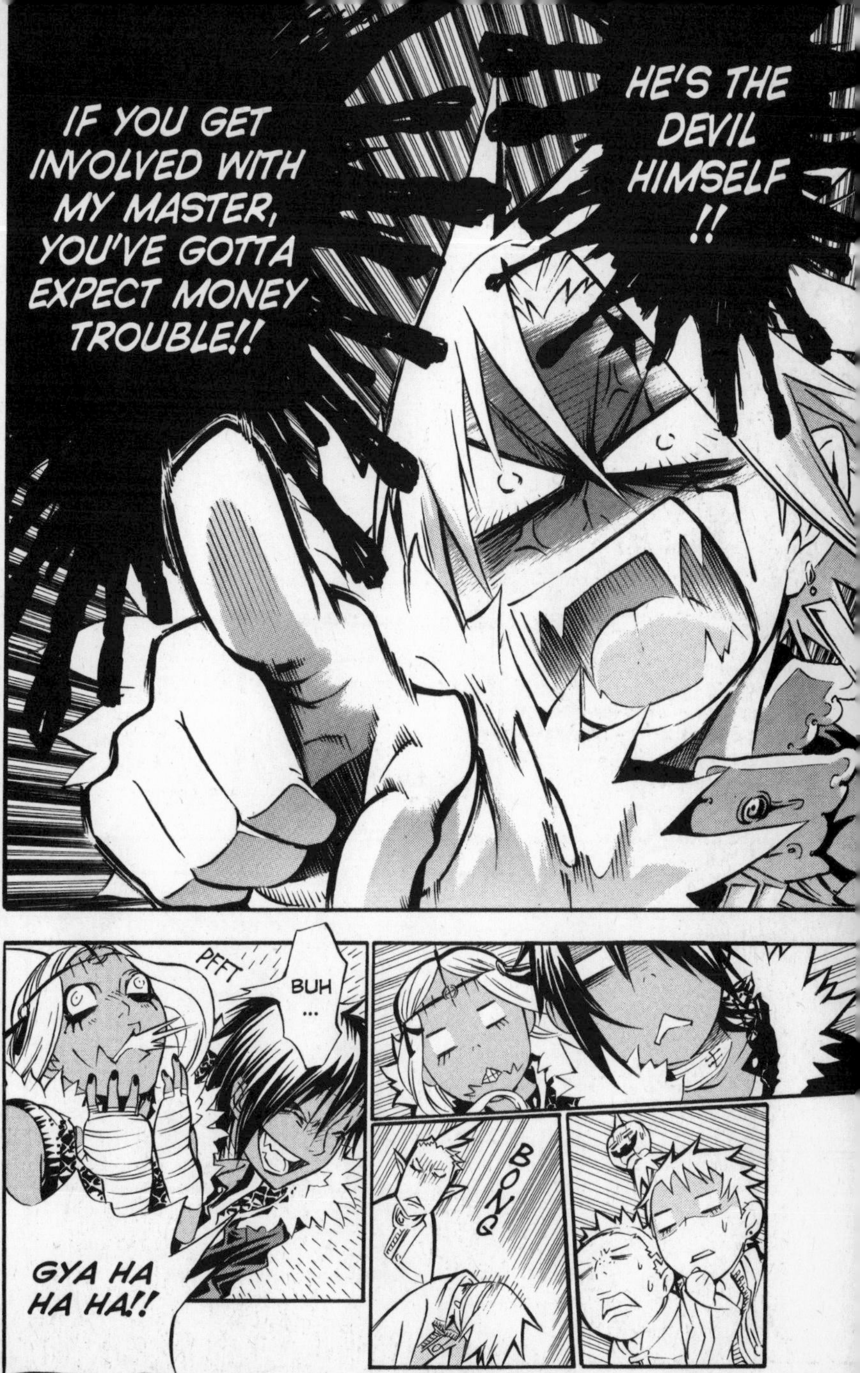
HE'S THE DEVIL HIMSELF!!
IF YOU GET INVOLVED WITH MY MASTER, YOU'VE GOTTA EXPECT MONEY TROUBLE!!
BONG
BUH ...
PFFT
GYA HA HA HA!!

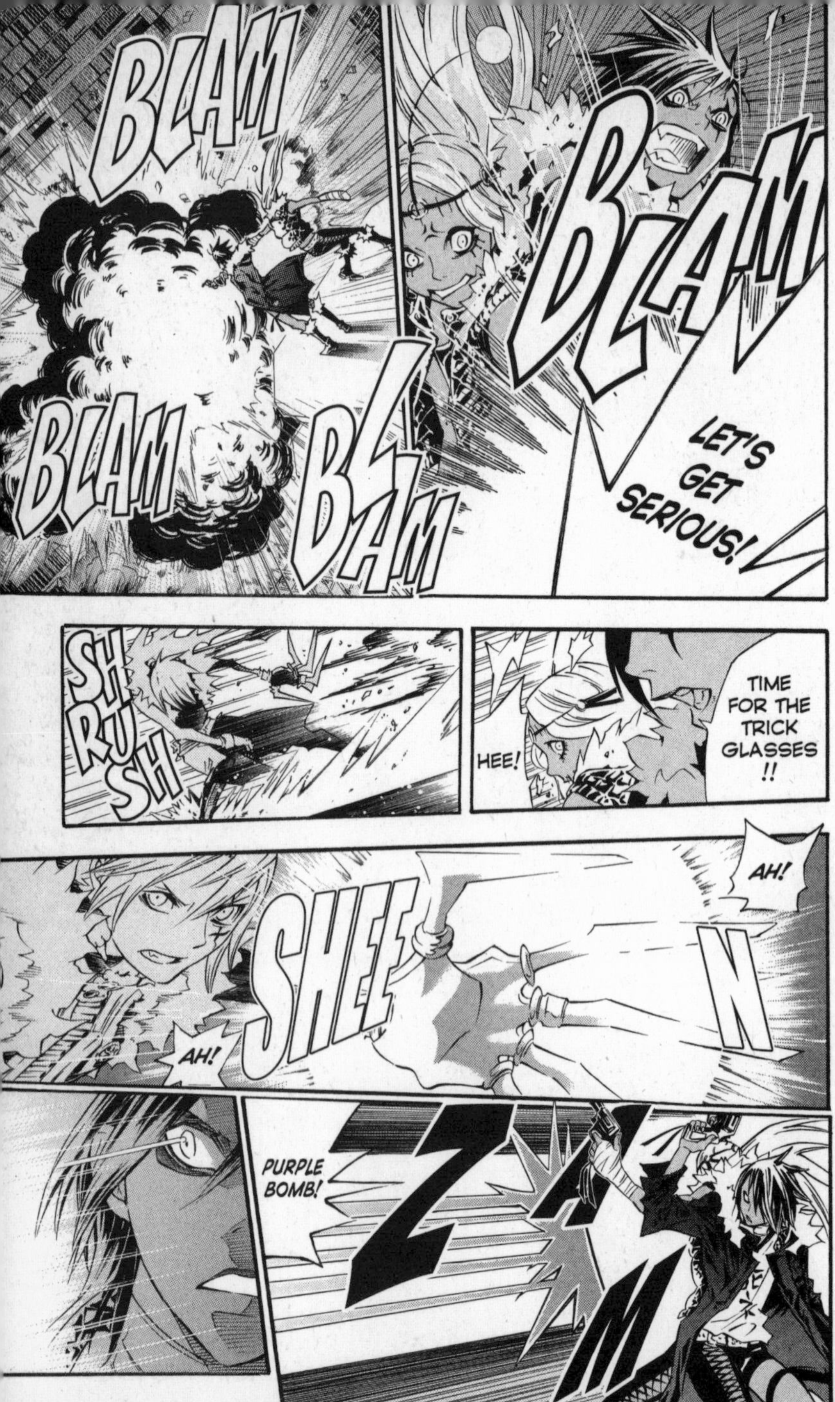
BLAM
LET'S GET SERIOUS!
BLAM
BLAM
BLAM
TIME FOR THE TRICK GLASSES !!
HEE!
SHRUSH
AH!
SHEEN
AH!
PURPLE BOMB!
ZZM

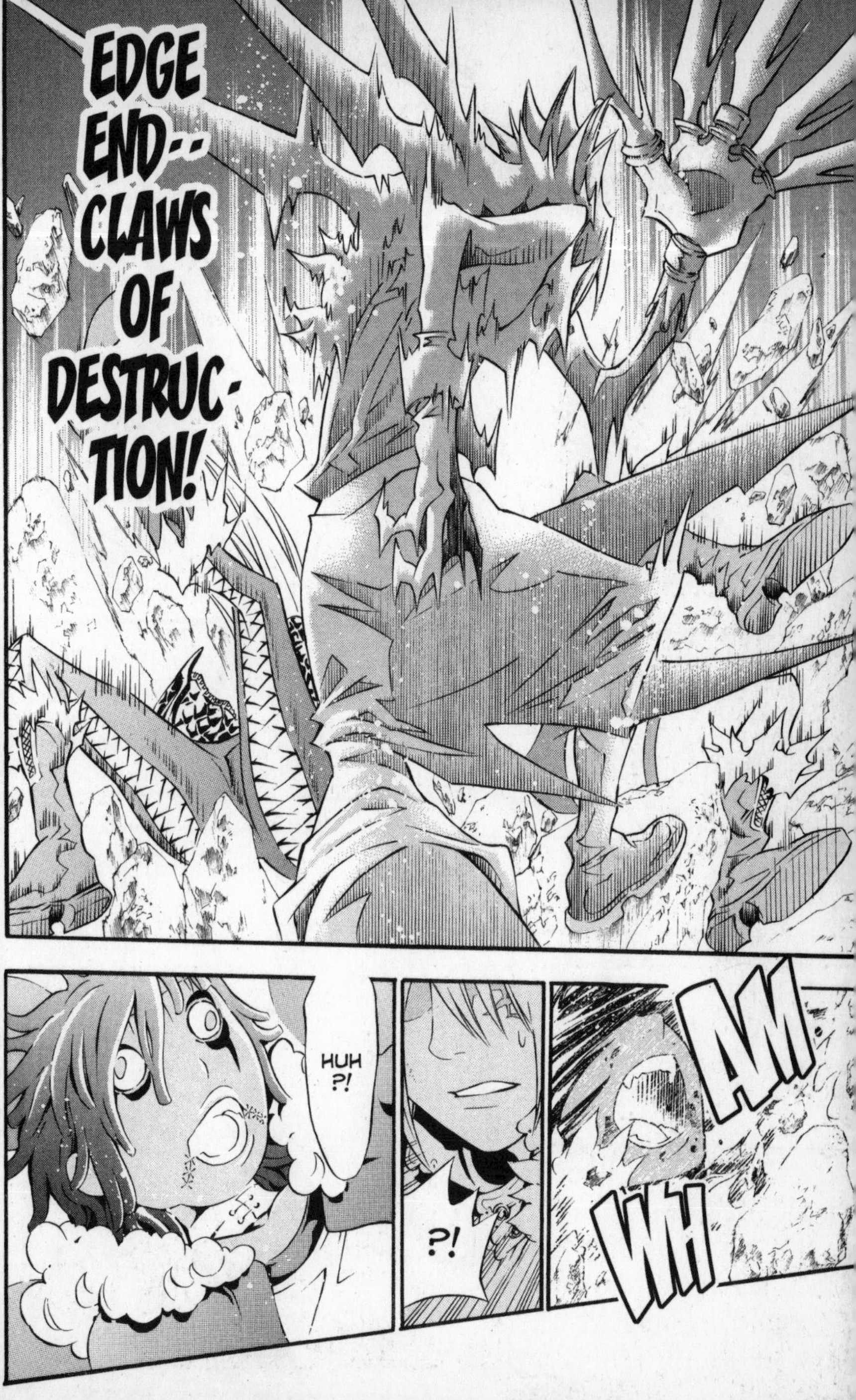
EDGE END-- CLAWS OF DESTRUC-TION!
WHAM
?!
HUH ?!

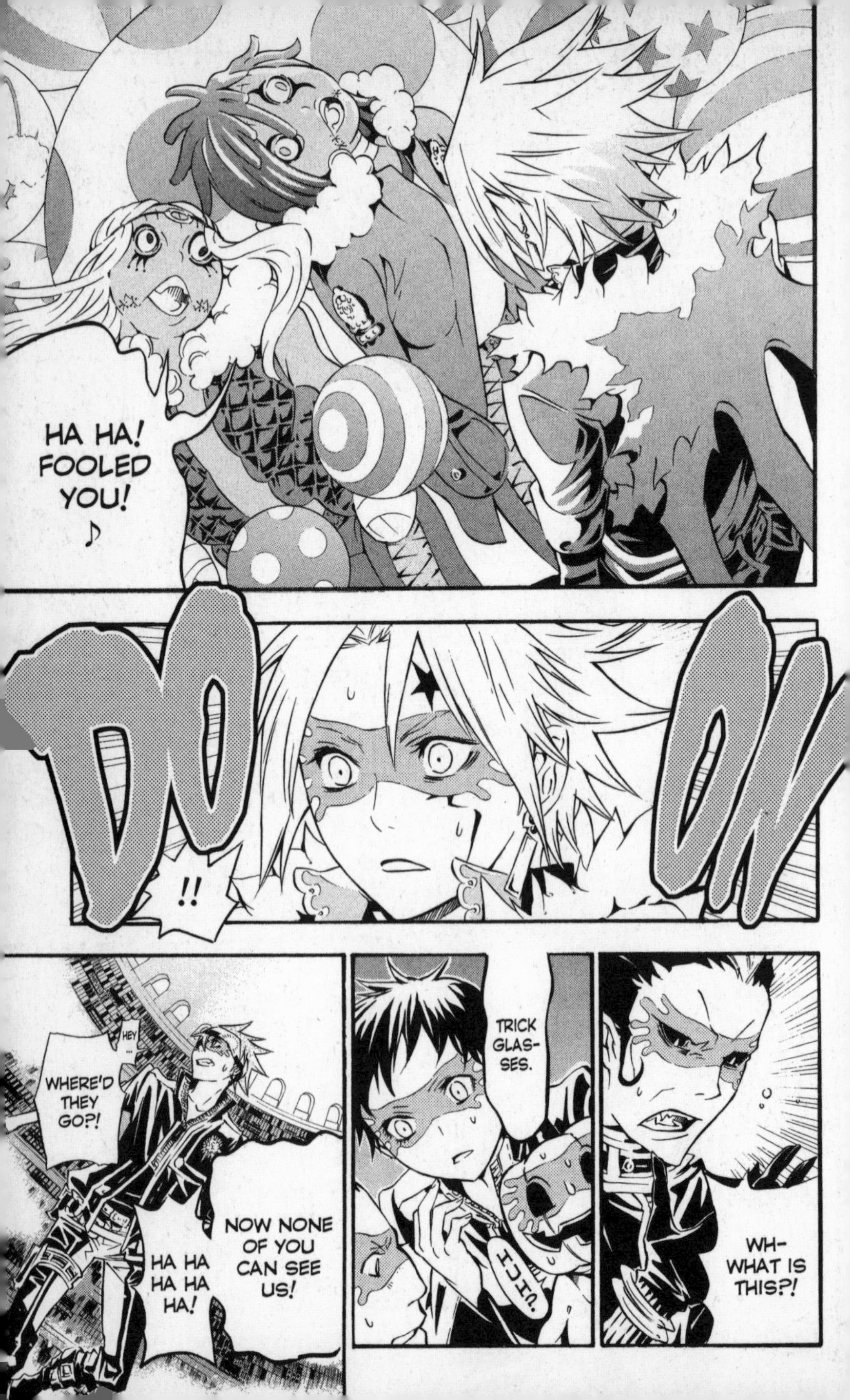
HA HA! FOOLED YOU! ♪
DOON
!!
WH- WHAT IS THIS?!
TRICK GLASSES.
HEY...
WHERE'D THEY GO?!
NOW NONE OF YOU CAN SEE US!
HA HA HA HA HA!

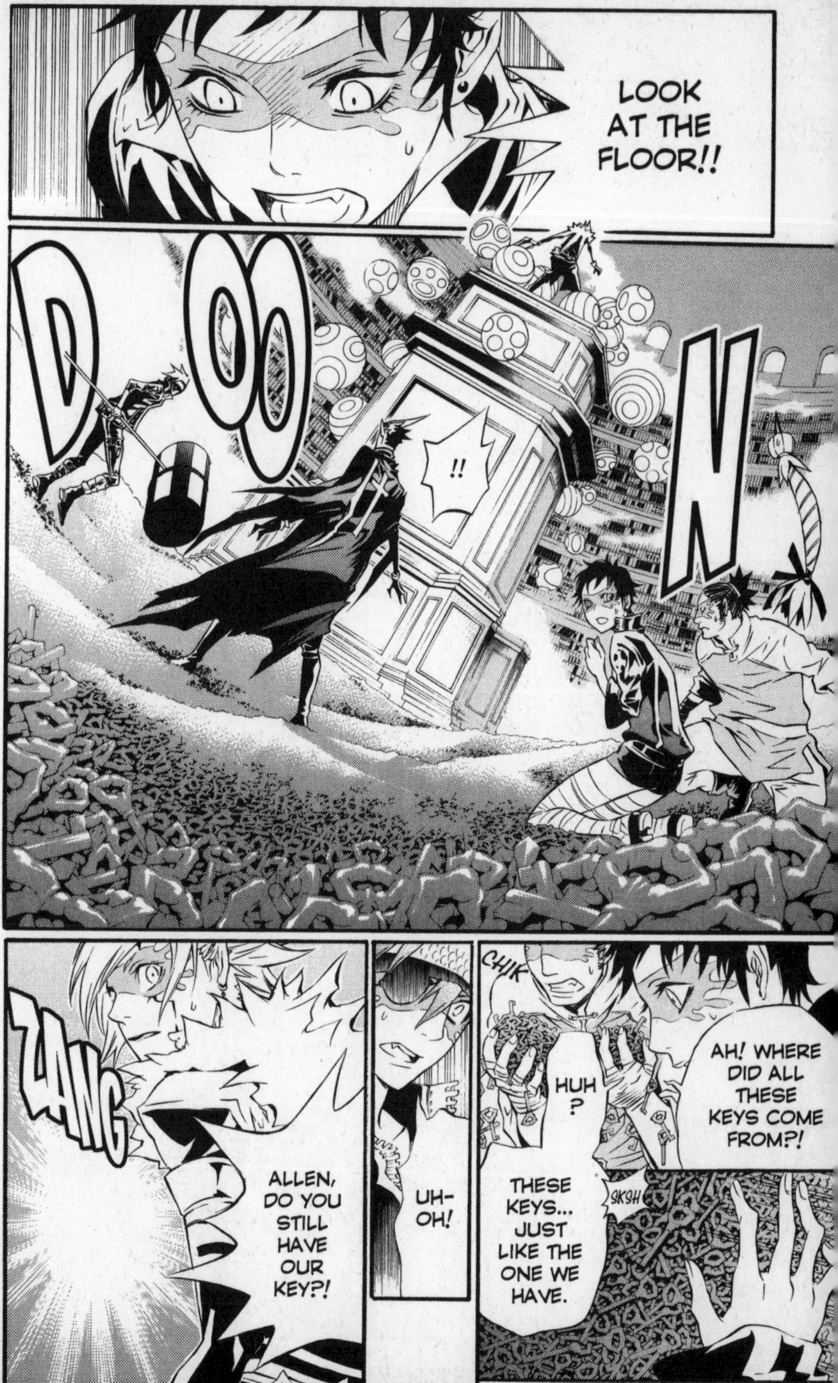
LOOK AT THE FLOOR!!
DOOON
!!
CHIK
AH! WHERE DID ALL THESE KEYS COME FROM?!
HUH?
SKSH
THESE KEYS... JUST LIKE THE ONE WE HAVE.
UH-OH!
ZANG
ALLEN, DO YOU STILL HAVE OUR KEY?!

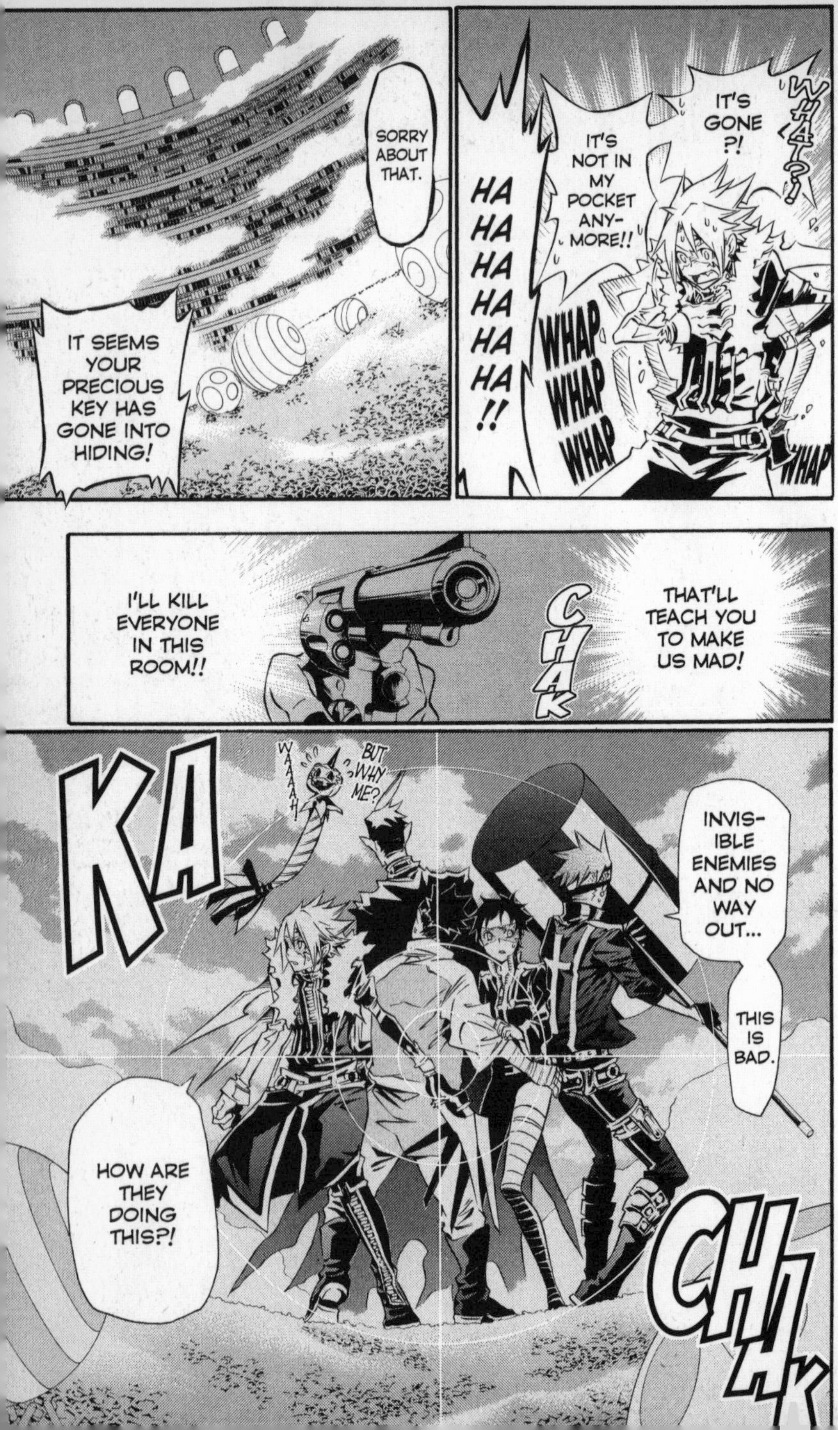
WHAT?!
IT'S GONE?!
IT'S NOT IN MY POCKET ANYMORE!!
WHAP WHAP WHAP
WHAP
HA HA HA HA HA HA HA!!
SORRY ABOUT THAT.
IT SEEMS YOUR PRECIOUS KEY HAS GONE INTO HIDING!
THAT'LL TEACH YOU TO MAKE US MAD!
CHAK
I'LL KILL EVERYONE IN THIS ROOM!!
INVISIBLE ENEMIES AND NO WAY OUT...
THIS IS BAD.
BUT WHY ME?
WAAAAAH!
KA
HOW ARE THEY DOING THIS?!
CHAK

Q: WHAT DO THE NOAH NORMALLY EAT?

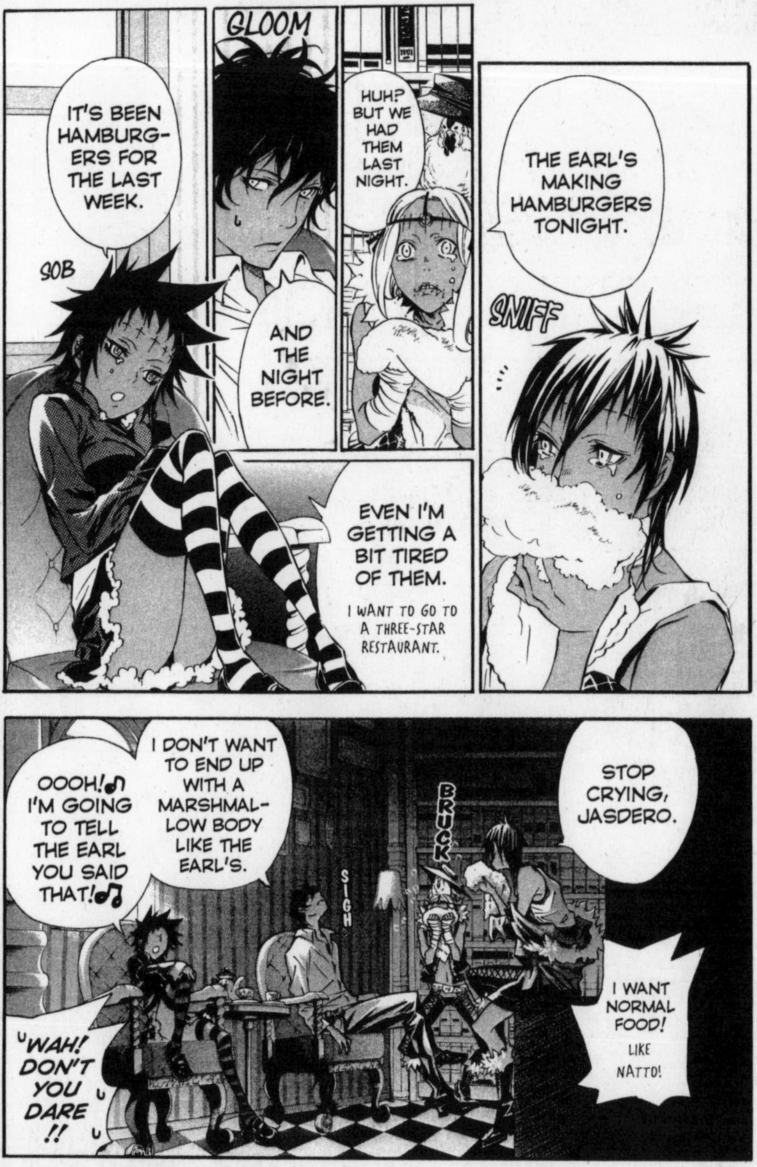
THE EARL'S MAKING HAMBURGERS TONIGHT.
SNIFF
HUH? BUT WE HAD THEM LAST NIGHT.
GLOOM
AND THE NIGHT BEFORE.
IT'S BEEN HAMBURGERS FOR THE LAST WEEK.
SOB
EVEN I'M GETTING A BIT TIRED OF THEM.
I WANT TO GO TO A THREE-STAR RESTAURANT.
STOP CRYING, JASDERO.
I WANT NORMAL FOOD!
LIKE NATTO!
BRUCK
SIGH
I DON'T WANT TO END UP WITH A MARSHMAL-LOW BODY LIKE THE EARL'S.
OOOH!♫ I'M GOING TO TELL THE EARL YOU SAID THAT!♫
WAH! DON'T YOU DARE!!

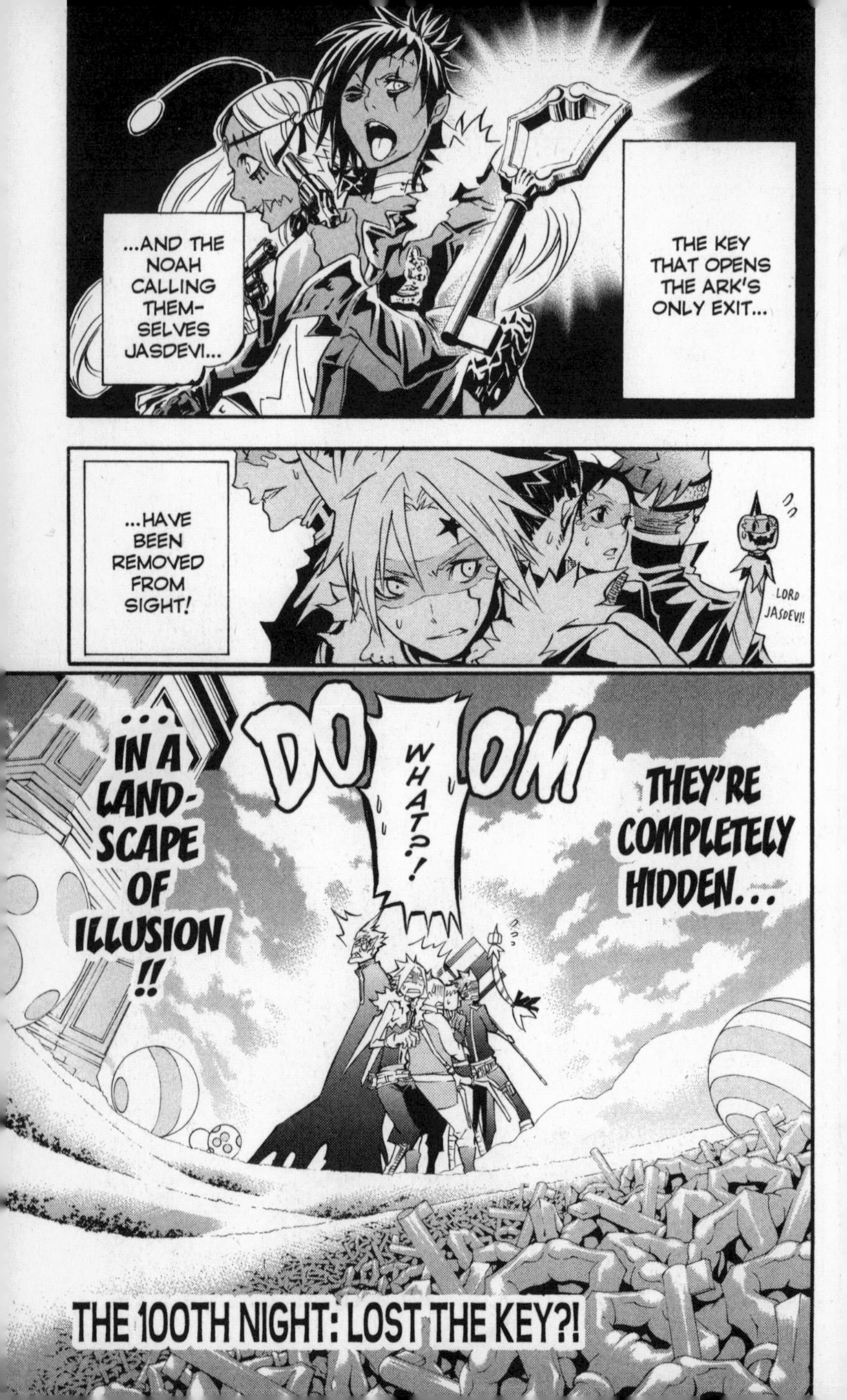
THE KEY THAT OPENS THE ARK'S ONLY EXIT...
...AND THE NOAH CALLING THEMSELVES JASDEVI...
LORD JASDEVI!
...HAVE BEEN REMOVED FROM SIGHT!
THEY'RE COMPLETELY HIDDEN...
DOOM
WHAT?!
...IN A LANDSCAPE OF ILLUSION!!
THE 100TH NIGHT: LOST THE KEY?!

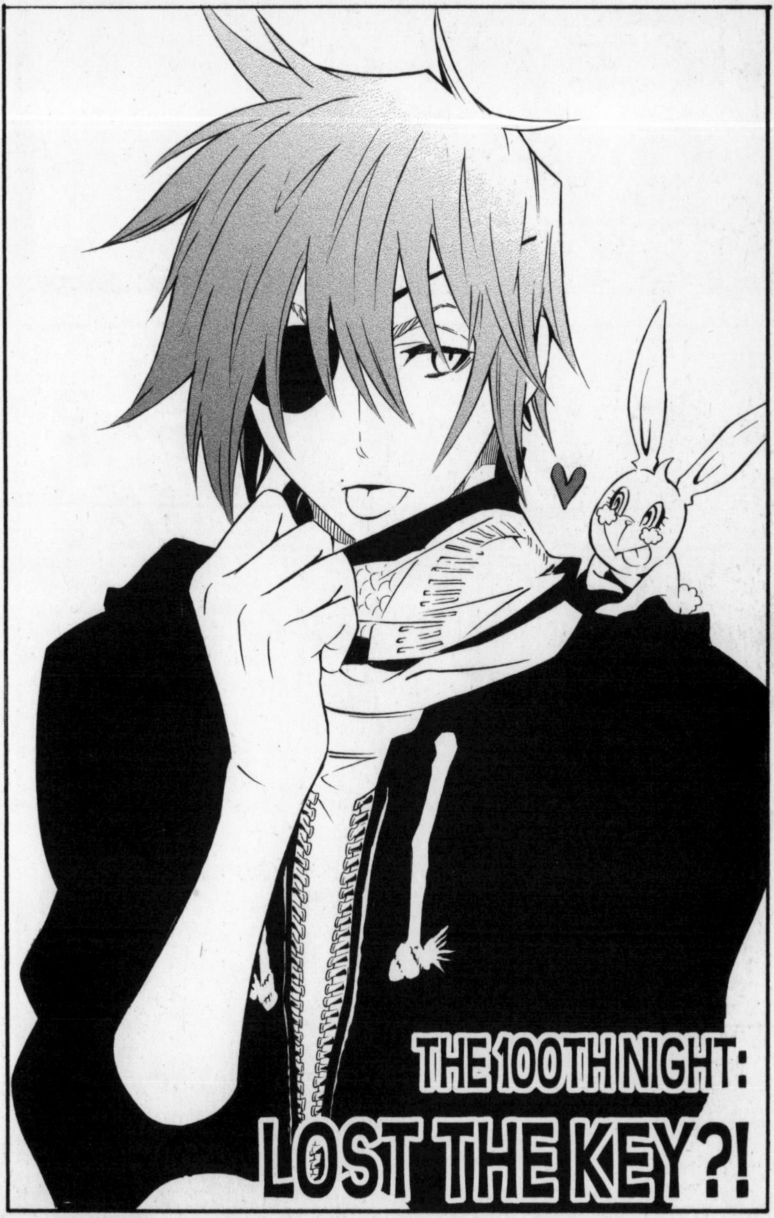
THE 100TH NIGHT:
LOST THE KEY?!

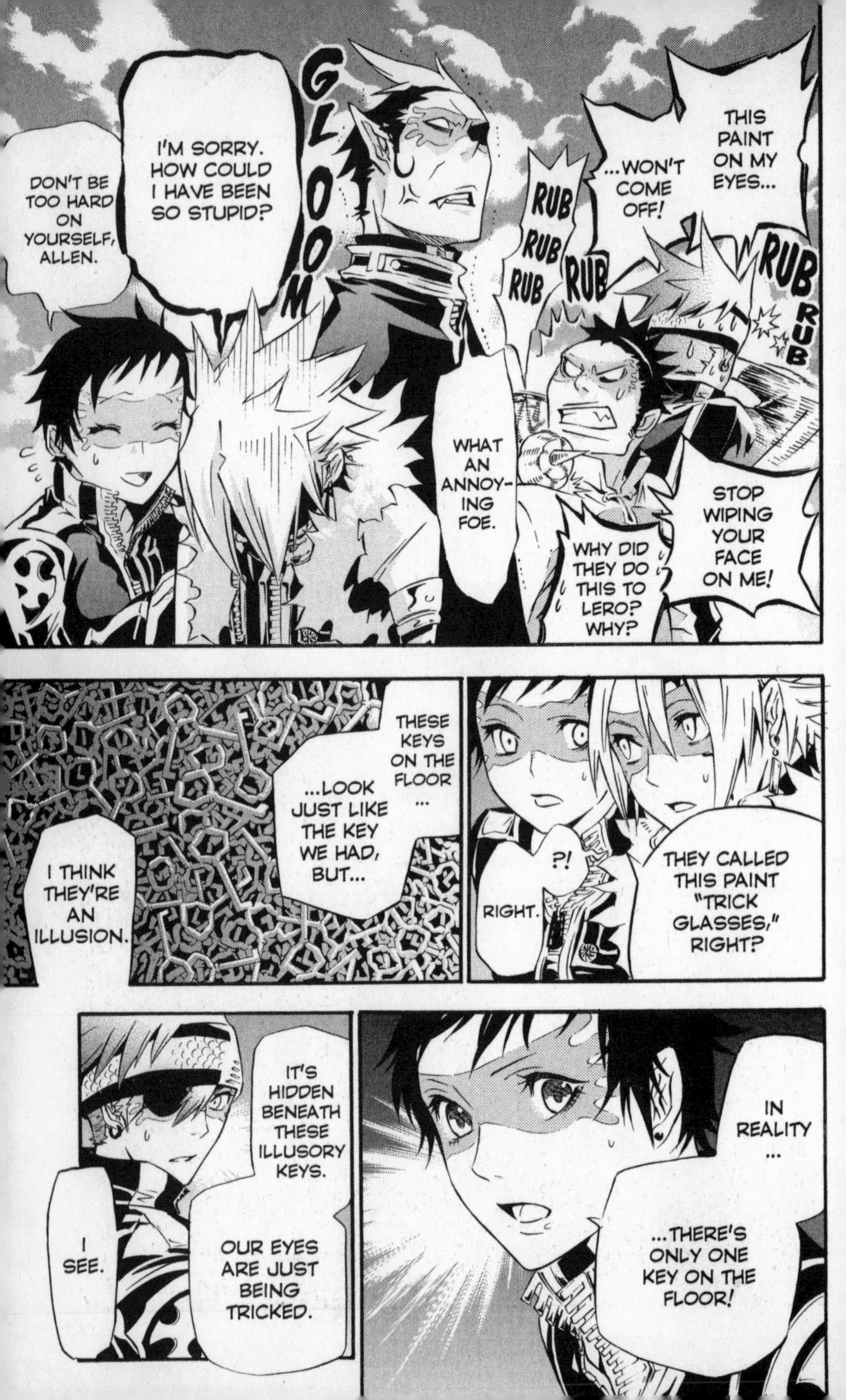
THIS PAINT ON MY EYES...
...WON'T COME OFF!
RUB RUB RUB RUB RUB RUB
STOP WIPING YOUR FACE ON ME!
WHY DID THEY DO THIS TO LERO? WHY?
WHAT AN ANNOYING FOE.
GLOOM
I'M SORRY. HOW COULD I HAVE BEEN SO STUPID?
DON'T BE TOO HARD ON YOURSELF, ALLEN.
THEY CALLED THIS PAINT "TRICK GLASSES," RIGHT?
?!
RIGHT.
THESE KEYS ON THE FLOOR...
...LOOK JUST LIKE THE KEY WE HAD, BUT...
I THINK THEY'RE AN ILLUSION.
IN REALITY...
...THERE'S ONLY ONE KEY ON THE FLOOR!
IT'S HIDDEN BENEATH THESE ILLUSORY KEYS.
OUR EYES ARE JUST BEING TRICKED.
I SEE.

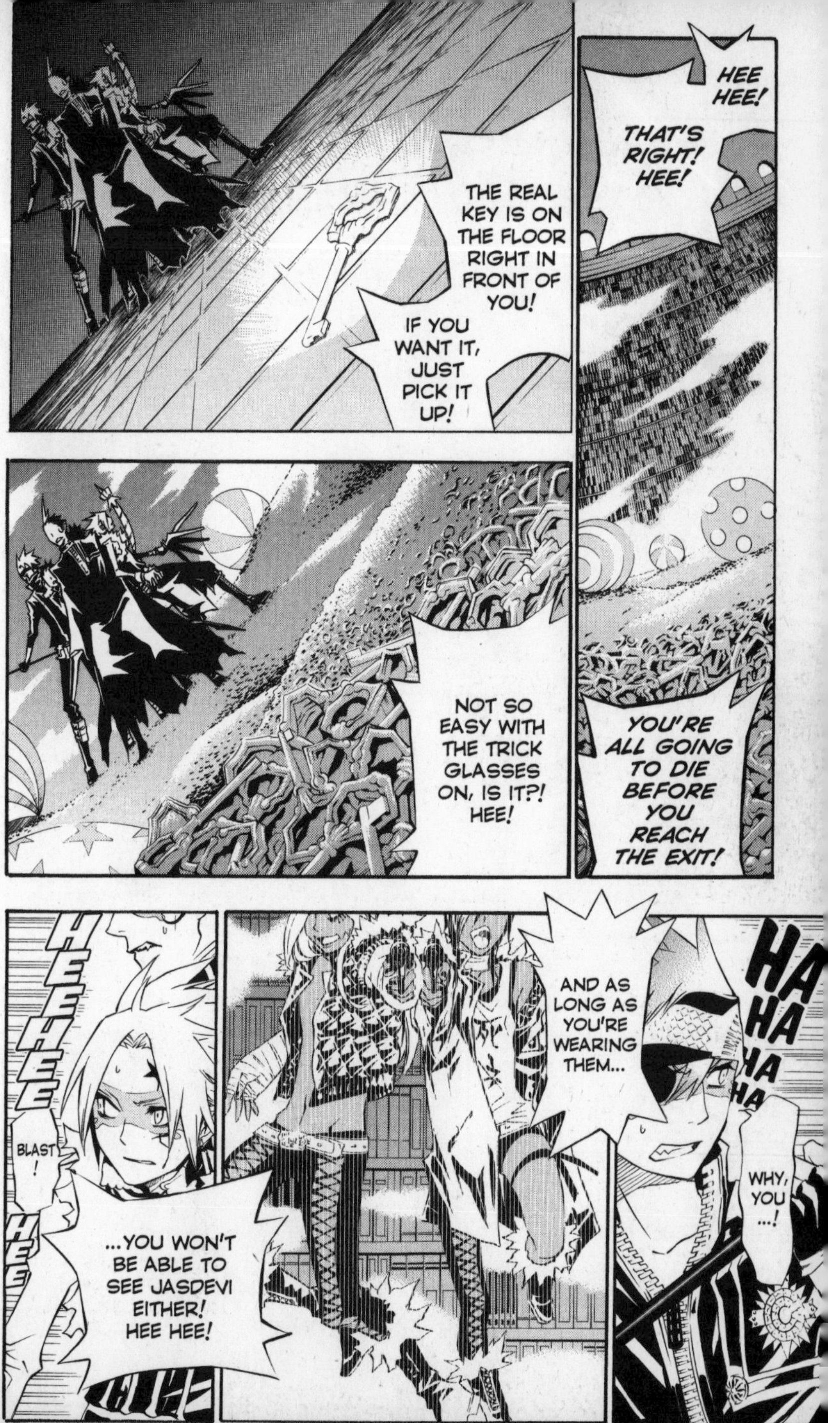
HEE HEE!
THAT'S RIGHT! HEE!
YOU'RE ALL GOING TO DIE BEFORE YOU REACH THE EXIT!
THE REAL KEY IS ON THE FLOOR RIGHT IN FRONT OF YOU!
IF YOU WANT IT, JUST PICK IT UP!
NOT SO EASY WITH THE TRICK GLASSES ON, IS IT?! HEE!
HAHAHAHA
WHY, YOU...!
AND AS LONG AS YOU'RE WEARING THEM...
...YOU WON'T BE ABLE TO SEE JASDEVI EITHER! HEE HEE!
HEEHEE
BLAST!
HEE

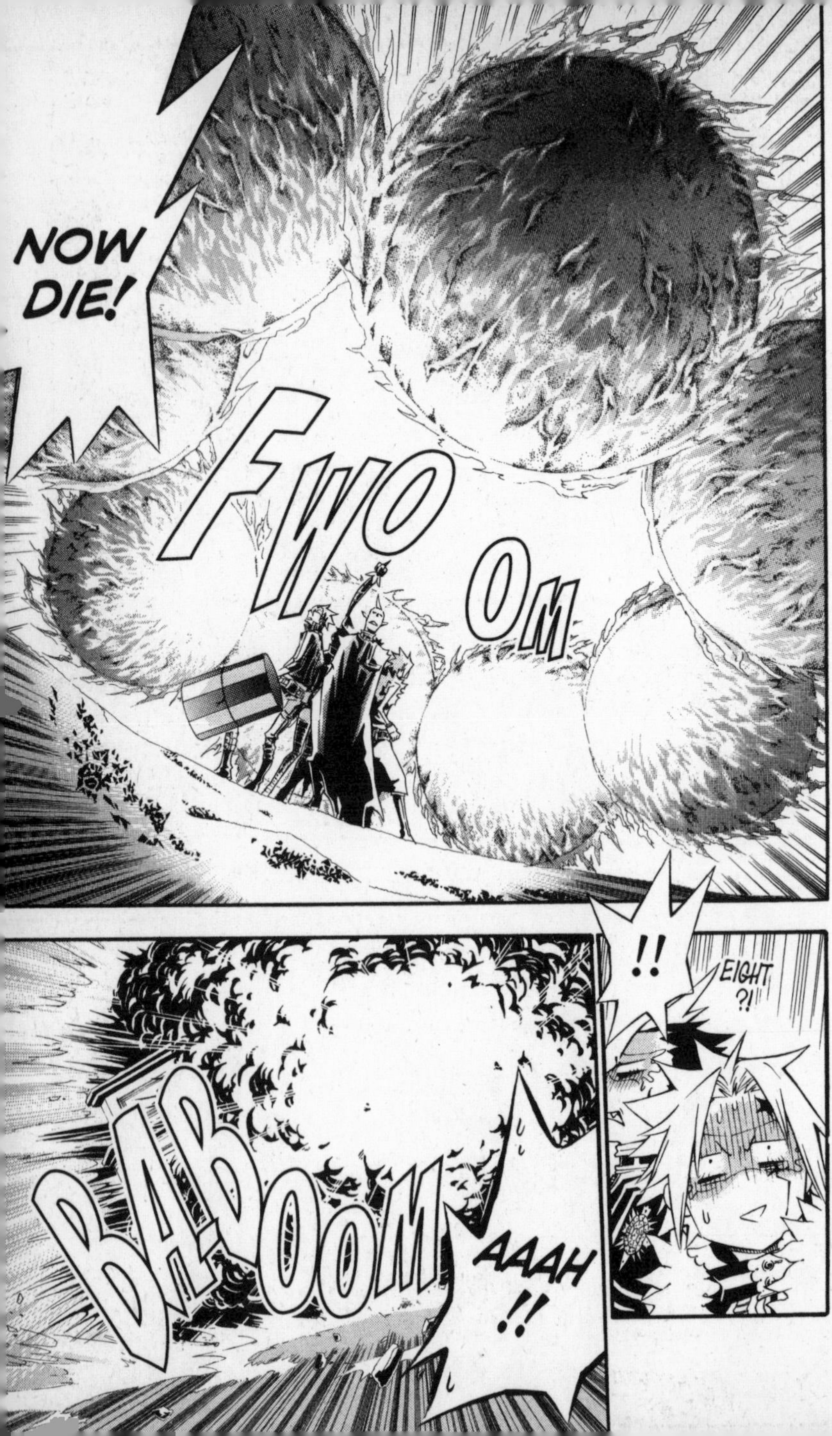
NOW DIE!
FWOOM
!!
EIGHT ?!
BABOOM
AAAH !!

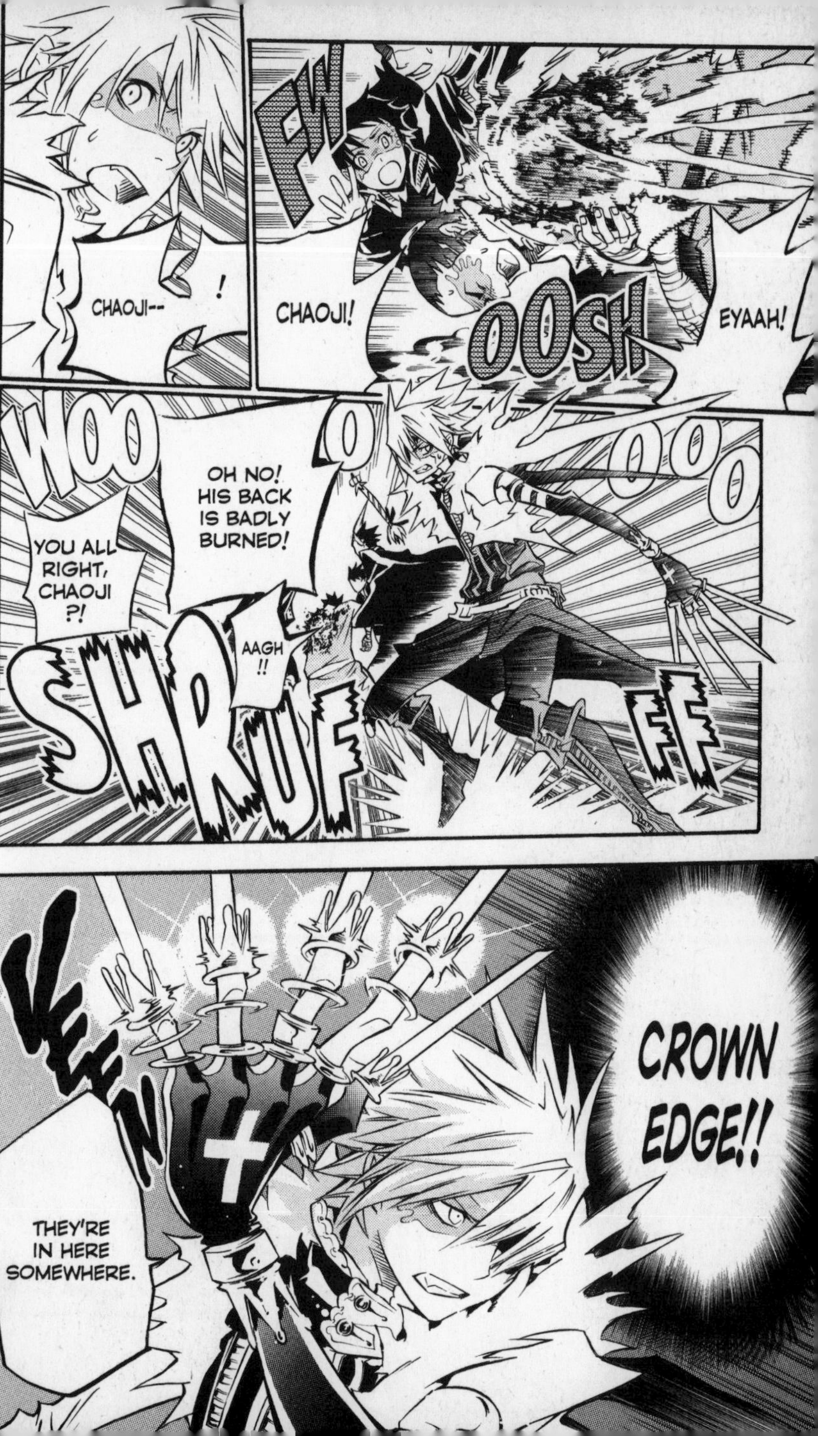
EYAAH!
OOSH
CHAOJI!
FW
!
CHAOJI--
OOO
O
OH NO! HIS BACK IS BADLY BURNED!
WOO
YOU ALL RIGHT, CHAOJI ?!
AAGH !!
FF
SHRUF
CROWN EDGE!!
THEY'RE IN HERE SOMEWHERE.

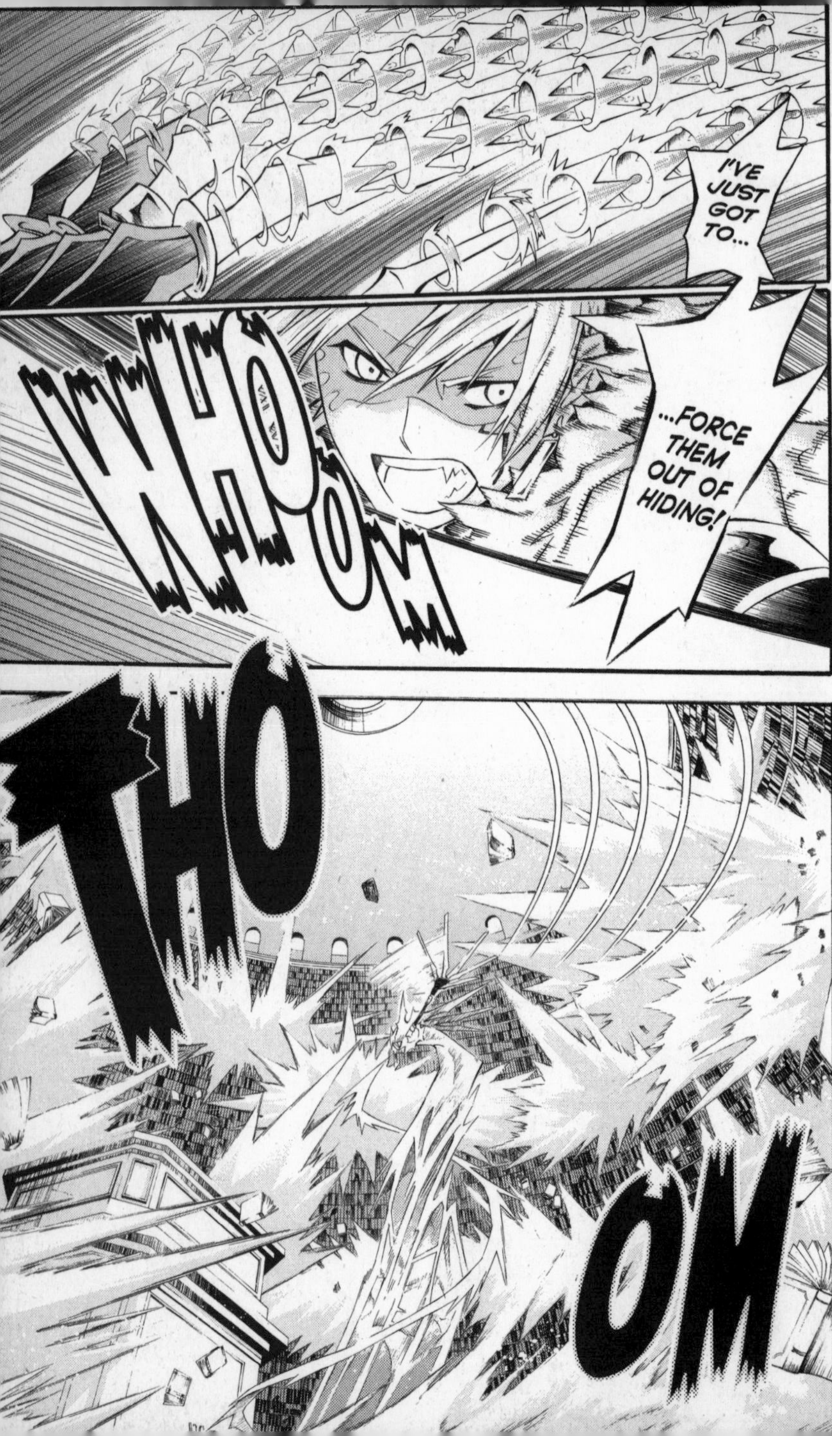
I'VE JUST GOT TO...
...FORCE THEM OUT OF HIDING!
WHOOM
THO
OM

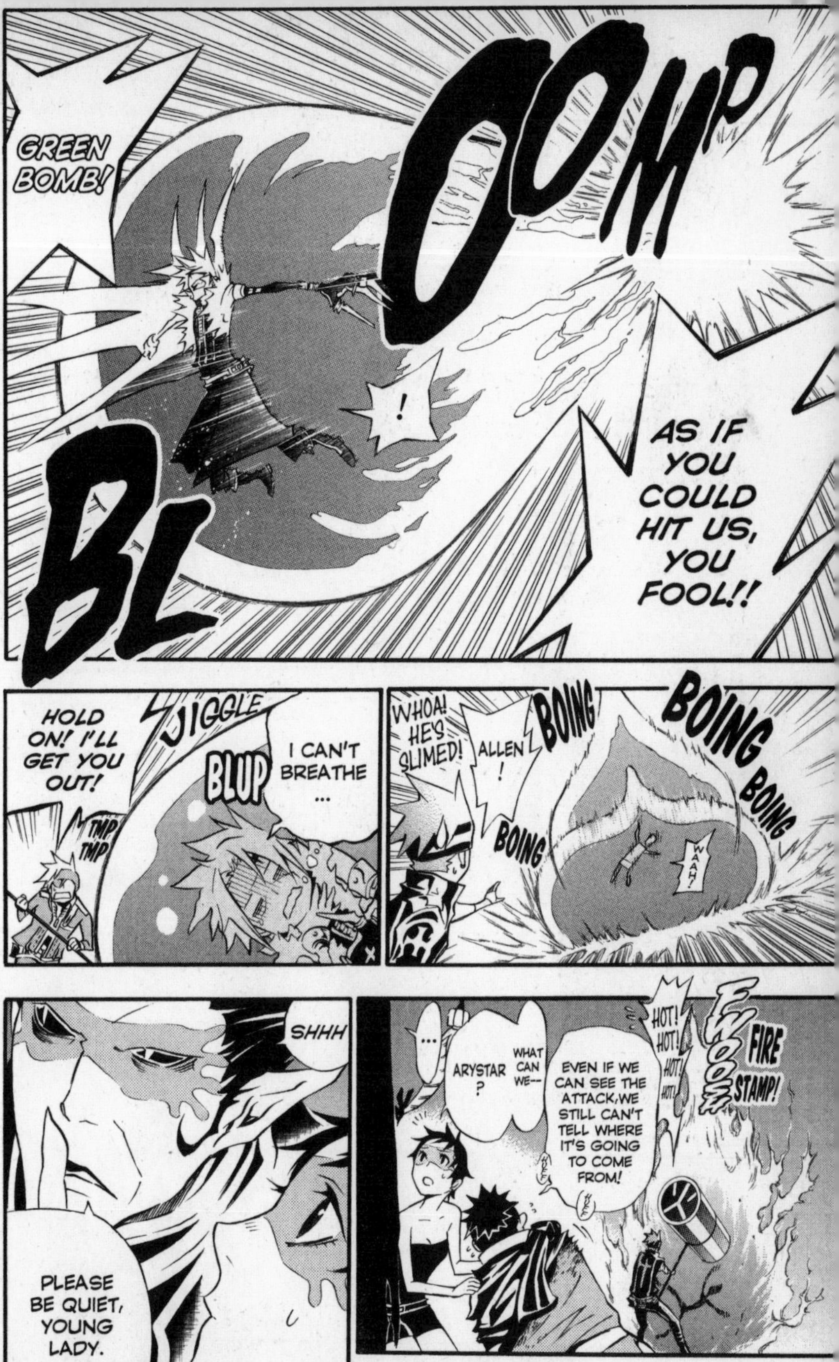
AS IF YOU COULD HIT US, YOU FOOL!!
OOMP
!
GREEN BOMB!
BL
BOING BOING BOING
WAAH!
BOING
ALLEN!
WHOA! HE'S SLIMED!
BOING
I CAN'T BREATHE ...
BLUP
JIGGLE
HOLD ON! I'LL GET YOU OUT!
TMP TMP
FIRE STAMP!
FWOOOM
HOT! HOT! HOT! HOT!
EVEN IF WE CAN SEE THE ATTACK, WE STILL CAN'T TELL WHERE IT'S GOING TO COME FROM!
WHAT CAN WE--
ARYSTAR?
...
SHHH
PLEASE BE QUIET, YOUNG LADY.

READ THIS WAY

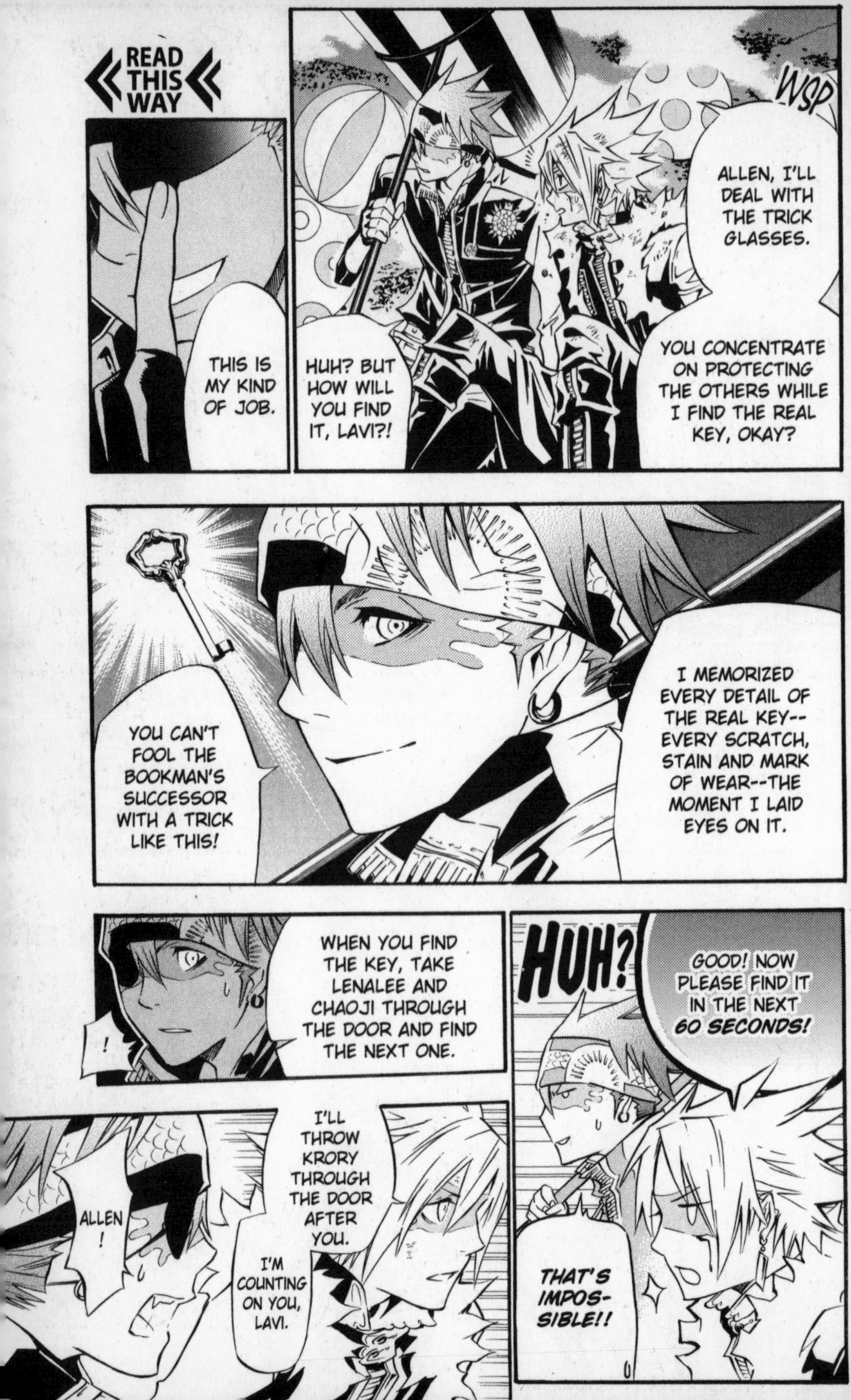
WSP
ALLEN, I'LL DEAL WITH THE TRICK GLASSES.
YOU CONCENTRATE ON PROTECTING THE OTHERS WHILE I FIND THE REAL KEY, OKAY?
HUH? BUT HOW WILL YOU FIND IT, LAVI?!
THIS IS MY KIND OF JOB.
I MEMORIZED EVERY DETAIL OF THE REAL KEY--EVERY SCRATCH, STAIN AND MARK OF WEAR--THE MOMENT I LAID EYES ON IT.
YOU CAN'T FOOL THE BOOKMAN'S SUCCESSOR WITH A TRICK LIKE THIS!
GOOD! NOW PLEASE FIND IT IN THE NEXT 60 SECONDS!
HUH?
THAT'S IMPOSSIBLE!!
WHEN YOU FIND THE KEY, TAKE LENALEE AND CHAOJI THROUGH THE DOOR AND FIND THE NEXT ONE.
!
I'LL THROW KRORY THROUGH THE DOOR AFTER YOU.
I'M COUNTING ON YOU, LAVI.
ALLEN!

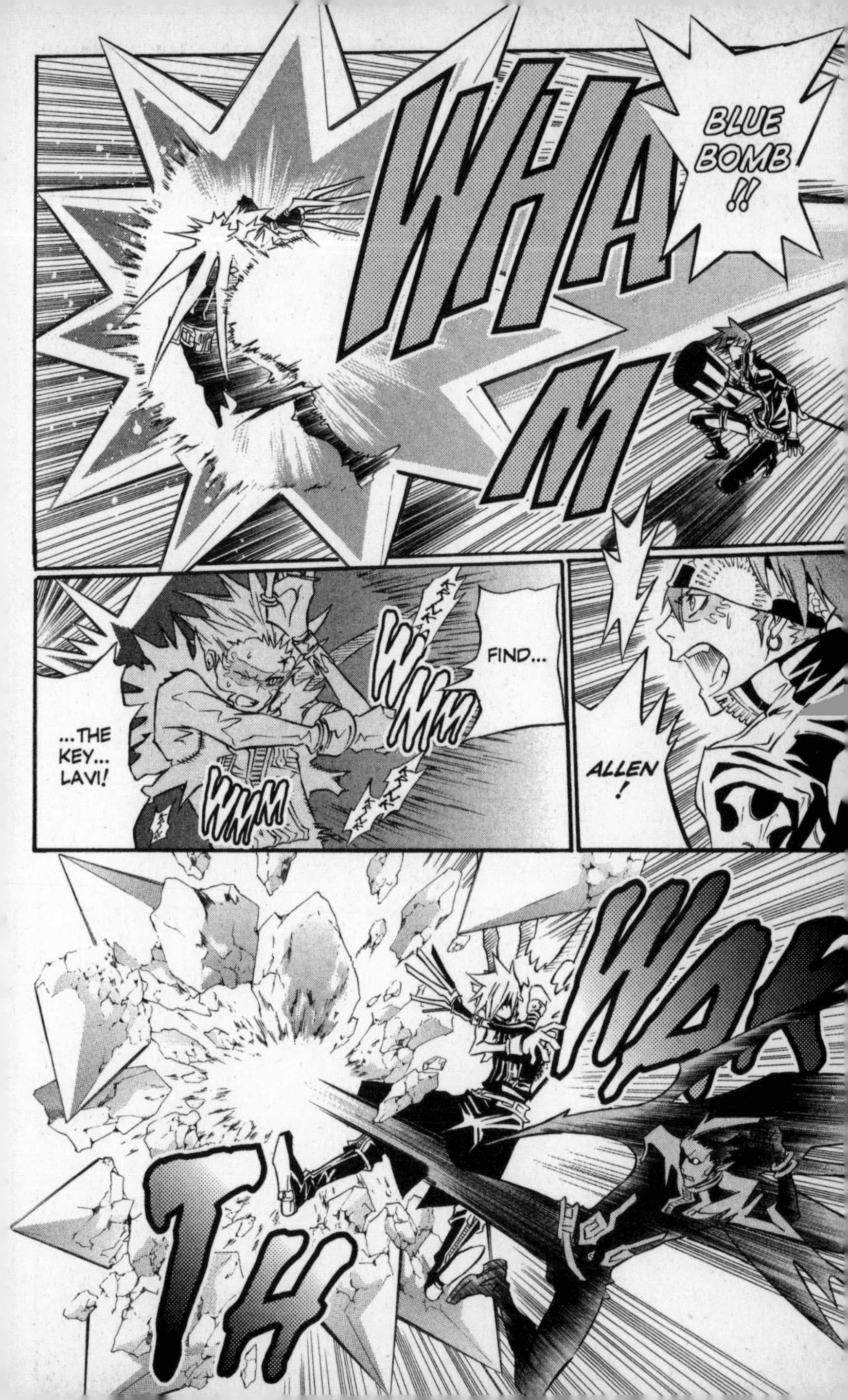
BLUE BOMB!!
WHAM
ALLEN!
FIND...
...THE KEY... LAVI!
WMM
WMM
WHA
TH

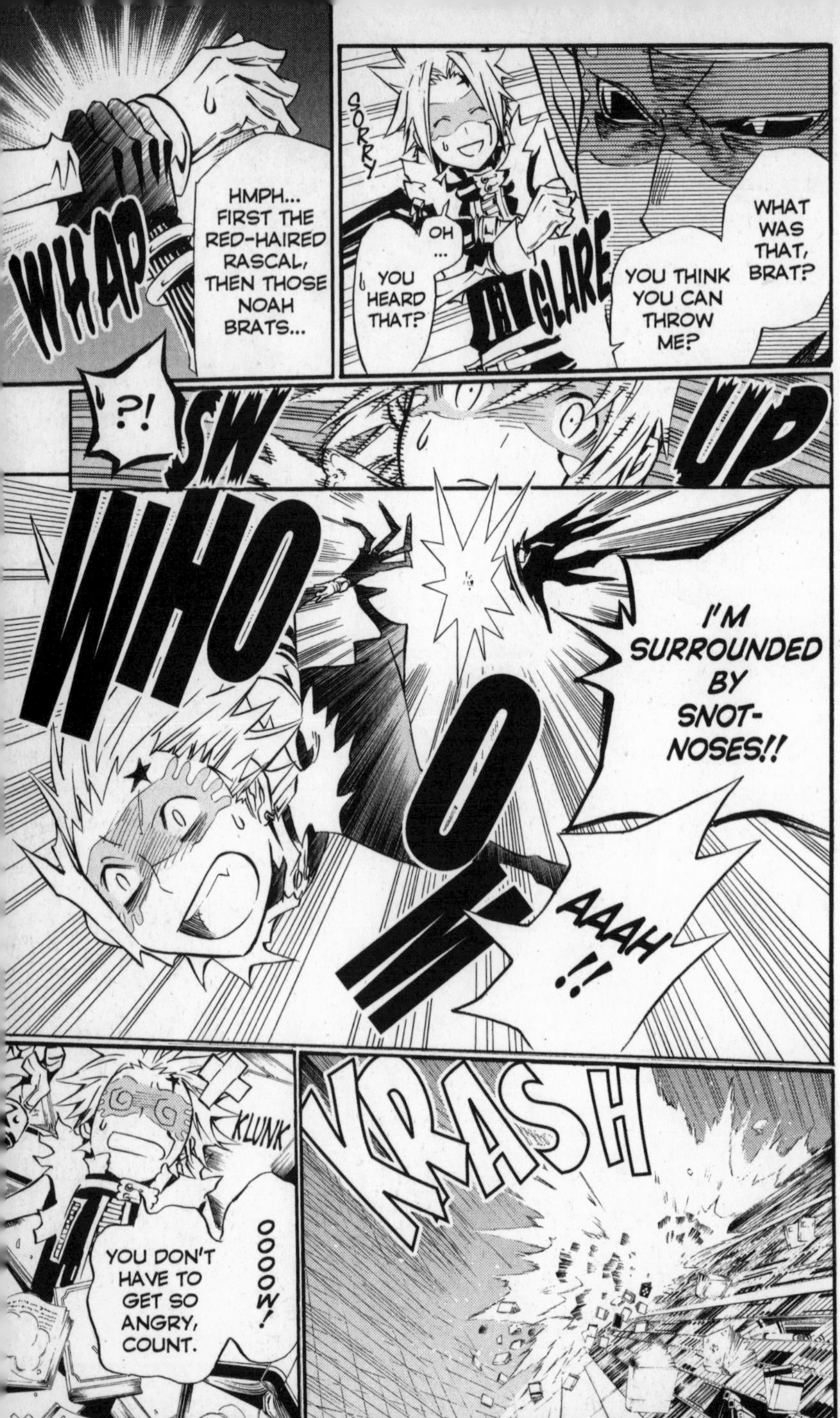
WHAT WAS THAT, BRAT?
YOU THINK YOU CAN THROW ME?
GLARE
SORRY
OH ...
YOU HEARD THAT?
HMPH... FIRST THE RED-HAIRED RASCAL, THEN THOSE NOAH BRATS...
WHAP!!!
UP
SW
?!
I'M SURROUNDED BY SNOT-NOSES!!
WHO
OM
AAAH!!
KRASH
KLUNK
OOOOOW!
YOU DON'T HAVE TO GET SO ANGRY, COUNT.

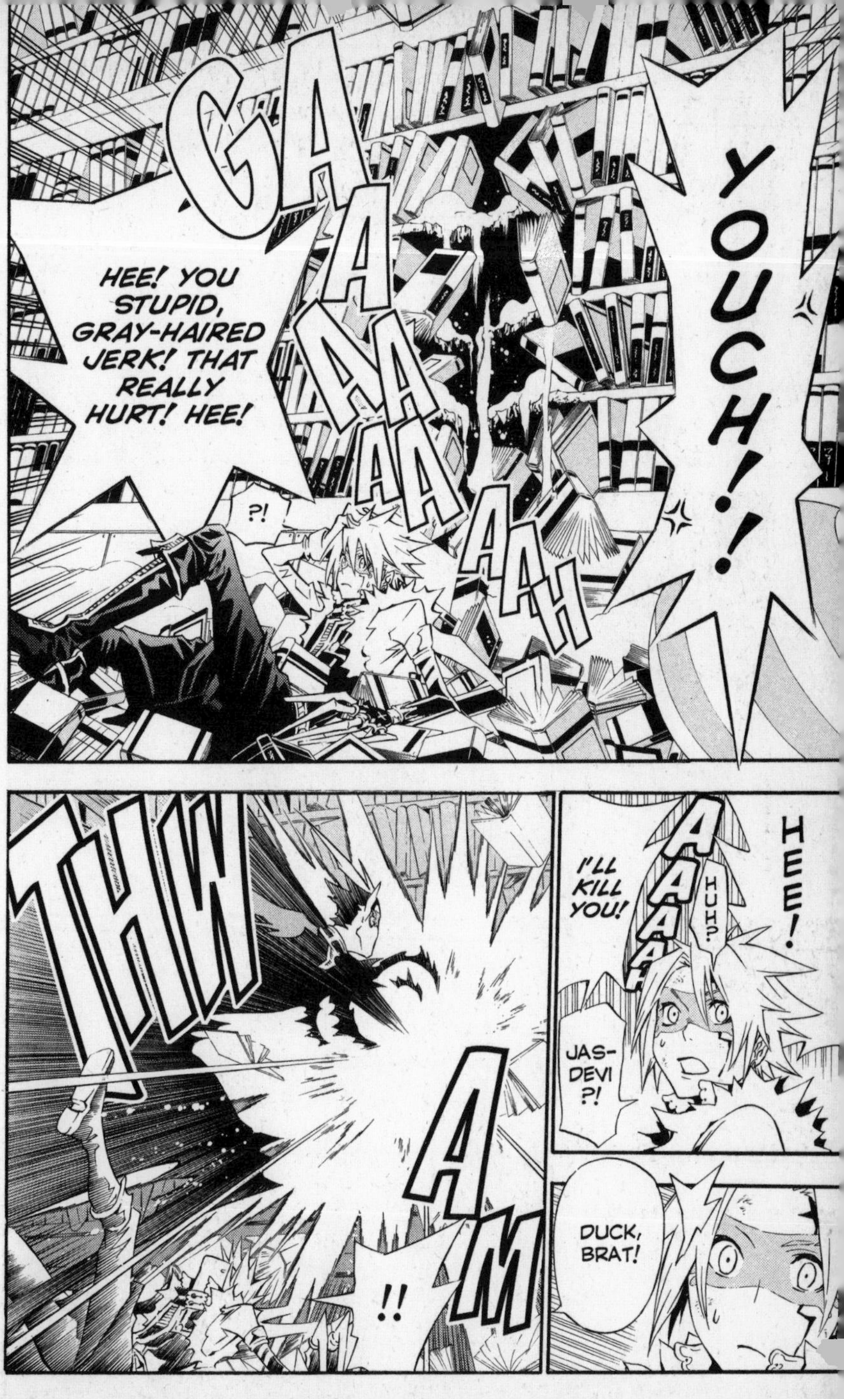
YOUCH!!
GAAAAAAAAH
HEE! YOU STUPID, GRAY-HAIRED JERK! THAT REALLY HURT! HEE!
?!
HEE!
HUH?
AAAAA
I'LL KILL YOU!
JAS-DEVI?!
DUCK, BRAT!
THWAAM
!!

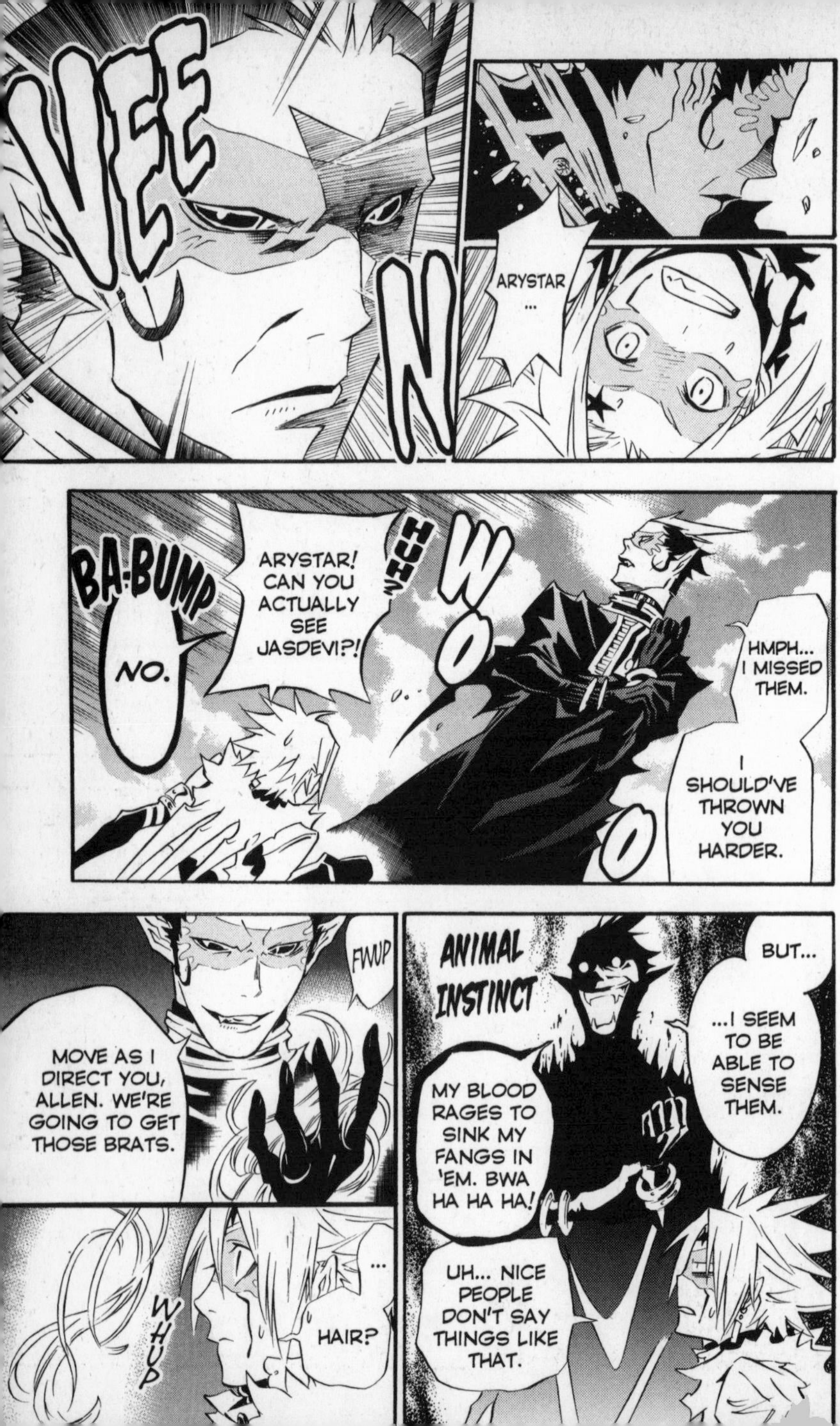
ARYSTAR ...
VEE
N
HMPH... I MISSED THEM.
I SHOULD'VE THROWN YOU HARDER.
WOO
HUH?!
ARYSTAR! CAN YOU ACTUALLY SEE JASDEVI?!
BA-BUMP
NO.
BUT...
...I SEEM TO BE ABLE TO SENSE THEM.
ANIMAL INSTINCT
MY BLOOD RAGES TO SINK MY FANGS IN 'EM. BWA HA HA HA!
UH... NICE PEOPLE DON'T SAY THINGS LIKE THAT.
FWUP
MOVE AS I DIRECT YOU, ALLEN. WE'RE GOING TO GET THOSE BRATS.
...
HAIR?
WHUP

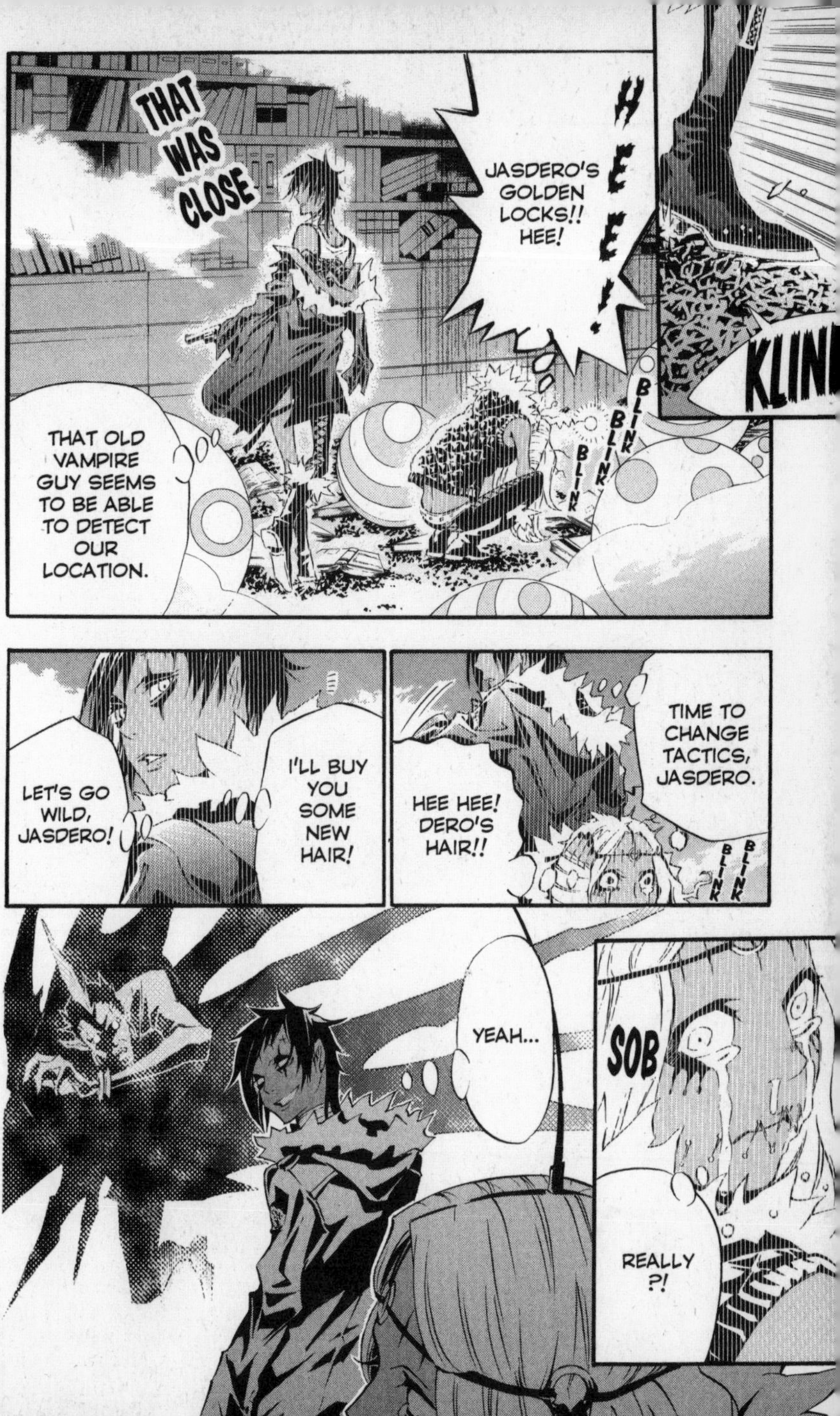
KLIN
HEE!
JASDERO'S GOLDEN LOCKS!! HEE!
THAT WAS CLOSE
BLINK BLINK BLINK
THAT OLD VAMPIRE GUY SEEMS TO BE ABLE TO DETECT OUR LOCATION.
TIME TO CHANGE TACTICS, JASDERO.
HEE HEE! DERO'S HAIR!!
BLINK BLINK
I'LL BUY YOU SOME NEW HAIR!
LET'S GO WILD, JASDERO!
SOB
REALLY ?!
YEAH...

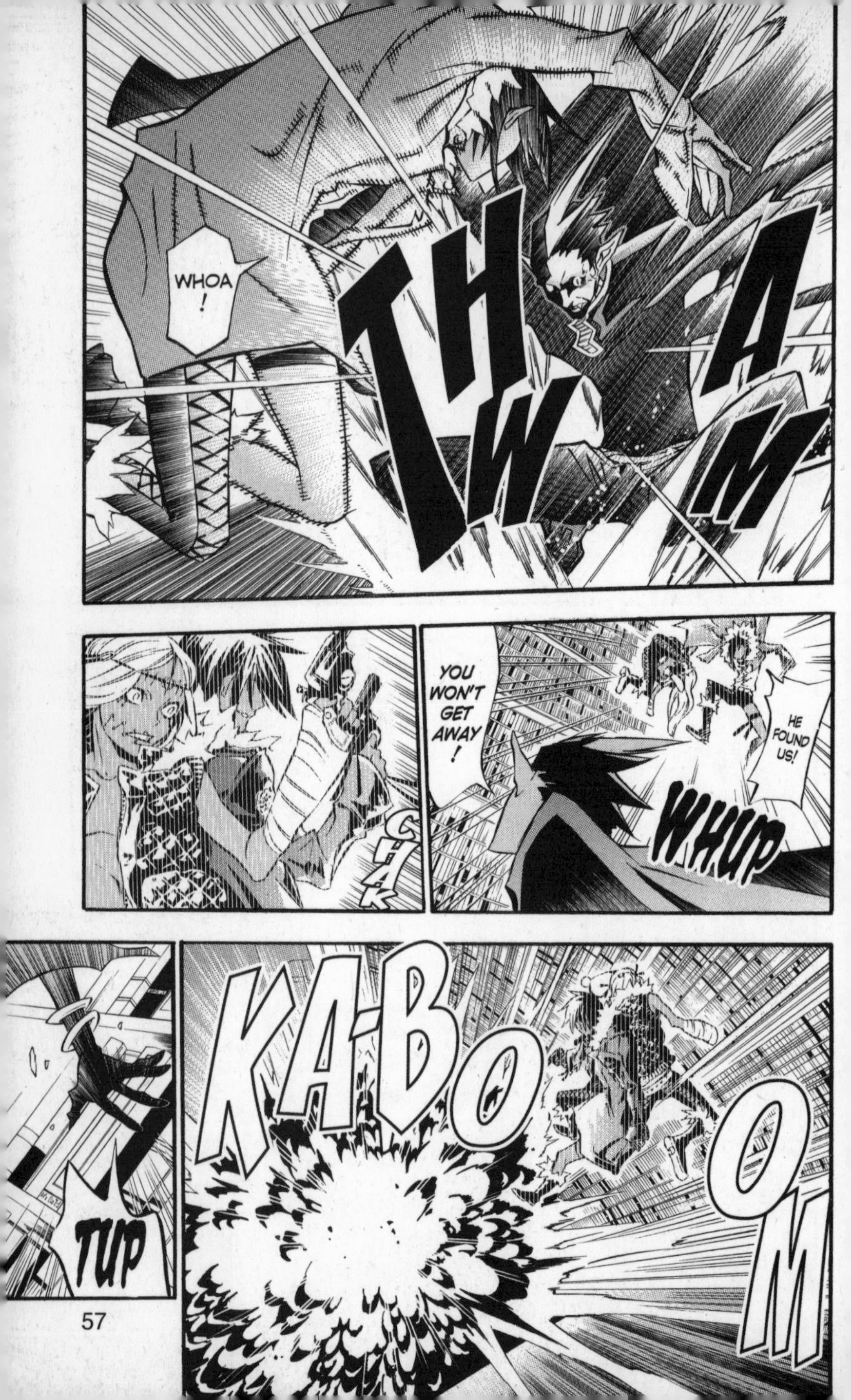
WHOA!
THWAM
HE FOUND US!
YOU WON'T GET AWAY!
WHUP
CHAK
KA-BOOM
TUP

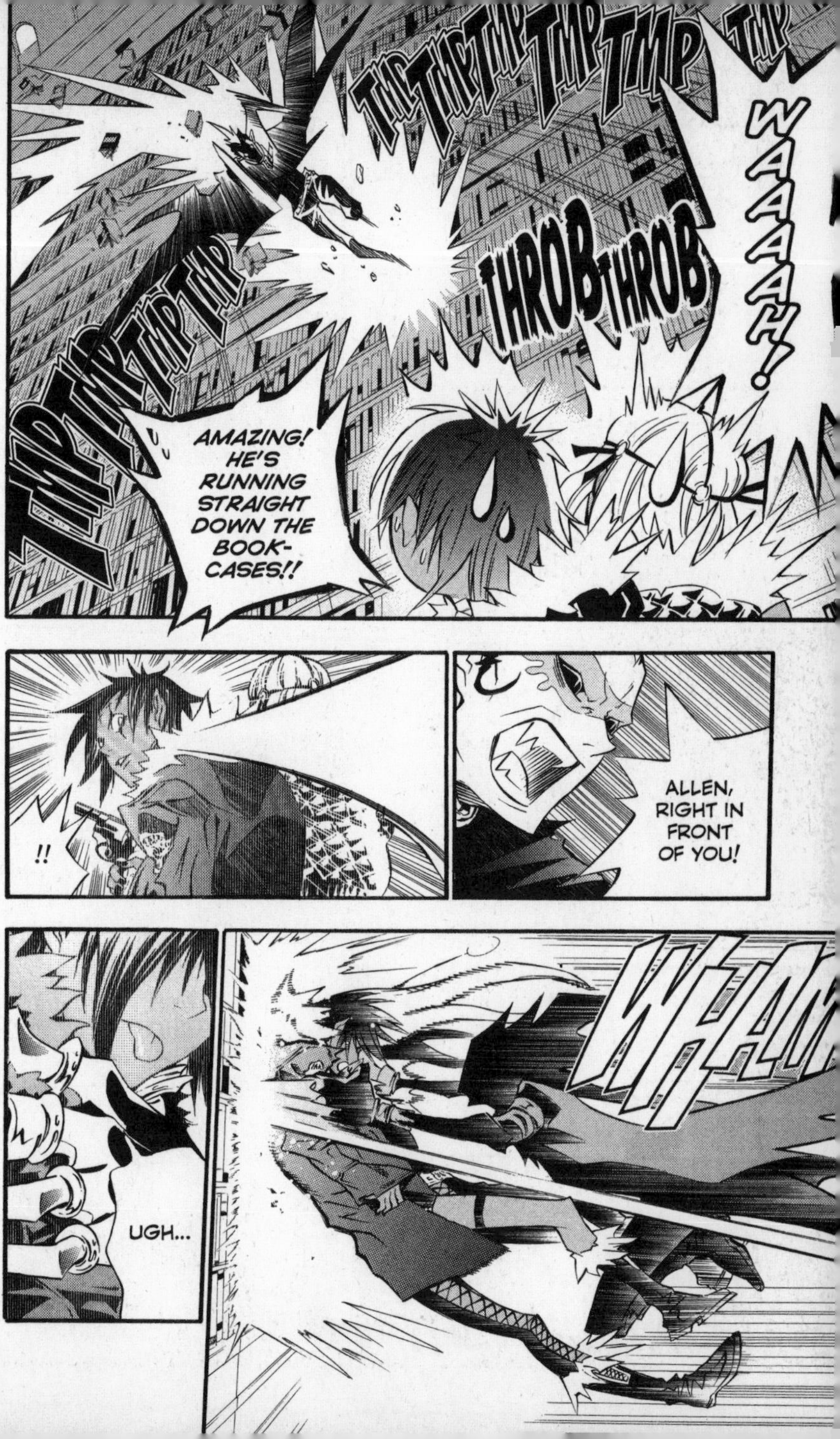

WAAAAAH!
TMP TMP TMP TMP TMP
THROB THROB
TMP TMP TMP TMP
AMAZING! HE'S RUNNING STRAIGHT DOWN THE BOOKCASES!!
ALLEN, RIGHT IN FRONT OF YOU!
!!
UGH...

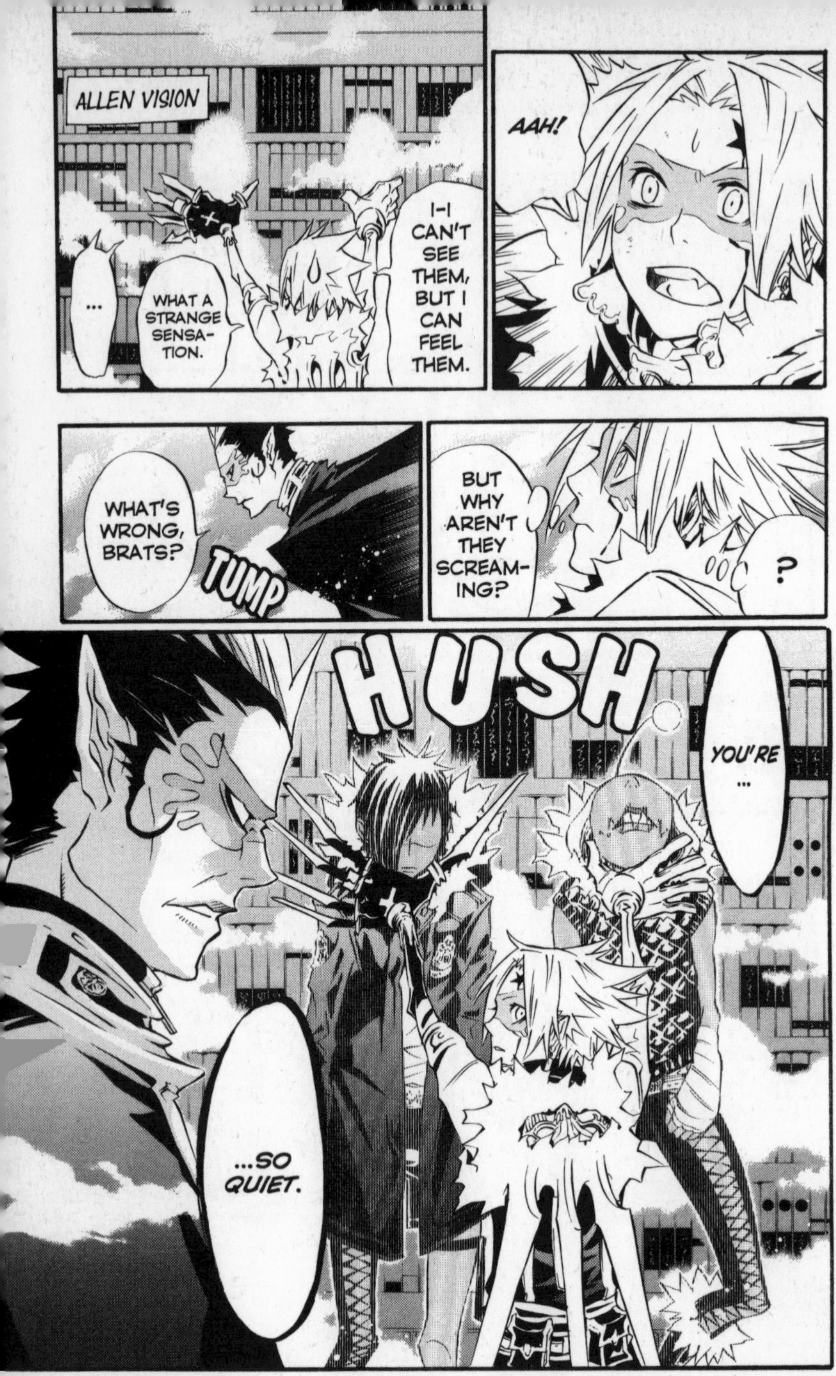
AAH!
ALLEN VISION
I-I CAN'T SEE THEM, BUT I CAN FEEL THEM.
WHAT A STRANGE SENSA-TION.
...
BUT WHY AREN'T THEY SCREAM-ING?
?
WHAT'S WRONG, BRATS?
TUMP
YOU'RE ...
HUSH
...SO QUIET.

Q: WHAT IS THAT ANTENNA THING ON JASDERO'S HEAD?

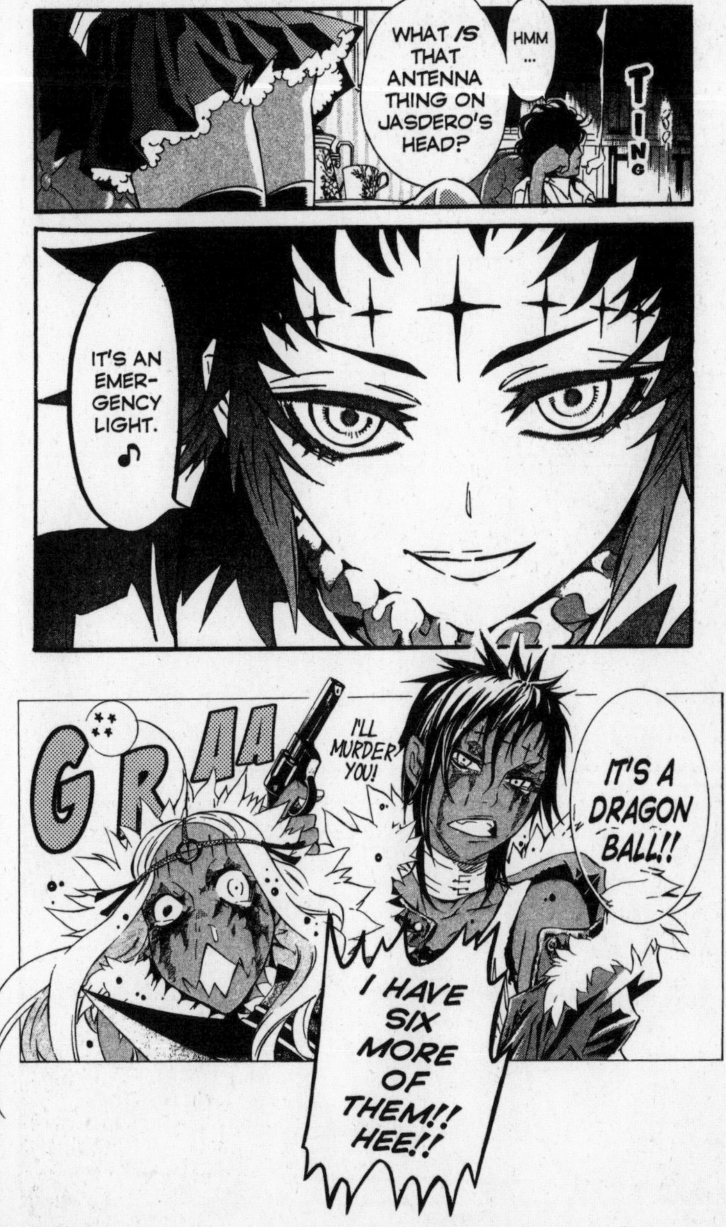
HMM ...
TING
WHAT IS THAT ANTENNA THING ON JASDERO'S HEAD?
IT'S AN EMERGENCY LIGHT. ♪
IT'S A DRAGON BALL!!
I'LL MURDER YOU!
GRAA
I HAVE SIX MORE OF THEM!! HEE!!

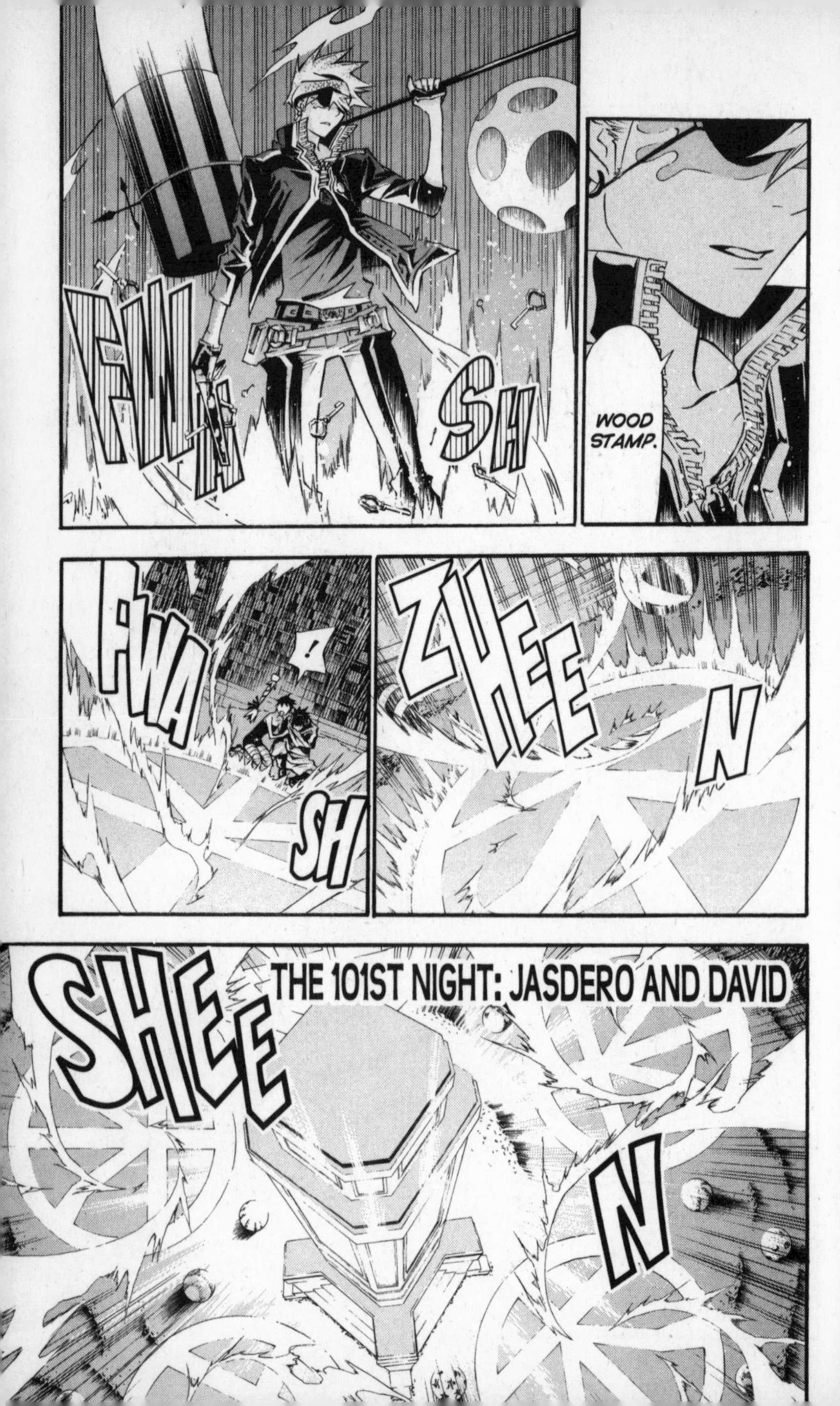
WOOD STAMP.
F'WA
SH
ZHEEN
F'WA
!
SH
THE 101ST NIGHT: JASDERO AND DAVID
SHEEN

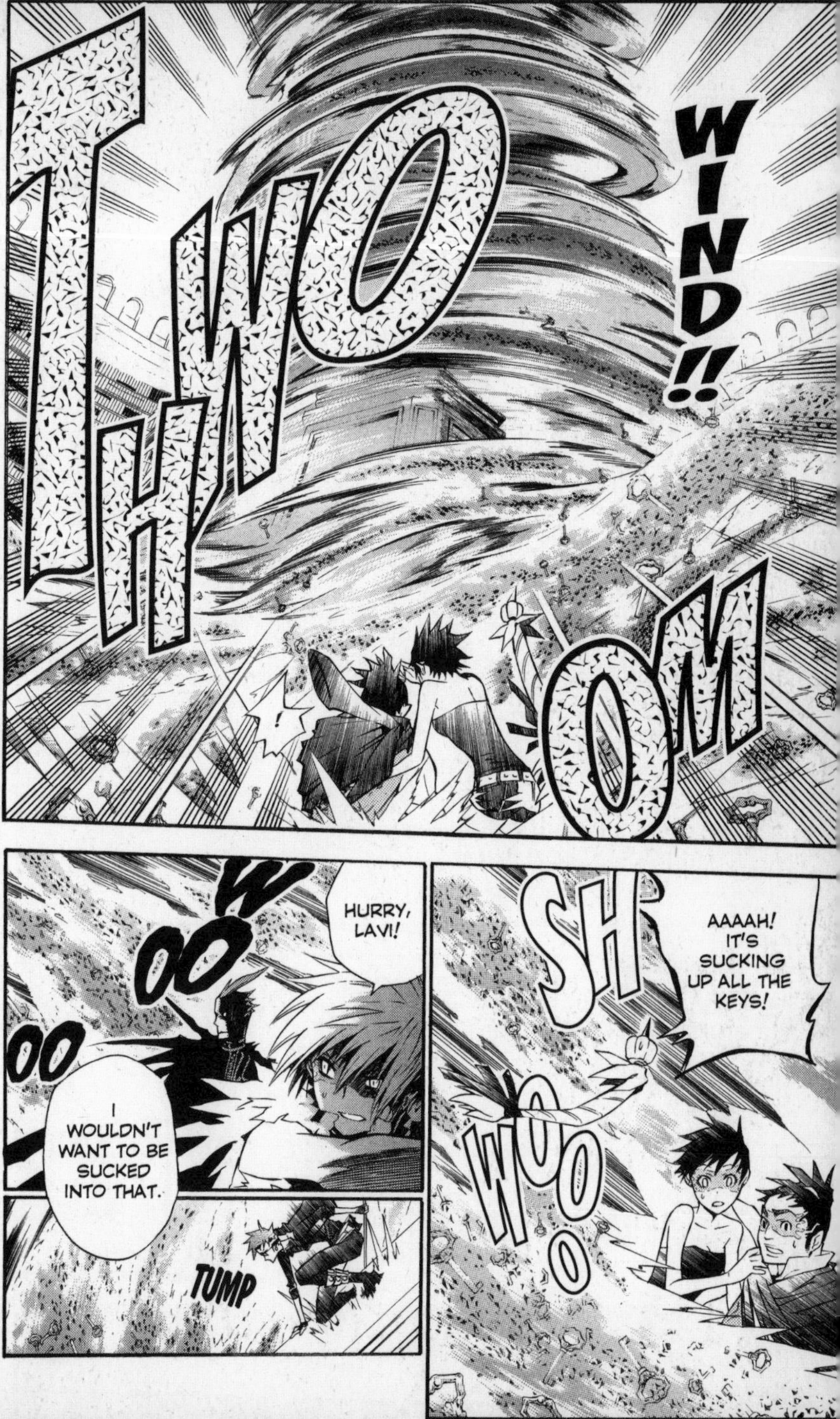
WIND!!
AAAAH! IT'S SUCKING UP ALL THE KEYS!
HURRY, LAVI!
I WOULDN'T WANT TO BE SUCKED INTO THAT.
TUMP

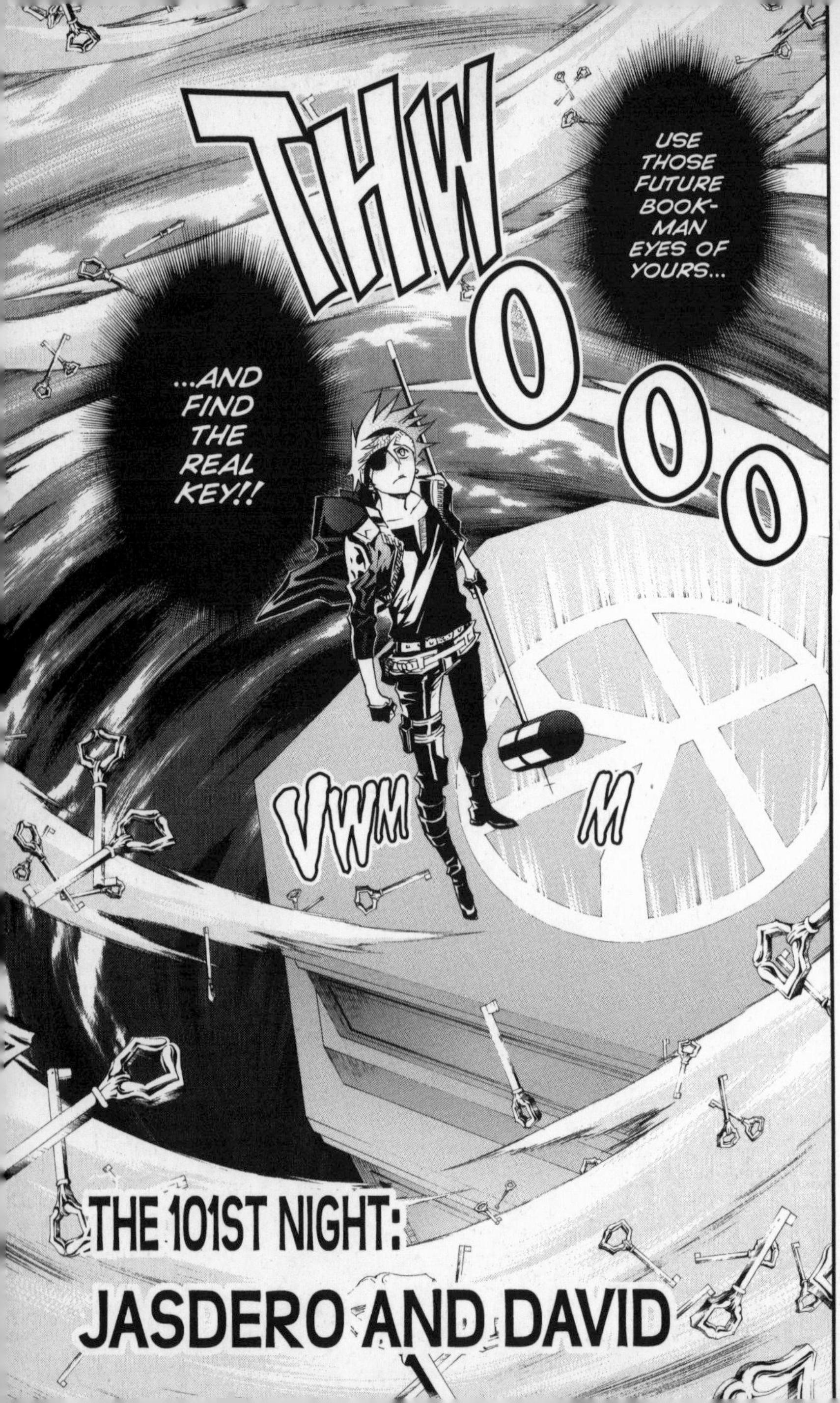
USE THOSE FUTURE BOOK-MAN EYES OF YOURS...
THWOOOO
...AND FIND THE REAL KEY!!
VWMM
THE 101ST NIGHT:
JASDERO AND DAVID

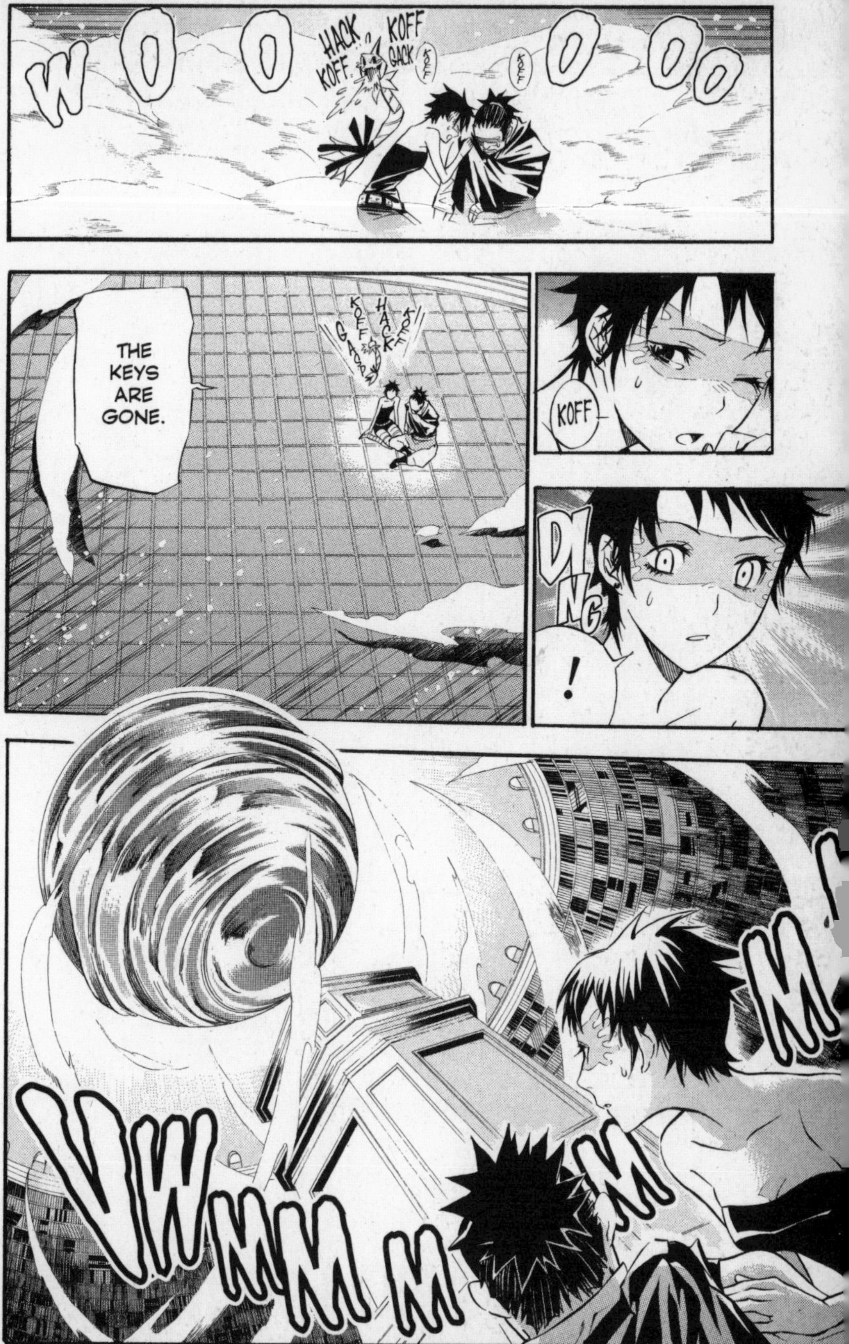 WOOOOOOO
HACK KOFF
KOFF GACK
KOFF
KOFF
KOFF
DING
!
HACK KOFF
KOFF GASP
THE KEYS ARE GONE.
VWMMMMMMM

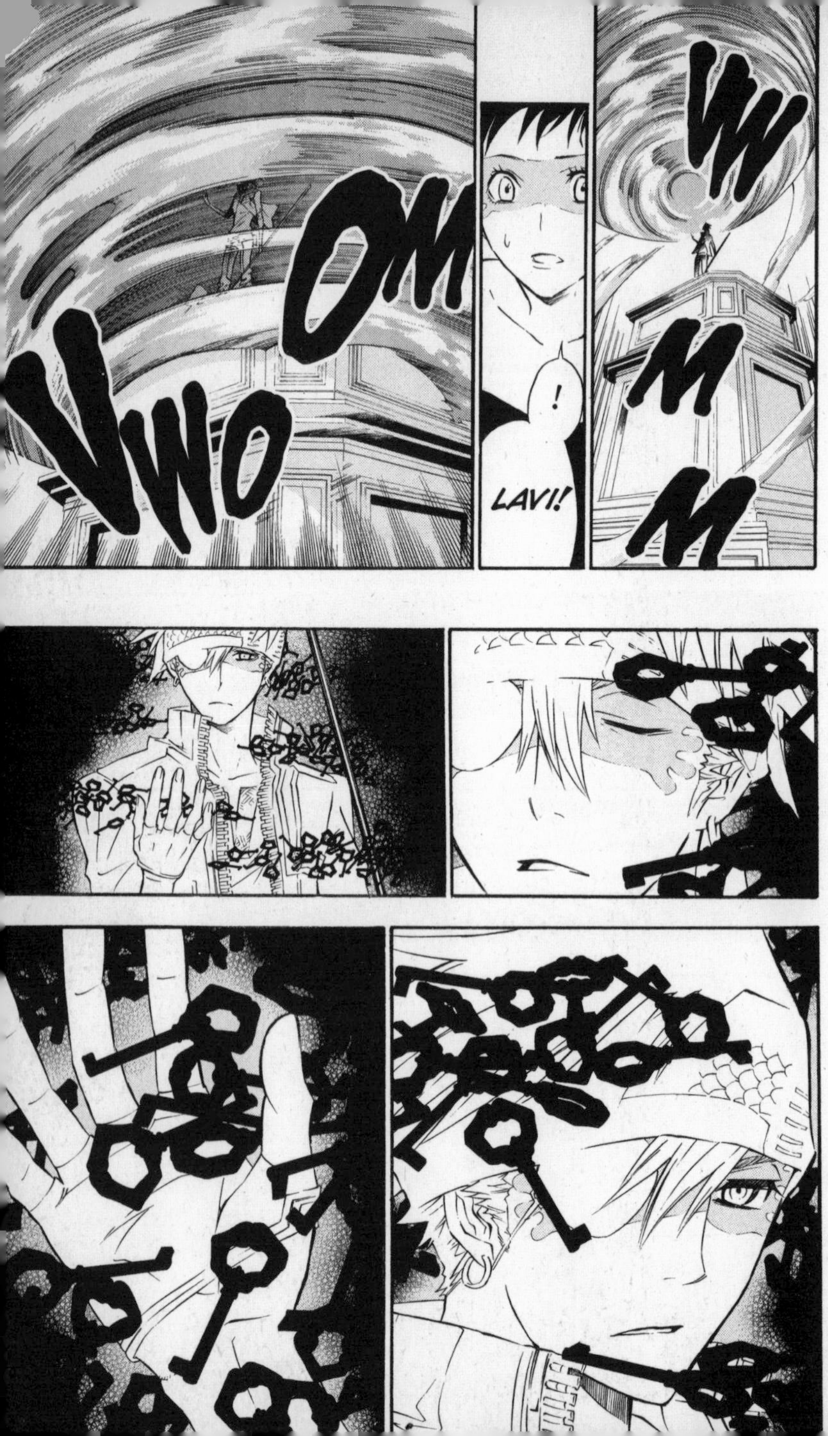

WWMMM
!
LAVI!
VWOOM

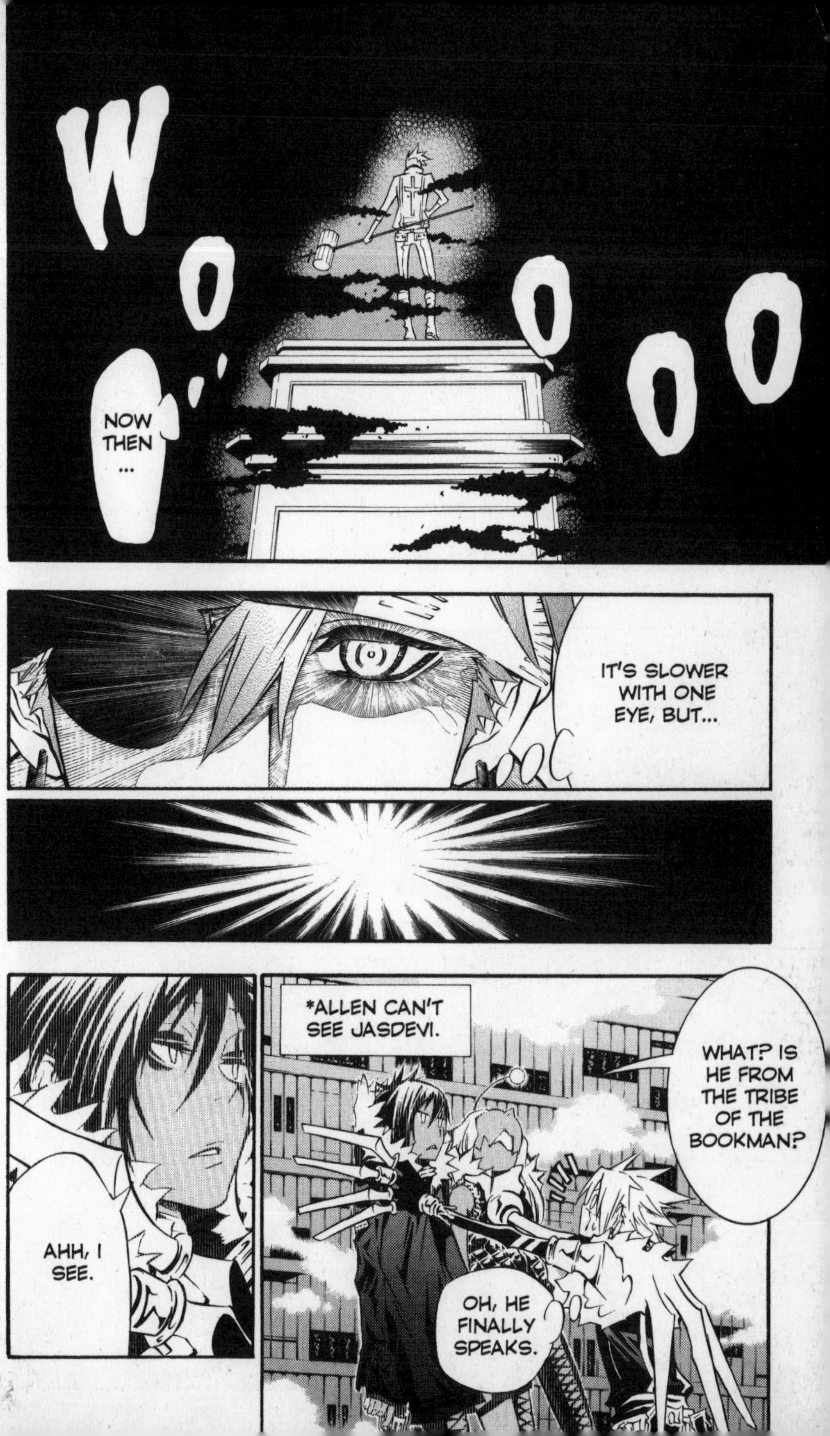
WOOOOO
NOW THEN ...
IT'S SLOWER WITH ONE EYE, BUT...
WHAT? IS HE FROM THE TRIBE OF THE BOOKMAN?
*ALLEN CAN'T SEE JASDEVI.
OH, HE FINALLY SPEAKS.
AHH, I SEE.

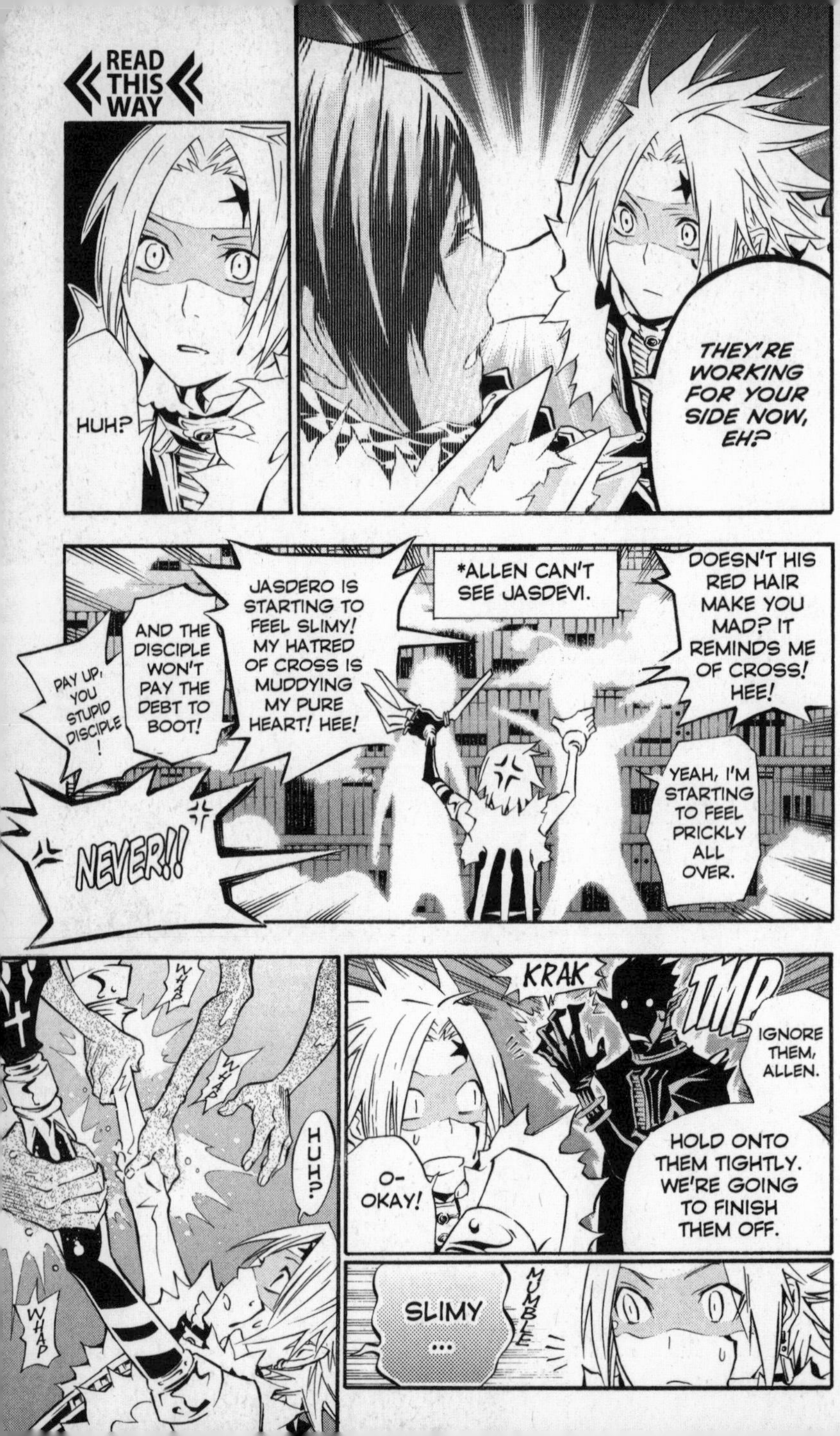
READ THIS WAY
THEY'RE WORKING FOR YOUR SIDE NOW, EH?
HUH?
DOESN'T HIS RED HAIR MAKE YOU MAD? IT REMINDS ME OF CROSS! HEE!
YEAH, I'M STARTING TO FEEL PRICKLY ALL OVER.
*ALLEN CAN'T SEE JASDEVI.
JASDERO IS STARTING TO FEEL SLIMY! MY HATRED OF CROSS IS MUDDYING MY PURE HEART! HEE!
AND THE DISCIPLE WON'T PAY THE DEBT TO BOOT!
PAY UP, YOU STUPID DISCIPLE!
NEVER!!
KRAK
TMP
IGNORE THEM, ALLEN.
HOLD ONTO THEM TIGHTLY. WE'RE GOING TO FINISH THEM OFF.
O-OKAY!
MUMBLE
SLIMY...
WHAP
WHAP
HUH?
WHAP

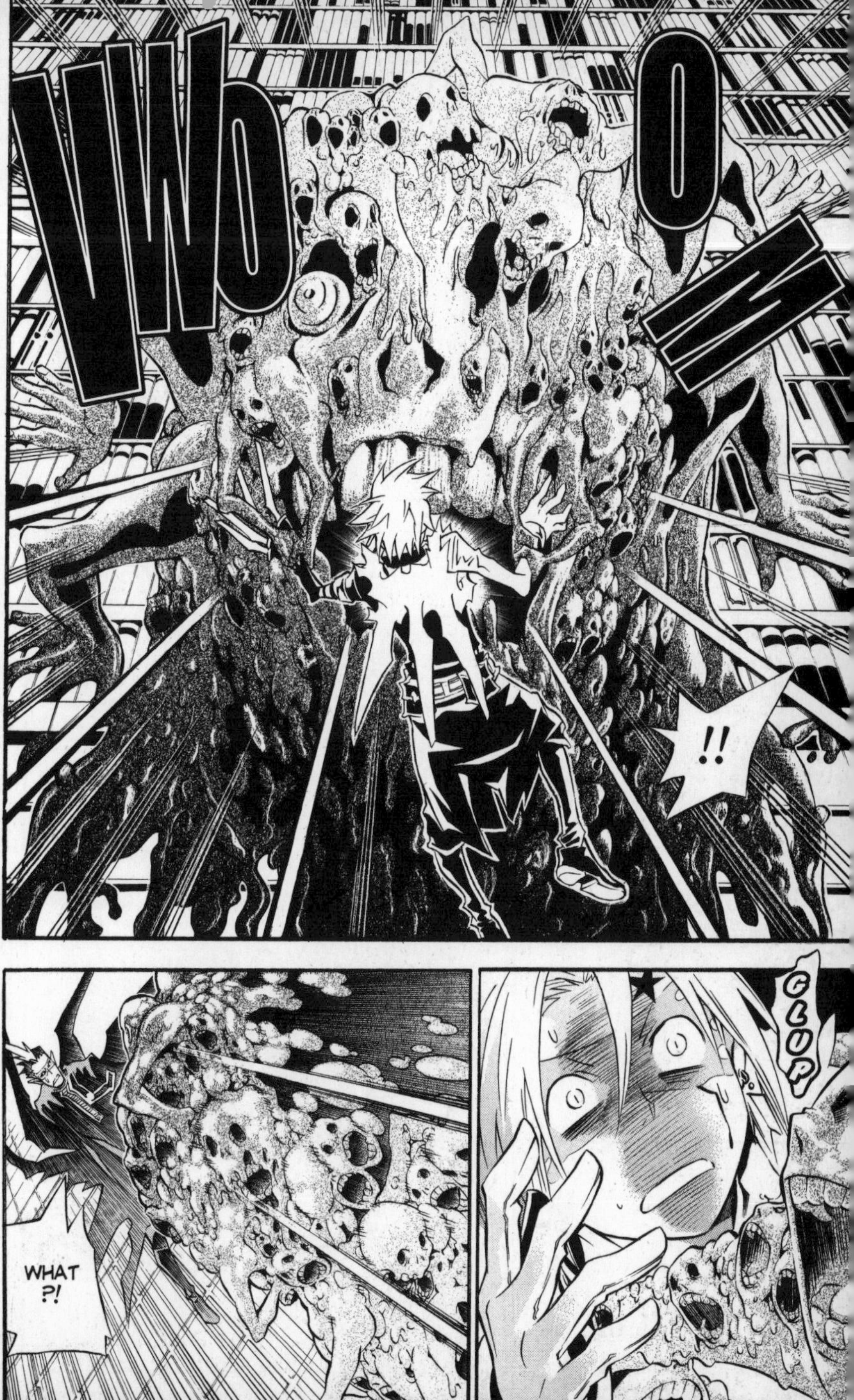
VWOOM
!!
GLUP
WHAT ?!

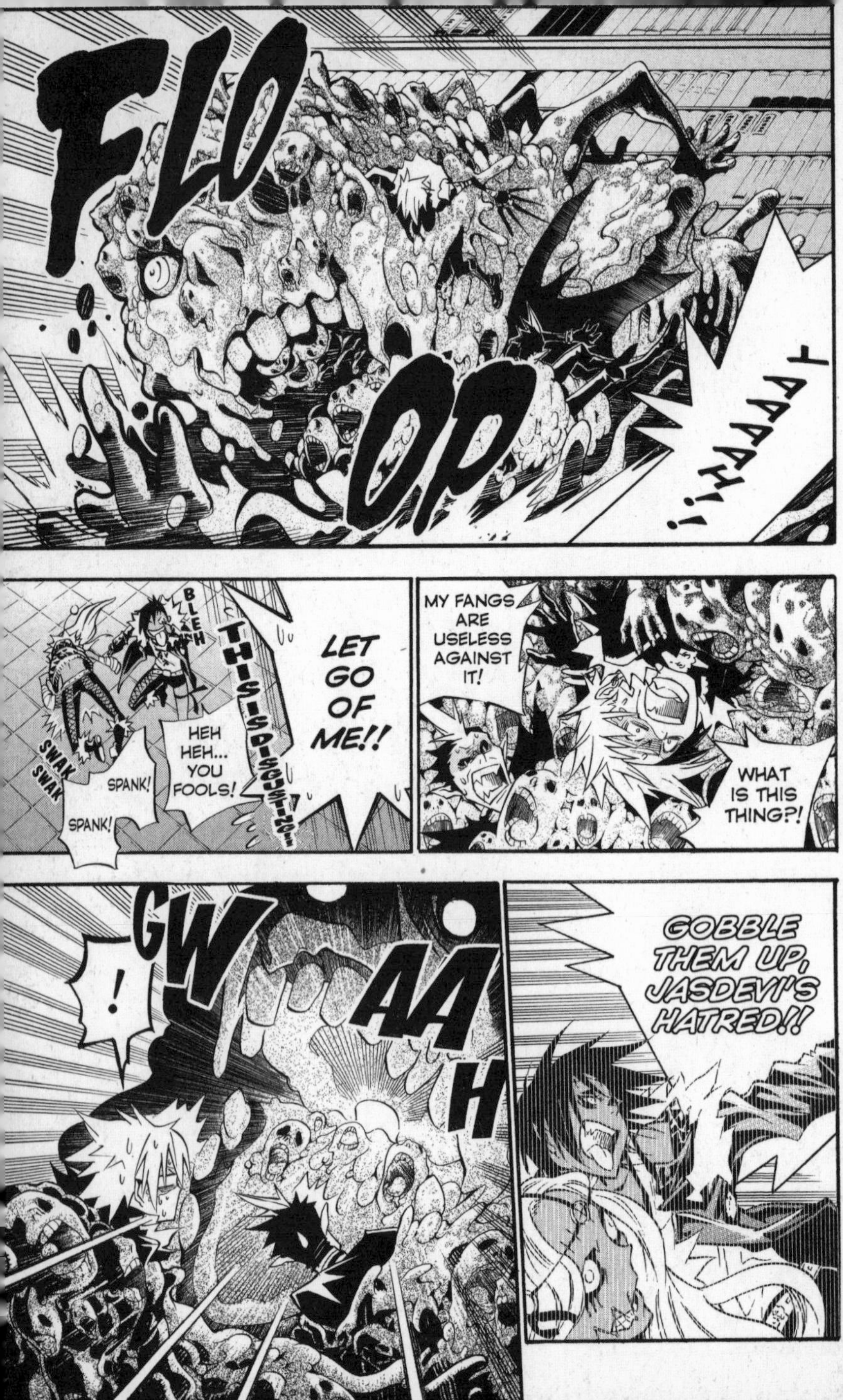
AAAAAH!!
FLOOP
MY FANGS ARE USELESS AGAINST IT!
WHAT IS THIS THING?!
LET GO OF ME!!
THIS IS DISGUSTING!!
BLEH
HEH HEH... YOU FOOLS!
SPANK!
SPANK!
SWAK
SWAK
GOBBLE THEM UP, JASDEVI'S HATRED!!
GWAAH
!

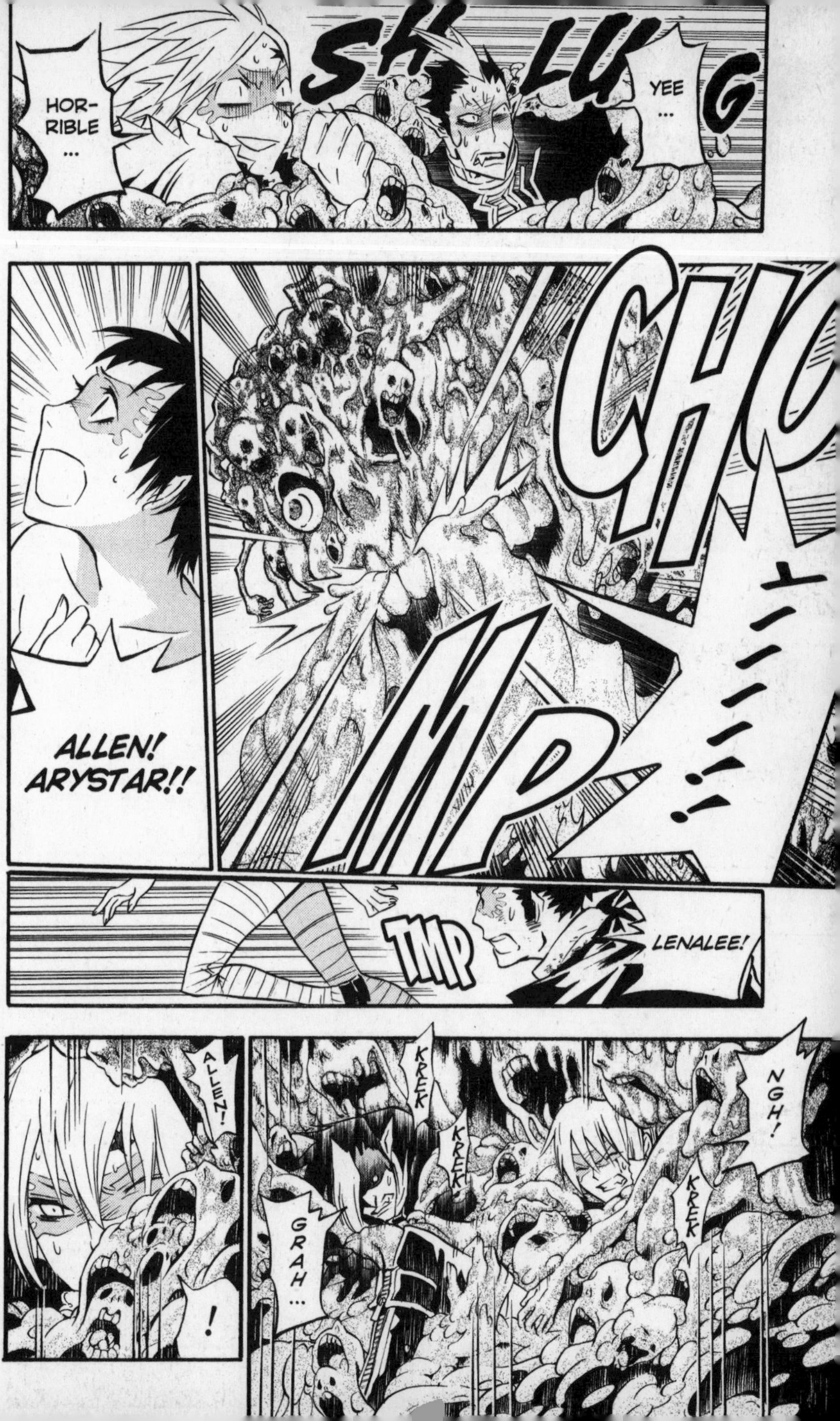
YEE...
SHLUG
HOR-RIBLE...
CHOMP!!
ALLEN! ARYSTAR!!
LENALEE!
TMP
NGH!
KREK
KREK
KREK
GRAH...
ALLEN!
!

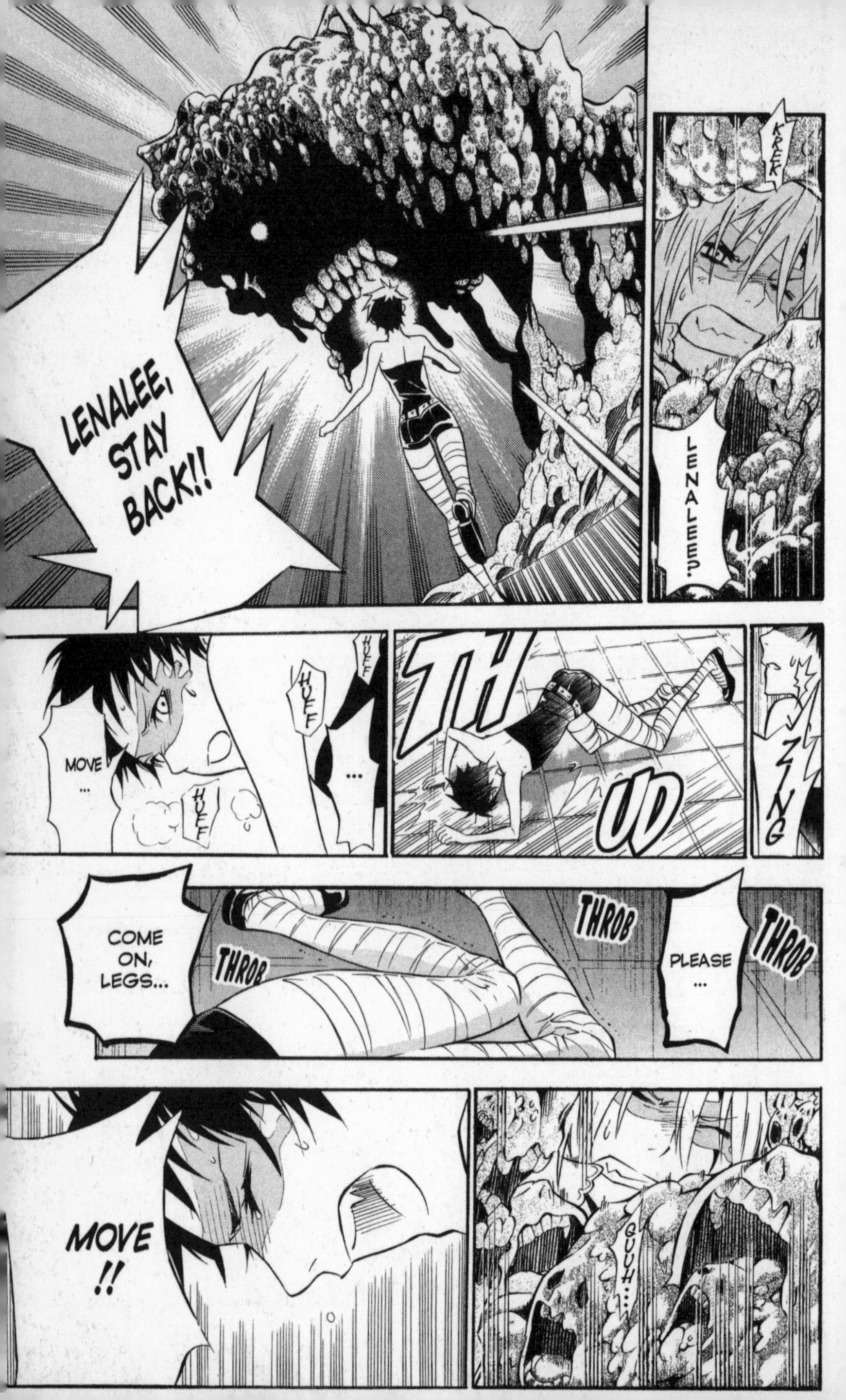

KREK
LENALEE?
LENALEE, STAY BACK!!
UM
ZING
THUD
HUFF
HUFF
...
HUFF
MOVE ...
THROB
PLEASE ...
THROB
THROB
COME ON, LEGS...
GUUH...
MOVE !!

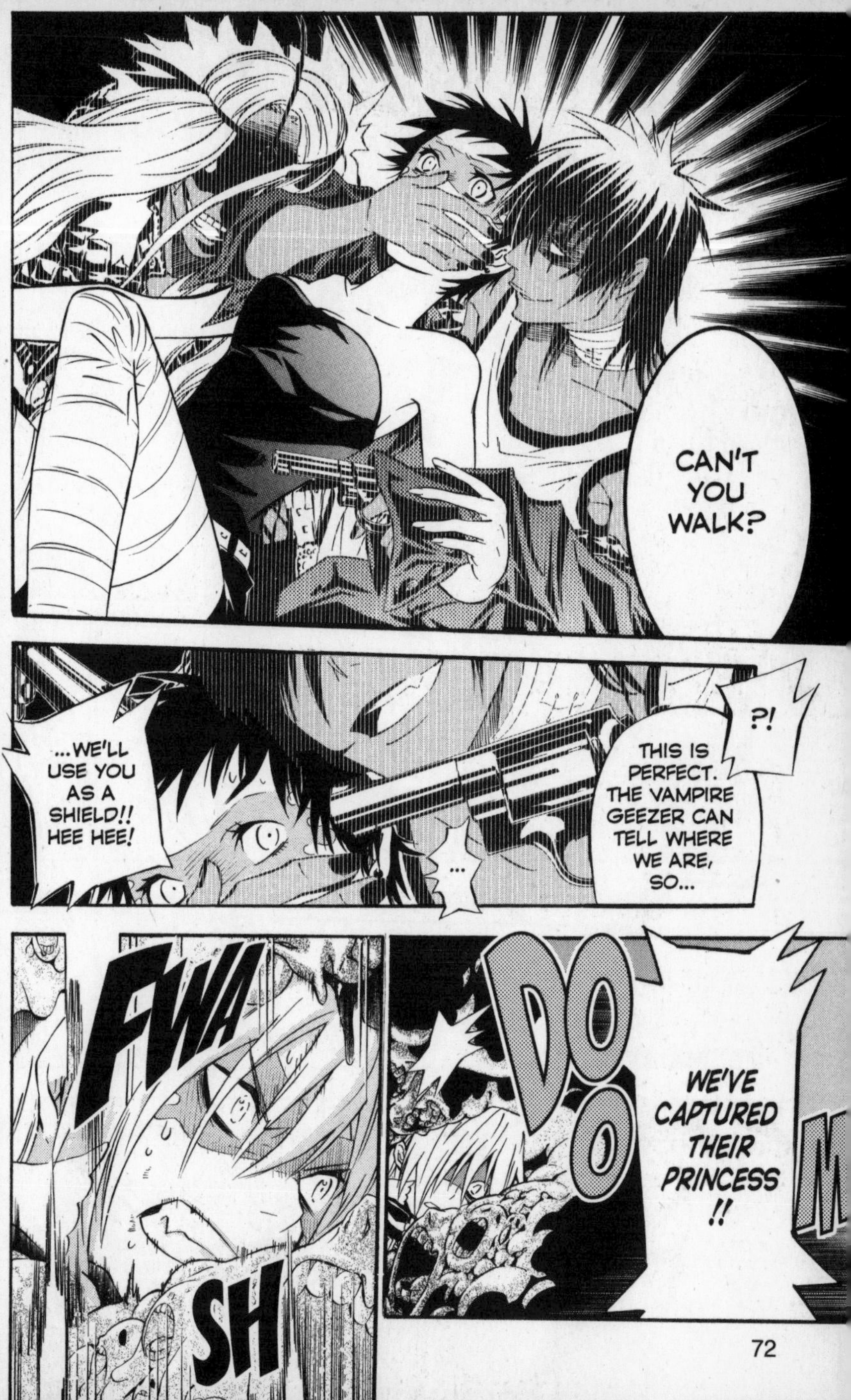
CAN'T YOU WALK?
THIS IS PERFECT. THE VAMPIRE GEEZER CAN TELL WHERE WE ARE, SO...
?!
...
...WE'LL USE YOU AS A SHIELD!! HEE HEE!
DOOM
WE'VE CAPTURED THEIR PRINCESS !!
FWASH

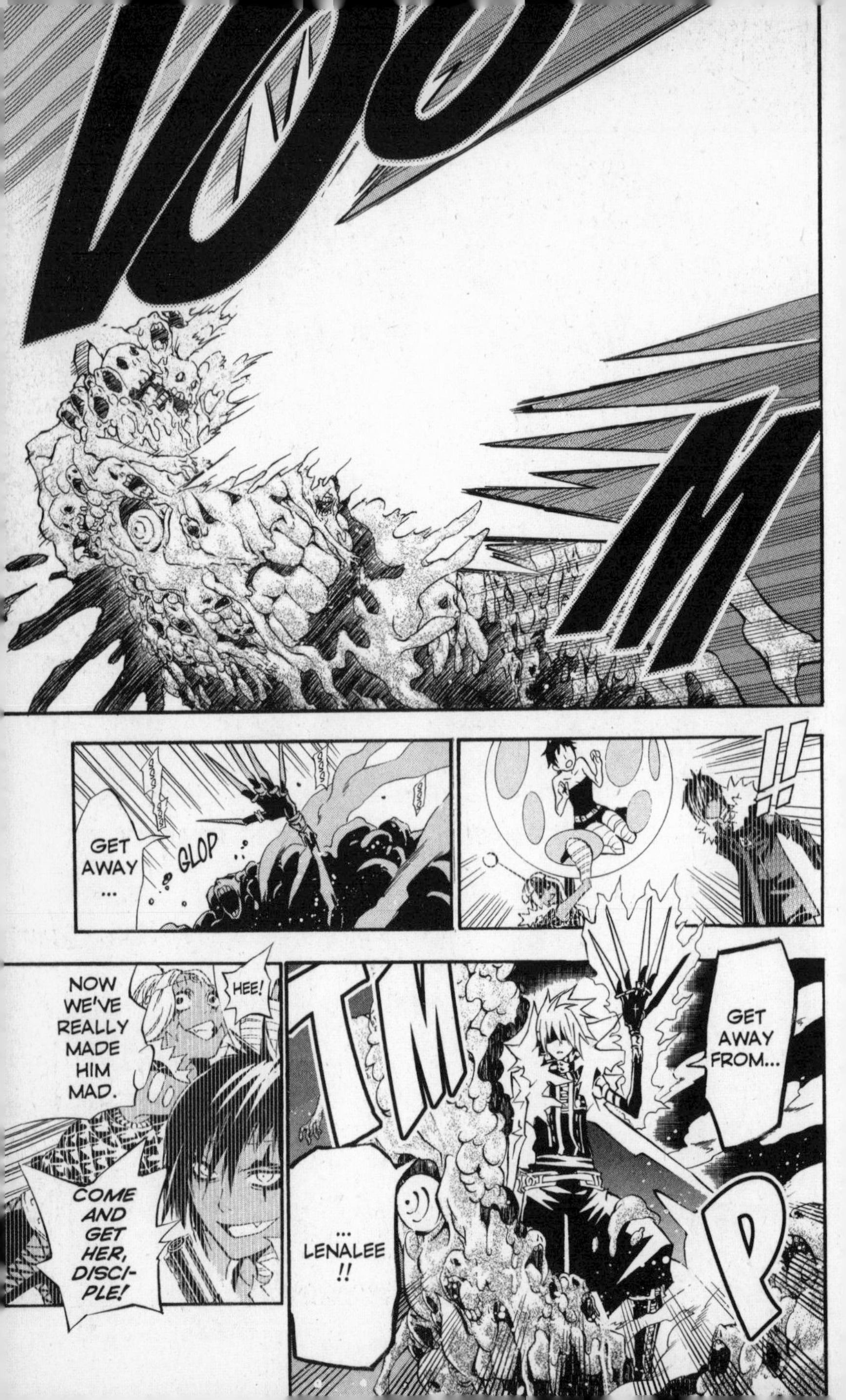
VOOM
!!
GET AWAY ...
GLOP
GET AWAY FROM...
TMP
... LENALEE !!
HEE!
NOW WE'VE REALLY MADE HIM MAD.
COME AND GET HER, DISCIPLE!

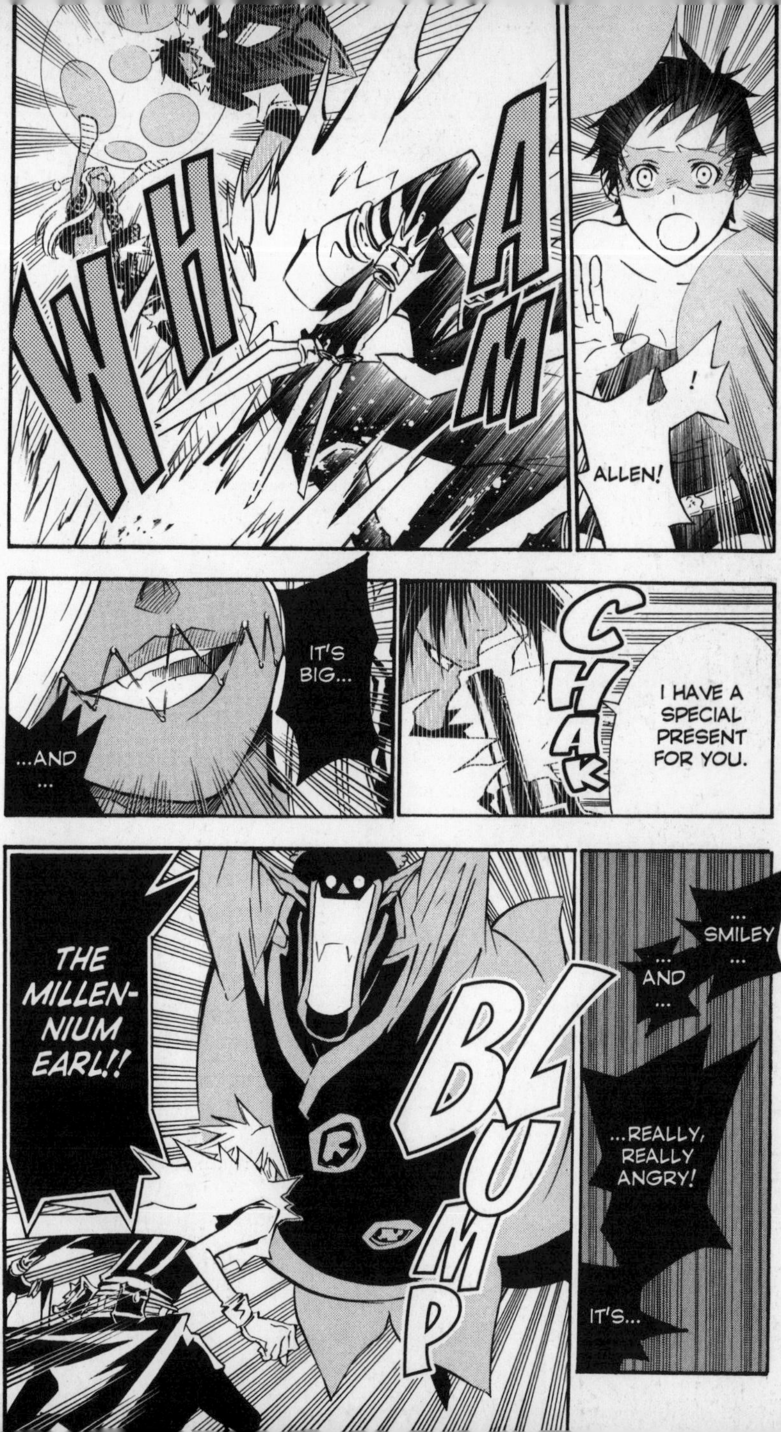
!
ALLEN!
WHAM
I HAVE A SPECIAL PRESENT FOR YOU.
CHAK
IT'S BIG...
...AND ...
... SMILEY ...
... AND ...
...REALLY, REALLY ANGRY!
IT'S...
BLUMP
THE MILLEN-NIUM EARL!!

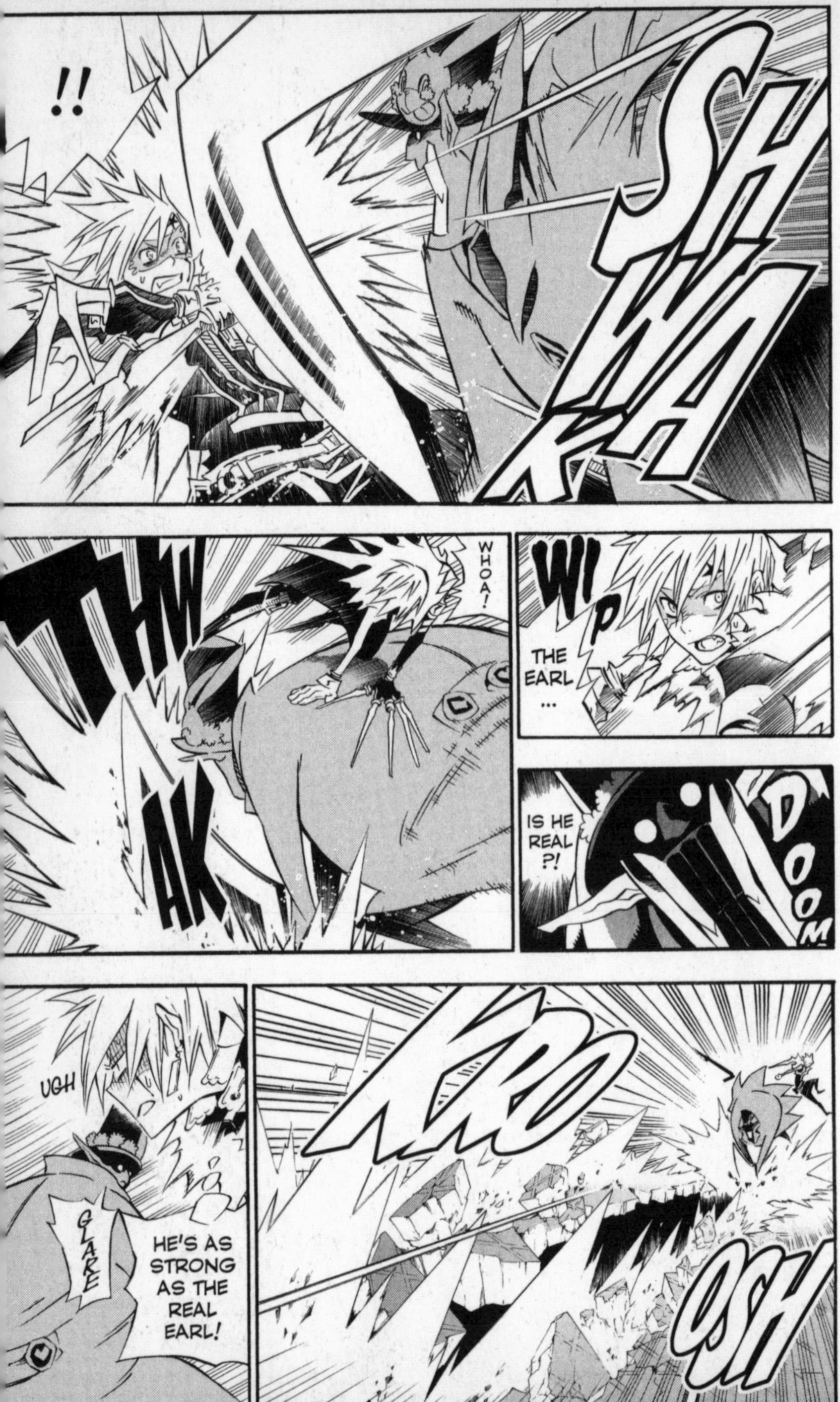
SHAAK
!!
WIP
THE EARL ...
IS HE REAL ?!
DOOOM
WHOA!
THWAK
KROOSH
UGH
GLARE
HE'S AS STRONG AS THE REAL EARL!

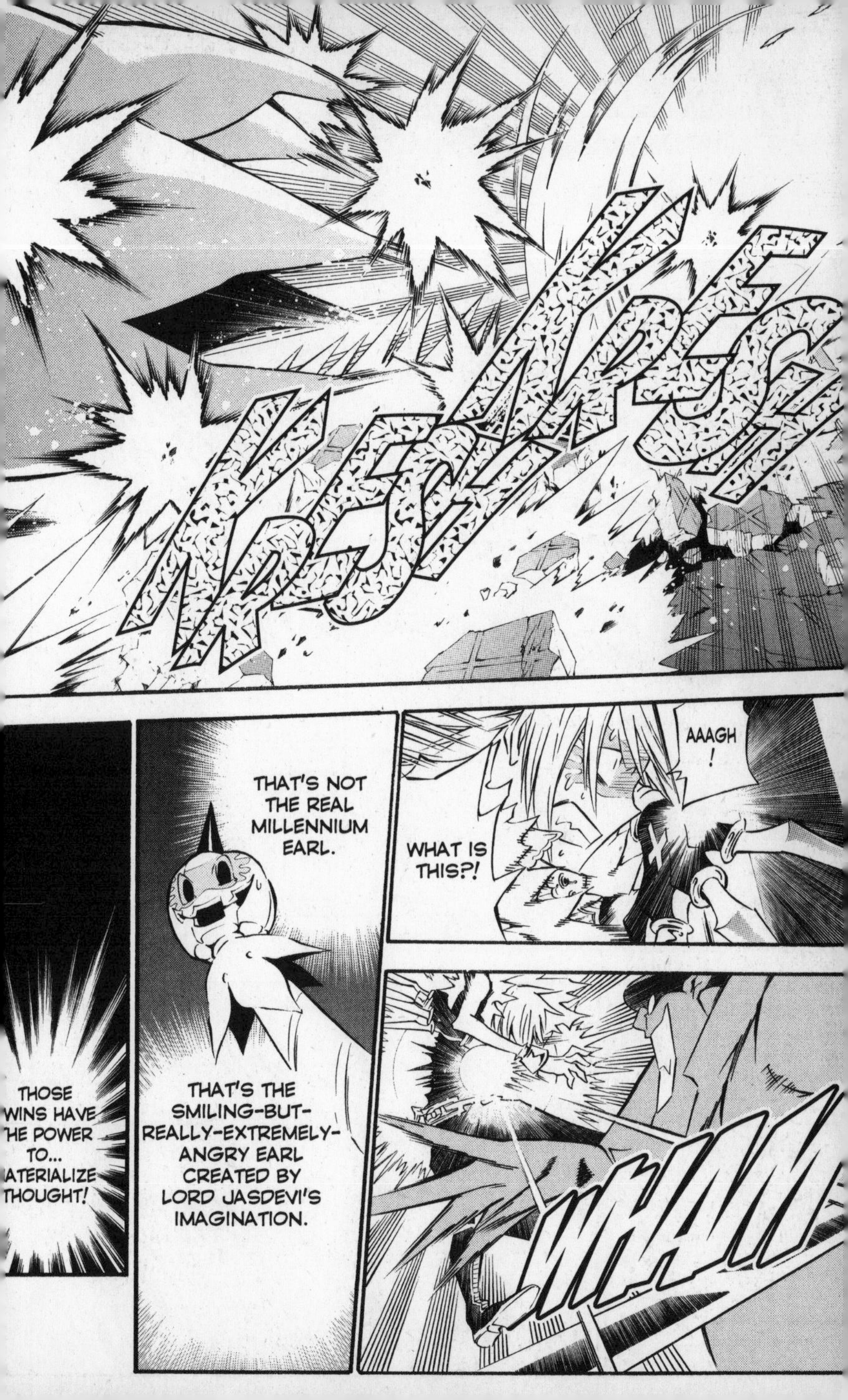
AAAGH!
WHAT IS THIS?!
THAT'S NOT THE REAL MILLENNIUM EARL.
THAT'S THE SMILING-BUT-REALLY-EXTREMELY-ANGRY EARL CREATED BY LORD JASDEVI'S IMAGINATION.
THOSE WINS HAVE HE POWER TO... ATERIALIZE THOUGHT!

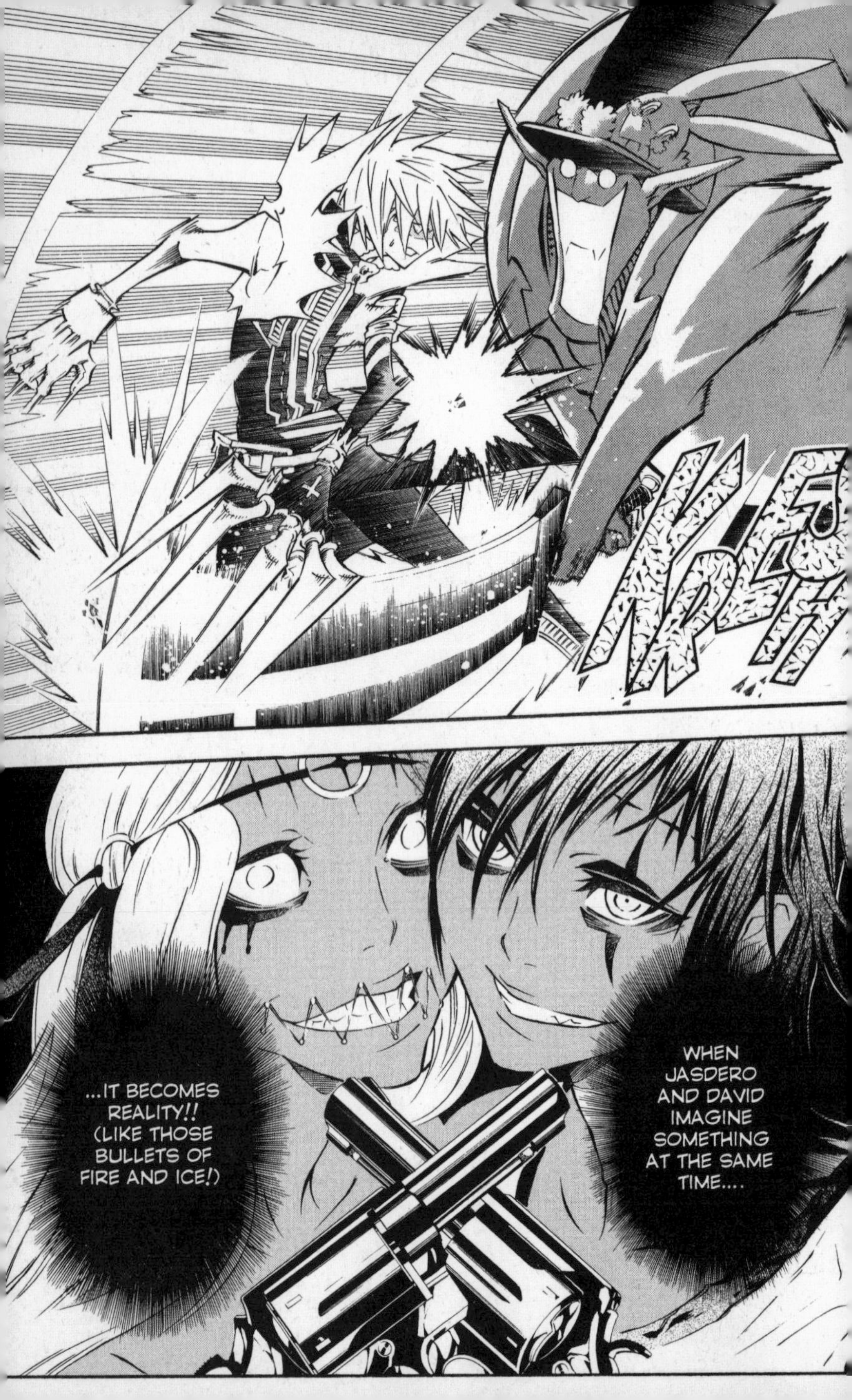
WHEN JASDERO AND DAVID IMAGINE SOMETHING AT THE SAME TIME....
...IT BECOMES REALITY!! (LIKE THOSE BULLETS OF FIRE AND ICE!)

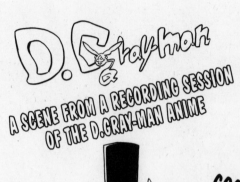

D.Gray-man
A SCENE FROM A RECORDING SESSION OF THE D.GRAY-MAN ANIME
GOOD FRIENDS
HEE HEE HEE
HA HA HA HA
SCRIPT
SCRIPT

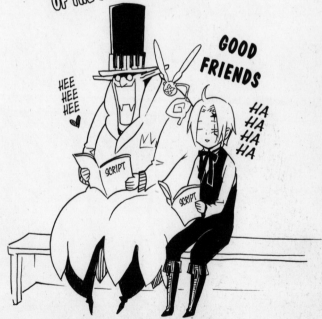

DURING THE RECORDING SESSIONS, TAKIZAWA, WHO VOICES THE MILLENNIUM EARL, ALWAYS SITS NEXT TO SANAE KOBAYASHI, WHO DOES THE VOICE OF ALLEN.

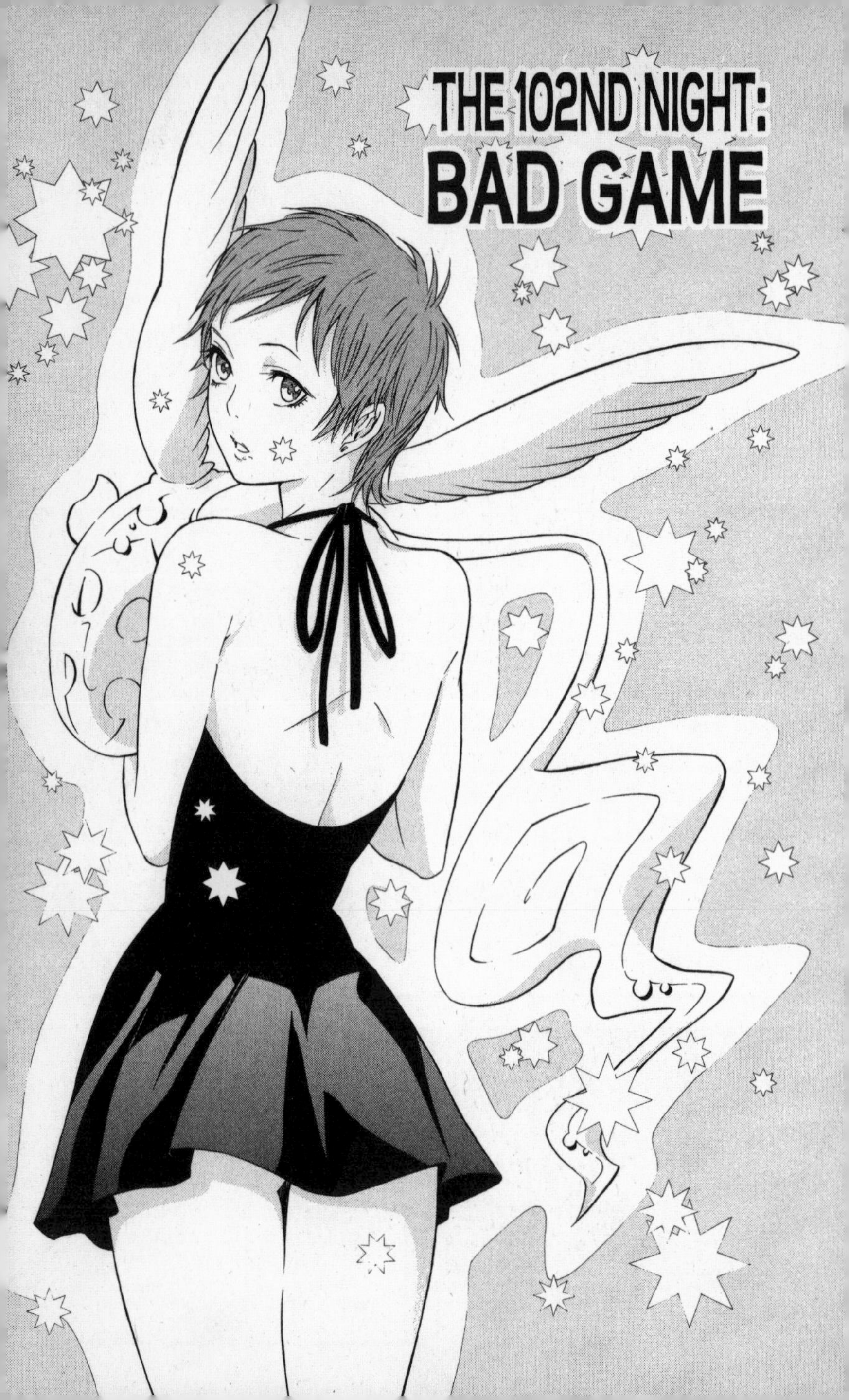
THE 102ND NIGHT:
BAD GAME

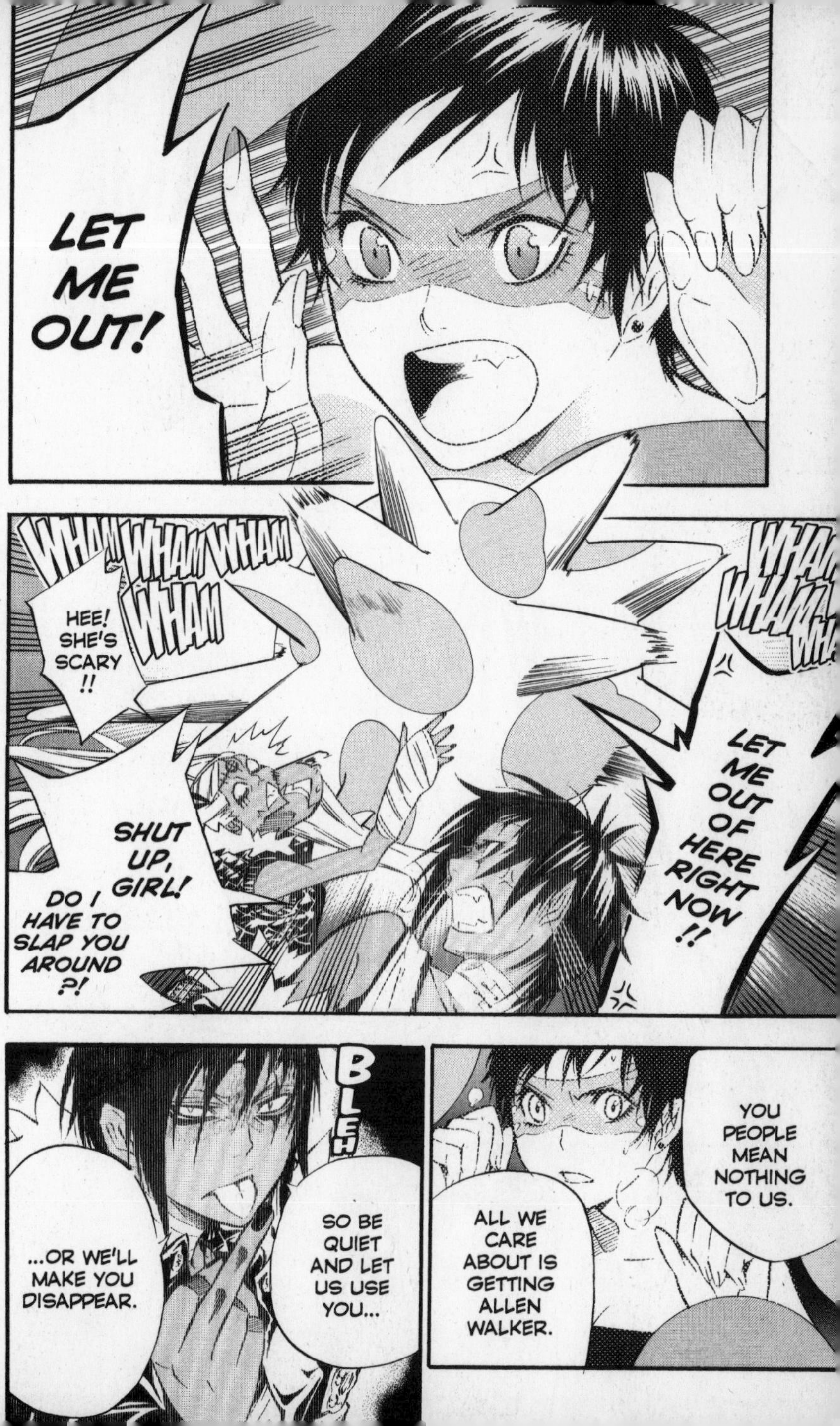
LET ME OUT!
WHAM WHAM
LET ME OUT OF HERE RIGHT NOW!!
WHAM WHAM WHAM WHAM
HEE! SHE'S SCARY!!
SHUT UP, GIRL!
DO I HAVE TO SLAP YOU AROUND?!
YOU PEOPLE MEAN NOTHING TO US.
ALL WE CARE ABOUT IS GETTING ALLEN WALKER.
BLEH
SO BE QUIET AND LET US USE YOU...
...OR WE'LL MAKE YOU DISAPPEAR.

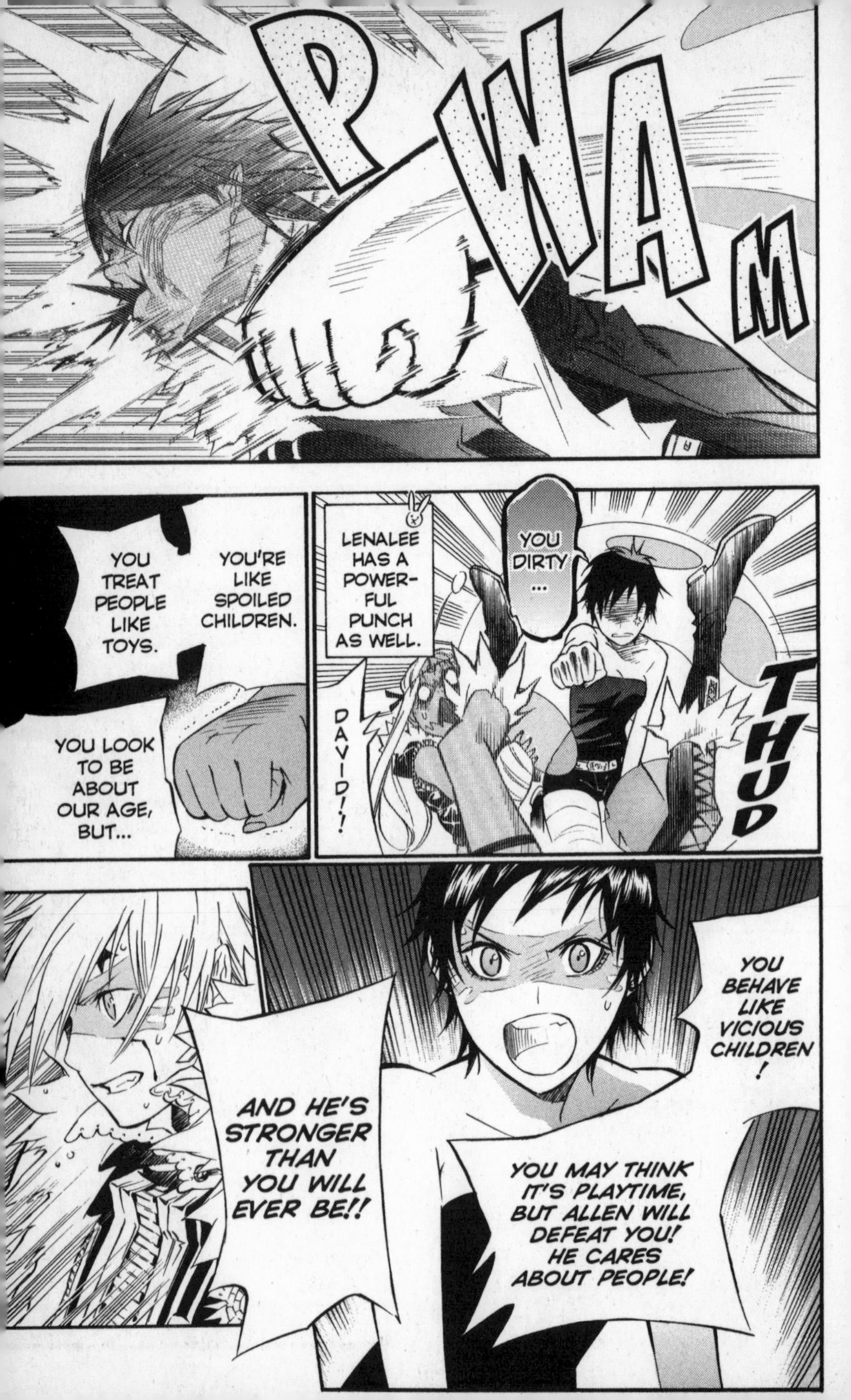
PWAM
YOU DIRTY ...
LENALEE HAS A POWER-FUL PUNCH AS WELL.
THUD
DAVID!!
YOU'RE LIKE SPOILED CHILDREN.
YOU TREAT PEOPLE LIKE TOYS.
YOU LOOK TO BE ABOUT OUR AGE, BUT...
YOU BEHAVE LIKE VICIOUS CHILDREN!
YOU MAY THINK IT'S PLAYTIME, BUT ALLEN WILL DEFEAT YOU! HE CARES ABOUT PEOPLE!
AND HE'S STRONGER THAN YOU WILL EVER BE!!

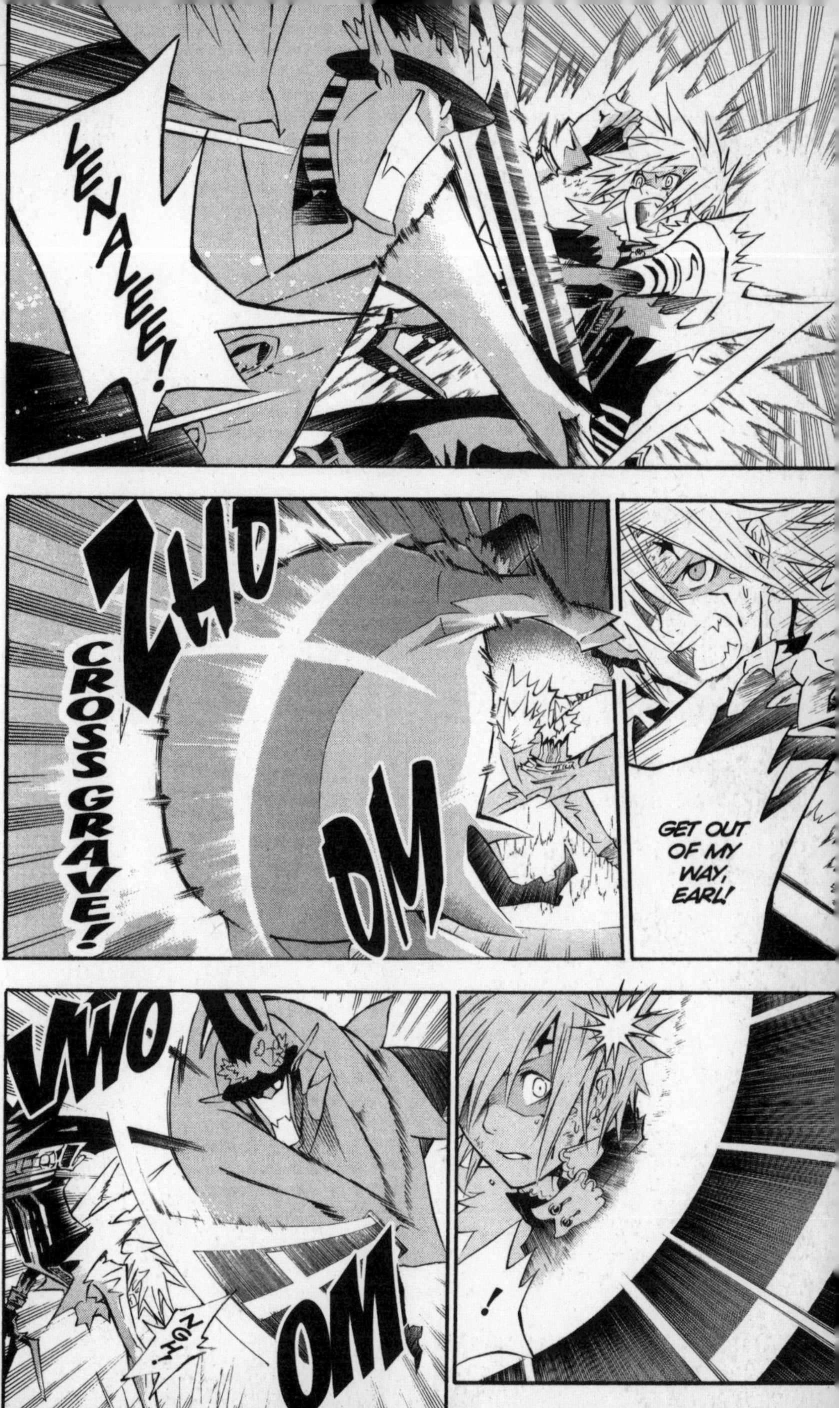
LENALEEE!
GET OUT OF MY WAY, EARL!
ZHO
DM
CROSS GRAVE!
!
VWO
OM
NGH!

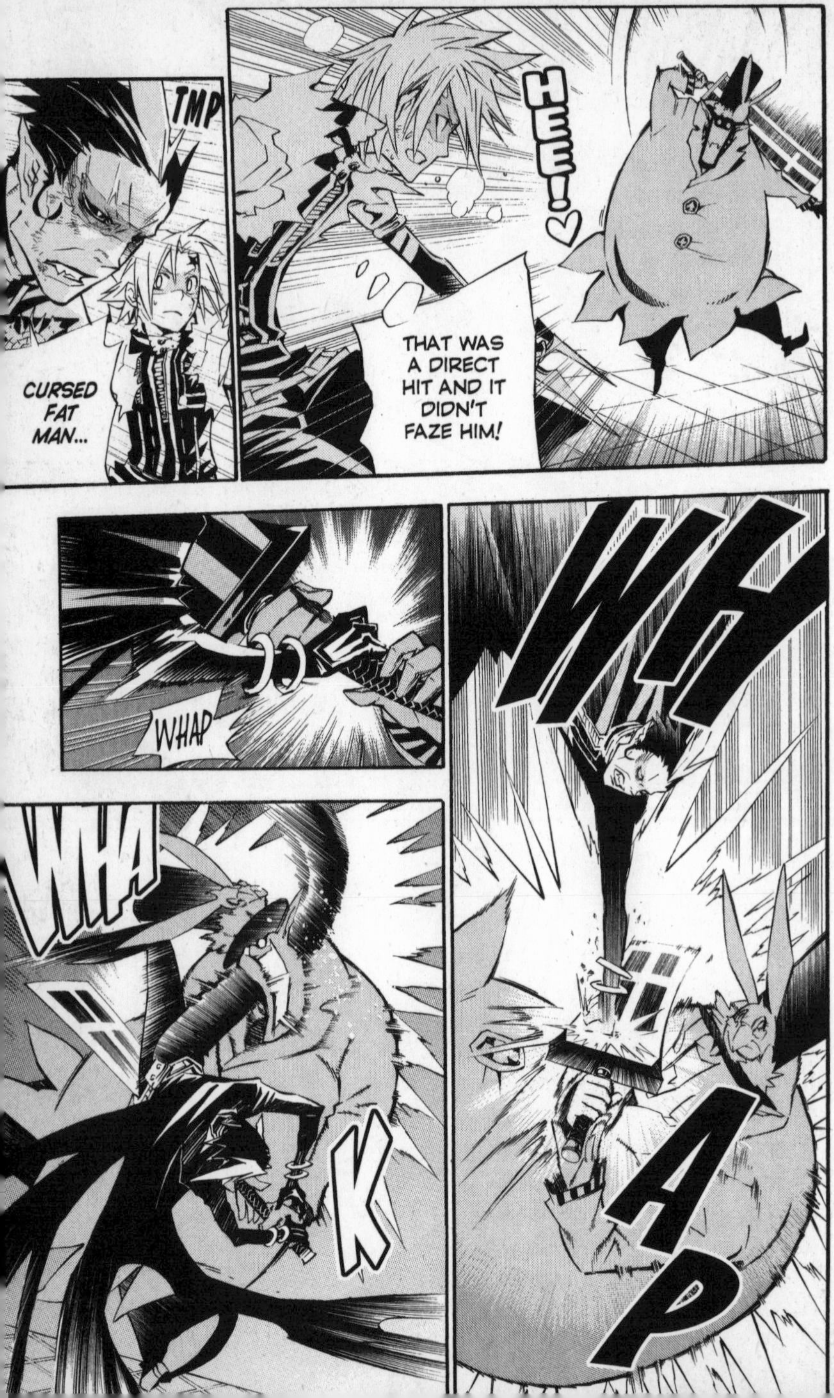
HEE! ♥
THAT WAS A DIRECT HIT AND IT DIDN'T FAZE HIM!
TMP
CURSED FAT MAN...
WH
AP
WHAP
WHA
K

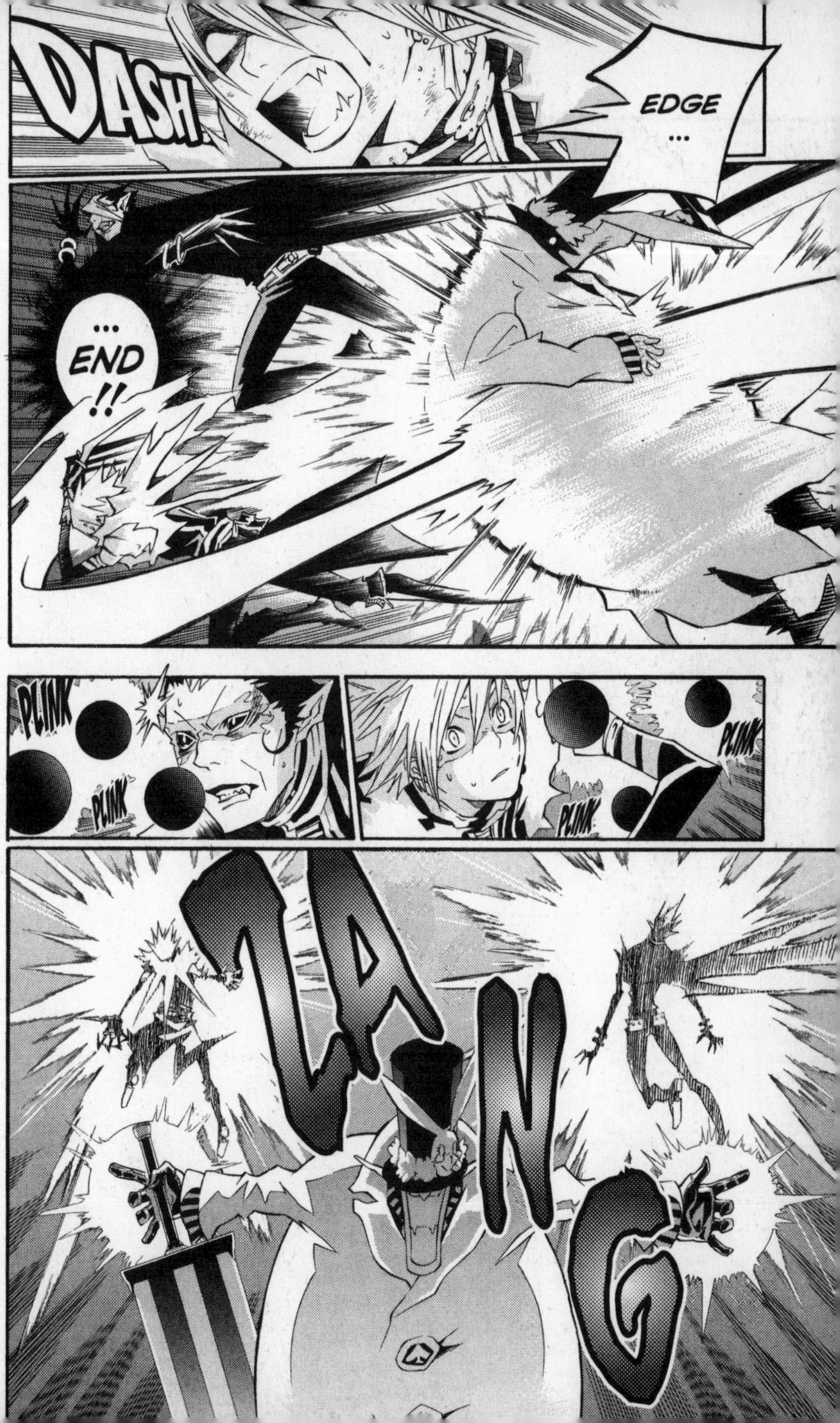
EDGE ...
DASH
... END !!
PLINK
PLINK
PLINK
PLINK
ZANG

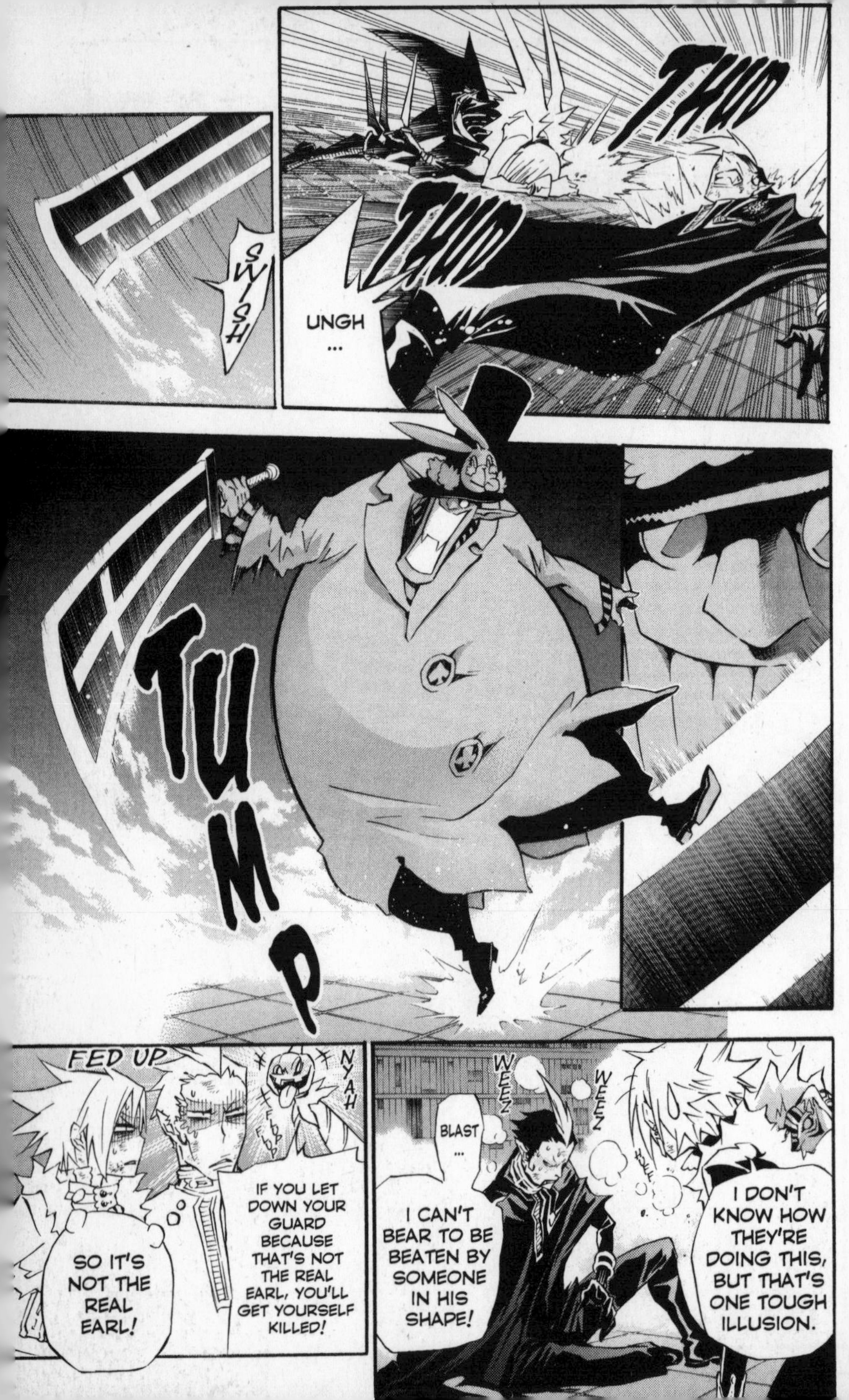
THUD
THUD
UNGH ...
SWISH
TUMP
I DON'T KNOW HOW THEY'RE DOING THIS, BUT THAT'S ONE TOUGH ILLUSION.
WEEZ
WEEZ
BLAST ...
I CAN'T BEAR TO BE BEATEN BY SOMEONE IN HIS SHAPE!
NYAH
FED UP
IF YOU LET DOWN YOUR GUARD BECAUSE THAT'S NOT THE REAL EARL, YOU'LL GET YOURSELF KILLED!
SO IT'S NOT THE REAL EARL!

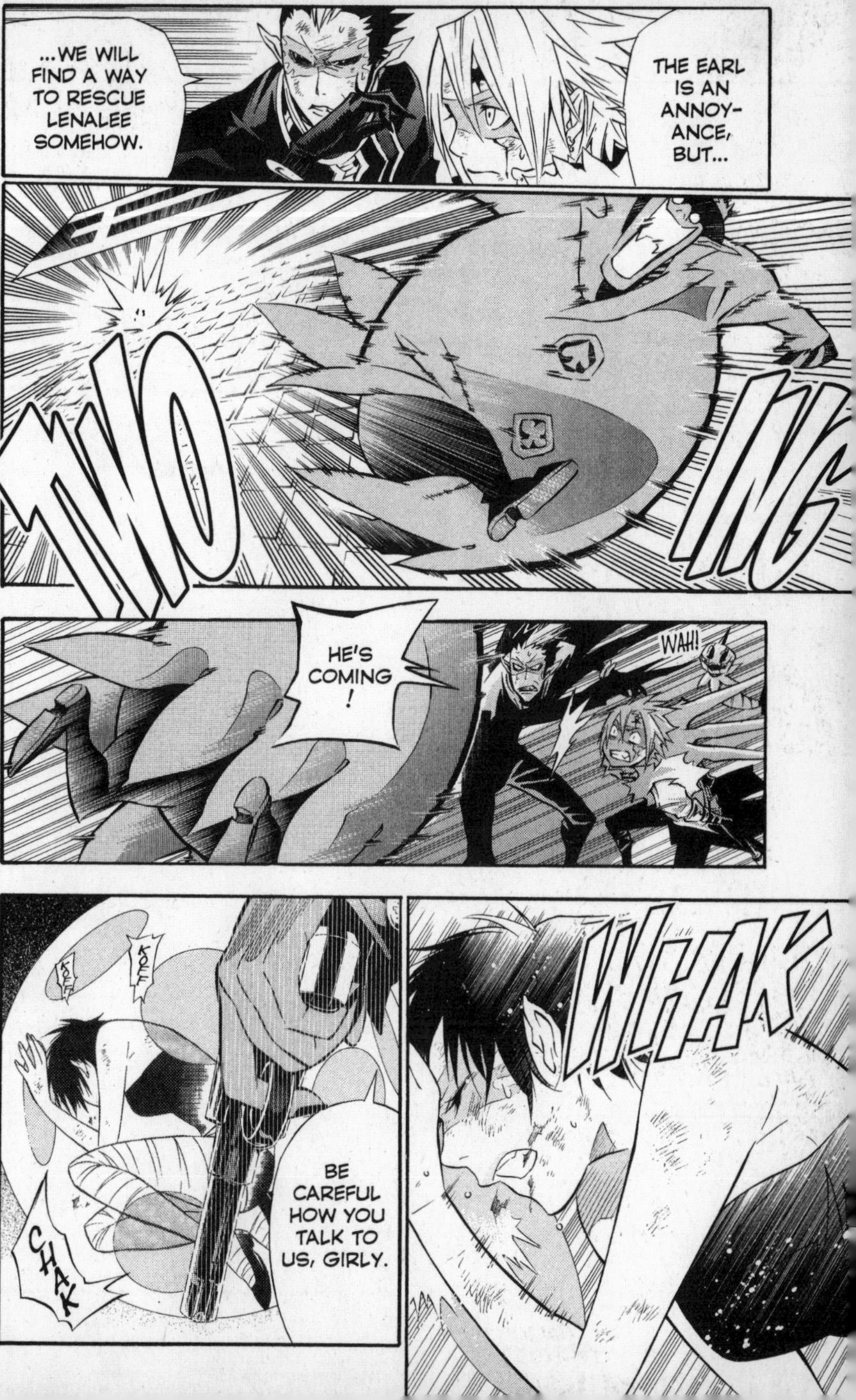
THE EARL IS AN ANNOY-ANCE, BUT...
...WE WILL FIND A WAY TO RESCUE LENALEE SOMEHOW.
TWO ING
WAH!
HE'S COMING!
WHAK
KOFF
KOFF
BE CAREFUL HOW YOU TALK TO US, GIRLY.
CHAK

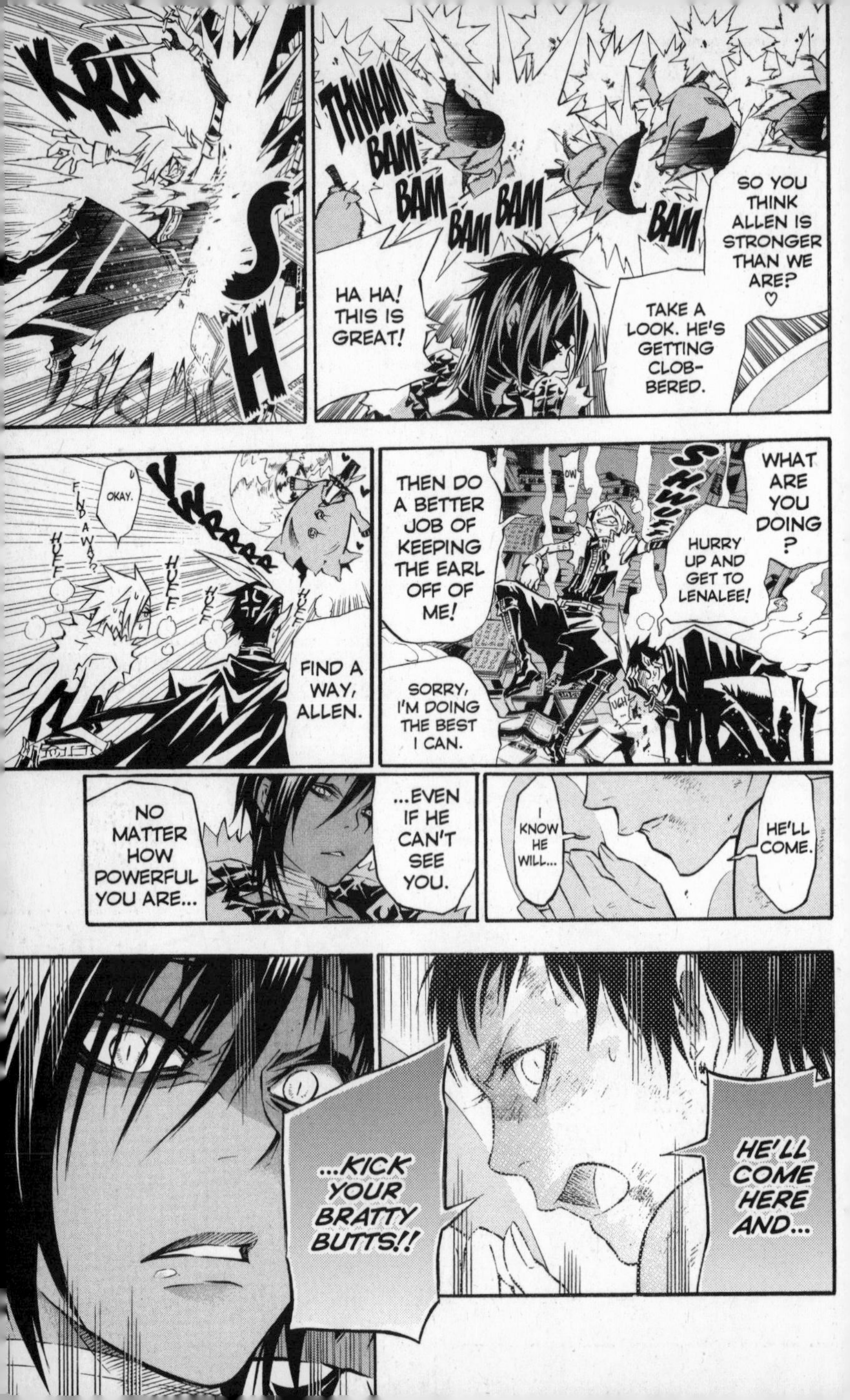
THWAM
BAM
BAM
BAM
BAM
BAM
SO YOU THINK ALLEN IS STRONGER THAN WE ARE? ♡
TAKE A LOOK. HE'S GETTING CLOB-BERED.
HA HA! THIS IS GREAT!
KRASSH
SHWUFF
WHAT ARE YOU DOING?
HURRY UP AND GET TO LENALEE!
OW...
THEN DO A BETTER JOB OF KEEPING THE EARL OFF OF ME!
UGH...
SORRY, I'M DOING THE BEST I CAN.
VWRRRR
OKAY.
FIND A WAY?!
HUFF
HUFF
HUFF
HUFF
FIND A WAY, ALLEN.
HE'LL COME.
I KNOW HE WILL...
...EVEN IF HE CAN'T SEE YOU.
NO MATTER HOW POWERFUL YOU ARE...
HE'LL COME HERE AND...
...KICK YOUR BRATTY BUTTS!!

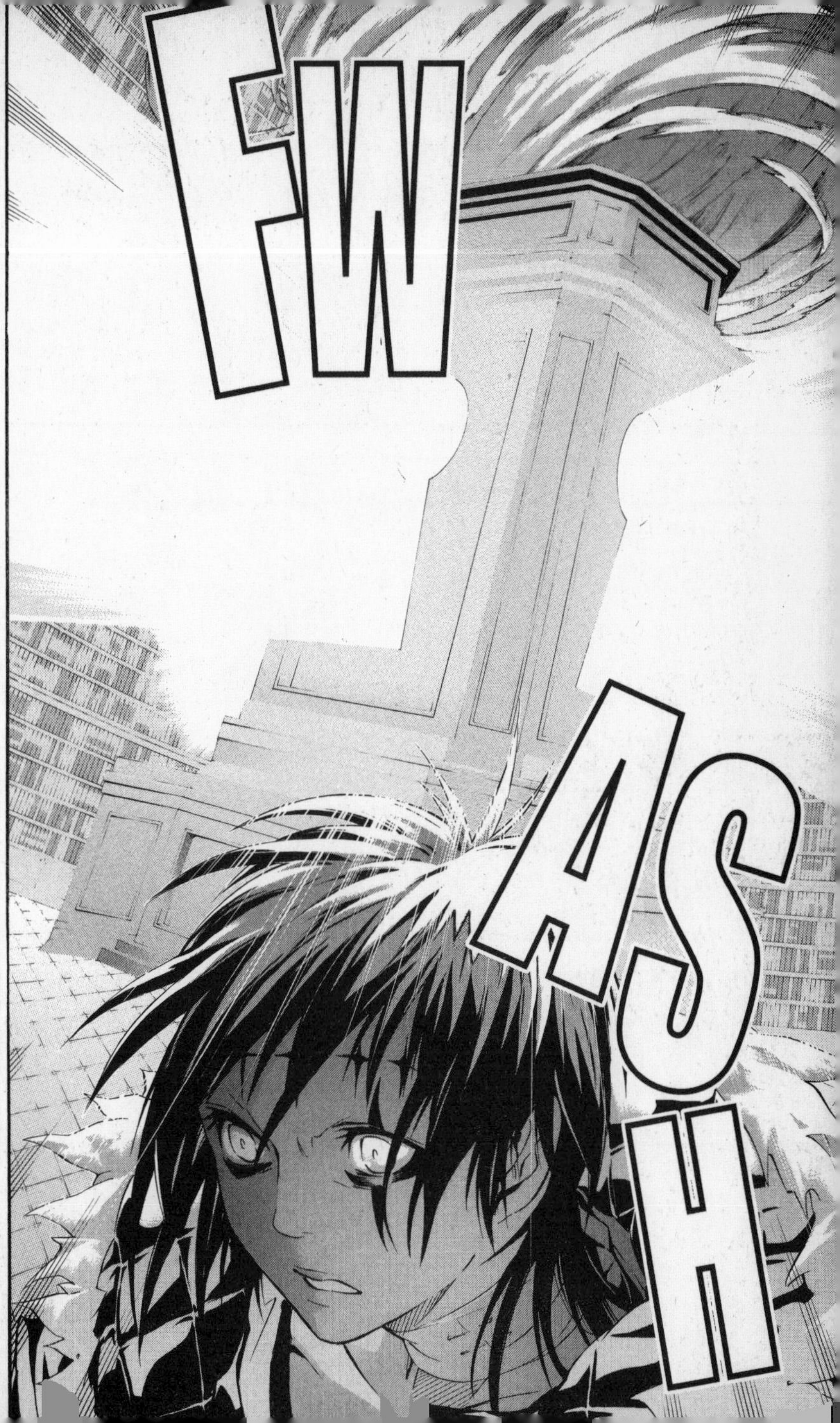
FWASH

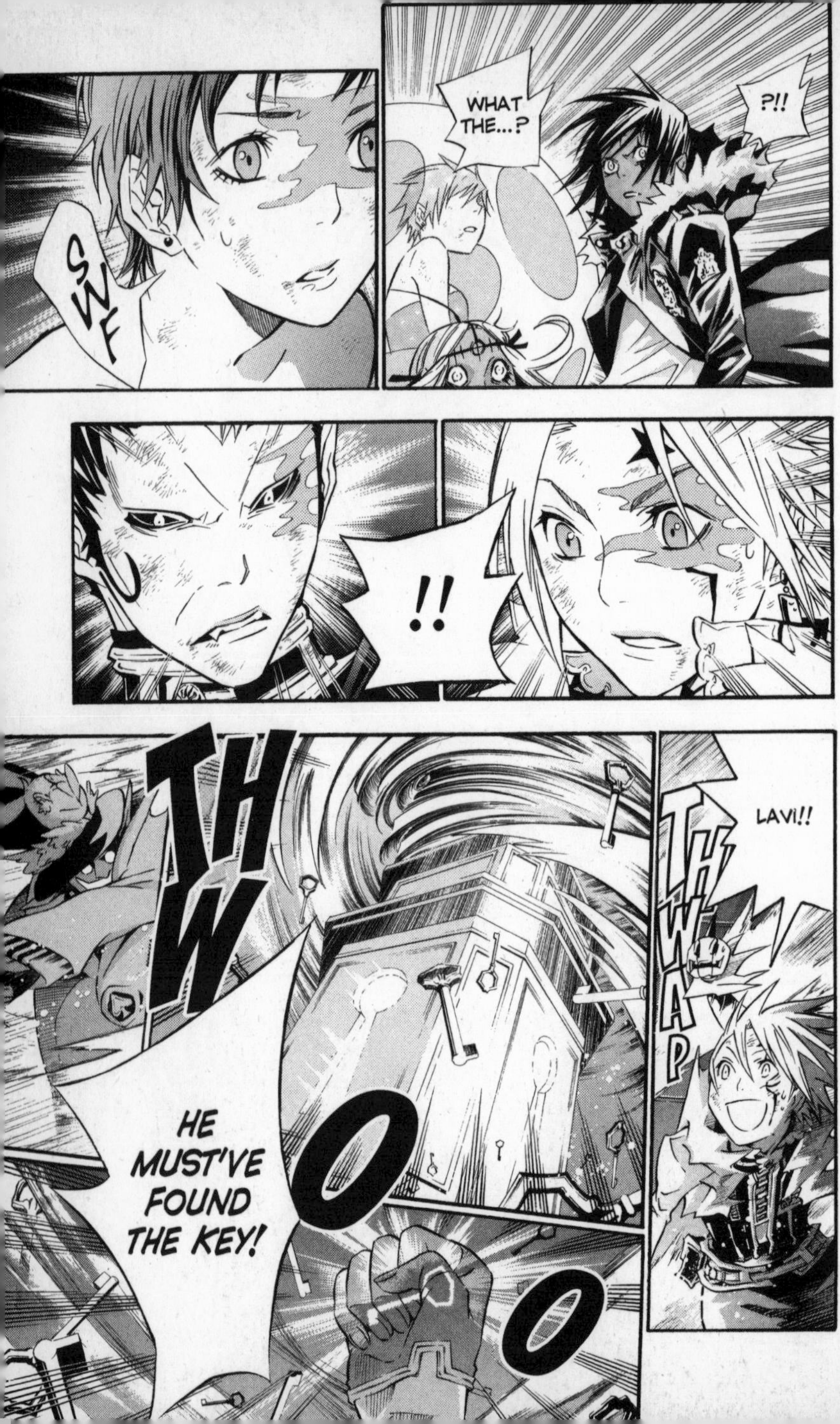
?!!
WHAT THE...?
SWF
!!
LAVI!!
THWAP
THW
OO
HE MUST'VE FOUND THE KEY!

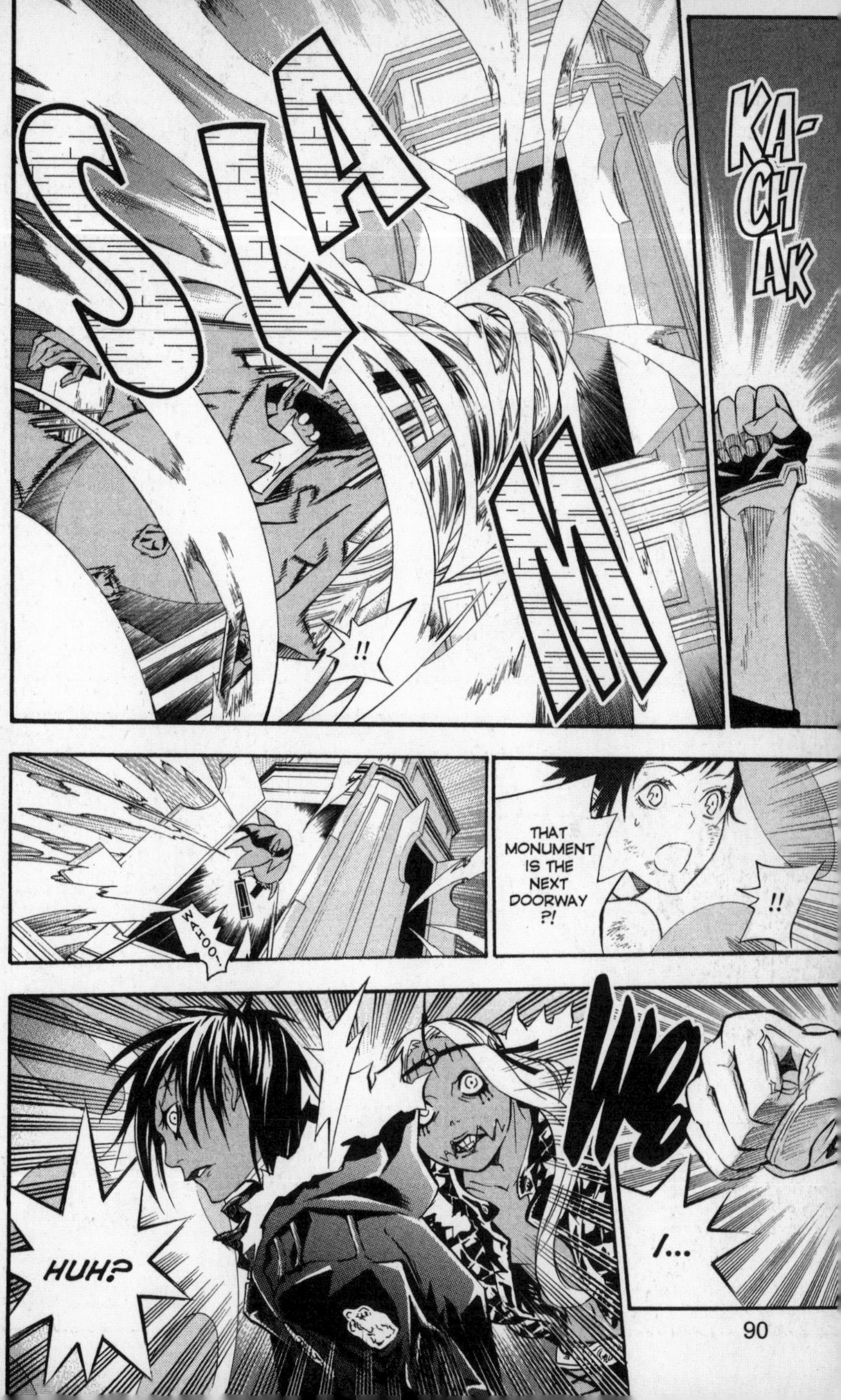
KA-CH AK
SLAM
!!
THAT MONUMENT IS THE NEXT DOORWAY ?!
!!
WAIOO!
I...
HUH?

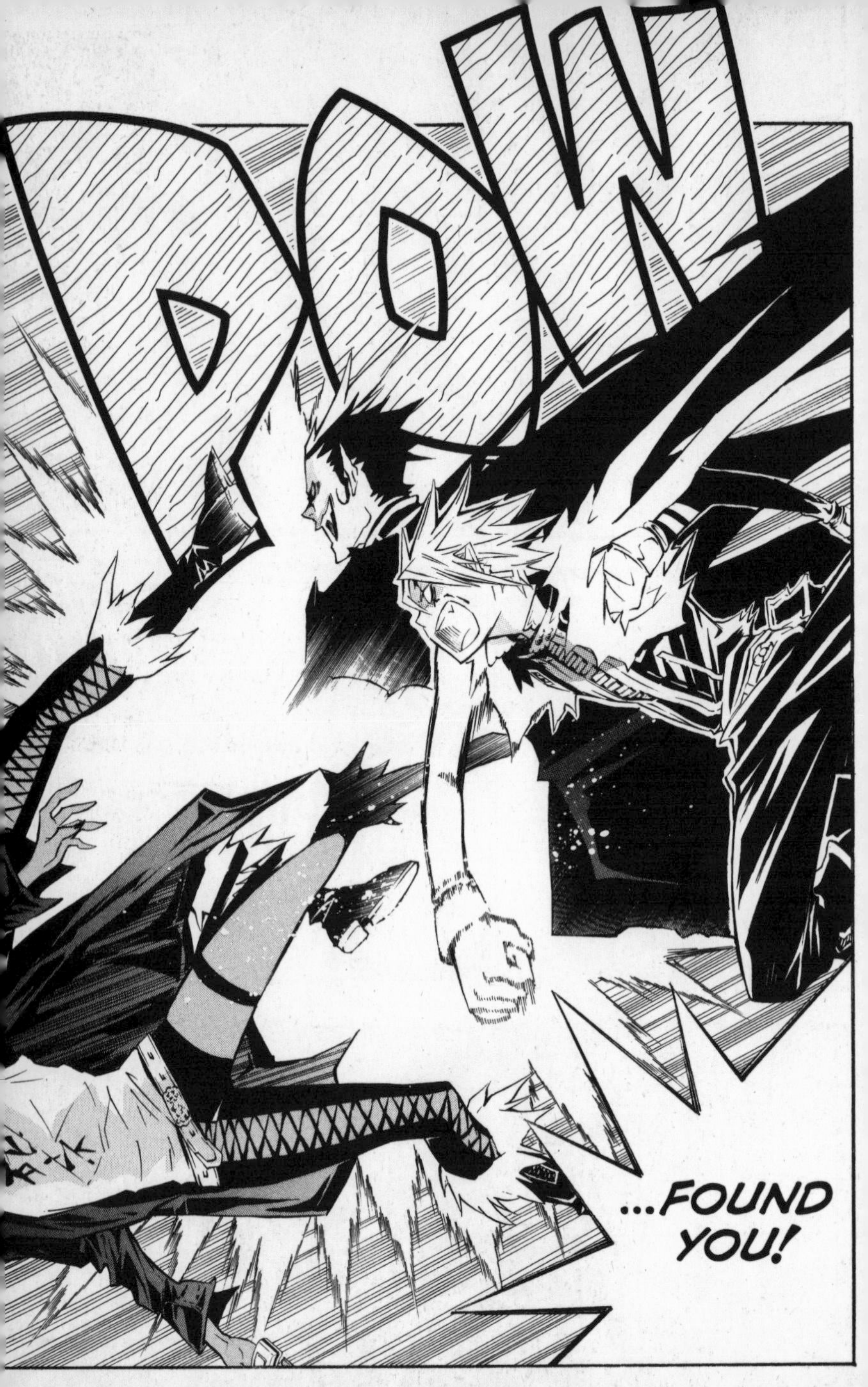
BOOM!
...FOUND YOU!

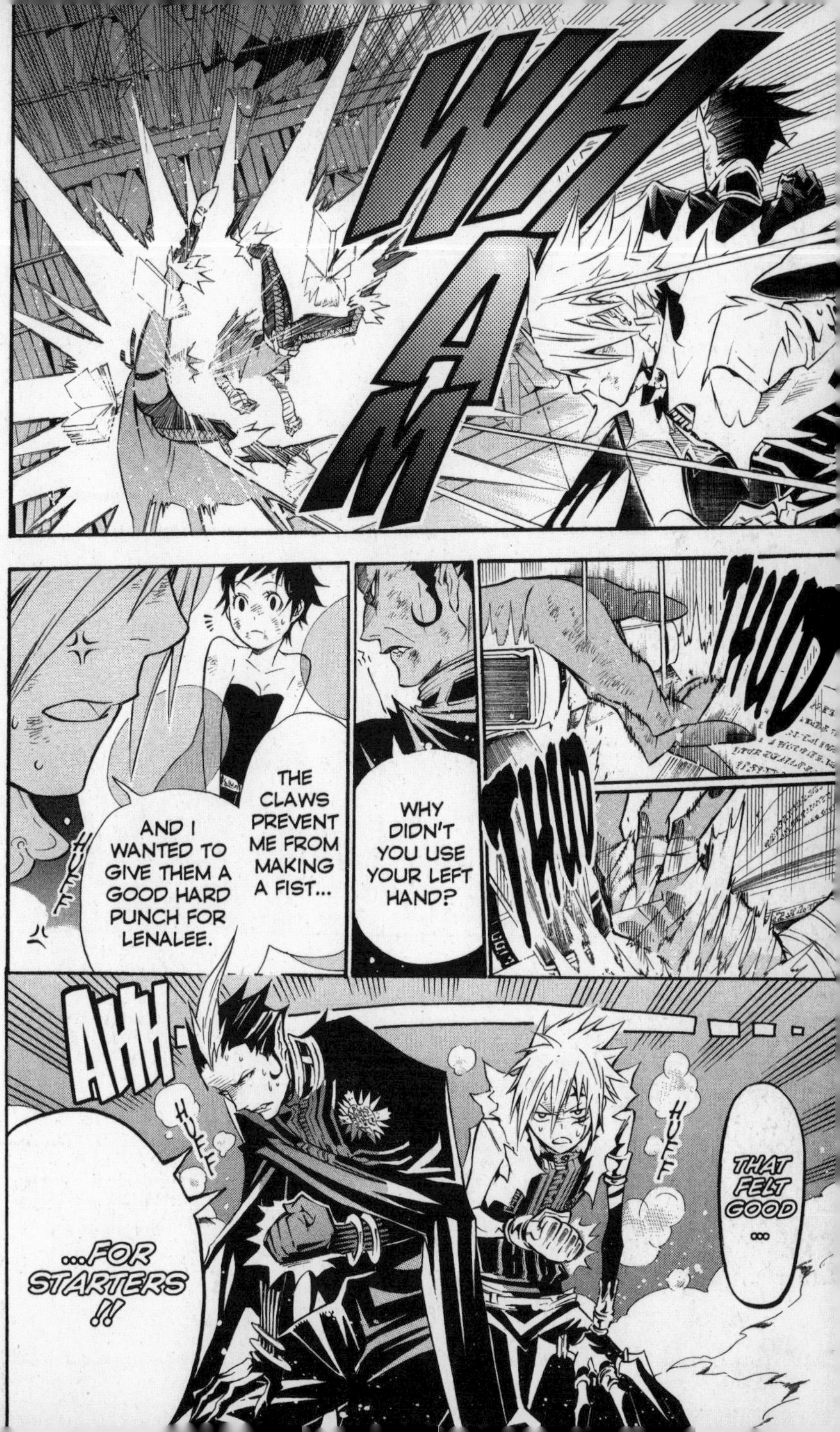
WHAM
THUD
THUD
WHY DIDN'T YOU USE YOUR LEFT HAND?
THE CLAWS PREVENT ME FROM MAKING A FIST...
AND I WANTED TO GIVE THEM A GOOD HARD PUNCH FOR LENALEE.
HUFF
THAT FELT GOOD ...
HUFF
AHH-.........
HUFF
...FOR STARTERS !!

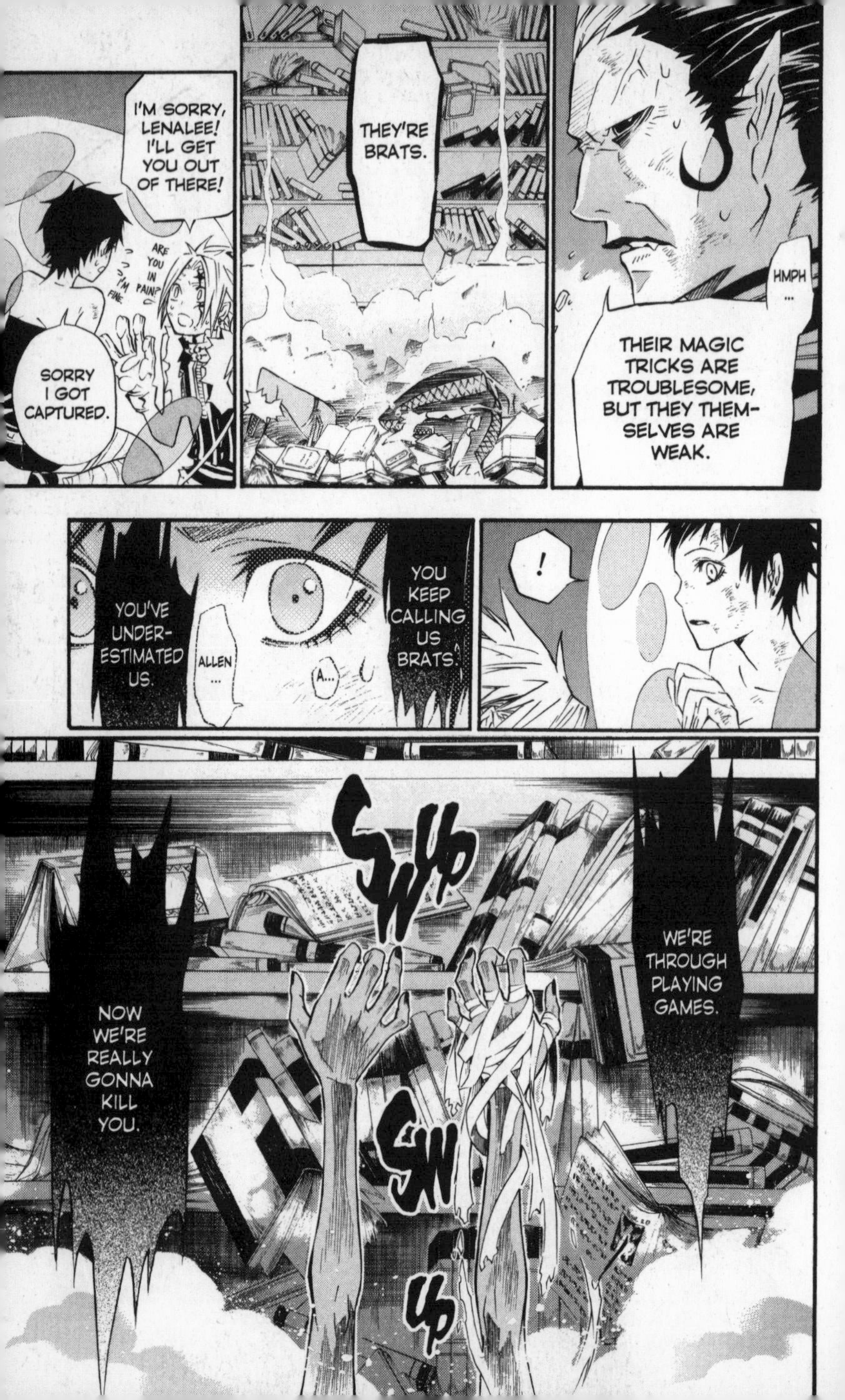
HMPH...
THEIR MAGIC TRICKS ARE TROUBLESOME, BUT THEY THEM-SELVES ARE WEAK.
THEY'RE BRATS.
I'M SORRY, LENALEE! I'LL GET YOU OUT OF THERE!
ARE YOU IN PAIN?
I'M FINE
SORRY I GOT CAPTURED.
!
YOU KEEP CALLING US BRATS.
A...
ALLEN...
YOU'VE UNDER-ESTIMATED US.
WE'RE THROUGH PLAYING GAMES.
SWUP
NOW WE'RE REALLY GONNA KILL YOU.
SWUP

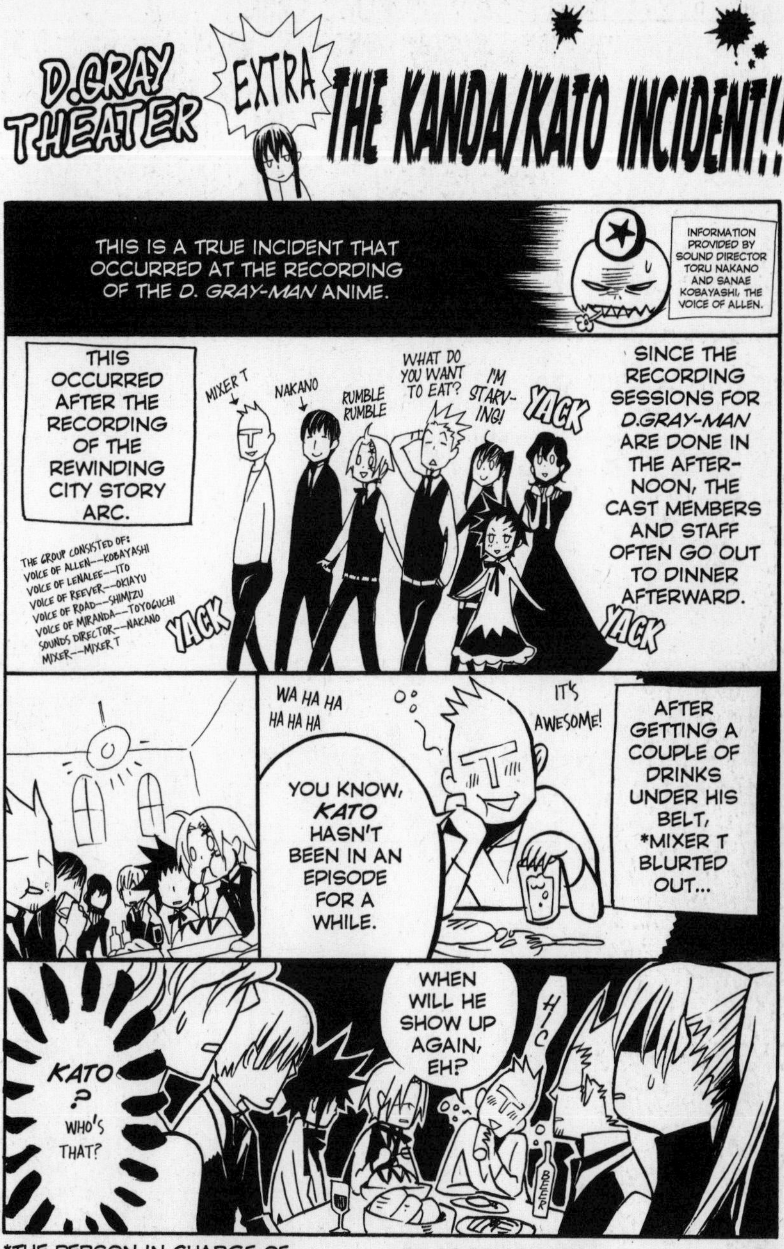
D.GRAY THEATER
EXTRA
THE KANDA/KATO INCIDENT!!
INFORMATION PROVIDED BY SOUND DIRECTOR TORU NAKANO AND SANAE KOBAYASHI, THE VOICE OF ALLEN.
THIS IS A TRUE INCIDENT THAT OCCURRED AT THE RECORDING OF THE *D. GRAY-MAN* ANIME.
SINCE THE RECORDING SESSIONS FOR *D.GRAY-MAN* ARE DONE IN THE AFTER-NOON, THE CAST MEMBERS AND STAFF OFTEN GO OUT TO DINNER AFTERWARD.
YACK
YACK
I'M STARV-ING!
WHAT DO YOU WANT TO EAT?
RUMBLE RUMBLE
NAKANO
MIXER T
THIS OCCURRED AFTER THE RECORDING OF THE REWINDING CITY STORY ARC.
THE GROUP CONSISTED OF:
VOICE OF ALLEN--KOBAYASHI
VOICE OF LENALEE--ITO
VOICE OF REEVER--OKIAYU
VOICE OF ROAD--SHIMIZU
VOICE OF MIRANDA--TOYOGUCHI
SOUNDS DIRECTOR--NAKANO
MIXER--MIXER T
YACK
AFTER GETTING A COUPLE OF DRINKS UNDER HIS BELT, *MIXER T BLURTED OUT...
IT'S AWESOME!
WA HA HA HA HA HA
YOU KNOW, *KATO* HASN'T BEEN IN AN EPISODE FOR A WHILE.
HIC
WHEN WILL HE SHOW UP AGAIN, EH?
BEER
KATO ? WHO'S THAT?

*THE PERSON IN CHARGE OF THE RECORDING EQUIPMENT

TO BE CONTINUED

THE 103RD NIGHT: AN UNRULY CHILD

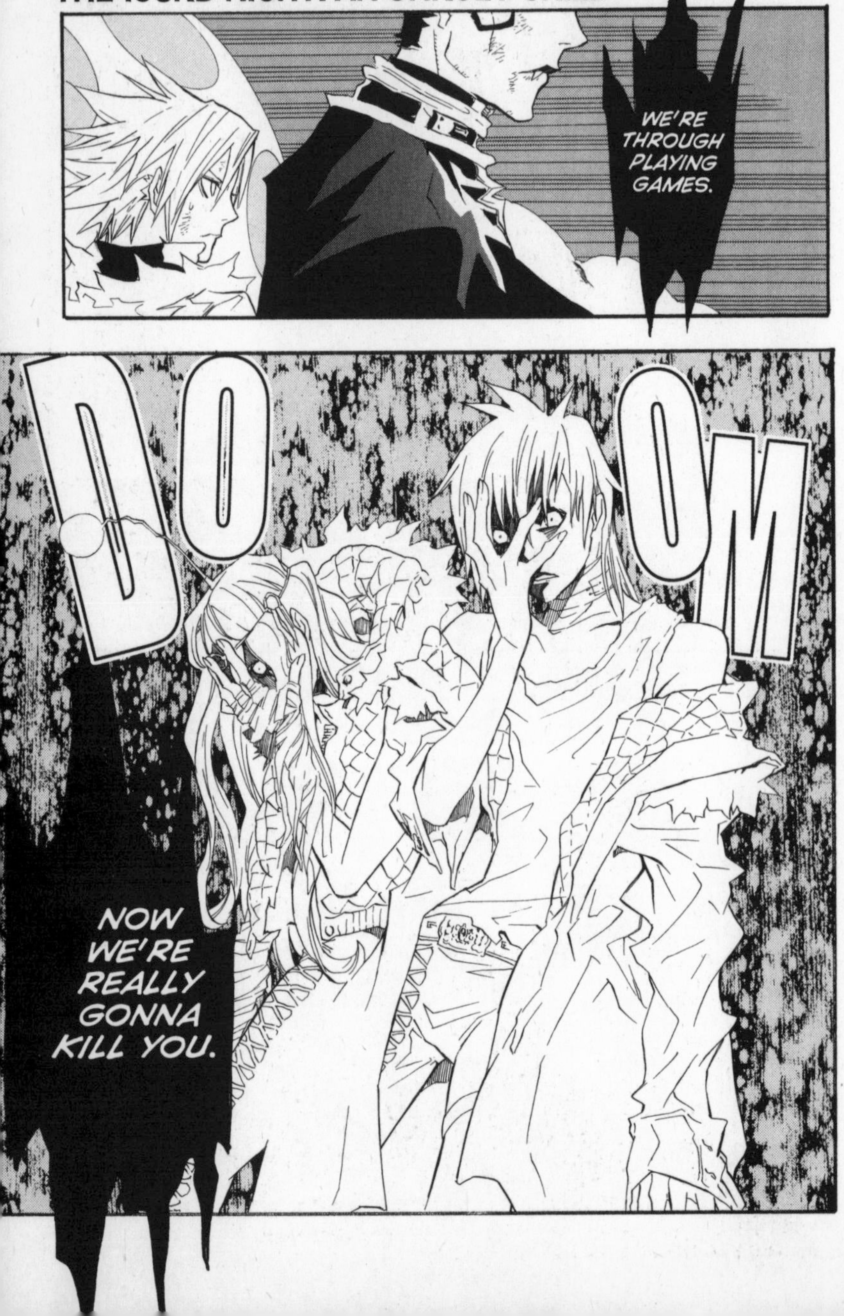
WE'RE THROUGH PLAYING GAMES.
DOOM
NOW WE'RE REALLY GONNA KILL YOU.

THE 103RD NIGHT: AN UNRULY CHILD

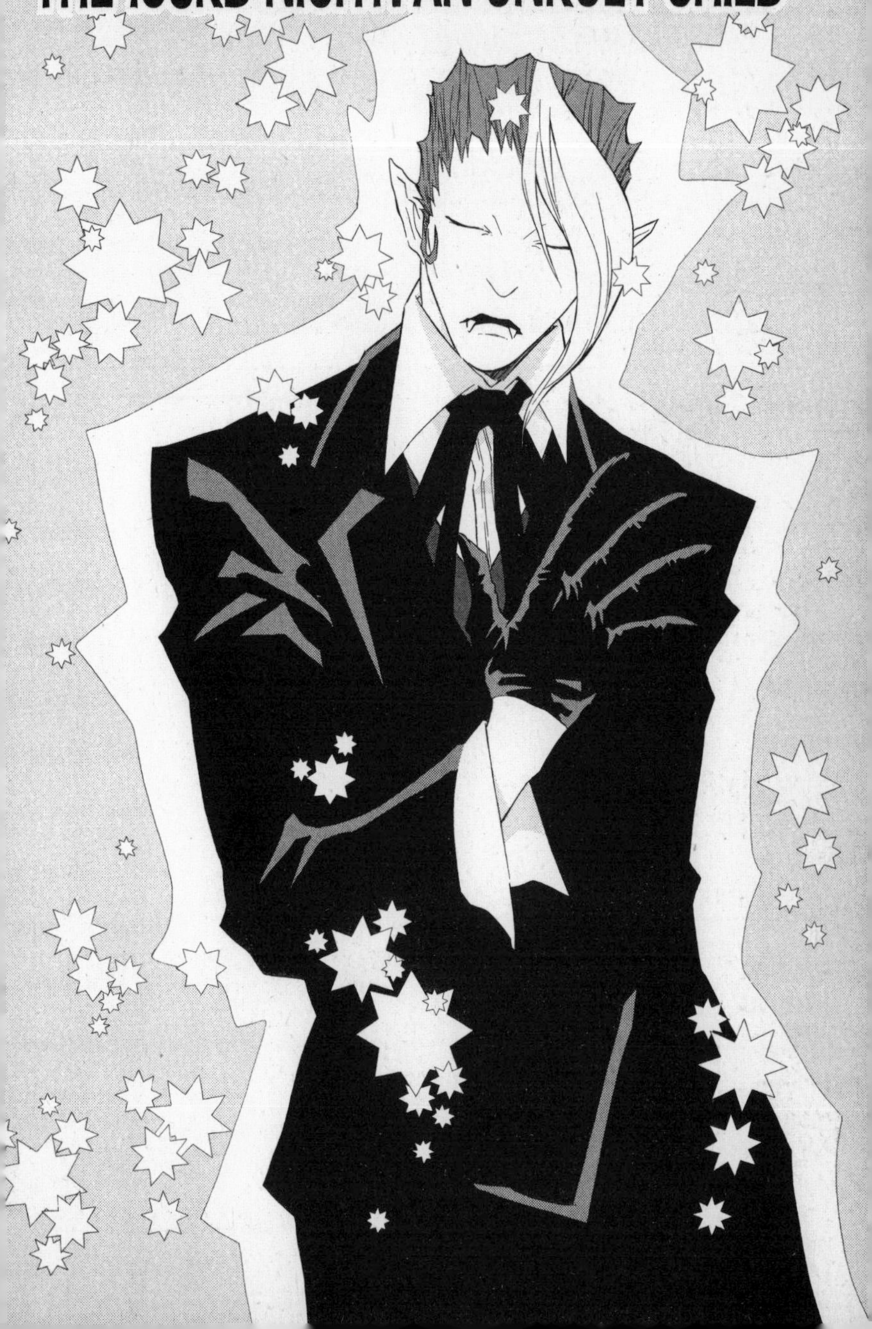

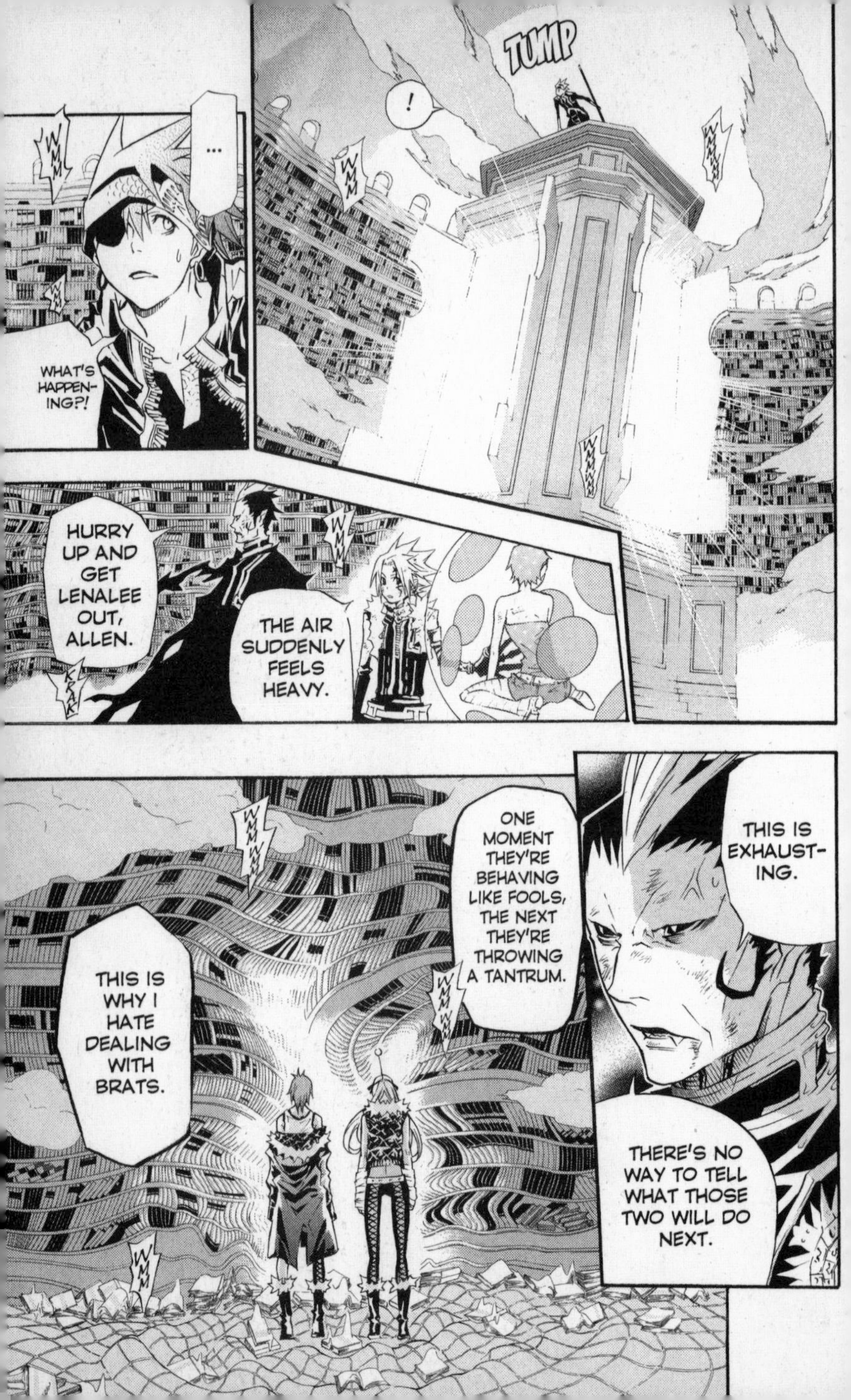
TUMP
!
WMM
WMM
...
WMM
WMM
WHAT'S HAPPEN-ING?!
WMMMM
WMM
THE AIR SUDDENLY FEELS HEAVY.
HURRY UP AND GET LENALEE OUT, ALLEN.
KRAK
THIS IS EXHAUST-ING.
ONE MOMENT THEY'RE BEHAVING LIKE FOOLS, THE NEXT THEY'RE THROWING A TANTRUM.
THERE'S NO WAY TO TELL WHAT THOSE TWO WILL DO NEXT.
WMMMM
WMMMM
THIS IS WHY I HATE DEALING WITH BRATS.
WMM

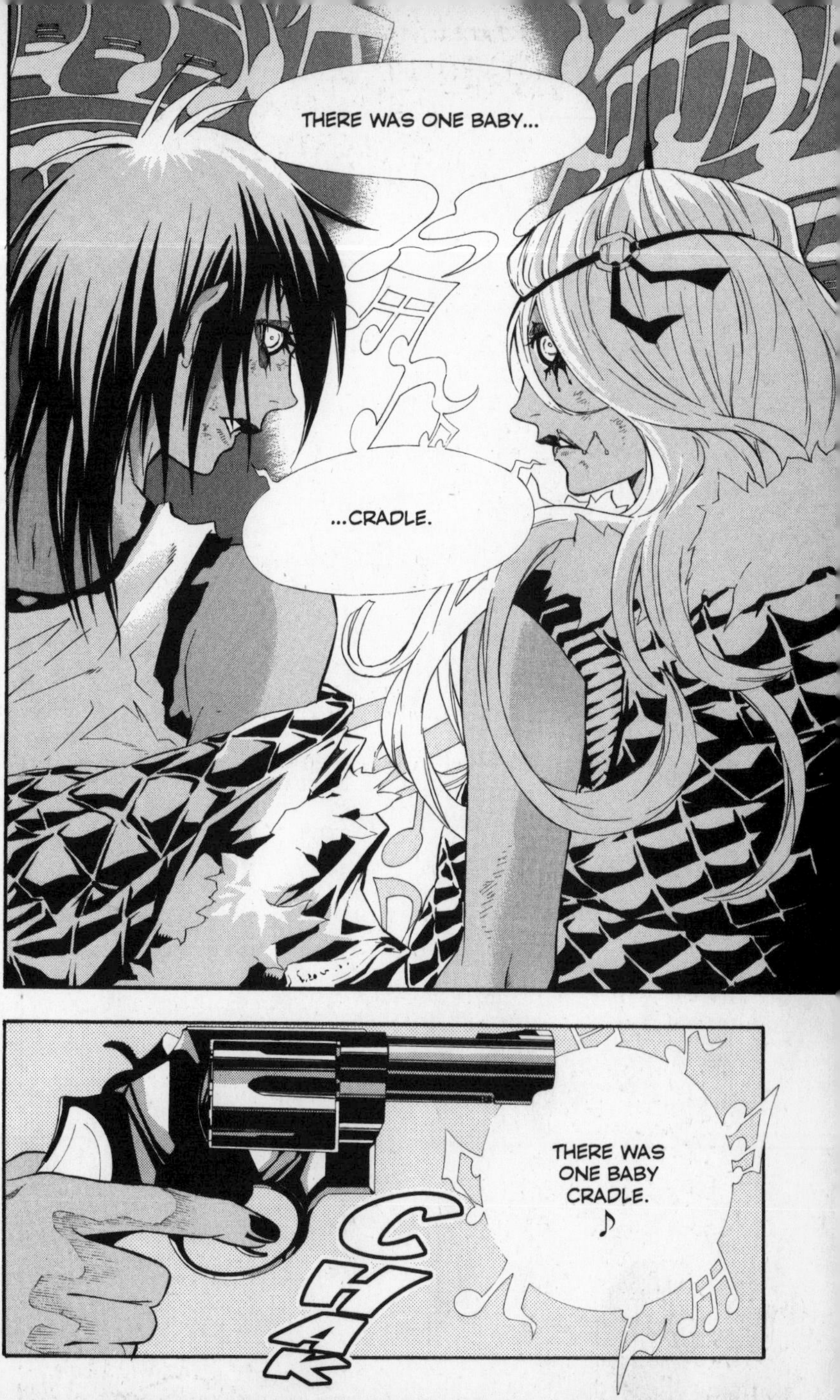
THERE WAS ONE BABY...
...CRADLE.
THERE WAS ONE BABY CRADLE. ♪
CHAK

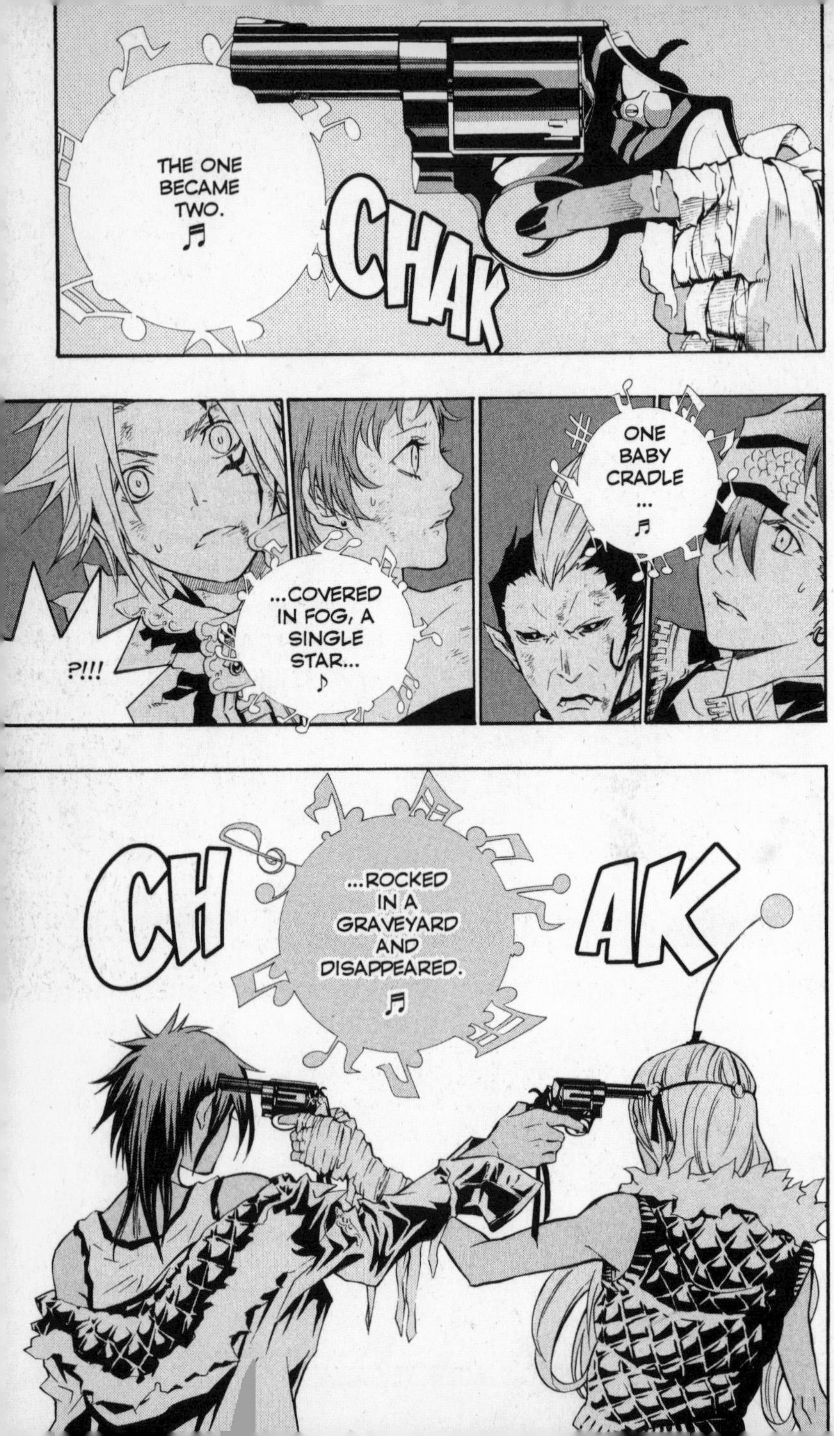
THE ONE BECAME TWO. ♬
CHAK
ONE BABY CRADLE ... ♬
...COVERED IN FOG, A SINGLE STAR... ♪
?!!!
...ROCKED IN A GRAVEYARD AND DISAPPEARED. ♬
CH AK

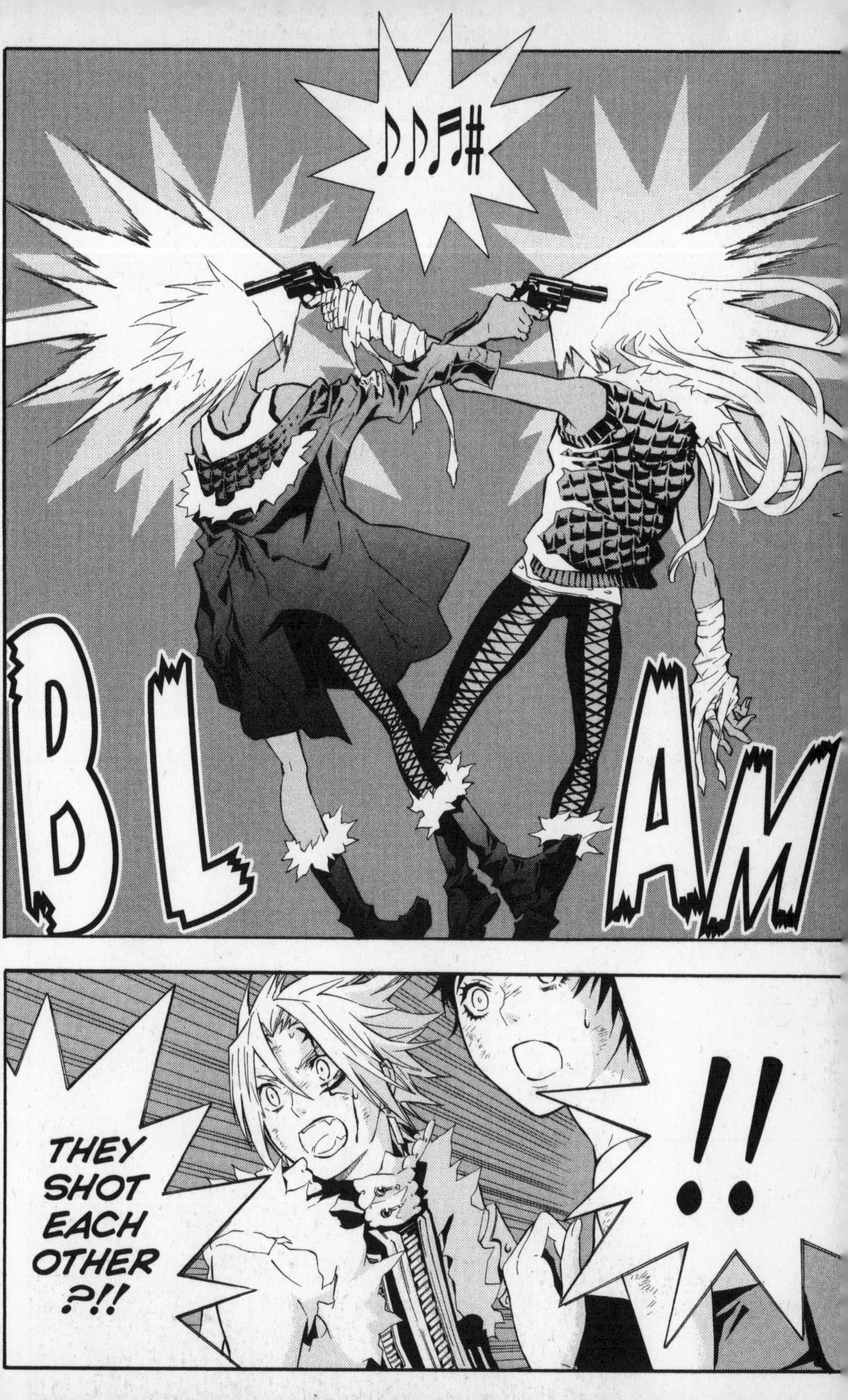
♪♪♬#
BLAM
!!
THEY SHOT EACH OTHER ?!!

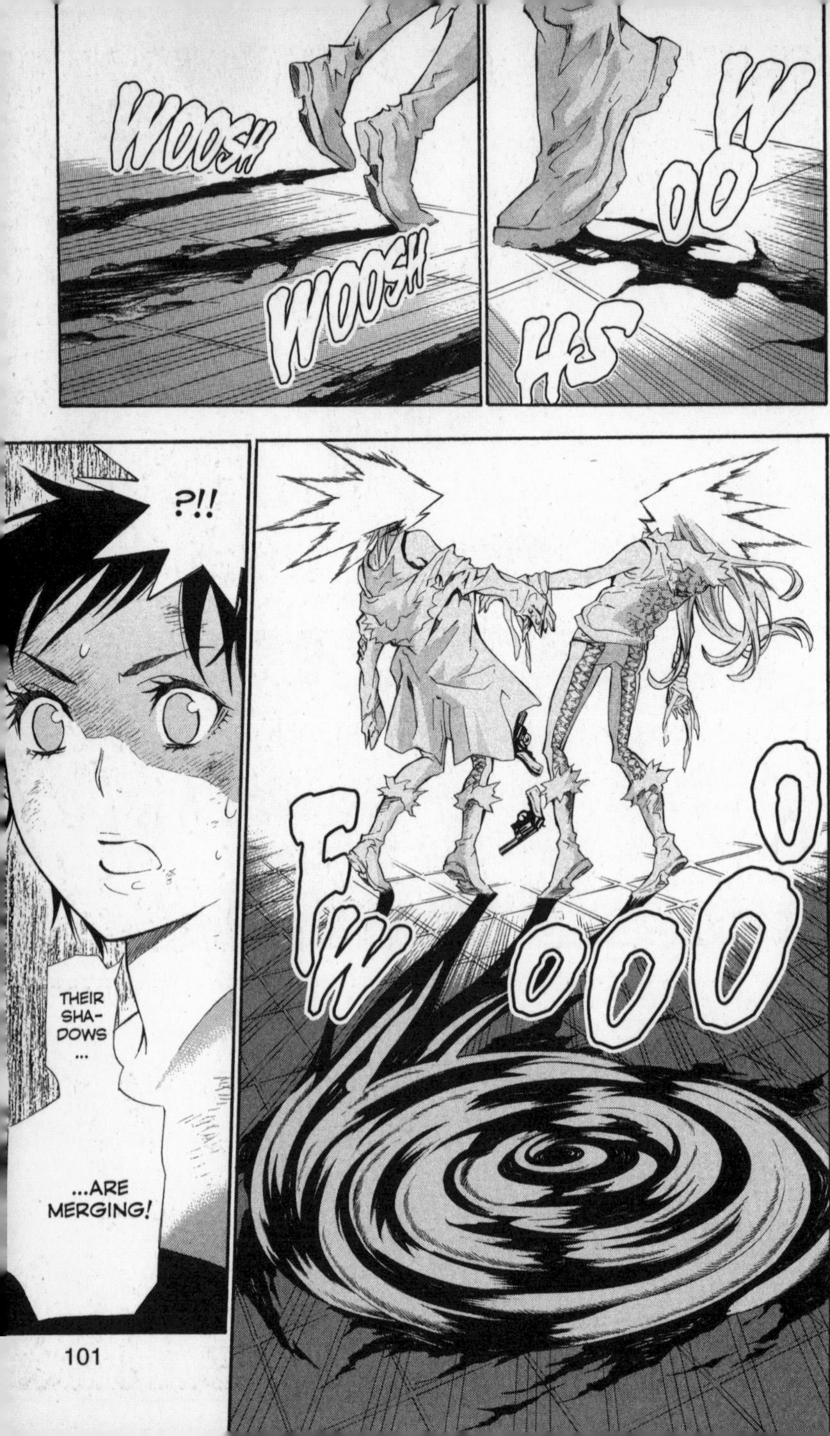
WOOSH
WOOSH
WOOSH
FWOOOO
?!!
THEIR SHA- DOWS ...
...ARE MERGING!

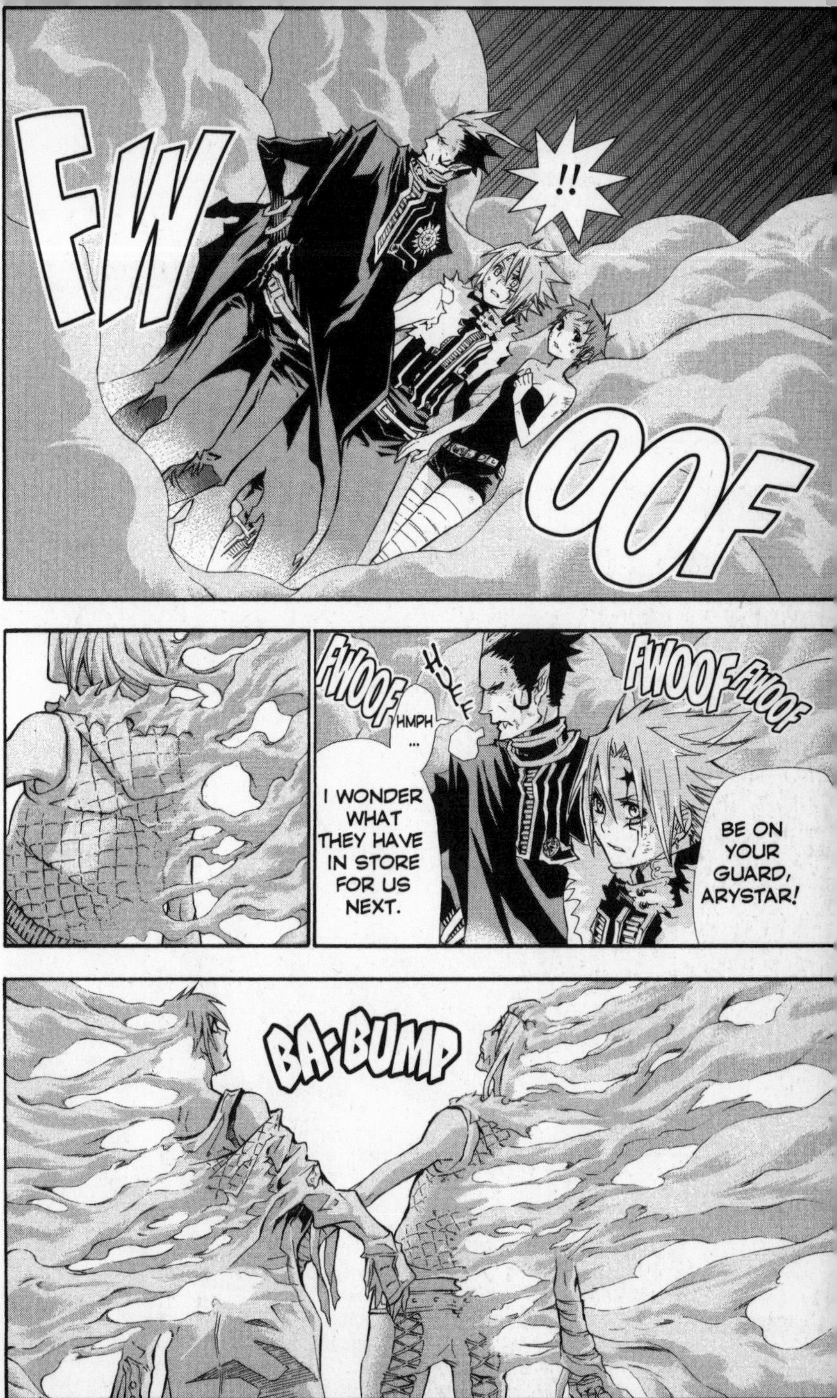
!!
FW
OOF
FWOOF FWOOF
BE ON YOUR GUARD, ARYSTAR!
HUFF
HMPH ...
FWOOF
I WONDER WHAT THEY HAVE IN STORE FOR US NEXT.
BA-BUMP

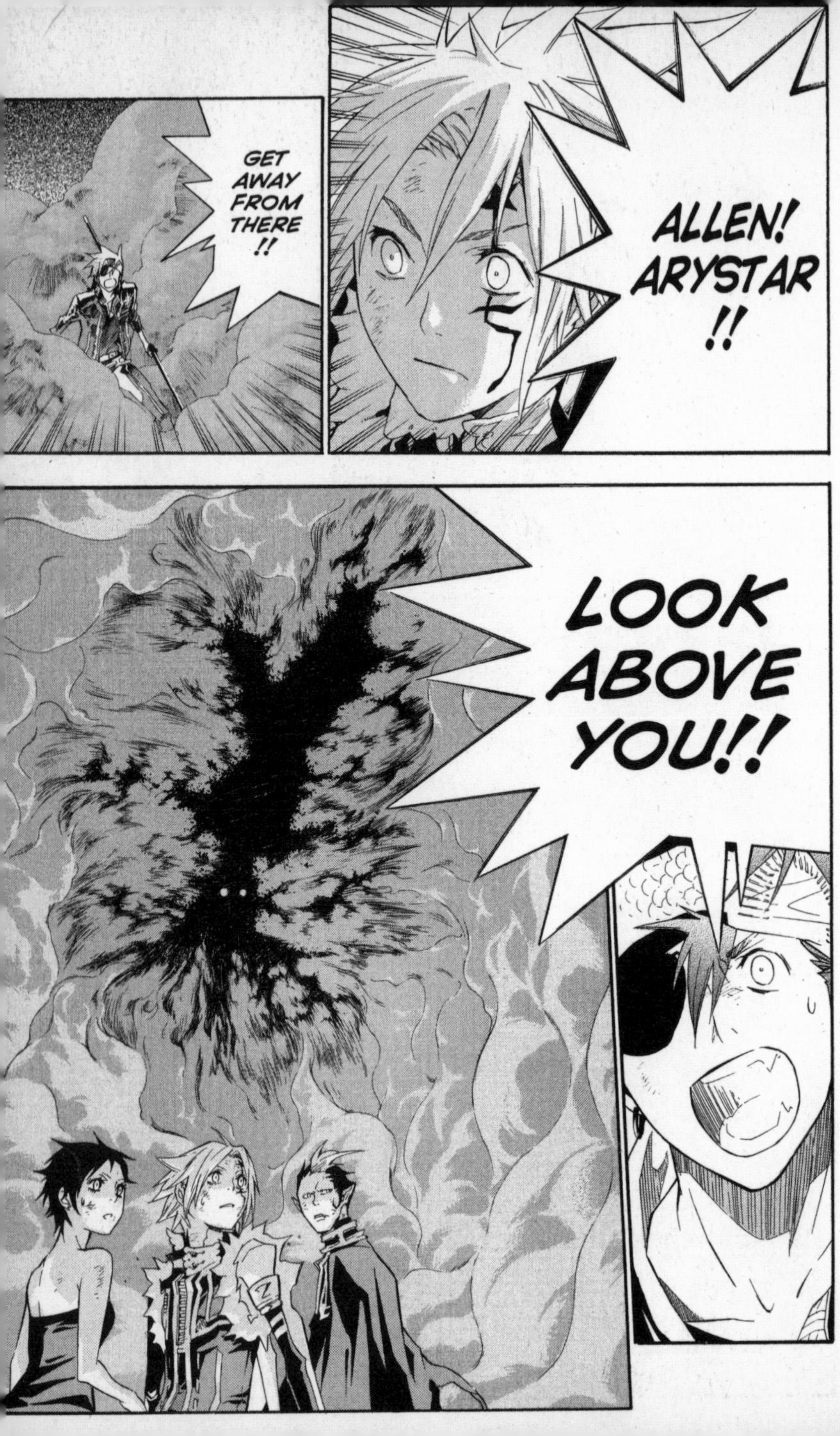
ALLEN! ARYSTAR !!
GET AWAY FROM THERE !!
LOOK ABOVE YOU!!

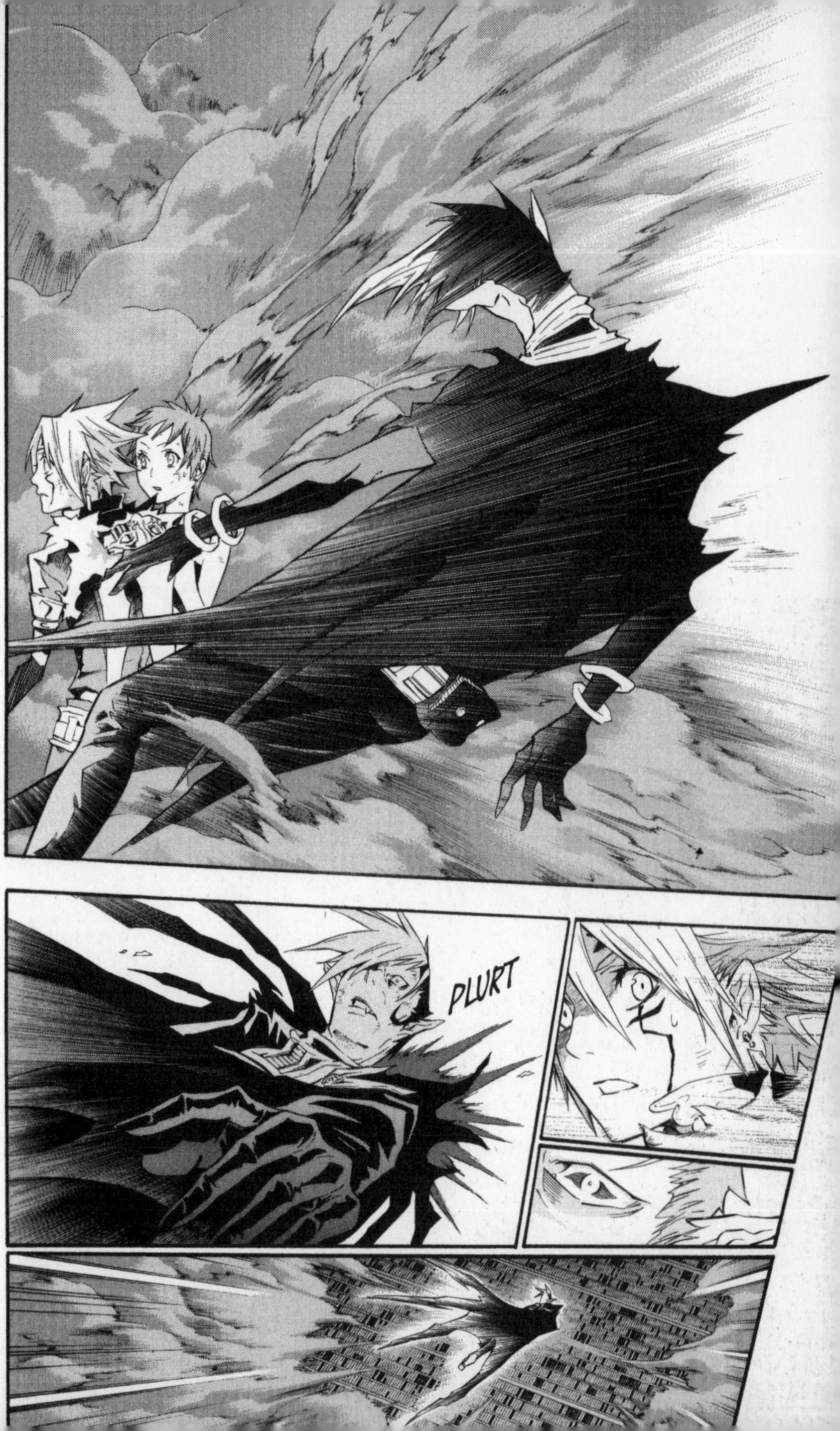
PLURT

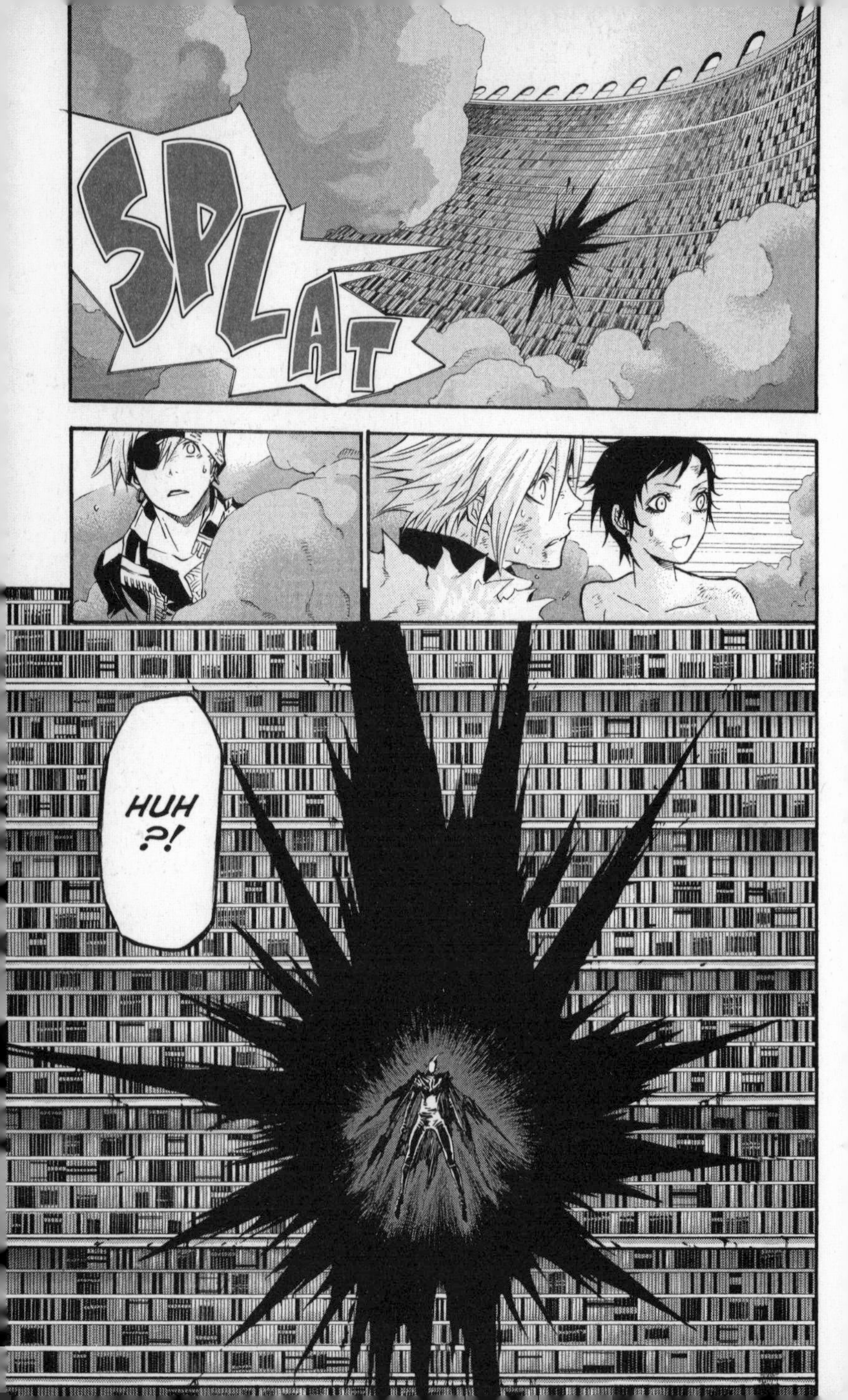
SPLAT
HUH ?!

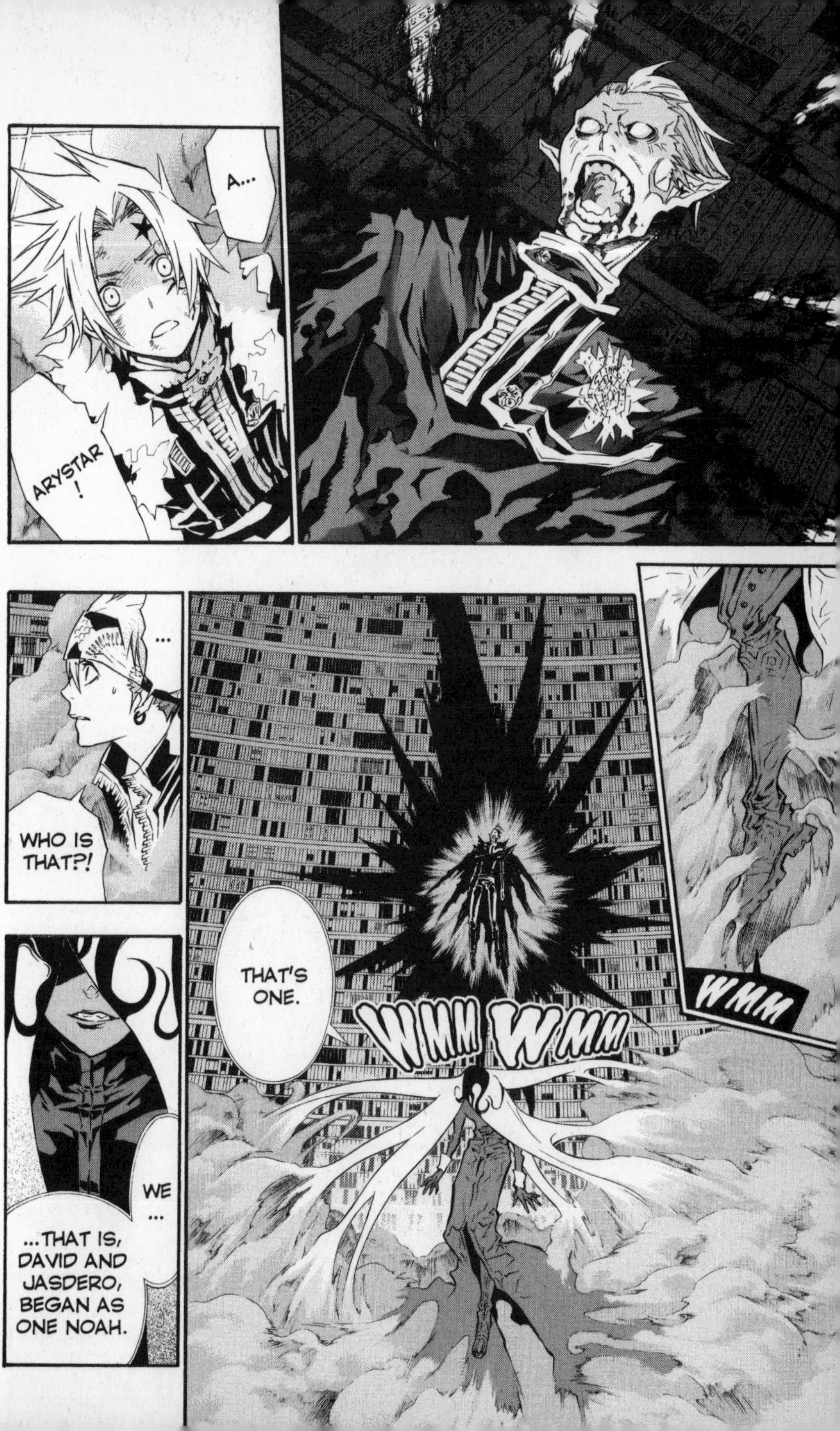
A...
ARYSTAR!
WMM
THAT'S ONE.
WMM WMM
...
WHO IS THAT?!
WE...
...THAT IS, DAVID AND JASDERO, BEGAN AS ONE NOAH.

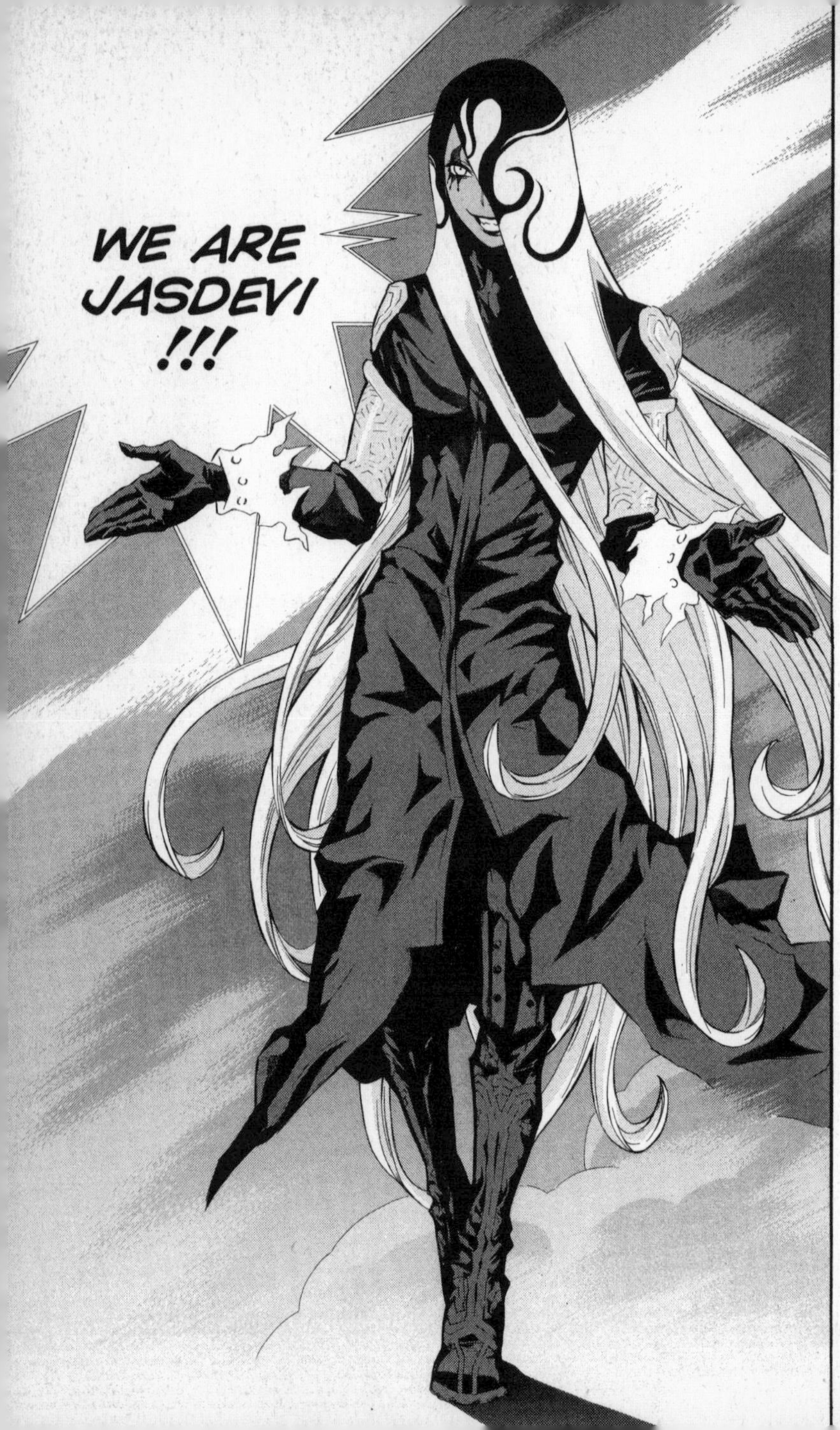
WE ARE JASDEVI !!!

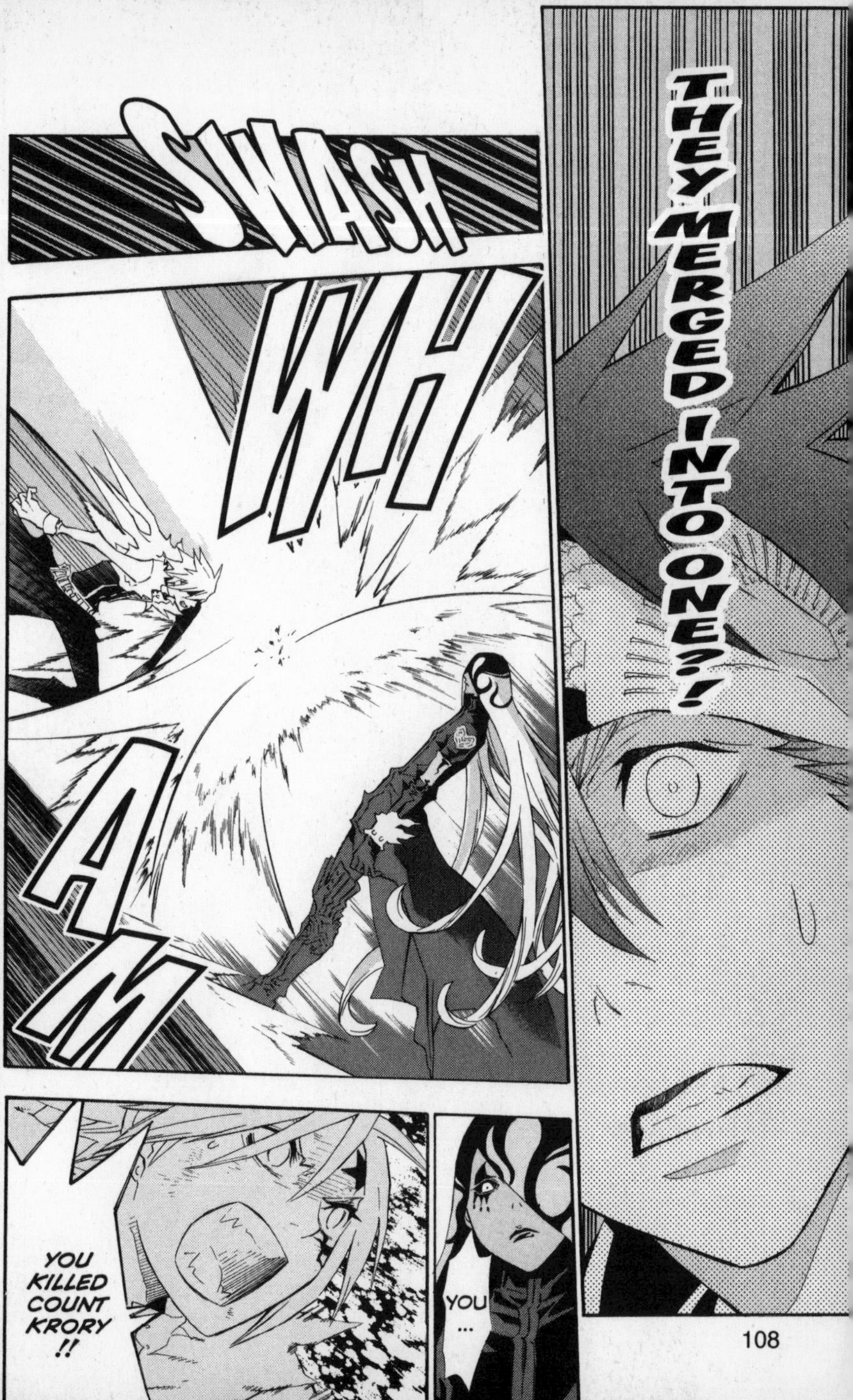
THEY MERGED INTO ONE?!
SWASH
WHAM
YOU ...
YOU KILLED COUNT KRORY!!

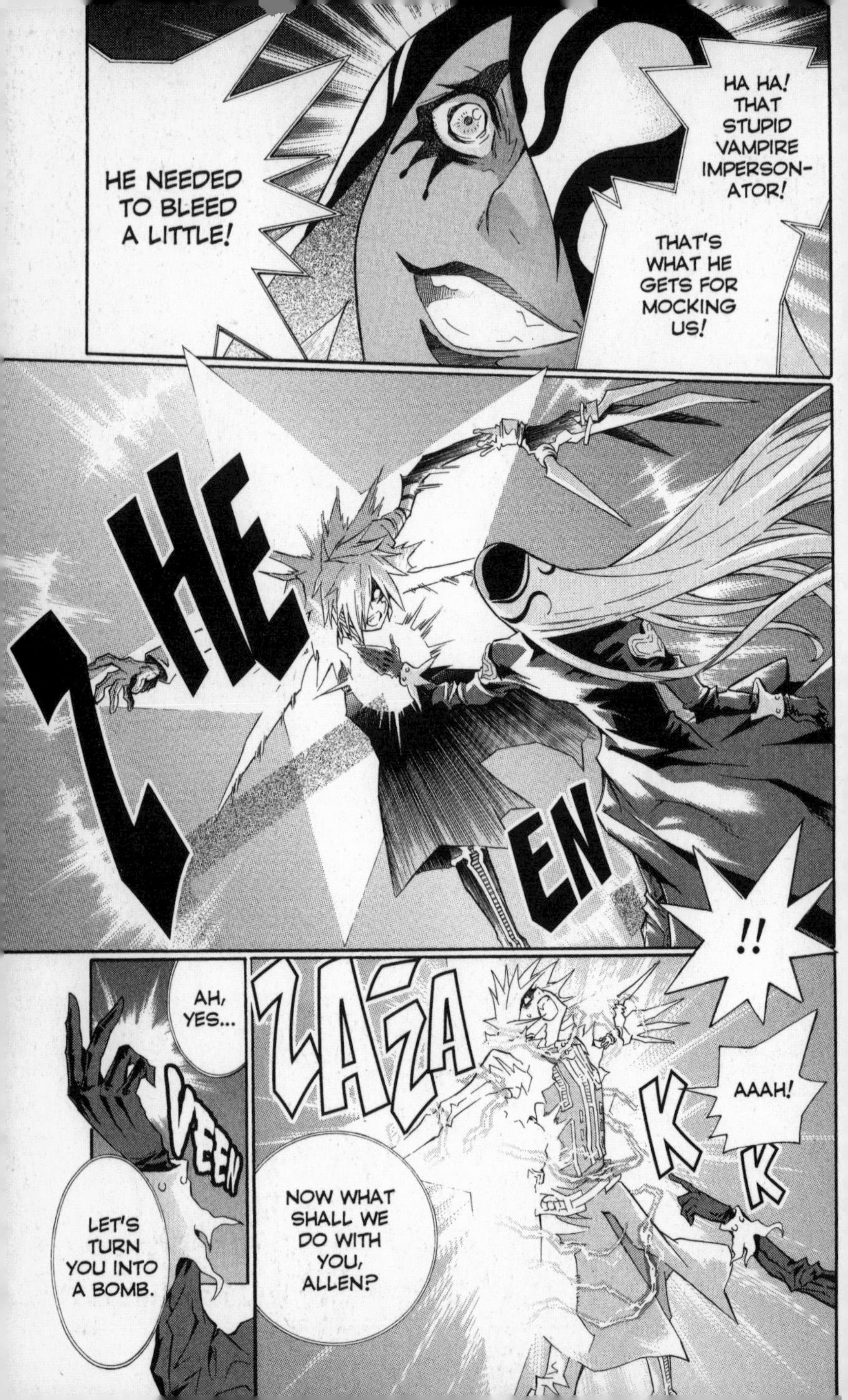
HA HA! THAT STUPID VAMPIRE IMPERSON-ATOR!
THAT'S WHAT HE GETS FOR MOCKING US!
HE NEEDED TO BLEED A LITTLE!
ZHE
EN
!!
AAAH!
K
K
ZAZA
AH, YES...
NOW WHAT SHALL WE DO WITH YOU, ALLEN?
VEEN
LET'S TURN YOU INTO A BOMB.

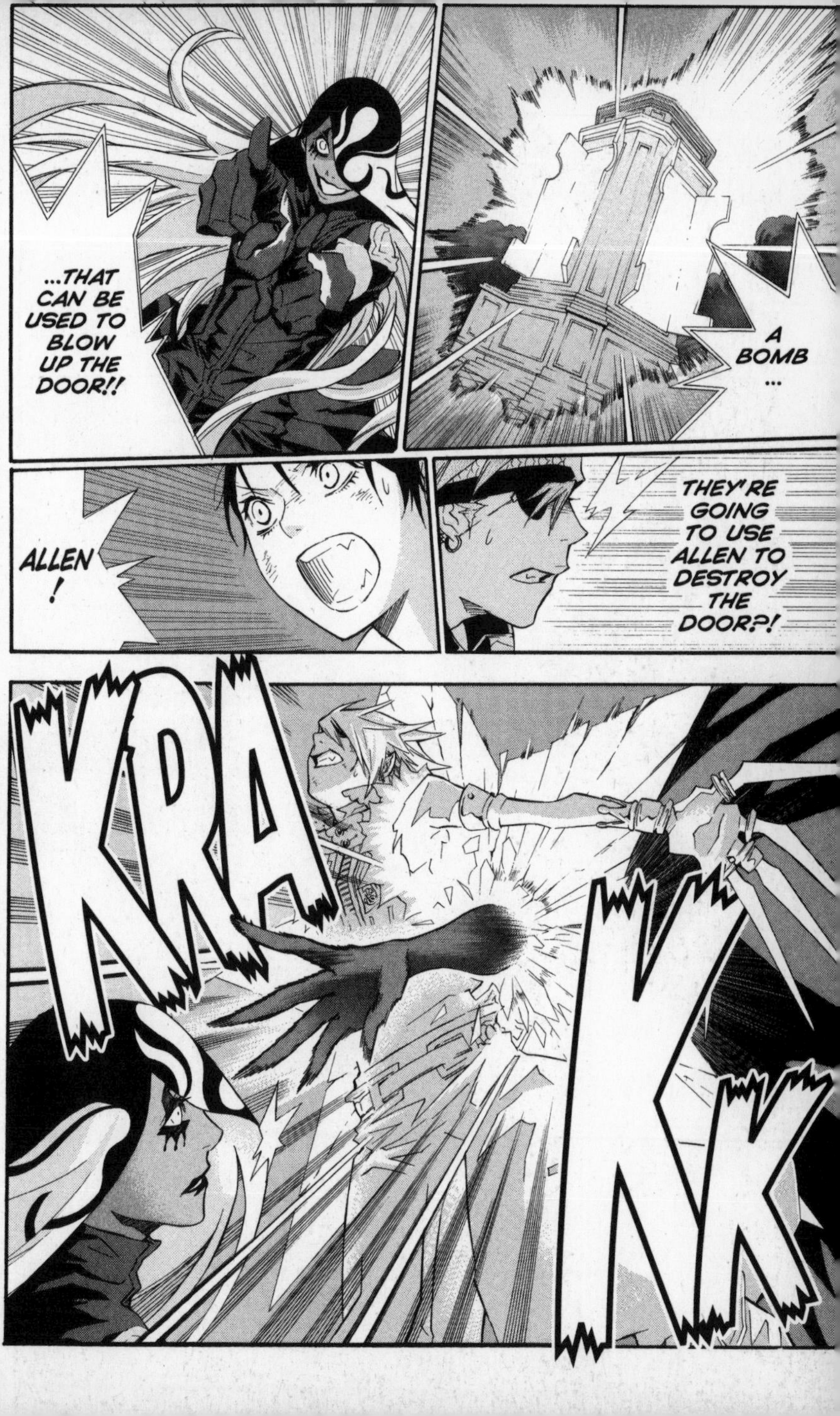
A BOMB ...
...THAT CAN BE USED TO BLOW UP THE DOOR!!
THEY'RE GOING TO USE ALLEN TO DESTROY THE DOOR?!
ALLEN !
KRAKK

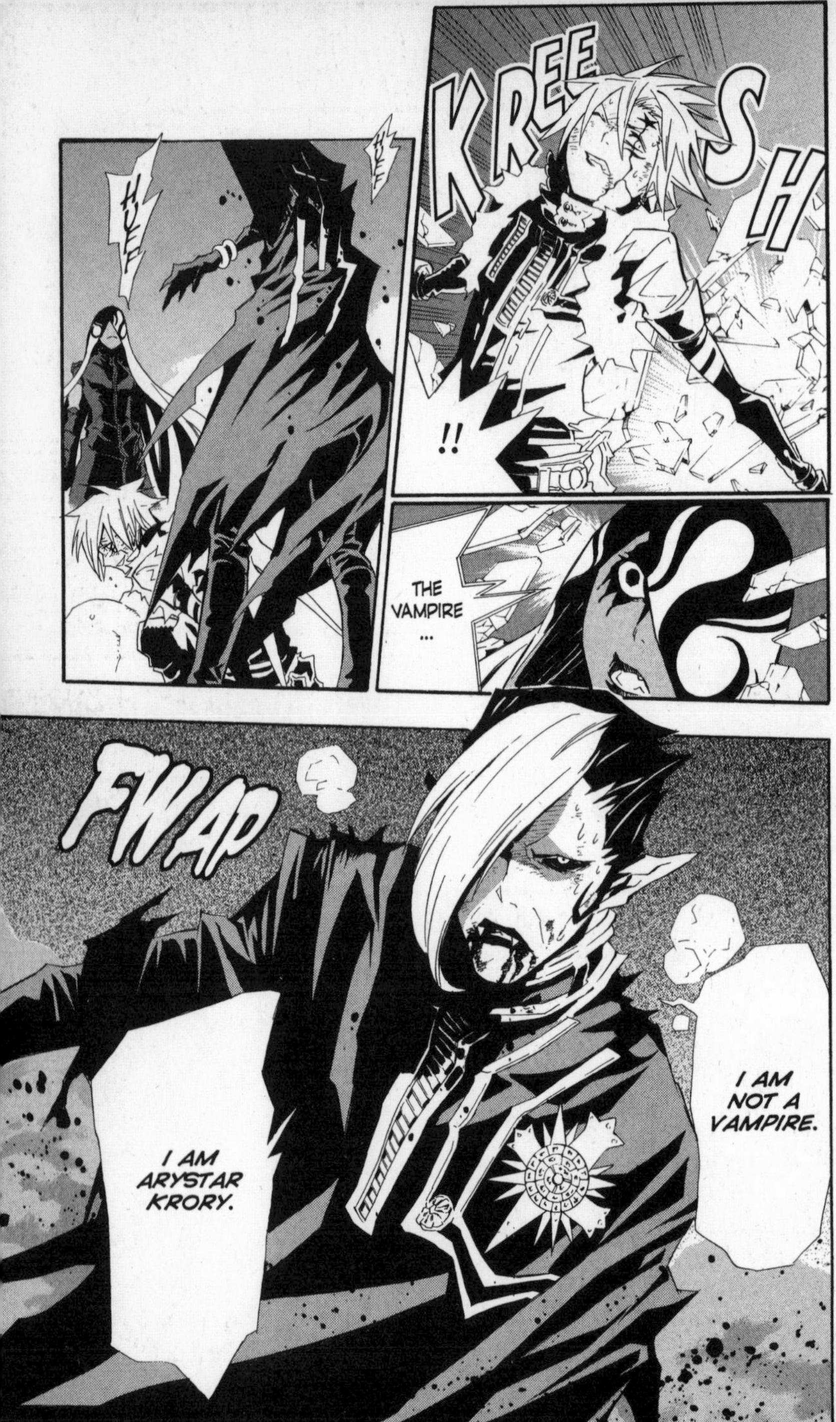
KREESH
!!
HUFF
HUFF
THE VAMPIRE ...
FWAP
I AM NOT A VAMPIRE.
I AM ARYSTAR KRORY.

THE KATO INCIDENT, PART II

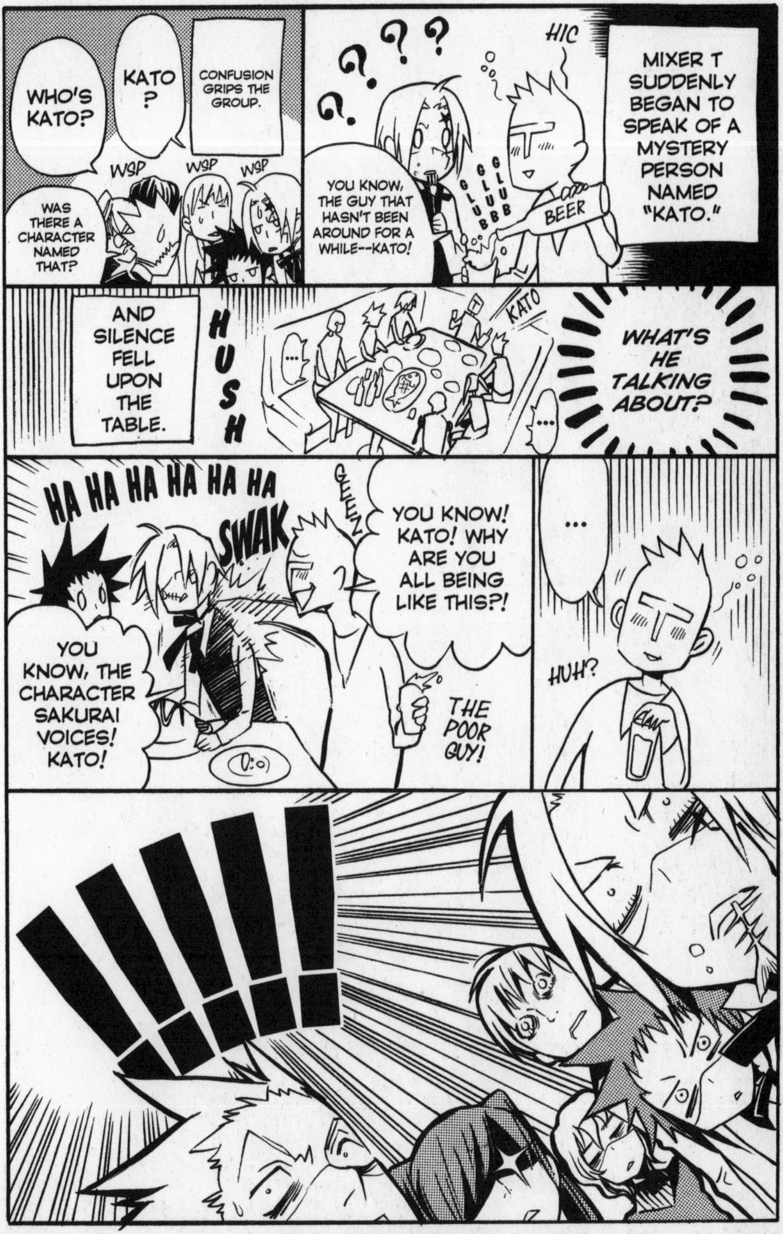
MIXER T SUDDENLY BEGAN TO SPEAK OF A MYSTERY PERSON NAMED "KATO."
HIC
? ? ? ?
GLUB GLUB GLUB
BEER
YOU KNOW, THE GUY THAT HASN'T BEEN AROUND FOR A WHILE--KATO!
CONFUSION GRIPS THE GROUP.
KATO ?
WHO'S KATO?
WSP WSP WSP
WAS THERE A CHARACTER NAMED THAT?
WHAT'S HE TALKING ABOUT?
...
KATO
...
HUSH
AND SILENCE FELL UPON THE TABLE.
...
HUH?
YOU KNOW! KATO! WHY ARE YOU ALL BEING LIKE THIS?!
GEEZ
THE POOR GUY!
SWAK
HA HA HA HA HA HA
YOU KNOW, THE CHARACTER SAKURAI VOICES! KATO!

REALIZATION. STILL TO BE CONTINUED.

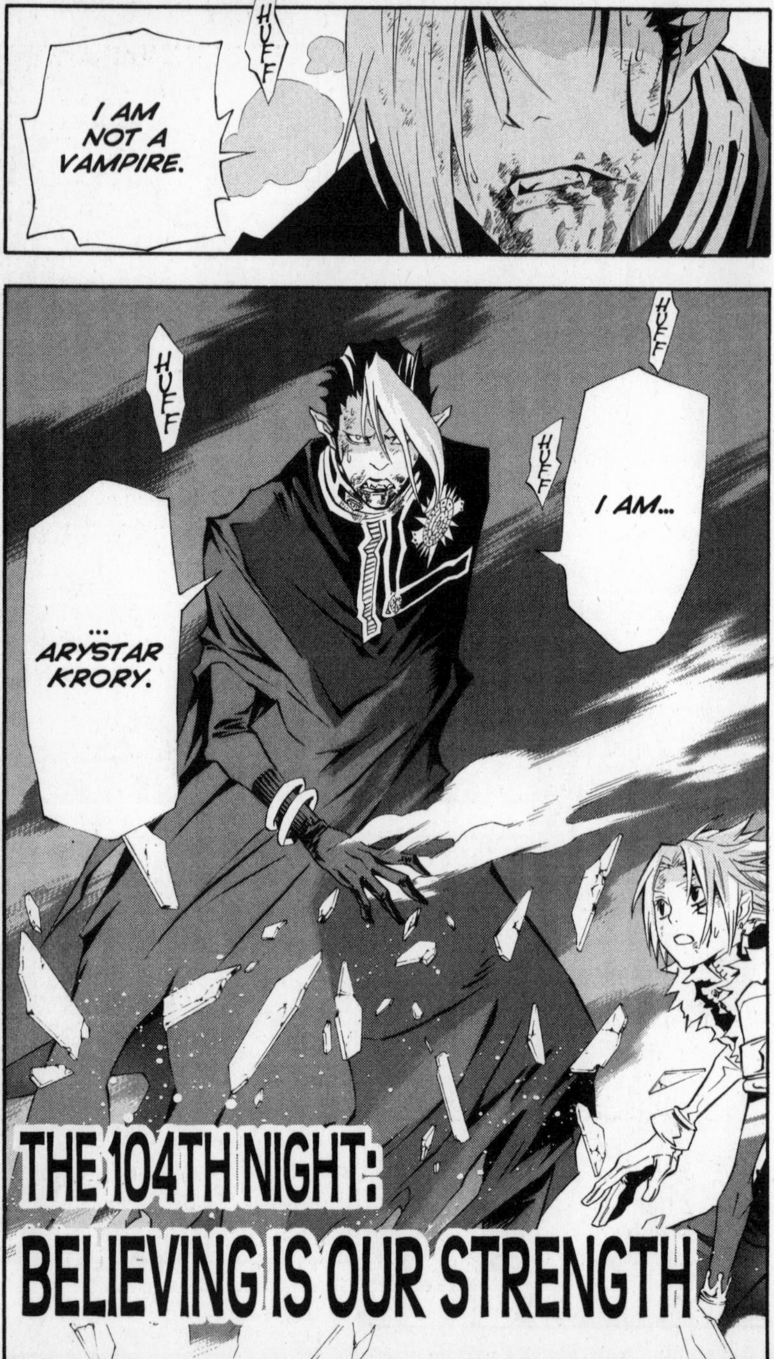
HUFF
I AM NOT A VAMPIRE.
HUFF
HUFF
I AM...
HUFF
... ARYSTAR KRORY.
THE 104TH NIGHT: BELIEVING IS OUR STRENGTH

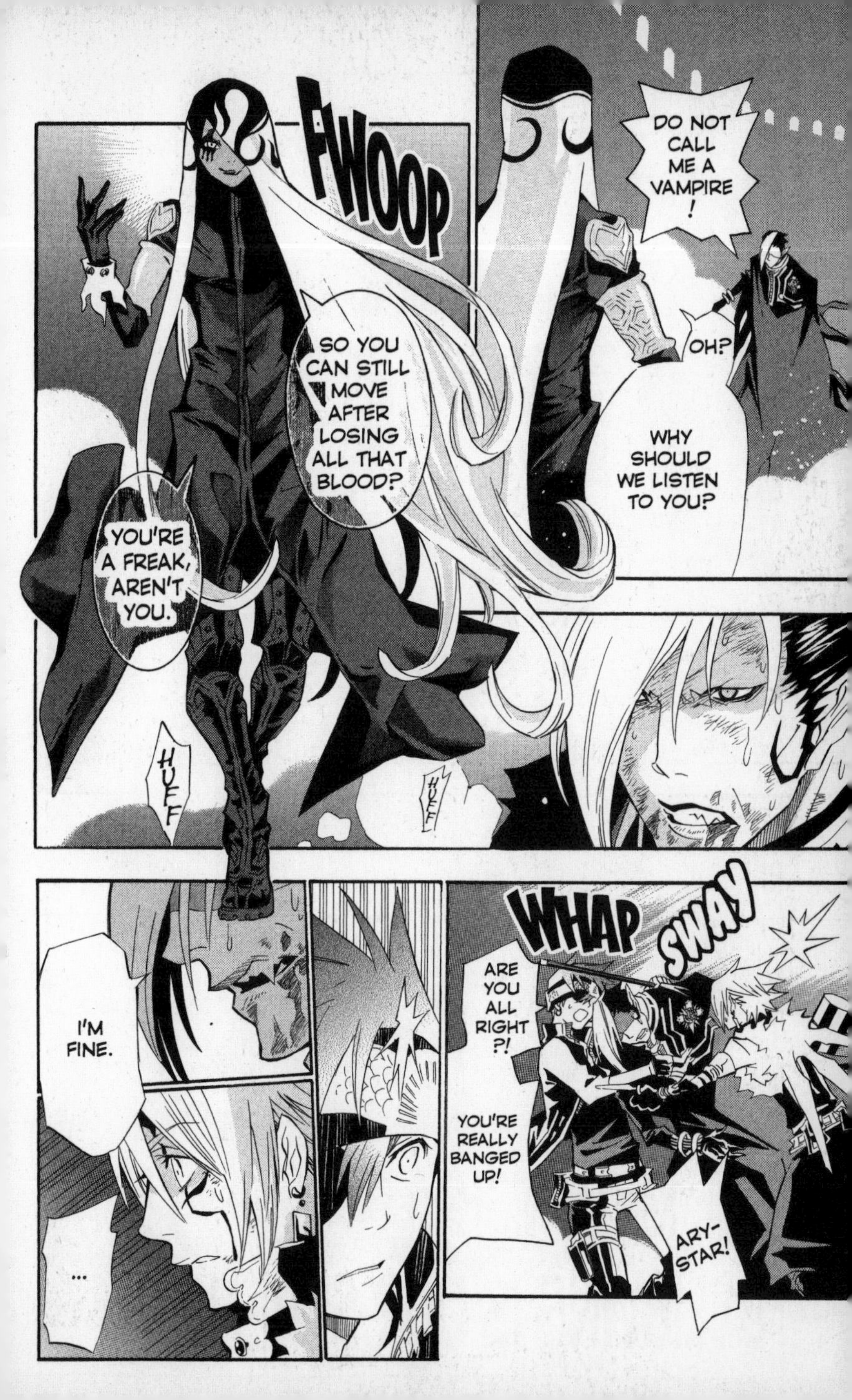
DO NOT CALL ME A VAMPIRE!
OH?
WHY SHOULD WE LISTEN TO YOU?
FWOOP
SO YOU CAN STILL MOVE AFTER LOSING ALL THAT BLOOD?
YOU'RE A FREAK, AREN'T YOU.
HUFF
HUFF
WHAP
SWAY
ARE YOU ALL RIGHT?!
YOU'RE REALLY BANGED UP!
ARY-STAR!
I'M FINE.
...

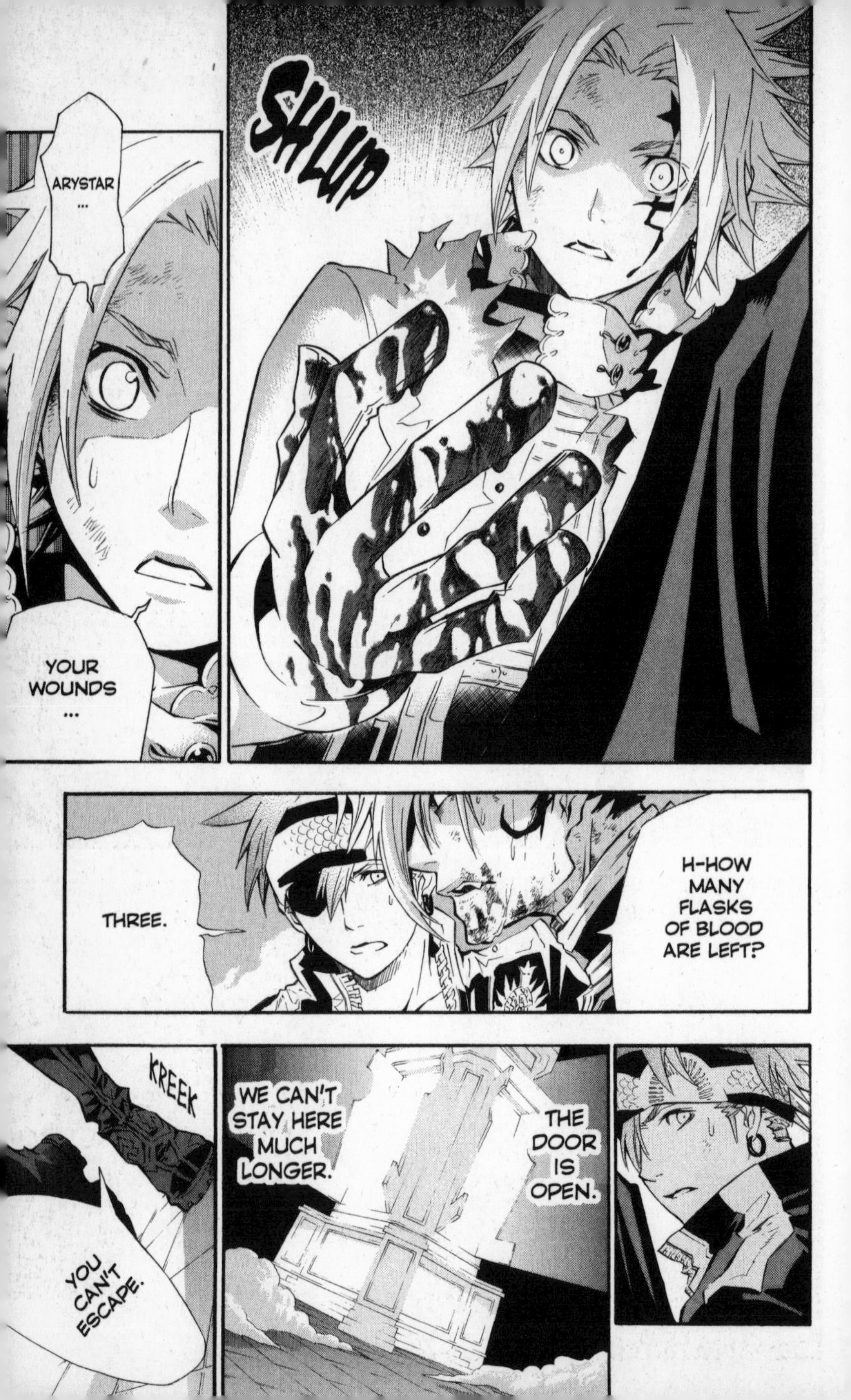
SHLUP
ARYSTAR ...
YOUR WOUNDS ...
H-HOW MANY FLASKS OF BLOOD ARE LEFT?
THREE.
THE DOOR IS OPEN.
WE CAN'T STAY HERE MUCH LONGER.
KREEK
YOU CAN'T ESCAPE.

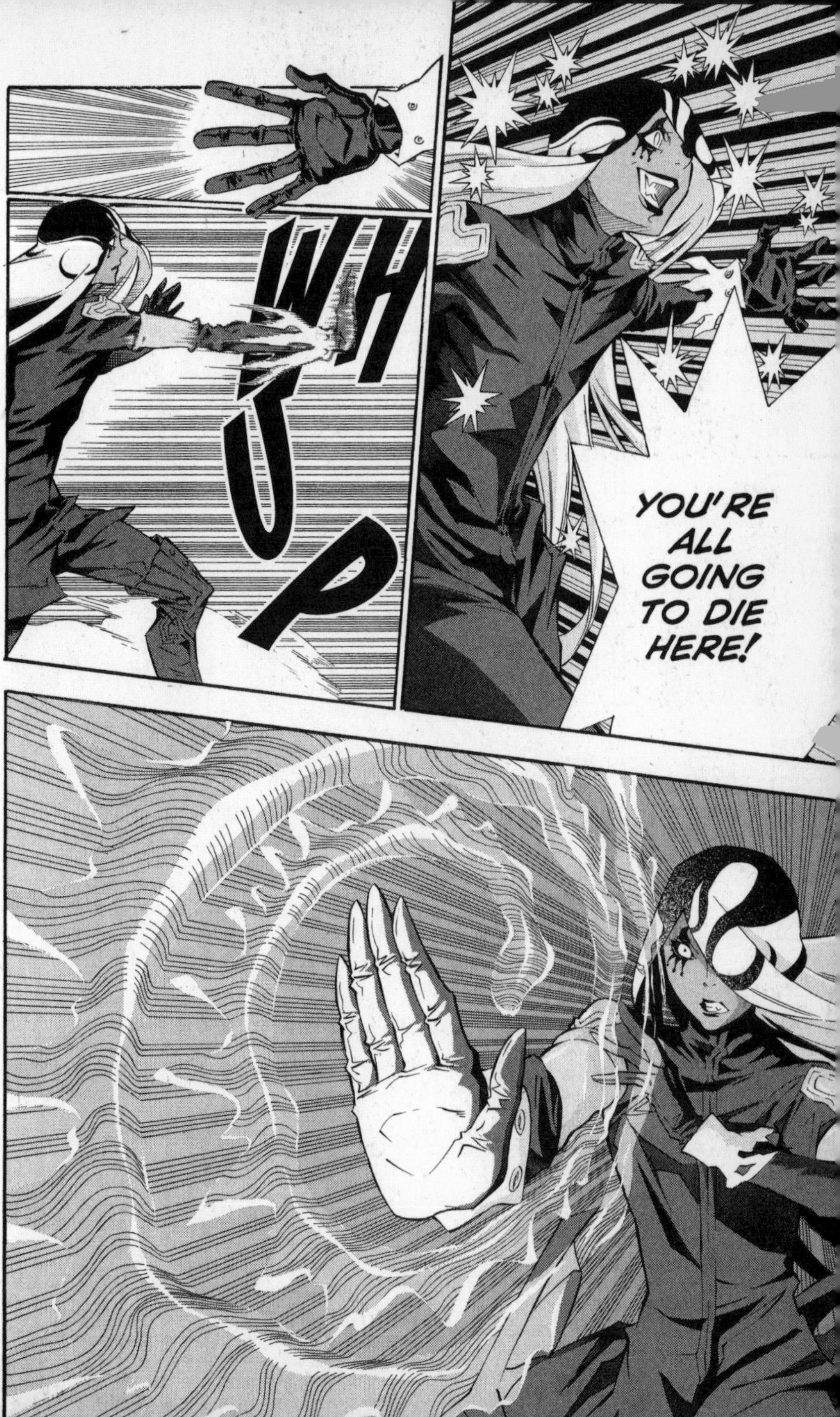
YOU'RE ALL GOING TO DIE HERE!
WHUP

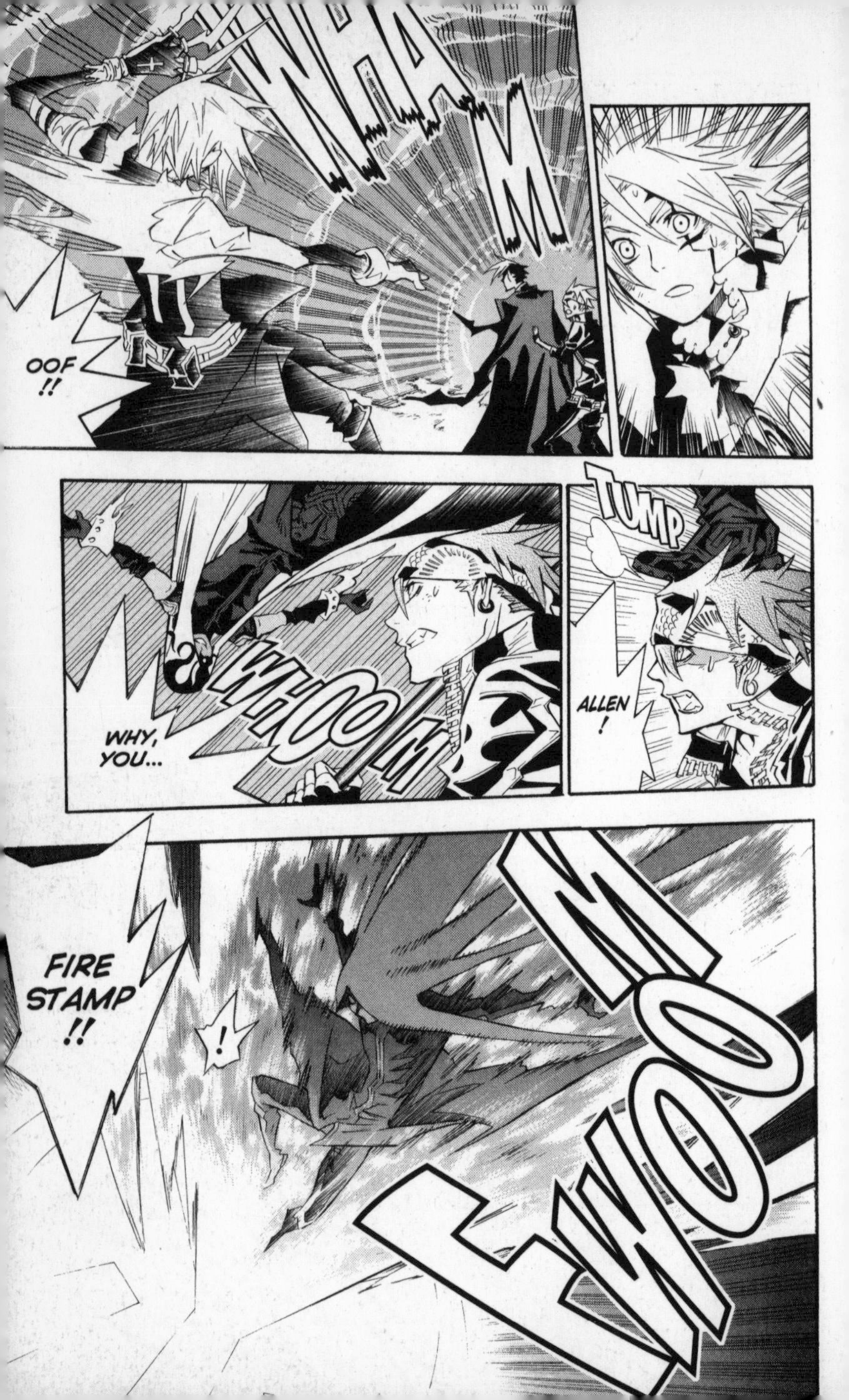
WHAM
OOF!!
TUMP
ALLEN!
WHOOM
WHY, YOU...
FIRE STAMP!!
!
WHOOM

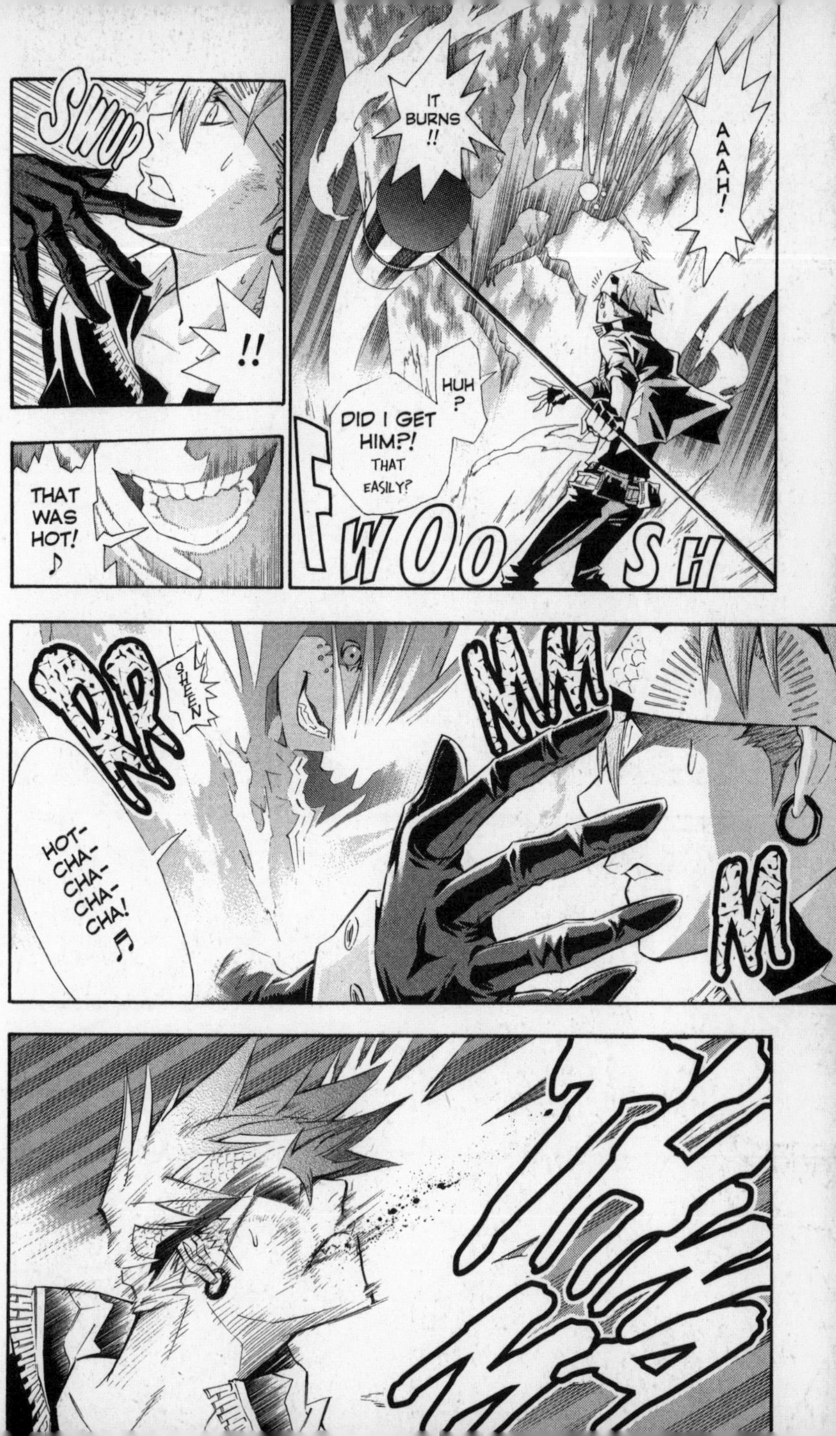
AAAH!
IT BURNS!!
HUH?
DID I GET HIM?! THAT EASILY?
FWOOSH
SWUP
!!
THAT WAS HOT! ♪
DRMMM
SHEEN
HOT-CHA-CHA-CHA-CHA! ♬

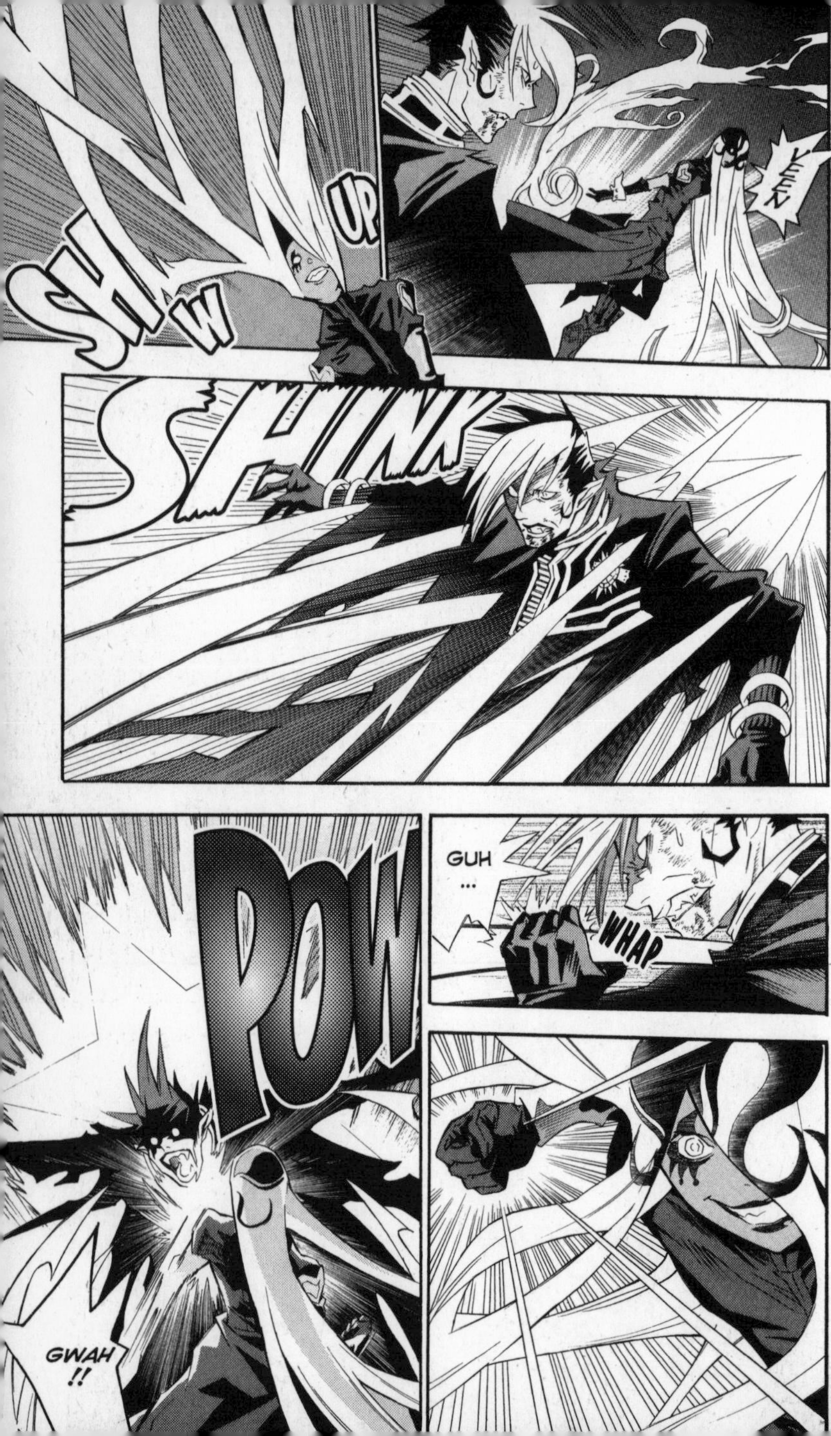
VEEN
SHWUP
SHINK
GUH ...
WHAP
POW
GWAH !!

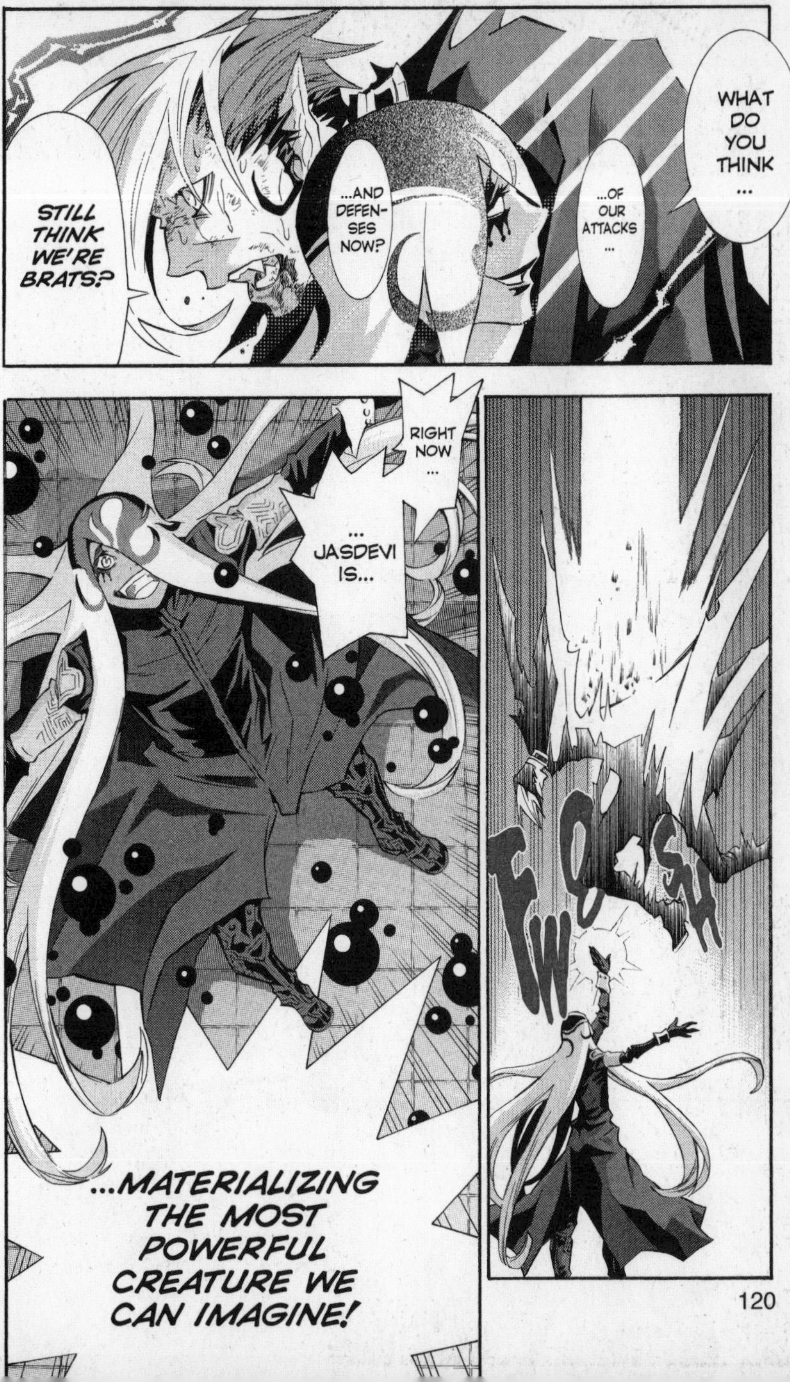
WHAT DO YOU THINK ...
...OF OUR ATTACKS ...
...AND DEFEN-SES NOW?
STILL THINK WE'RE BRATS?
FWOOSH
RIGHT NOW ...
... JASDEVI IS...
...MATERIALIZING THE MOST POWERFUL CREATURE WE CAN IMAGINE!

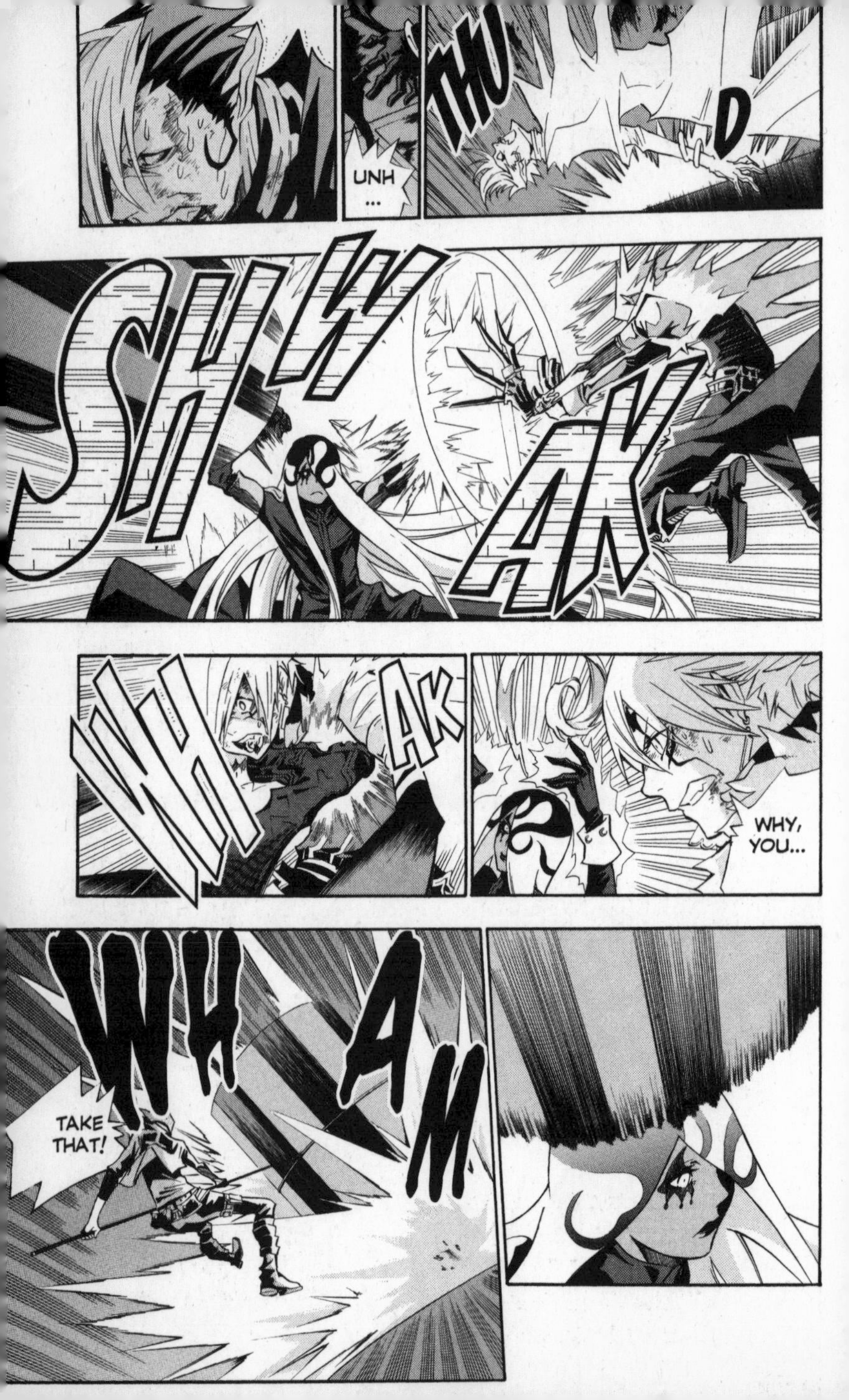
THUD
UNH ...
SHWAK
WHY, YOU...
WHAK
WHAM
TAKE THAT!

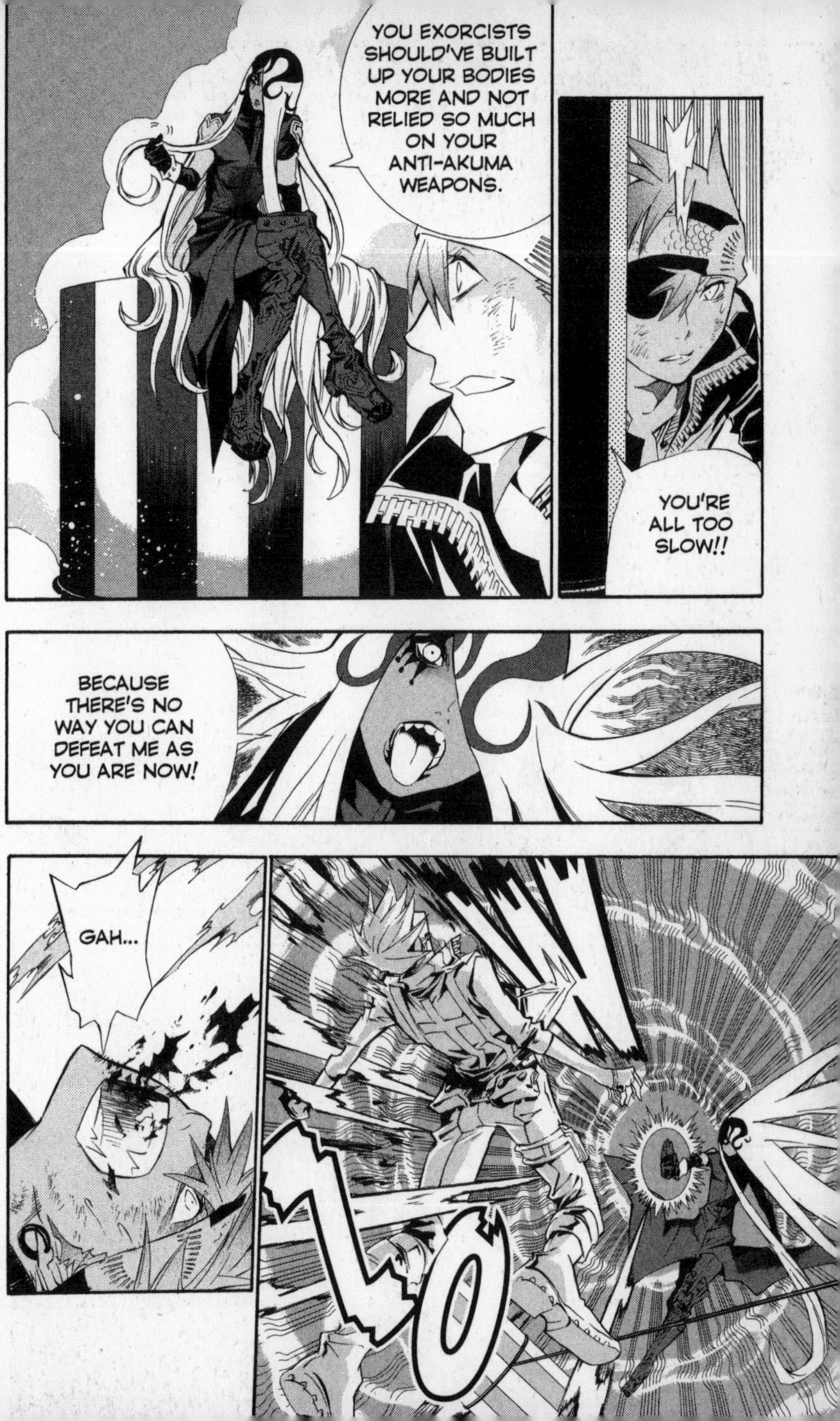
YOU'RE ALL TOO SLOW!!
YOU EXORCISTS SHOULD'VE BUILT UP YOUR BODIES MORE AND NOT RELIED SO MUCH ON YOUR ANTI-AKUMA WEAPONS.
BECAUSE THERE'S NO WAY YOU CAN DEFEAT ME AS YOU ARE NOW!
GAH...

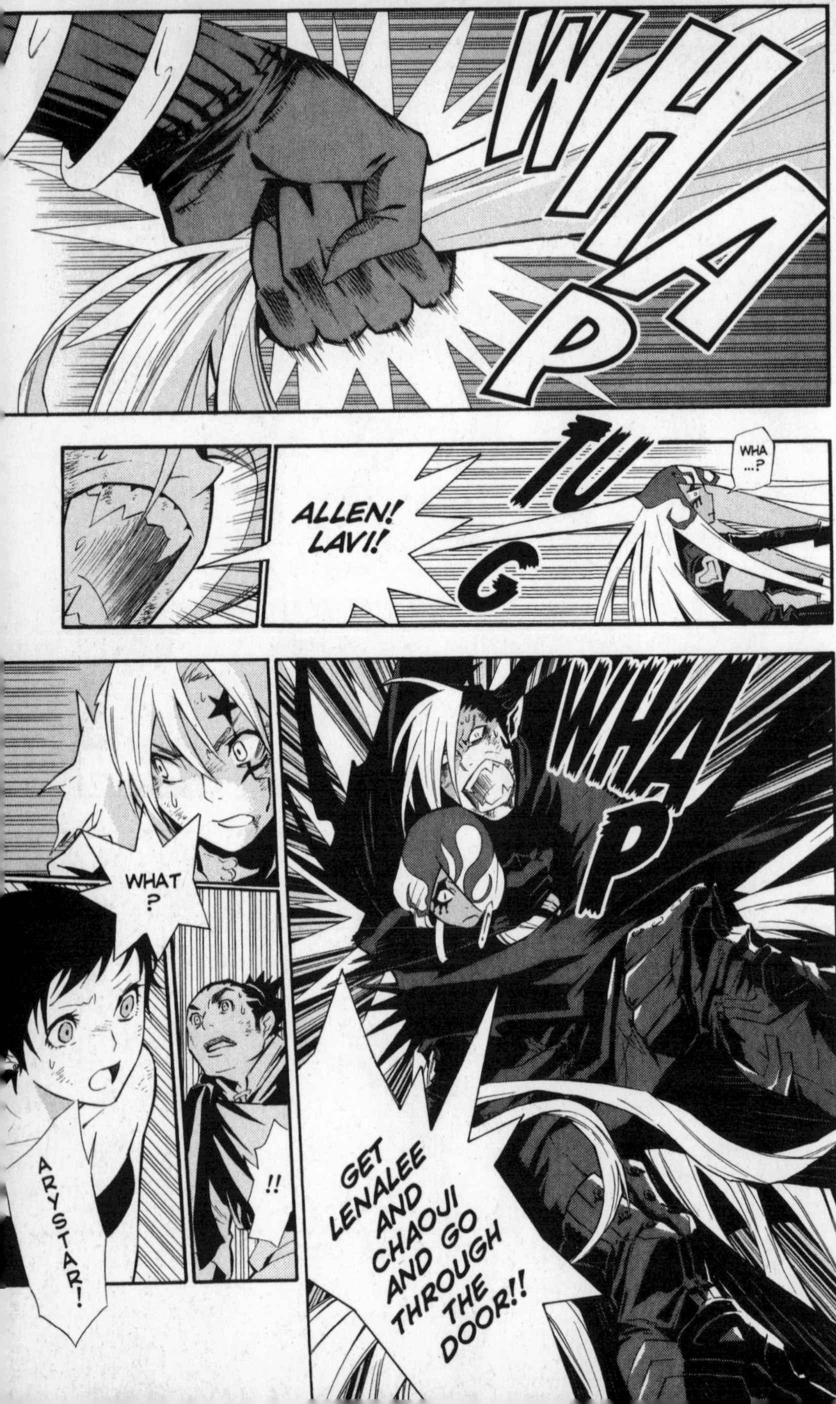

WHAP
WHA ...?
TUG
ALLEN! LAVI!
WHAP
GET LENALEE AND CHAOJI AND GO THROUGH THE DOOR!!
WHAT?
!!
ARYSTAR!

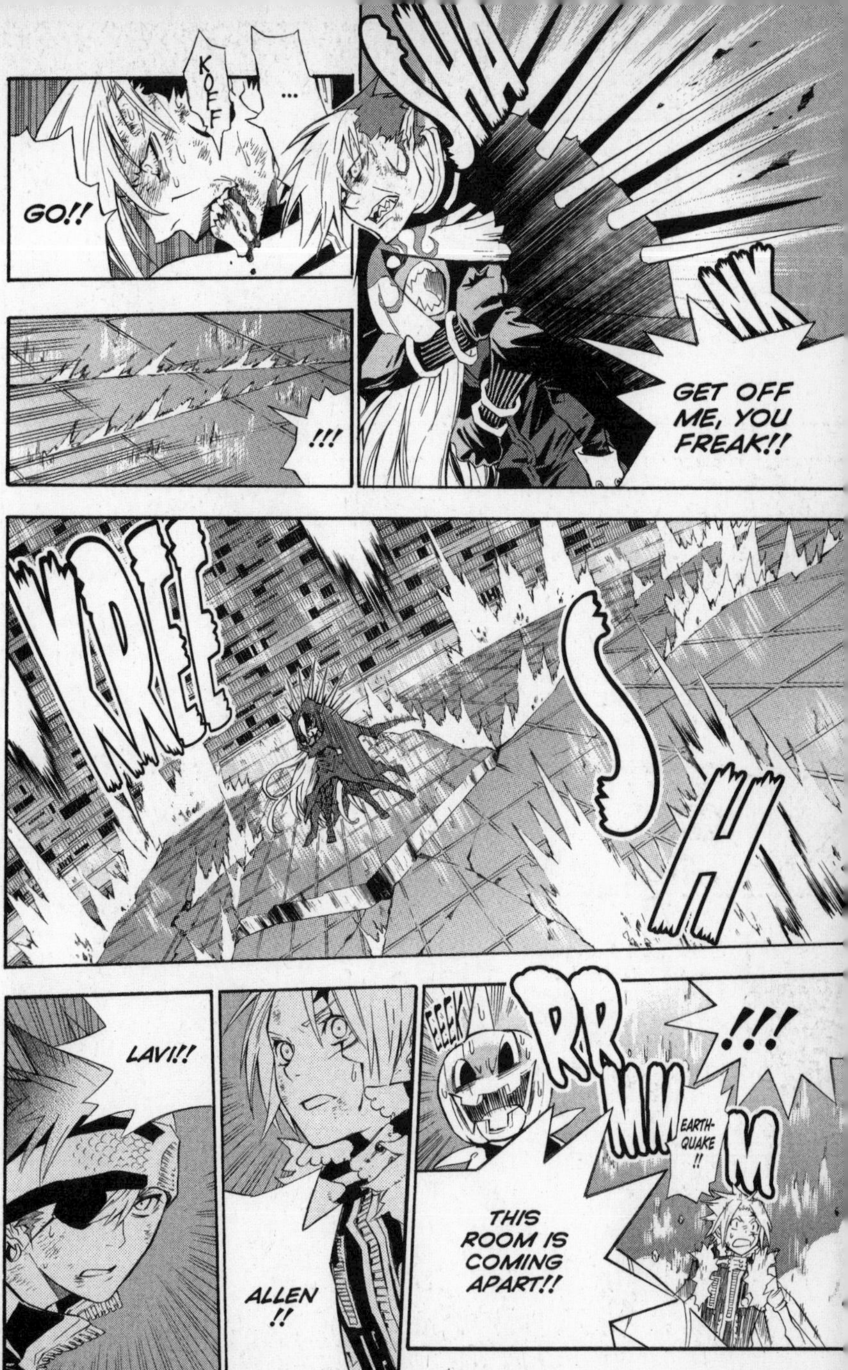
SHA
NK
GET OFF ME, YOU FREAK!!
KOFF
...
GO!!
!!!
KREE
SH
EEEK
RRMMM
!!!
EARTH-QUAKE !!
THIS ROOM IS COMING APART!!
ALLEN !!
LAVI!!

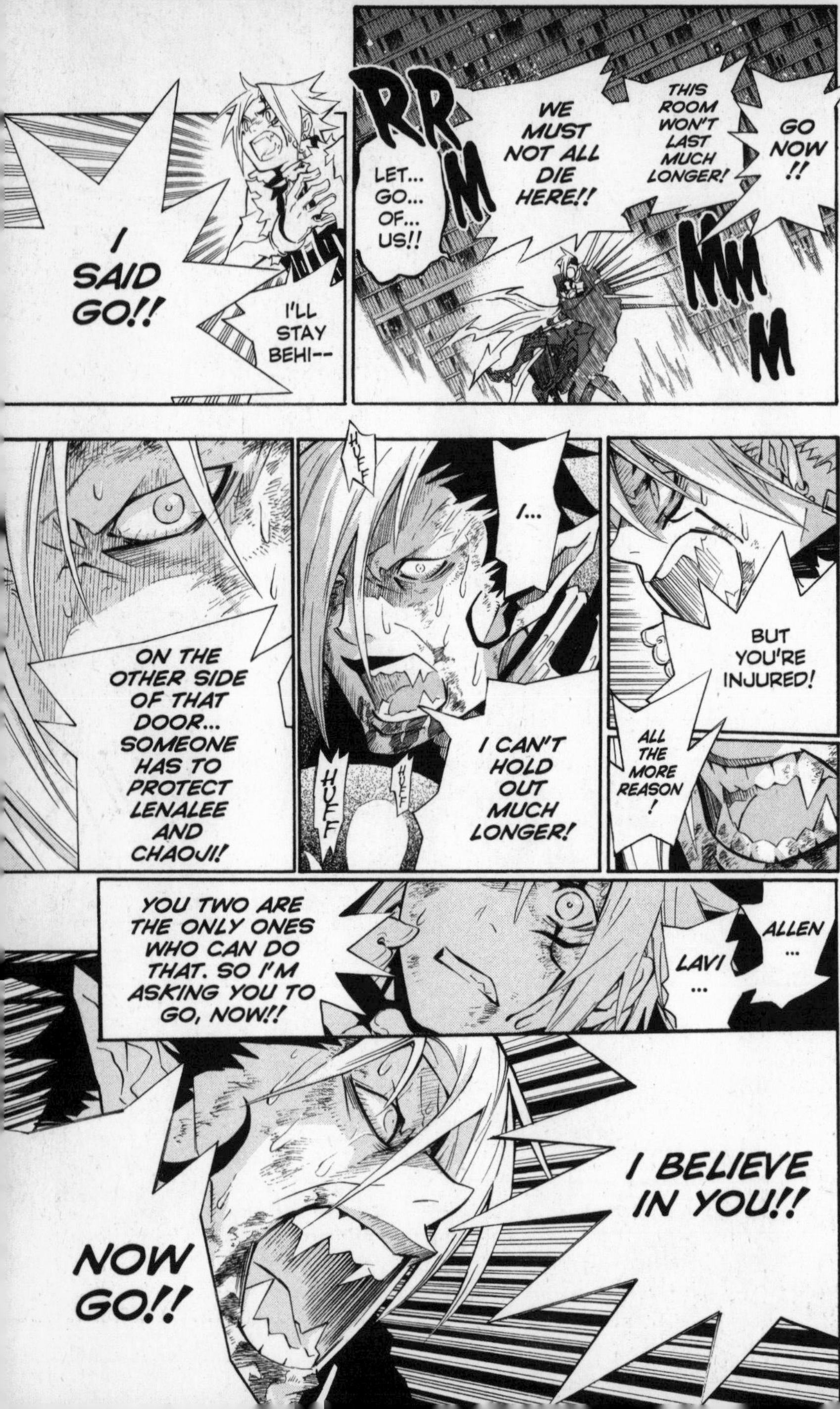
GO NOW!!
THIS ROOM WON'T LAST MUCH LONGER!
WE MUST NOT ALL DIE HERE!!
RRM
LET... GO... OF... US!!
MMM
I'LL STAY BEHI--
I SAID GO!!
BUT YOU'RE INJURED!
ALL THE MORE REASON!
HUFF
I...
I CAN'T HOLD OUT MUCH LONGER!
HUFF
HUFF
ON THE OTHER SIDE OF THAT DOOR... SOMEONE HAS TO PROTECT LENALEE AND CHAOJI!
ALLEN...
LAVI...
YOU TWO ARE THE ONLY ONES WHO CAN DO THAT. SO I'M ASKING YOU TO GO, NOW!!
I BELIEVE IN YOU!!
NOW GO!!

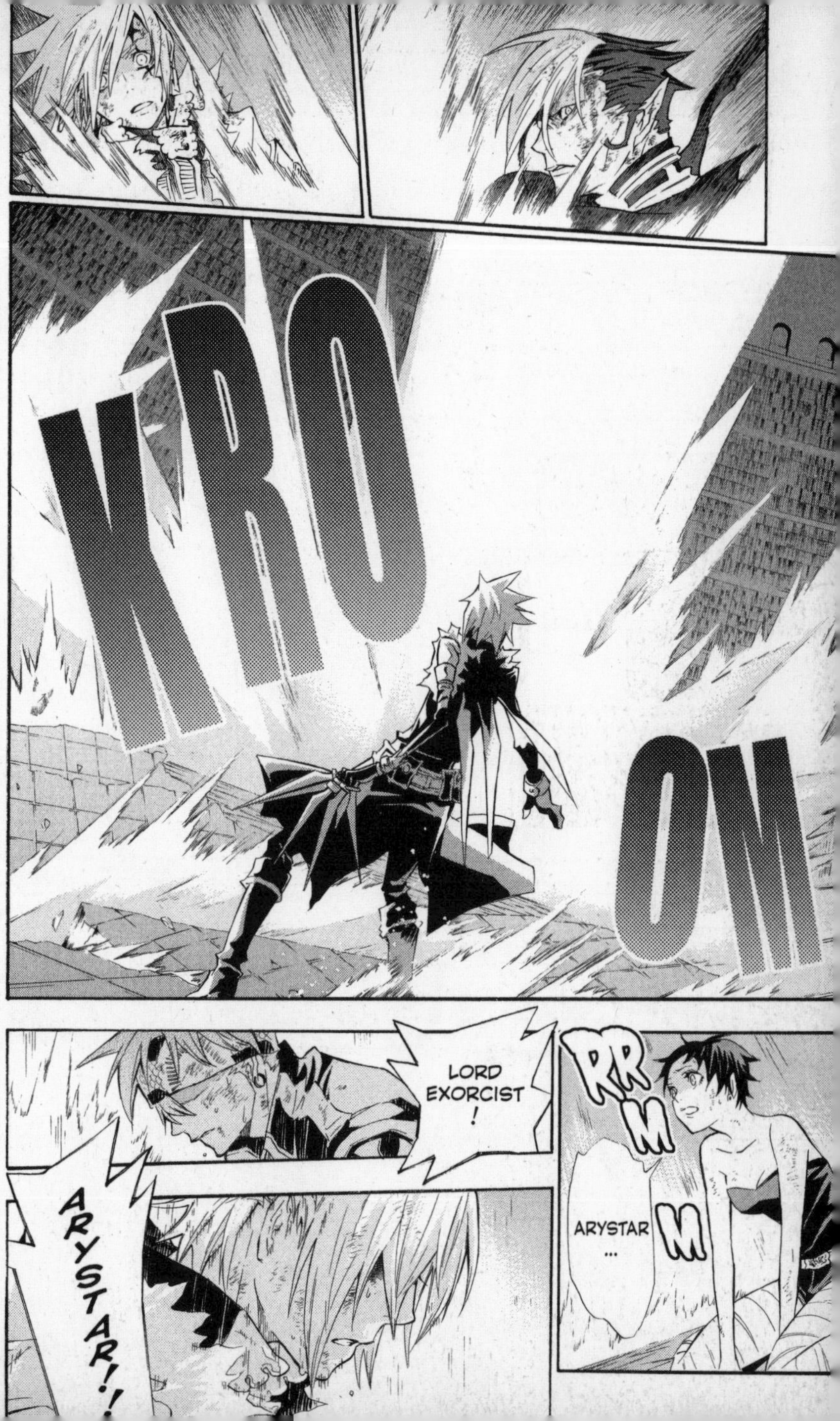
KROOM
RRMMM
ARYSTAR ...
LORD EXORCIST!
ARYSTAR!!

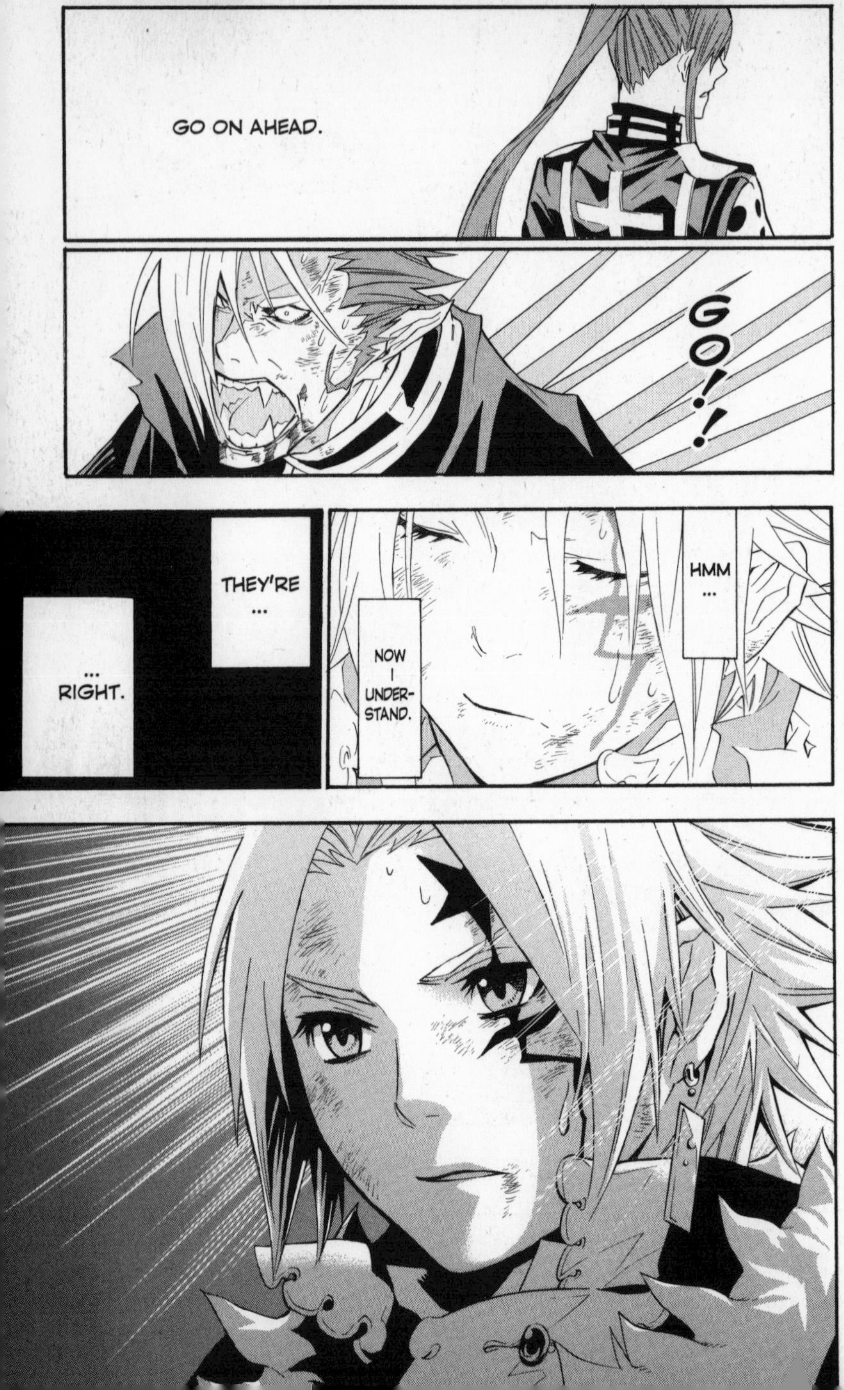
GO ON AHEAD.
GO!!
HMM...
NOW I UNDERSTAND.
THEY'RE...
...RIGHT.

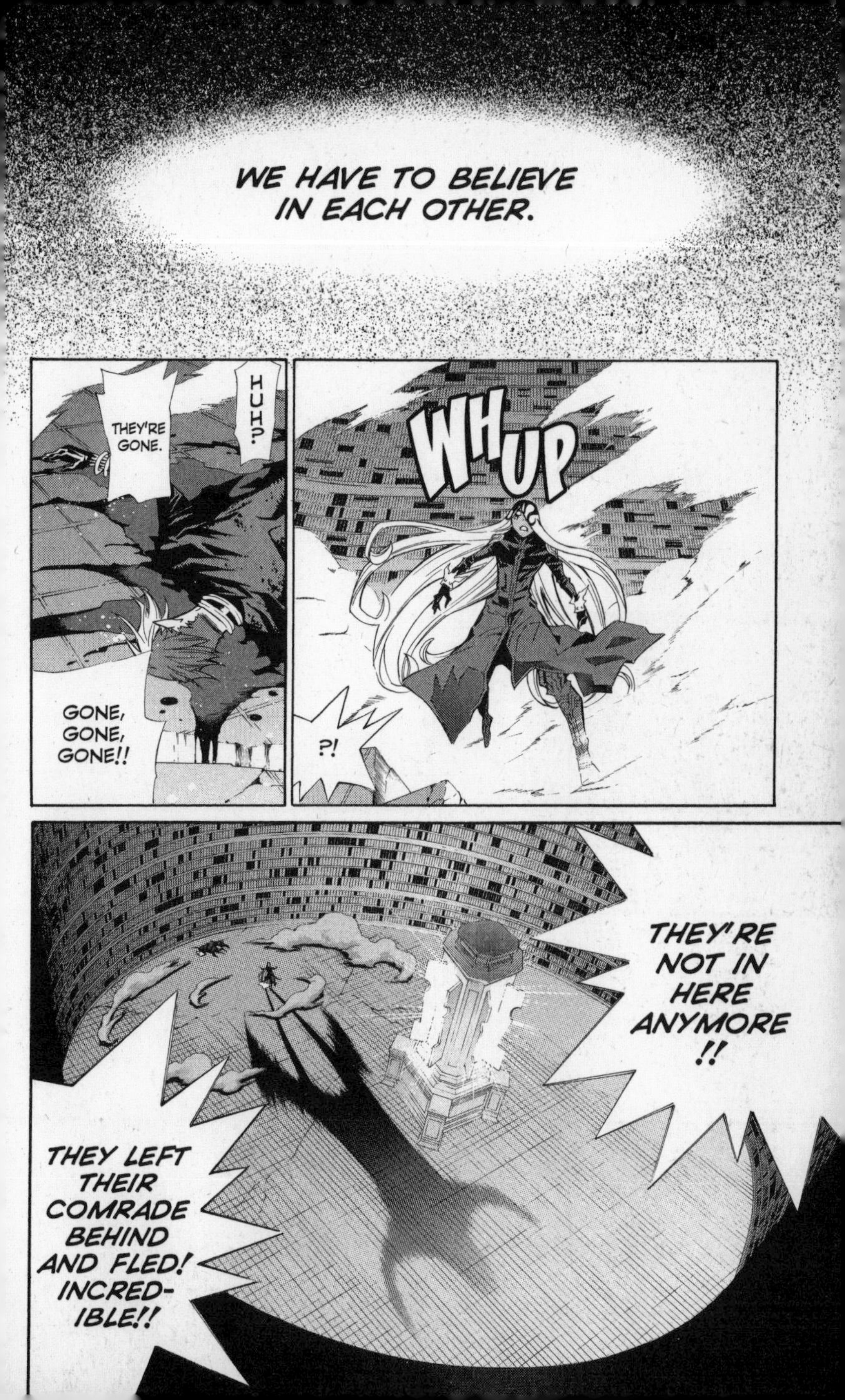
WE HAVE TO BELIEVE IN EACH OTHER.
WHUP
?!
HUH?
THEY'RE GONE.
GONE, GONE, GONE!!
THEY'RE NOT IN HERE ANYMORE!!
THEY LEFT THEIR COMRADE BEHIND AND FLED! INCRED-IBLE!!

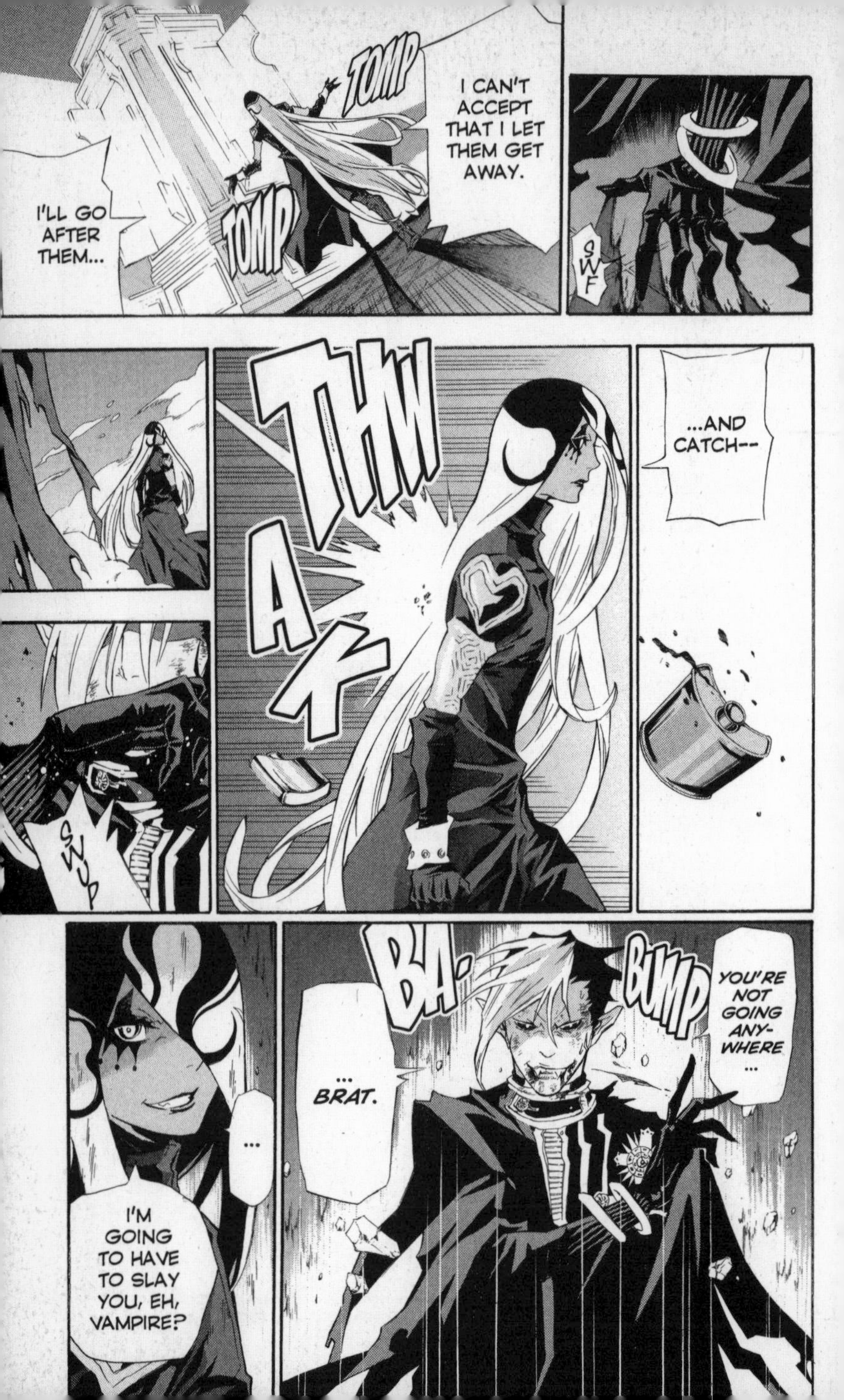
SWF
I CAN'T ACCEPT THAT I LET THEM GET AWAY.
TOMP
I'LL GO AFTER THEM...
TOMP
...AND CATCH--
THWAK
SWUP
BA-BUMP
YOU'RE NOT GOING ANYWHERE...
... BRAT.
...
I'M GOING TO HAVE TO SLAY YOU, EH, VAMPIRE?

THE KATO INCIDENT, PART 3

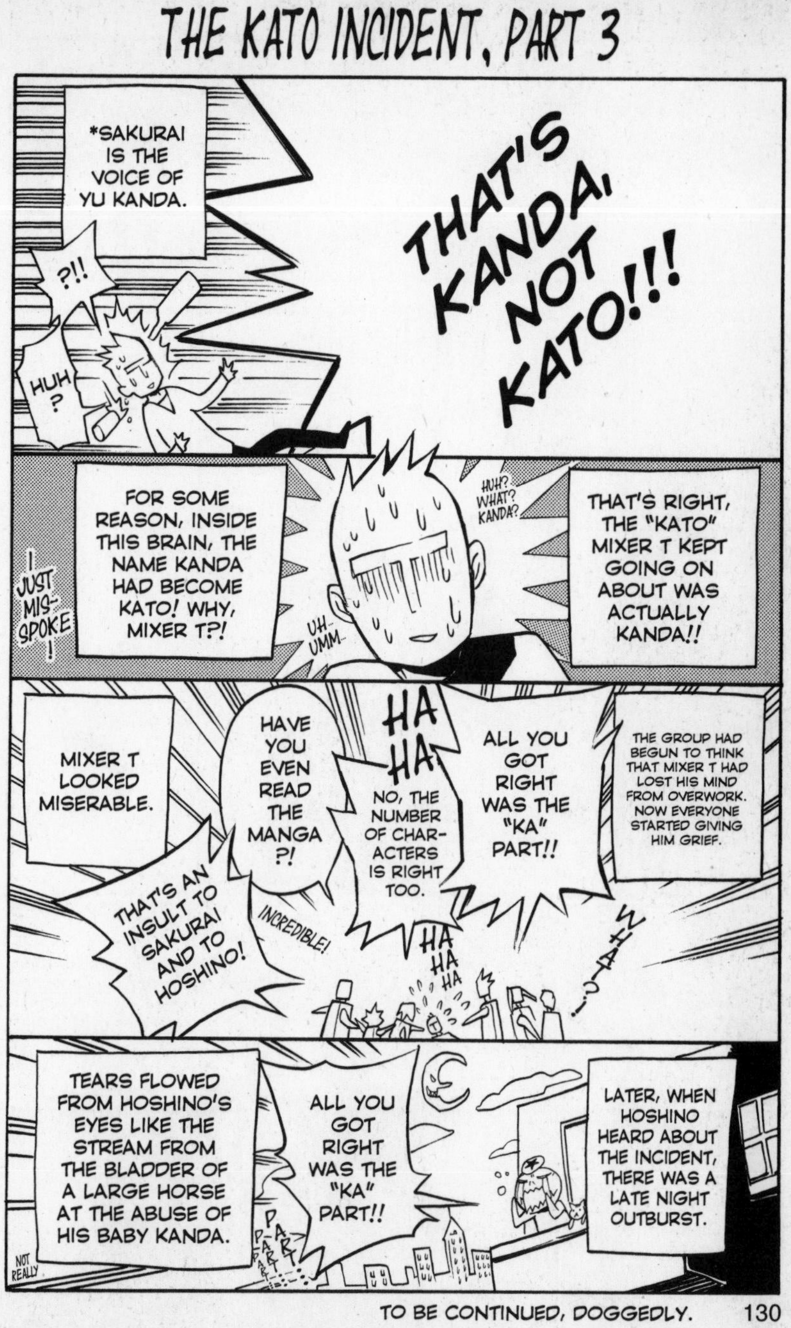
THAT'S KANDA, NOT KATO!!!
*SAKURAI IS THE VOICE OF YU KANDA.
?!!
HUH?
THAT'S RIGHT, THE "KATO" MIXER T KEPT GOING ON ABOUT WAS ACTUALLY KANDA!!
HUH? WHAT? KANDA?
FOR SOME REASON, INSIDE THIS BRAIN, THE NAME KANDA HAD BECOME KATO! WHY, MIXER T?!
UH... UMM...
I JUST MIS-SPOKE!
THE GROUP HAD BEGUN TO THINK THAT MIXER T HAD LOST HIS MIND FROM OVERWORK. NOW EVERYONE STARTED GIVING HIM GRIEF.
ALL YOU GOT RIGHT WAS THE "KA" PART!!
HA HA
NO, THE NUMBER OF CHARACTERS IS RIGHT TOO.
HAVE YOU EVEN READ THE MANGA?!
MIXER T LOOKED MISERABLE.
WHAT...?
HA HA HA
INCREDIBLE!
THAT'S AN INSULT TO SAKURAI AND TO HOSHINO!
LATER, WHEN HOSHINO HEARD ABOUT THE INCIDENT, THERE WAS A LATE NIGHT OUTBURST.
ALL YOU GOT RIGHT WAS THE "KA" PART!!
PART P-PART PART...
TEARS FLOWED FROM HOSHINO'S EYES LIKE THE STREAM FROM THE BLADDER OF A LARGE HORSE AT THE ABUSE OF HIS BABY KANDA.
NOT REALLY

TO BE CONTINUED, DOGGEDLY.

THE 105TH NIGHT: THE ROUGE STAGE

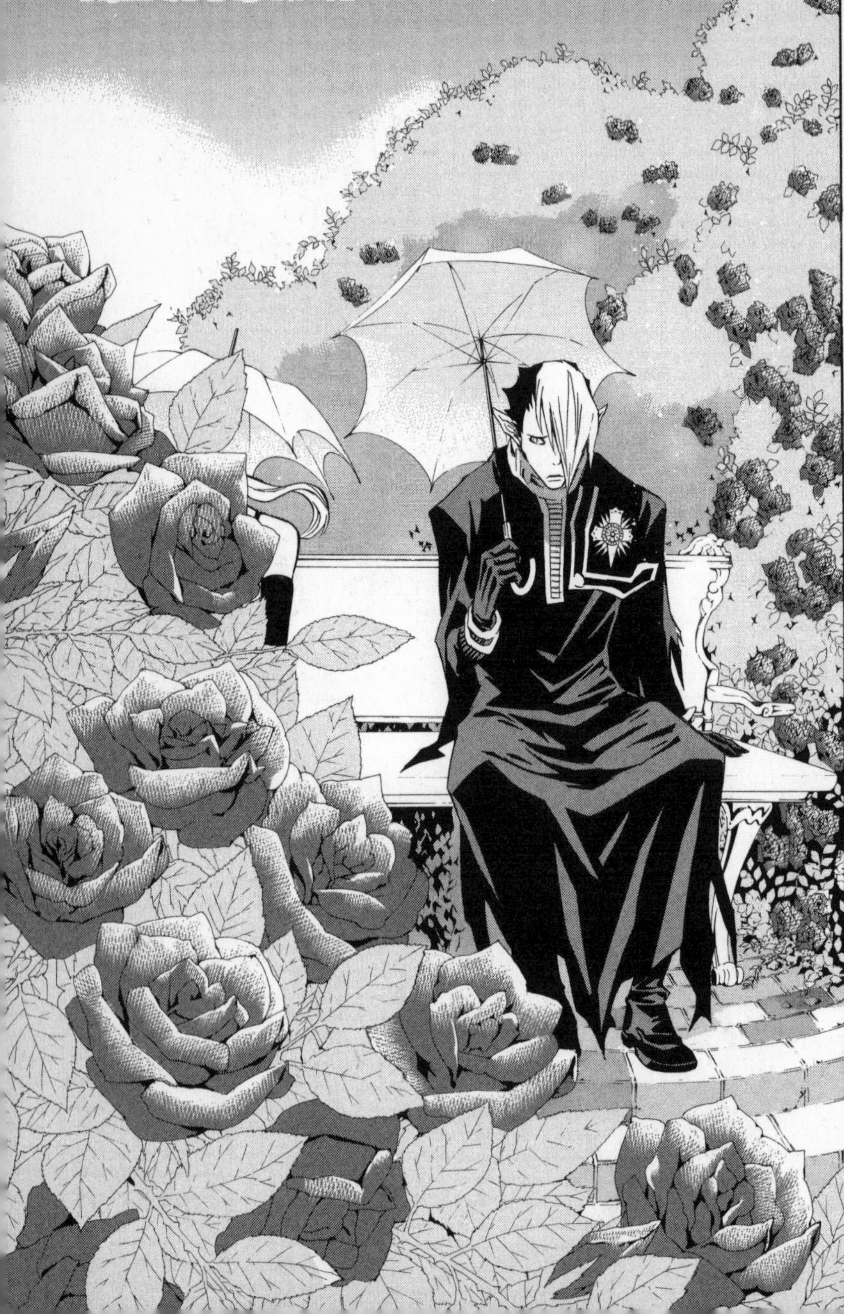

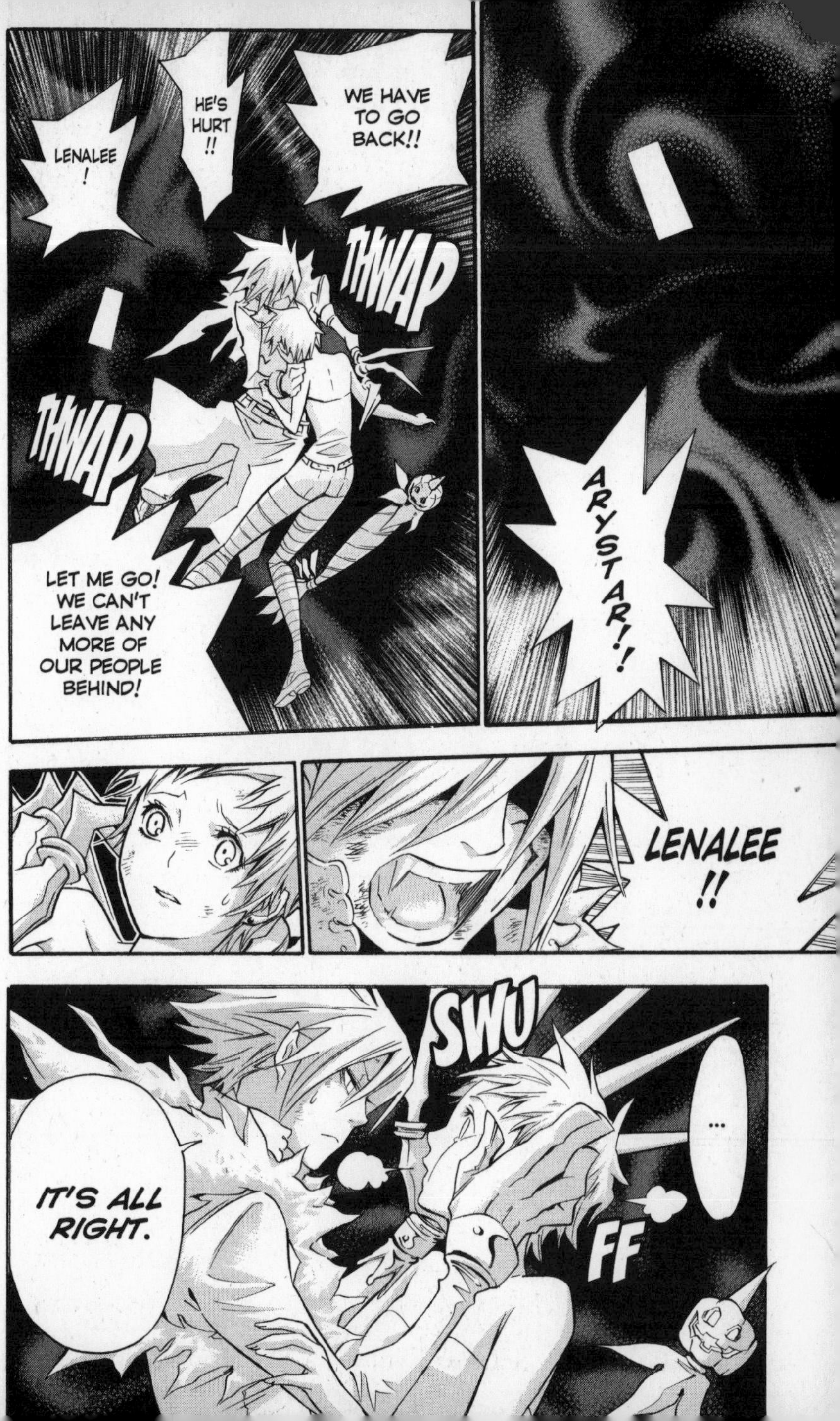
ARYSTAR!!
WE HAVE TO GO BACK!!
HE'S HURT!!
LENALEE!
THWAP
THWAP
LET ME GO! WE CAN'T LEAVE ANY MORE OF OUR PEOPLE BEHIND!
LENALEE!!
SWU
...
FF
IT'S ALL RIGHT.

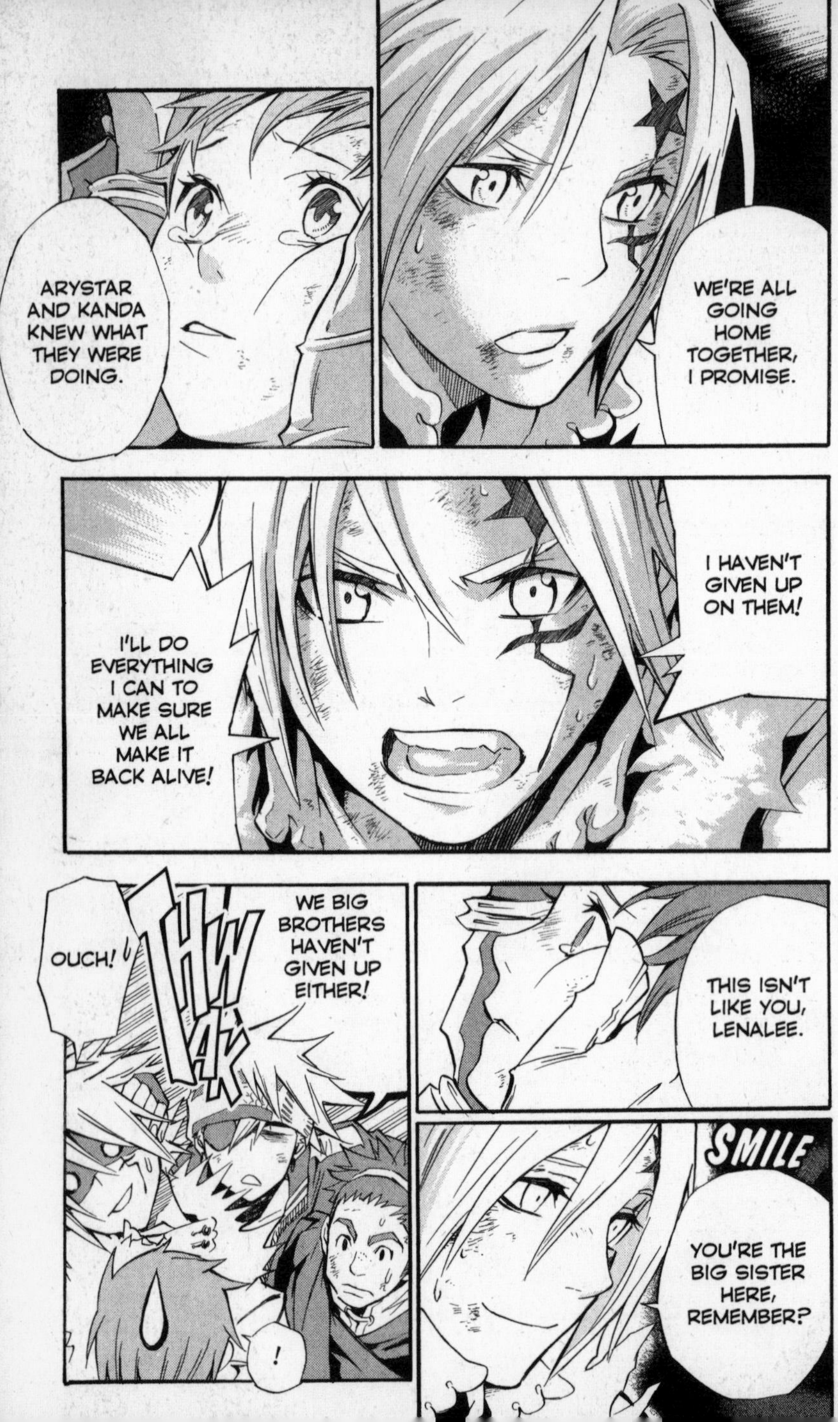
WE'RE ALL GOING HOME TOGETHER, I PROMISE.
ARYSTAR AND KANDA KNEW WHAT THEY WERE DOING.
I HAVEN'T GIVEN UP ON THEM!
I'LL DO EVERYTHING I CAN TO MAKE SURE WE ALL MAKE IT BACK ALIVE!
THIS ISN'T LIKE YOU, LENALEE.
SMILE
YOU'RE THE BIG SISTER HERE, REMEMBER?
WE BIG BROTHERS HAVEN'T GIVEN UP EITHER!
THWAK
OUCH!
!

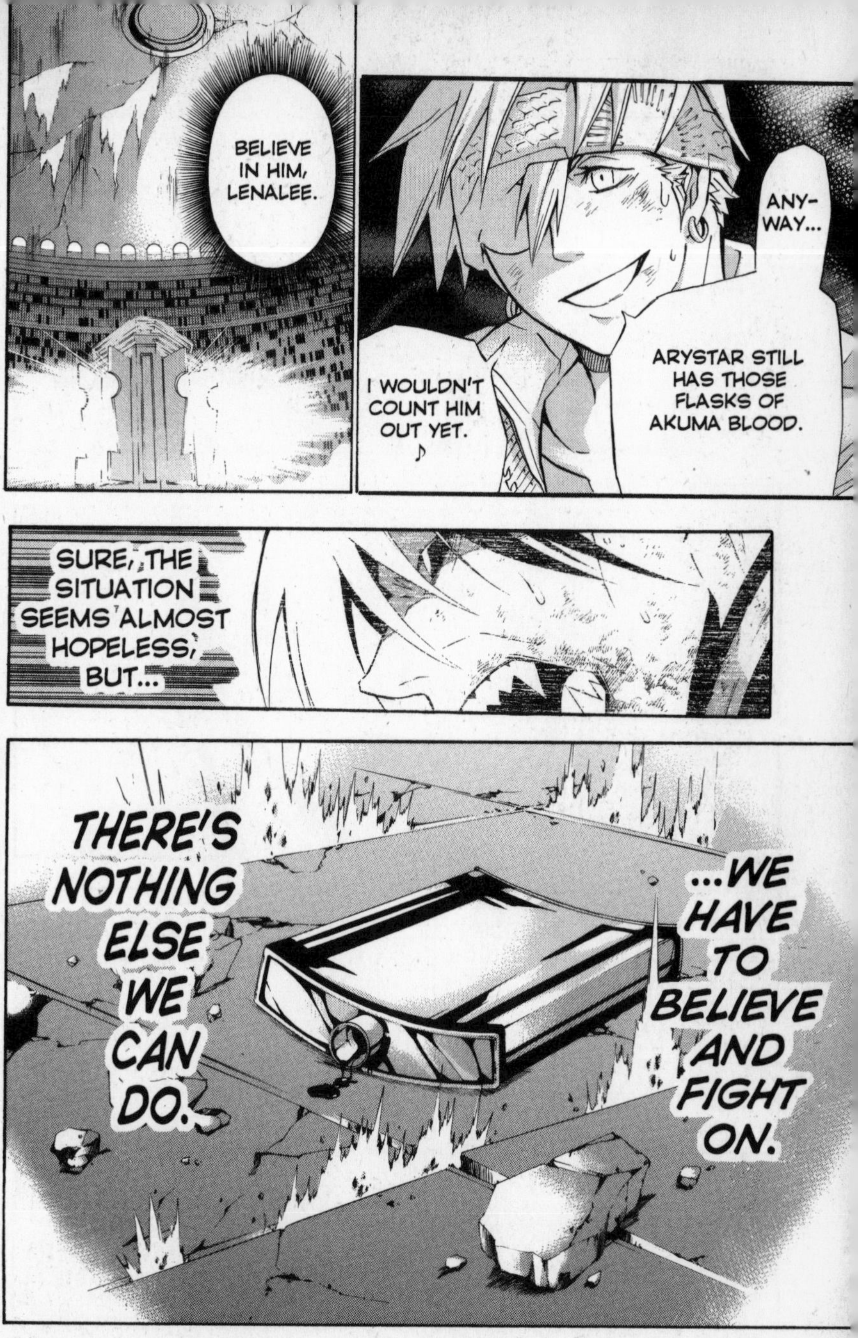
ANY-WAY...
ARYSTAR STILL HAS THOSE FLASKS OF AKUMA BLOOD.
I WOULDN'T COUNT HIM OUT YET. ♪
BELIEVE IN HIM, LENALEE.
SURE, THE SITUATION SEEMS ALMOST HOPELESS, BUT...
THERE'S NOTHING ELSE WE CAN DO.
...WE HAVE TO BELIEVE AND FIGHT ON.

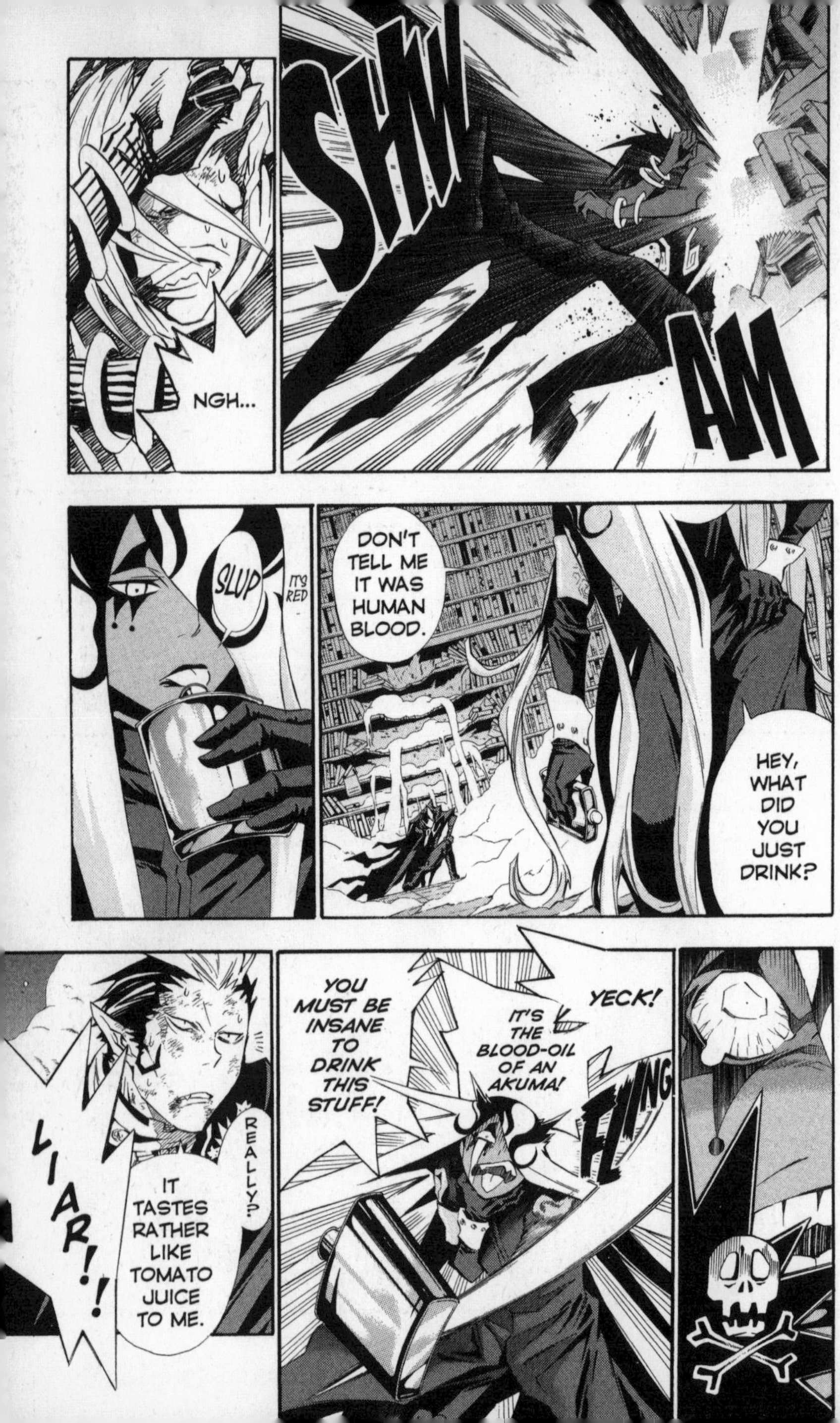
SHWAM
NGH...
HEY, WHAT DID YOU JUST DRINK?
DON'T TELL ME IT WAS HUMAN BLOOD.
SLUP
IT'S RED
YECK!
IT'S THE BLOOD-OIL OF AN AKUMA!
YOU MUST BE INSANE TO DRINK THIS STUFF!
FLING
REALLY?
IT TASTES RATHER LIKE TOMATO JUICE TO ME.
LIAR!!!

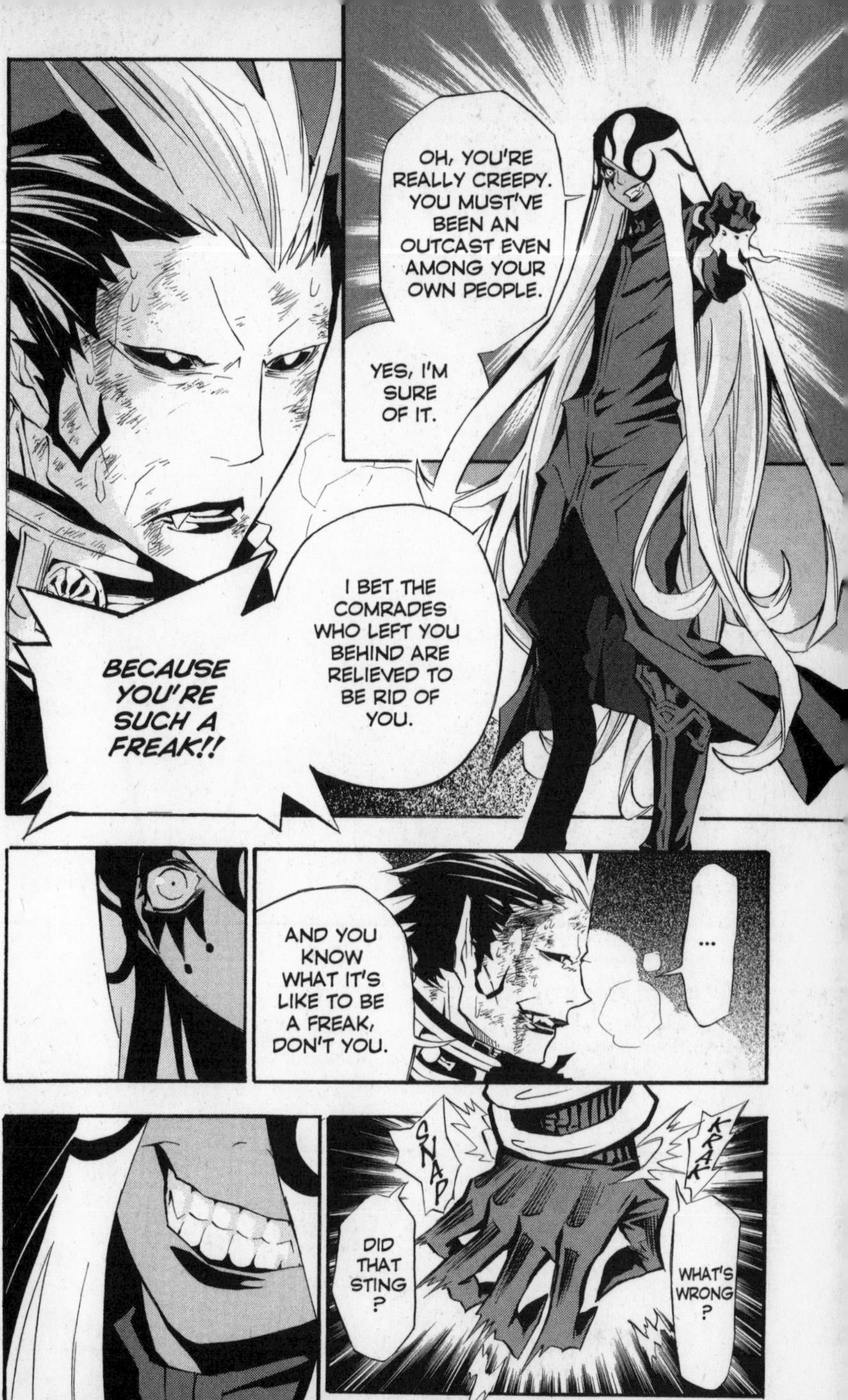
OH, YOU'RE REALLY CREEPY. YOU MUST'VE BEEN AN OUTCAST EVEN AMONG YOUR OWN PEOPLE.
YES, I'M SURE OF IT.
I BET THE COMRADES WHO LEFT YOU BEHIND ARE RELIEVED TO BE RID OF YOU.
BECAUSE YOU'RE SUCH A FREAK!!
...
AND YOU KNOW WHAT IT'S LIKE TO BE A FREAK, DON'T YOU.
KRAK
WHAT'S WRONG?
SNAP
DID THAT STING?

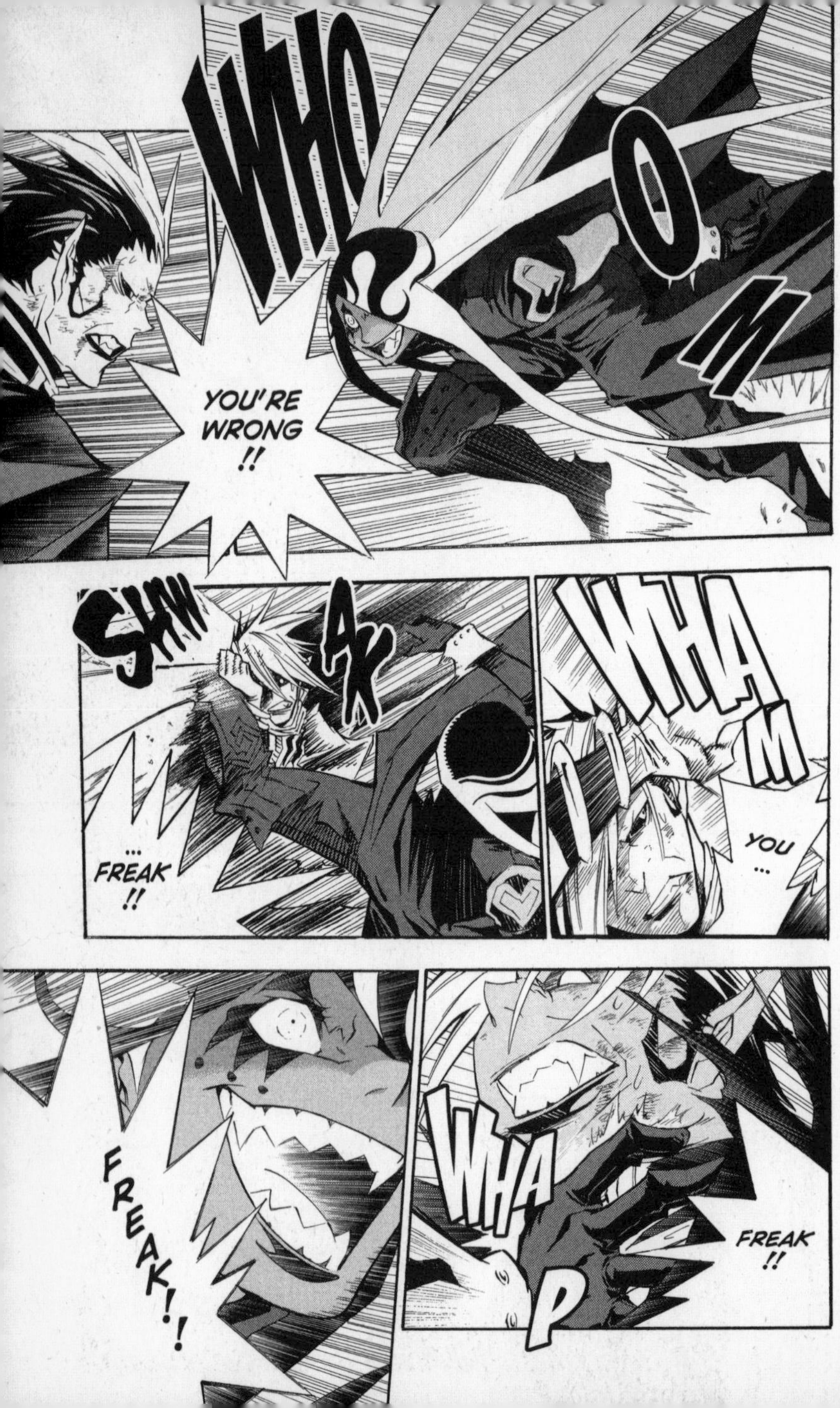
WHOOM
YOU'RE WRONG!!
WHAM
YOU...
SHWAK
...FREAK!!
WHAP
FREAK!!
FREAK!!!

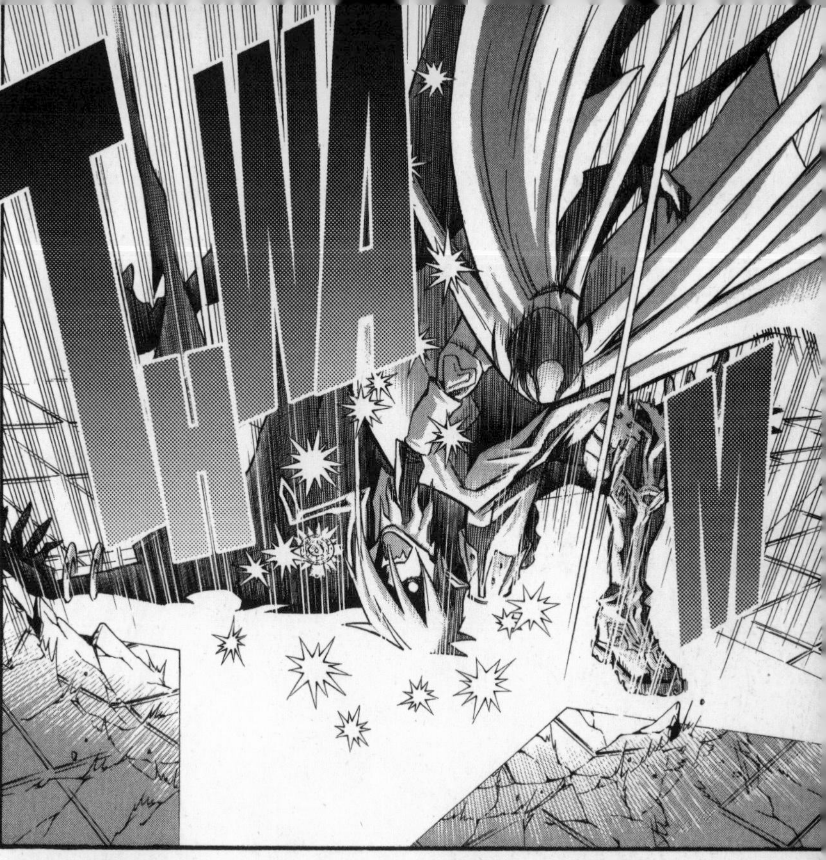
THWAM

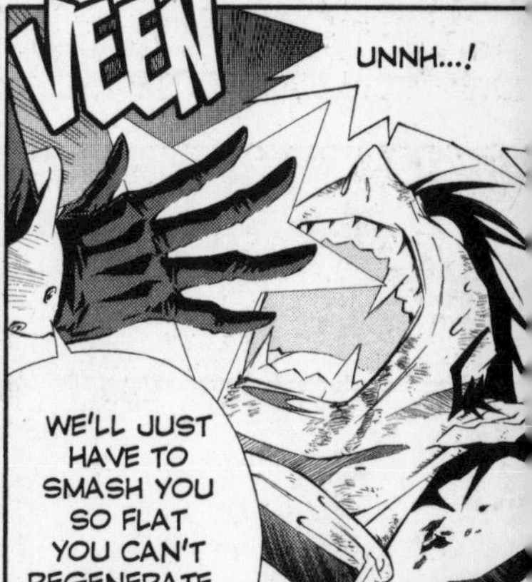
VEEN
UNNH...!
WE'LL JUST HAVE TO SMASH YOU SO FLAT YOU CAN'T REGENERATE.

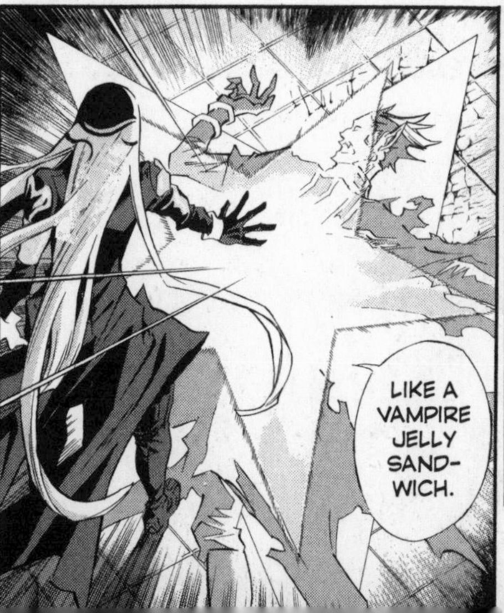
LIKE A VAMPIRE JELLY SAND-WICH.

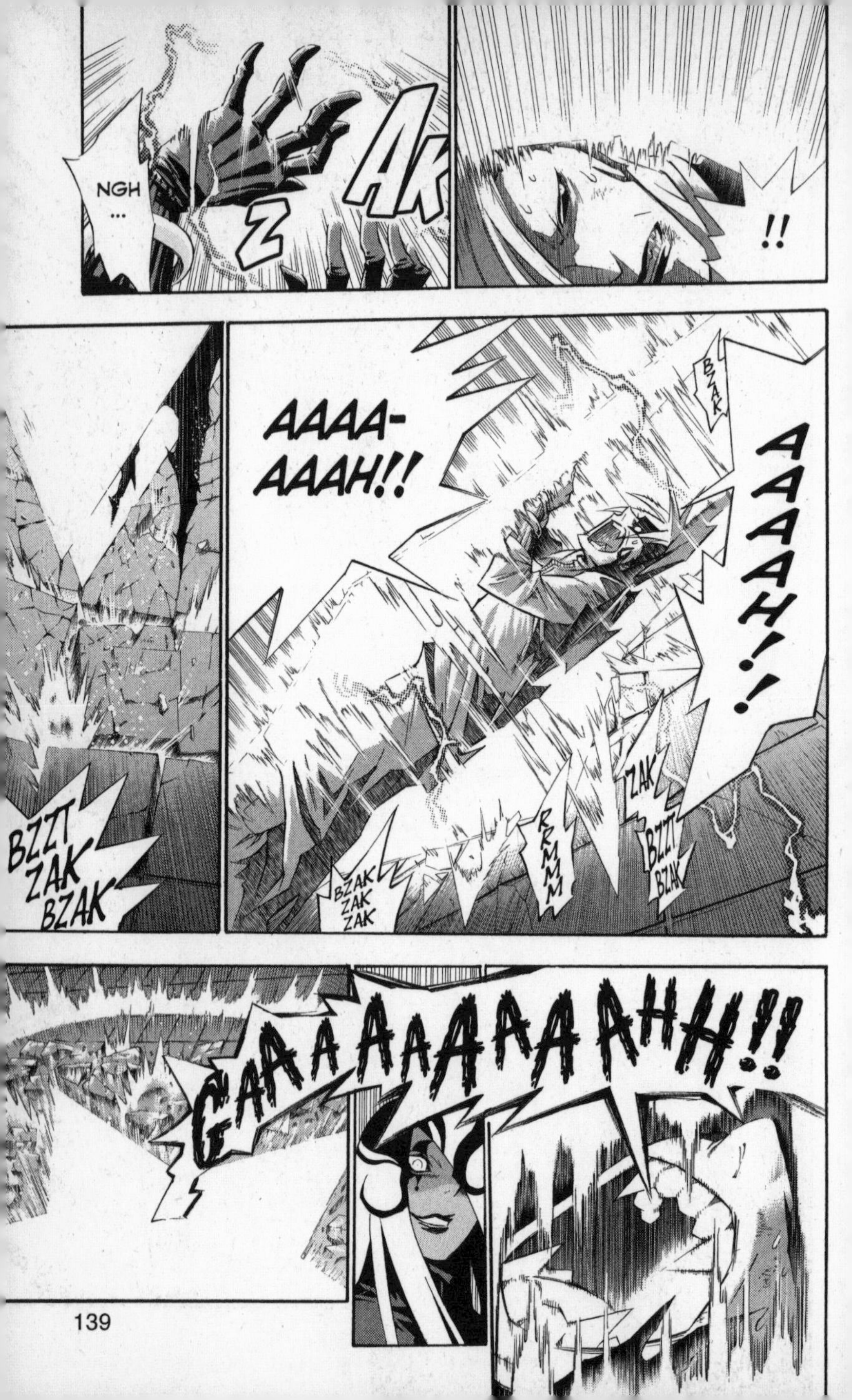
!!
AK
Z
NGH ...
BZAK
AAAAAH!!!
AAAA-AAAH!!
ZAK
BZZT BZAK
RRMMM
BZAK ZAK ZAK
BZZT ZAK BZAK
GAAAAAAAAHH!!

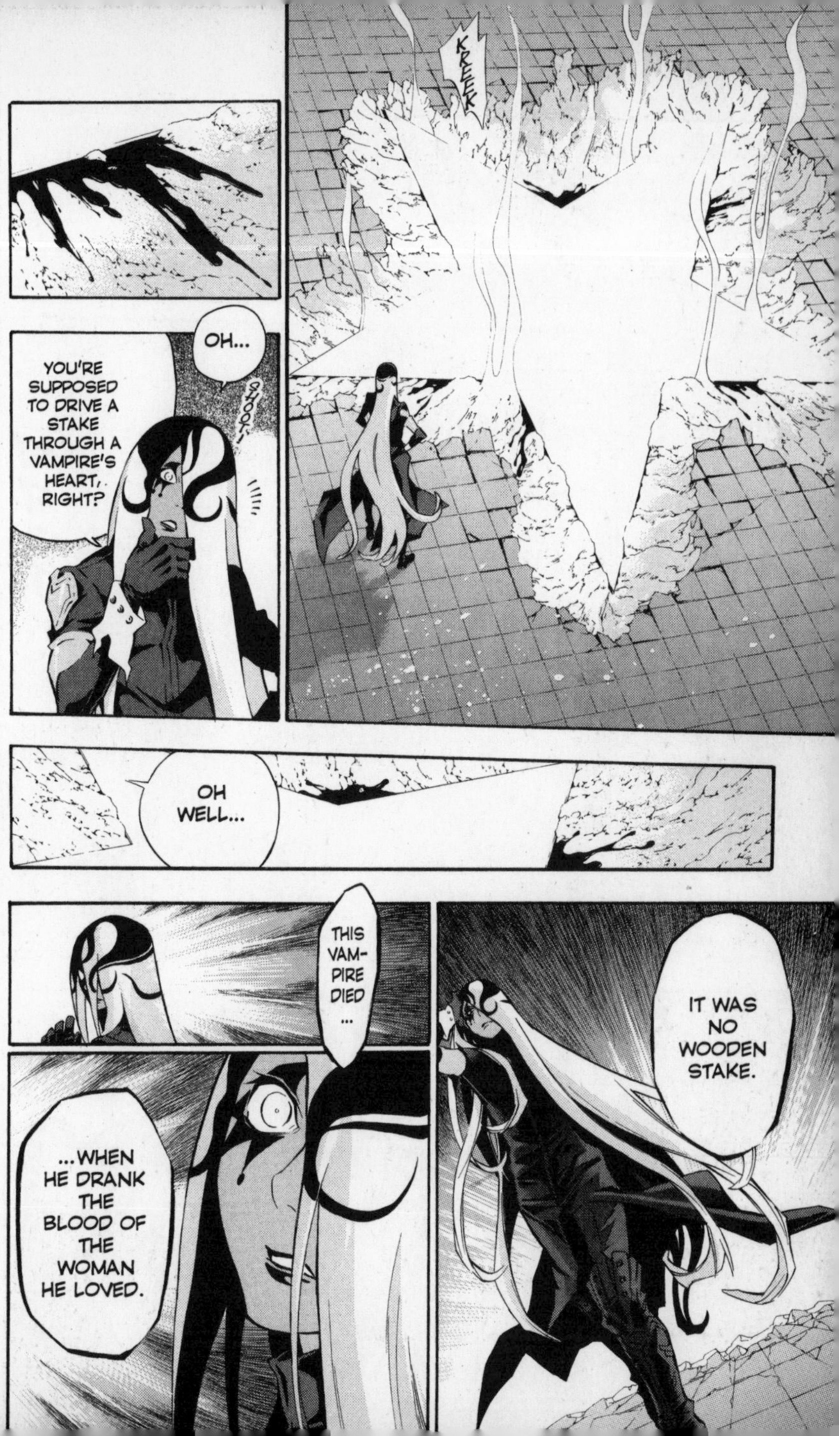
KREEK
OH...
SHOOT!
YOU'RE SUPPOSED TO DRIVE A STAKE THROUGH A VAMPIRE'S HEART, RIGHT?
OH WELL...
IT WAS NO WOODEN STAKE.
THIS VAM-PIRE DIED...
...WHEN HE DRANK THE BLOOD OF THE WOMAN HE LOVED.

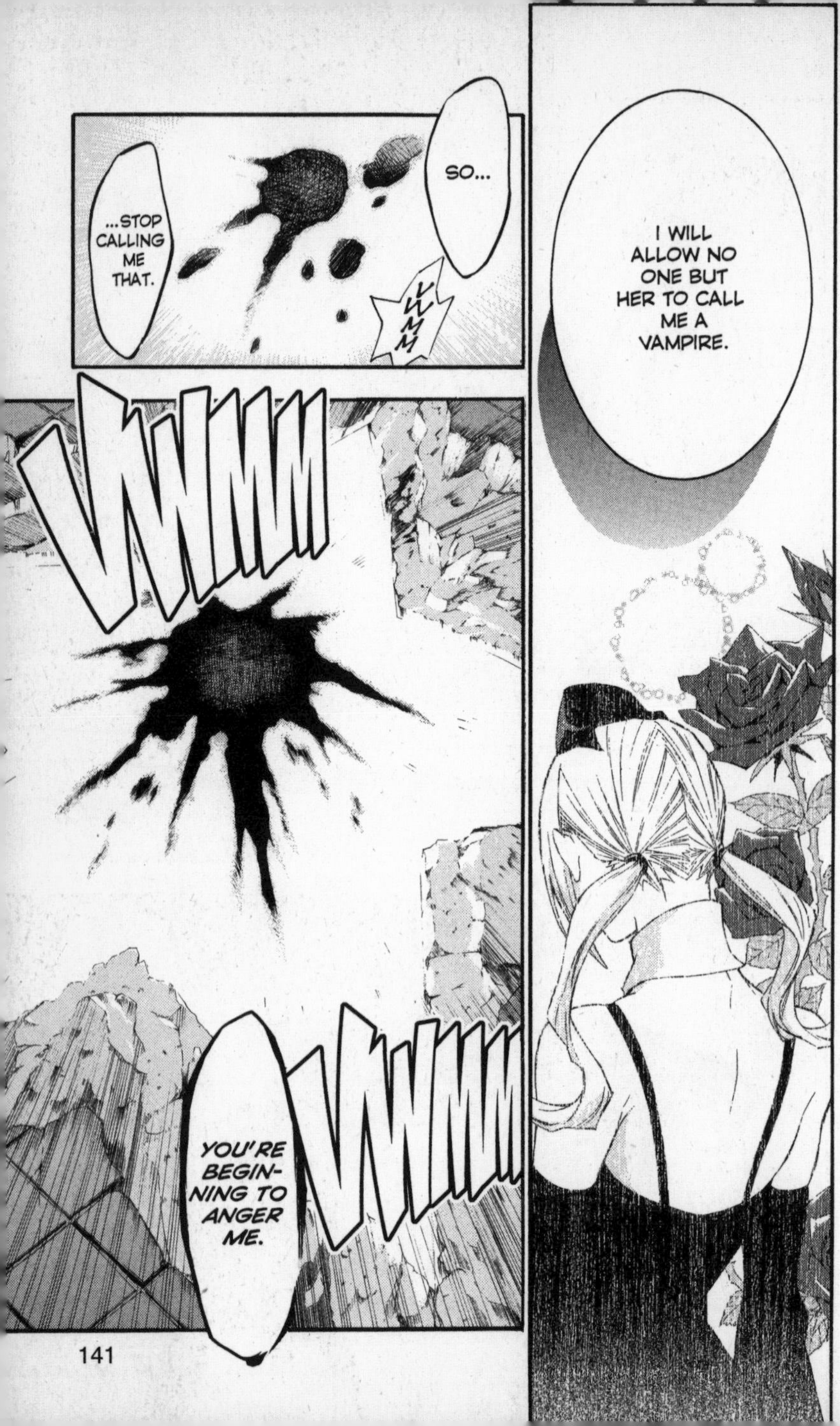
I WILL ALLOW NO ONE BUT HER TO CALL ME A VAMPIRE.
SO...
...STOP CALLING ME THAT.
YOU'RE BEGIN-NING TO ANGER ME.

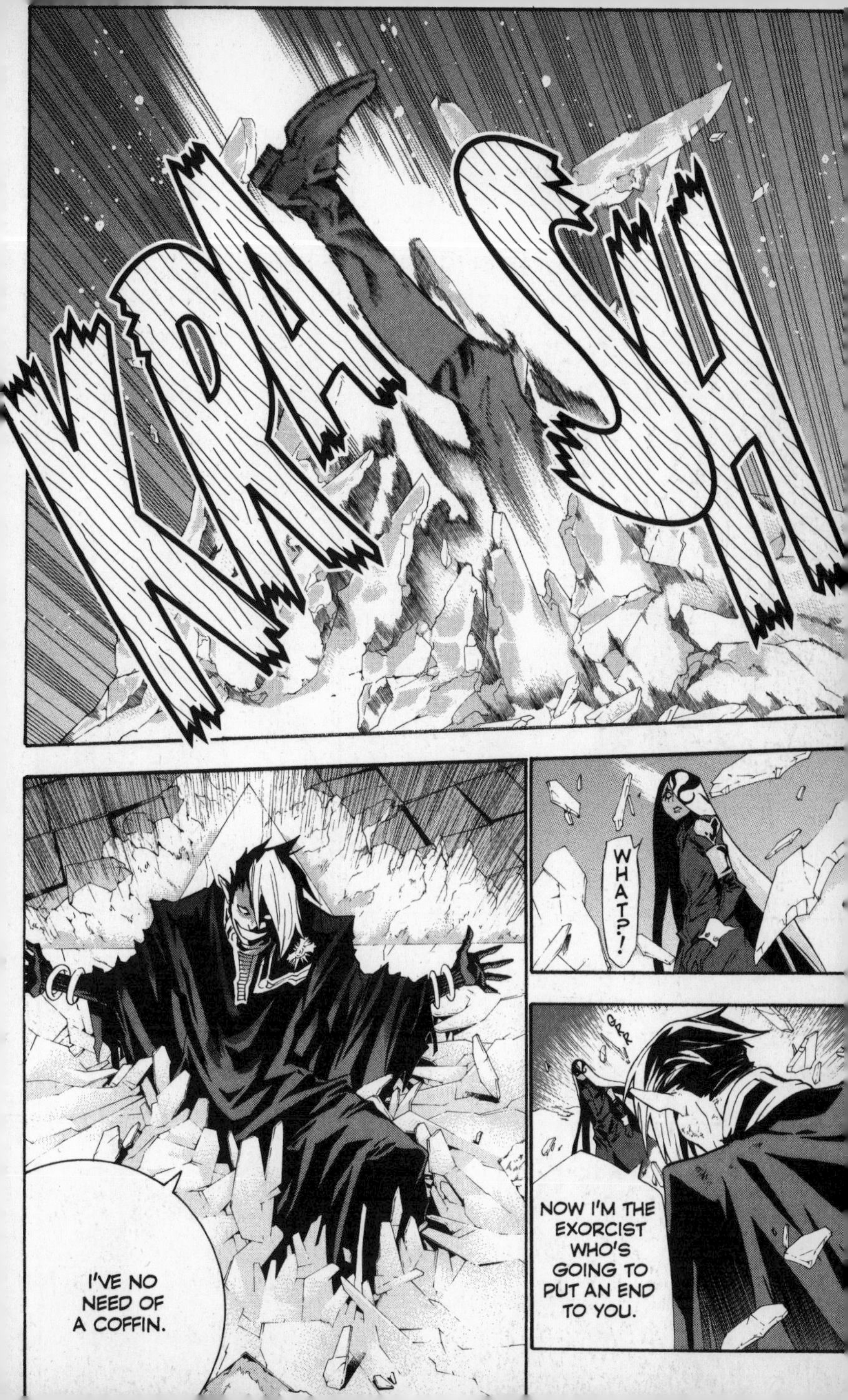
KRASH
WHAT?!
GRR
NOW I'M THE EXORCIST WHO'S GOING TO PUT AN END TO YOU.
I'VE NO NEED OF A COFFIN.

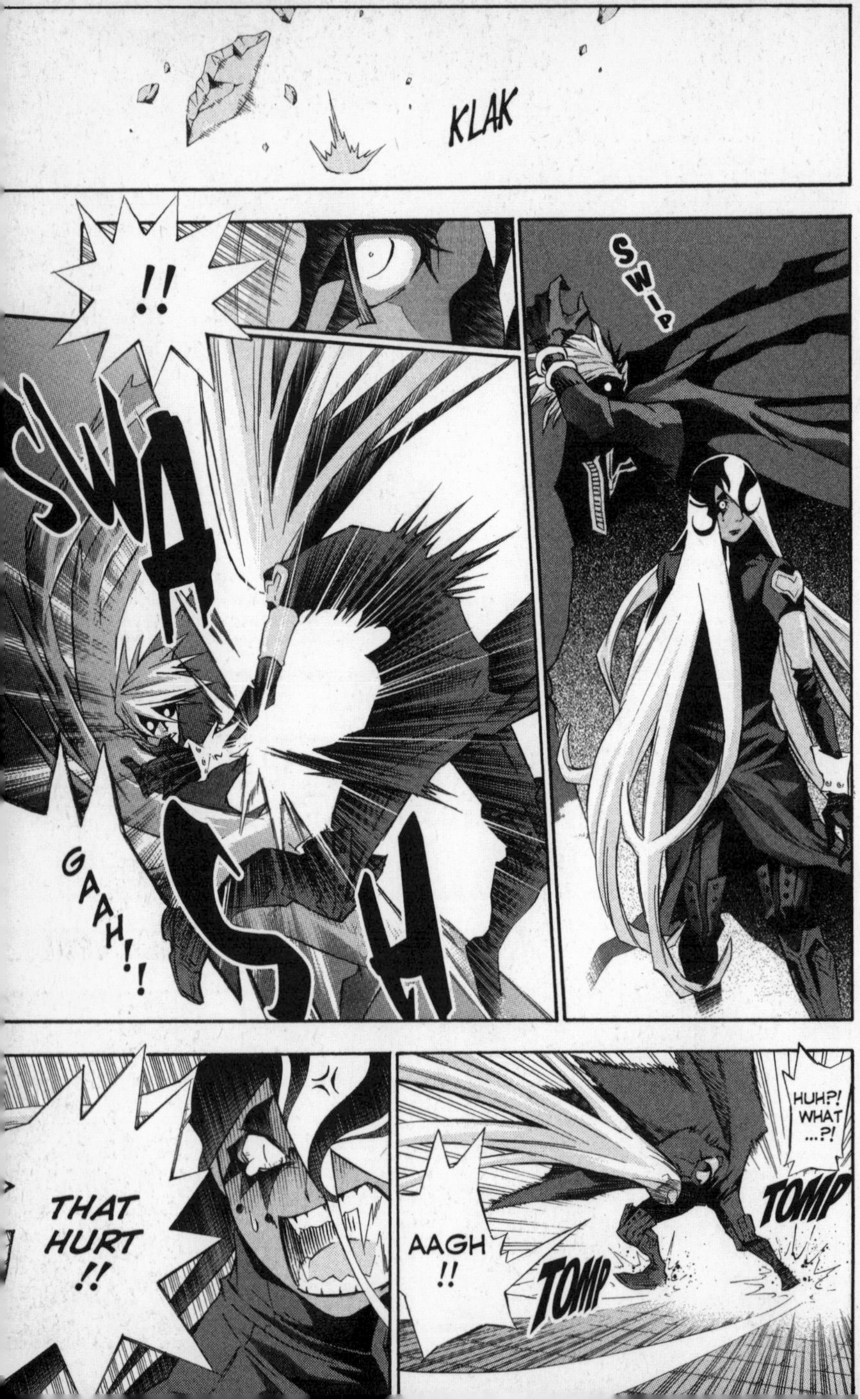
KLAK
SWIP
!!
SWASH
GAAH!!
HUH?! WHAT ...?!
TOMP
AAGH !!
TOMP
THAT HURT !!

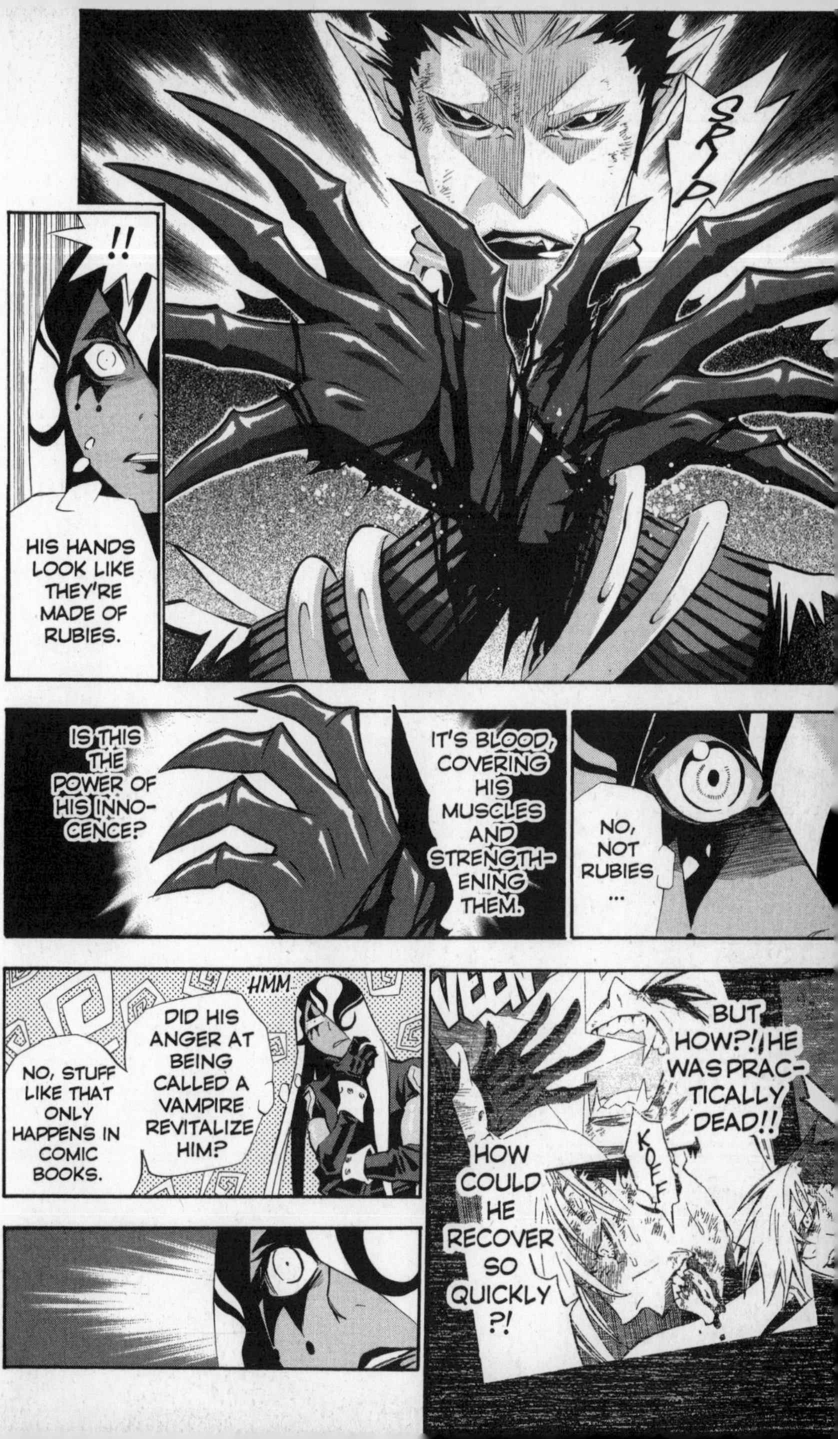
GRIP
!!
HIS HANDS LOOK LIKE THEY'RE MADE OF RUBIES.
NO, NOT RUBIES ...
IT'S BLOOD, COVERING HIS MUSCLES AND STRENGTHENING THEM.
IS THIS THE POWER OF HIS INNOCENCE?
BUT HOW?! HE WAS PRACTICALLY DEAD!!
KOFF
HOW COULD HE RECOVER SO QUICKLY?!
HMM
DID HIS ANGER AT BEING CALLED A VAMPIRE REVITALIZE HIM?
NO, STUFF LIKE THAT ONLY HAPPENS IN COMIC BOOKS.

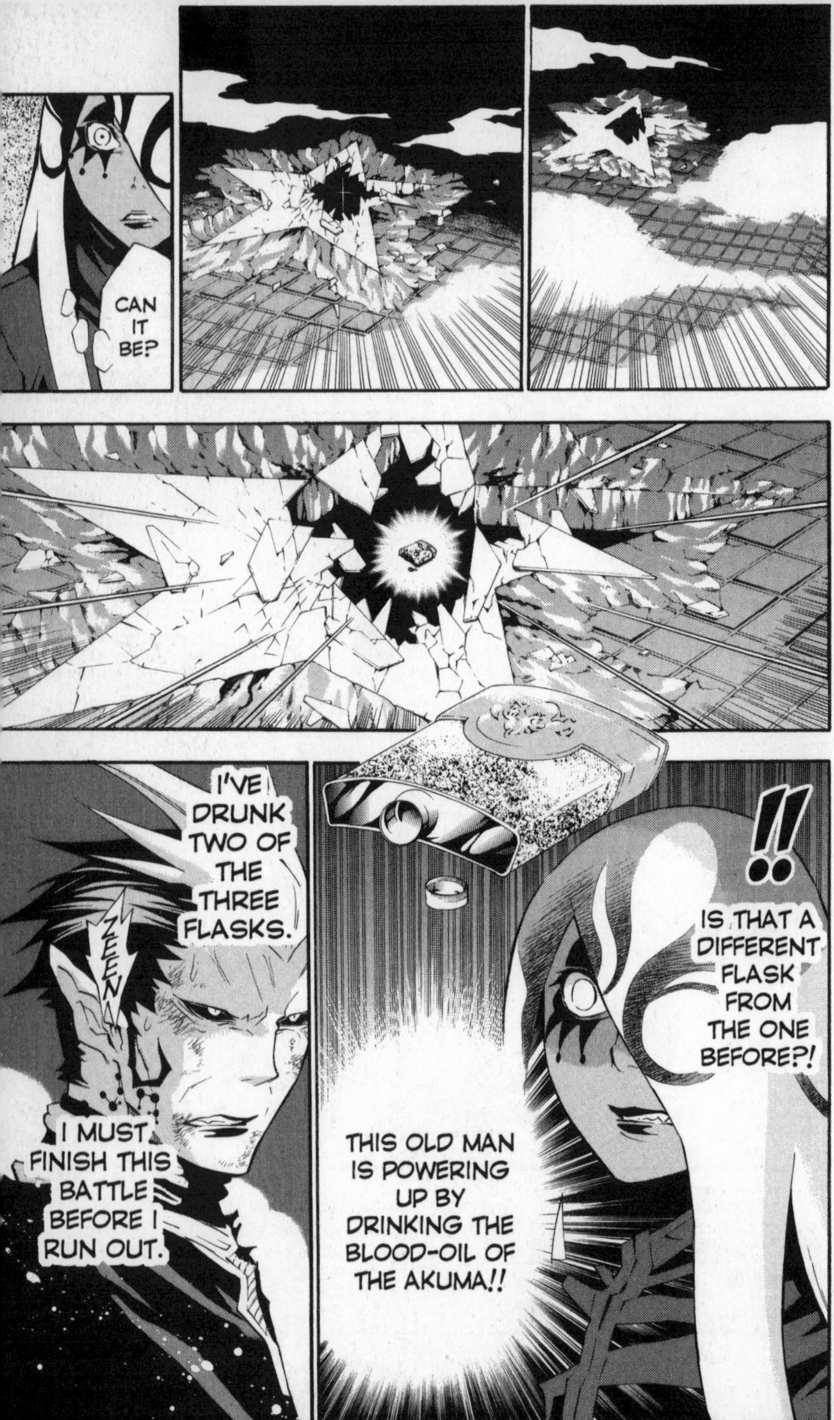
CAN IT BE?
!!
IS THAT A DIFFERENT FLASK FROM THE ONE BEFORE?!
THIS OLD MAN IS POWERING UP BY DRINKING THE BLOOD-OIL OF THE AKUMA!!
I'VE DRUNK TWO OF THE THREE FLASKS.
ZEEN
I MUST FINISH THIS BATTLE BEFORE I RUN OUT.

THE KATO INCIDENT, PART FOUR

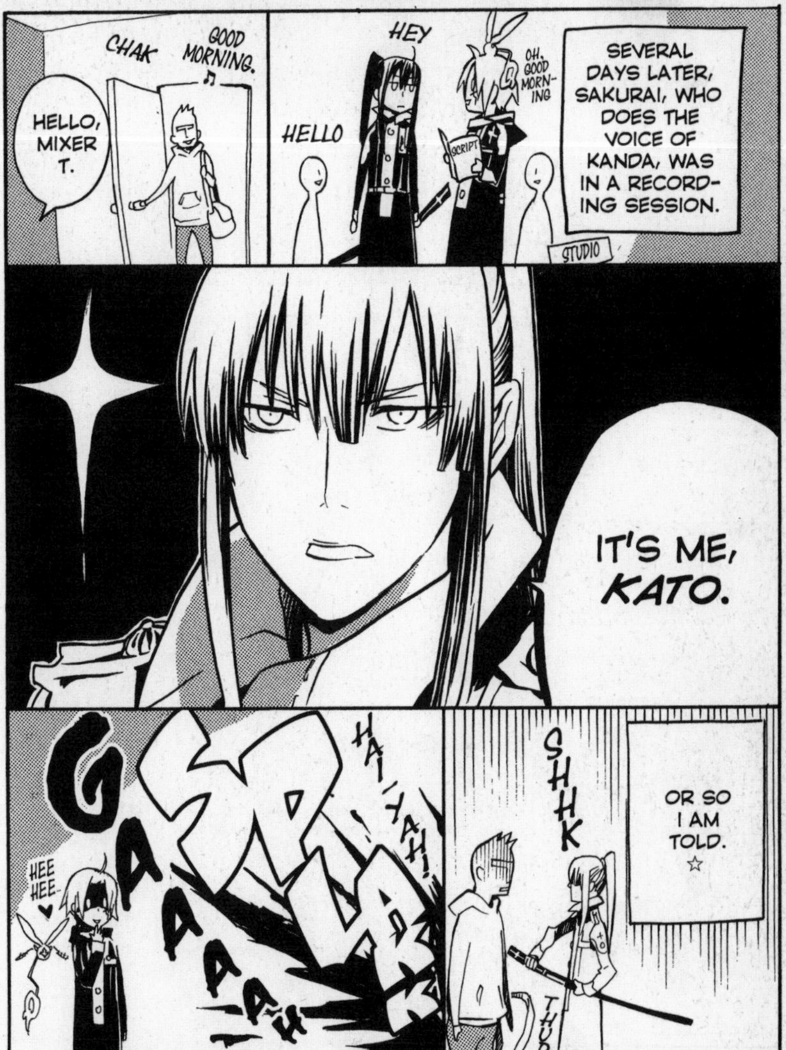
SEVERAL DAYS LATER, SAKURAI, WHO DOES THE VOICE OF KANDA, WAS IN A RECORDING SESSION.
OH, GOOD MORNING
HEY
SCRIPT
HELLO
STUDIO
GOOD MORNING. ♪
CHAK
HELLO, MIXER T.
IT'S ME, KATO.
SHHK
OR SO I AM TOLD. ☆
THUD
HAI-YAH!
GAAAAAH
HEE HEE ♥
SOON THE ENTIRE CREW HEARD ABOUT THE KATO/KANDA INCIDENT. I'M TOLD THAT NOW EVERYONE IN THE STUDIO REFERS TO KANDA AS KATO. SEE WHAT YOU'VE DONE, MIXER T?
THE END!

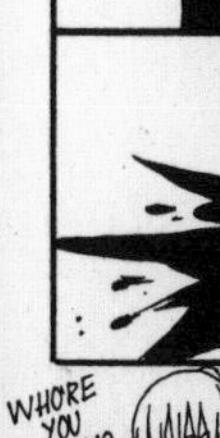
WHO'RE YOU CALLING KATO?!

THE 106TH NIGHT: CRIMSON SHAKE

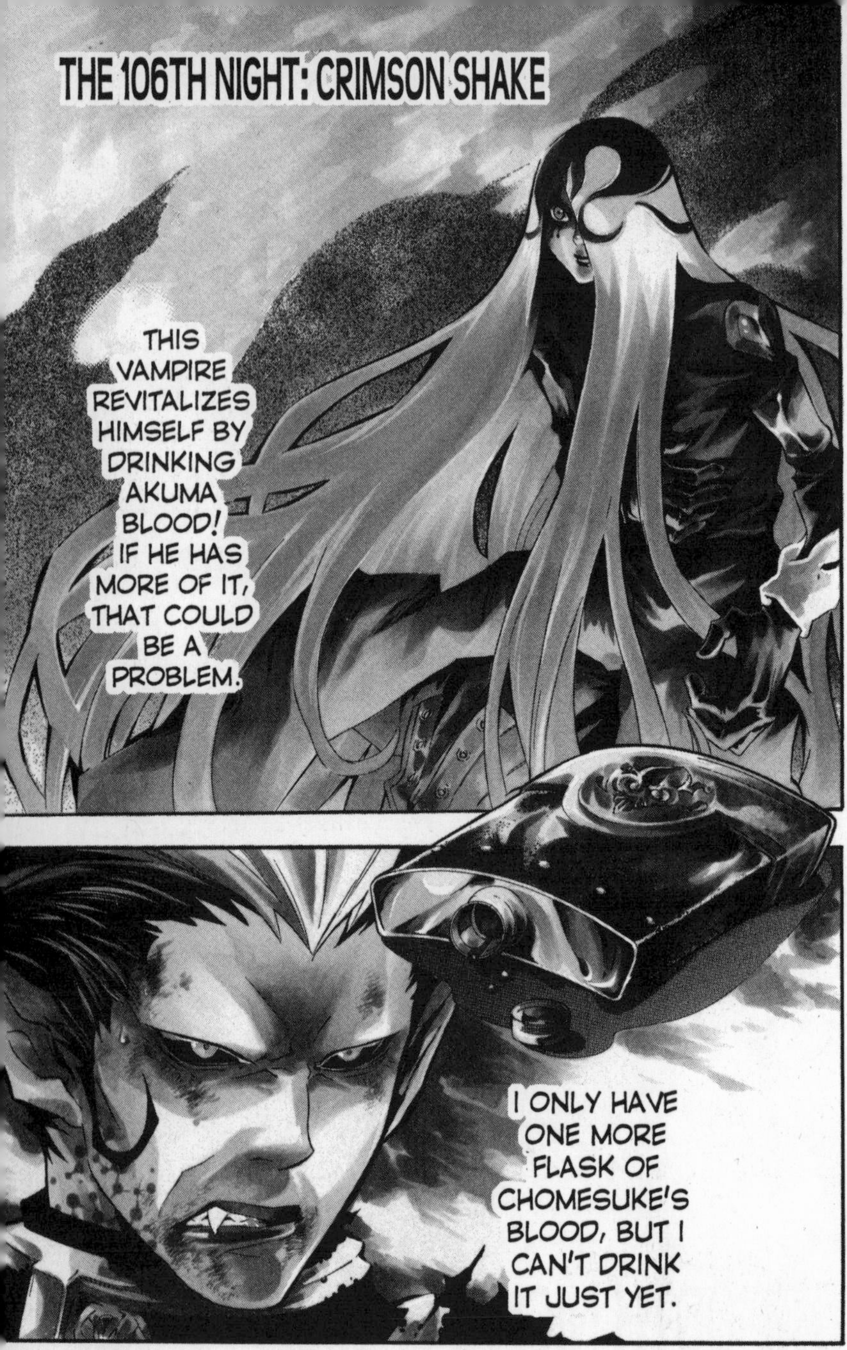
THIS VAMPIRE REVITALIZES HIMSELF BY DRINKING AKUMA BLOOD! IF HE HAS MORE OF IT, THAT COULD BE A PROBLEM.
I ONLY HAVE ONE MORE FLASK OF CHOMESUKE'S BLOOD, BUT I CAN'T DRINK IT JUST YET.

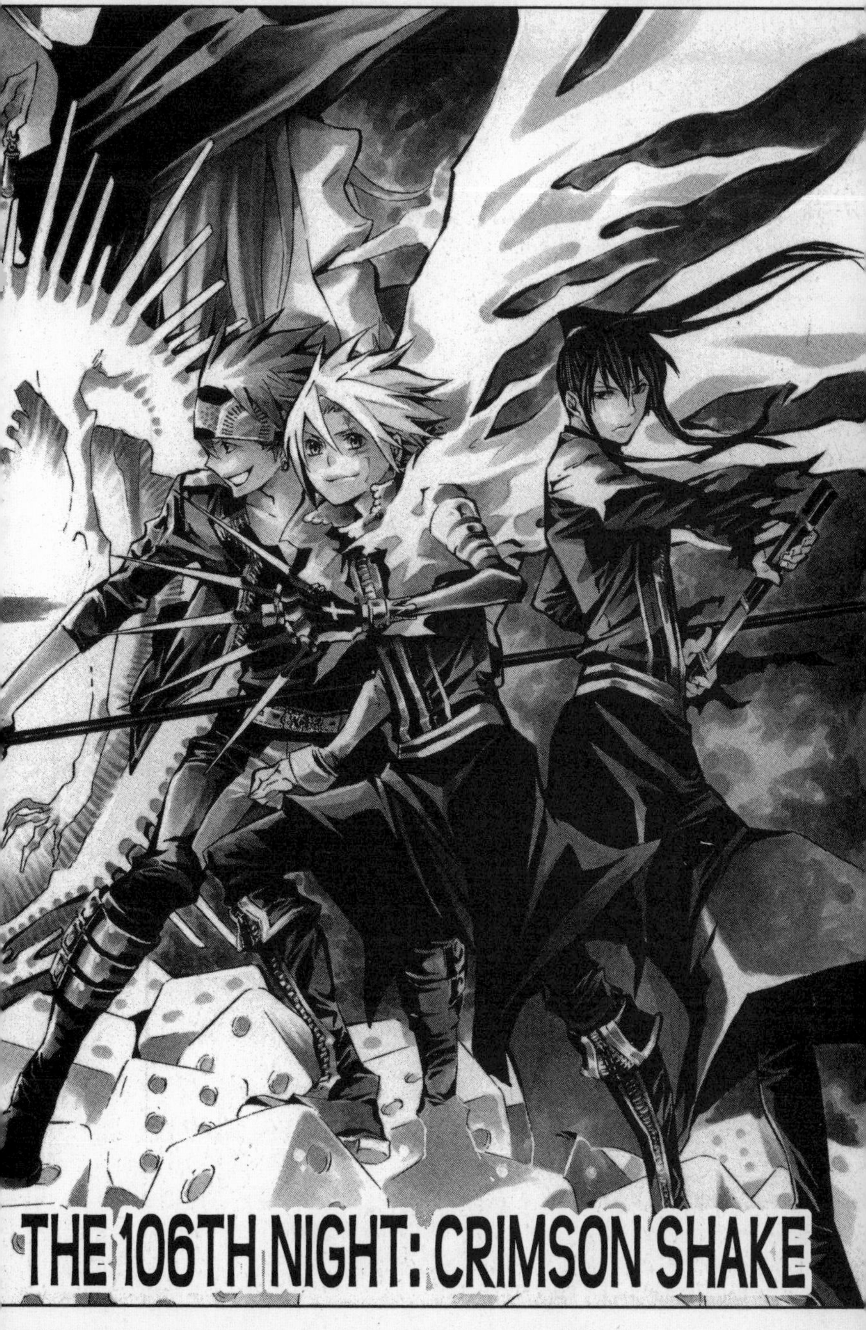
THE 106TH NIGHT: CRIMSON SHAKE

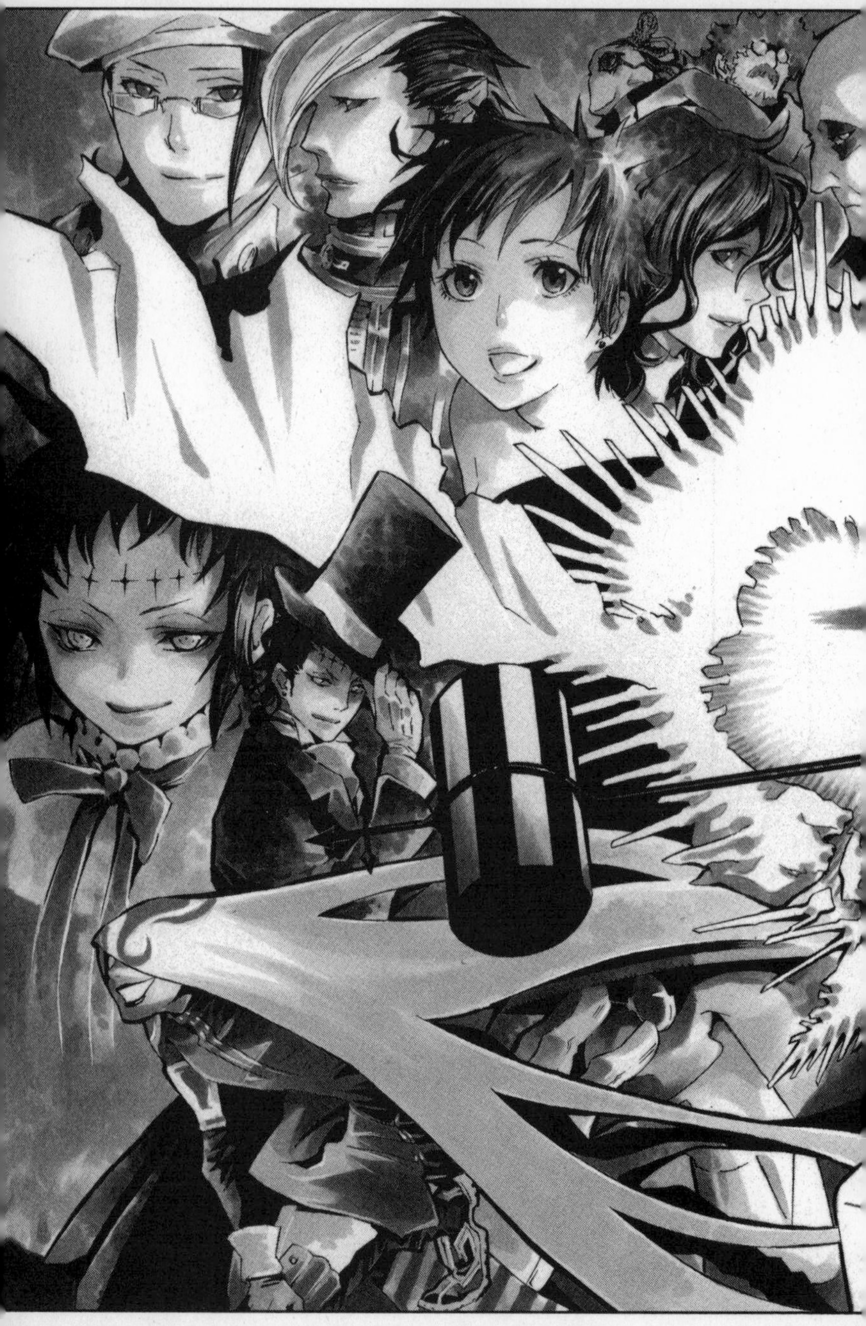

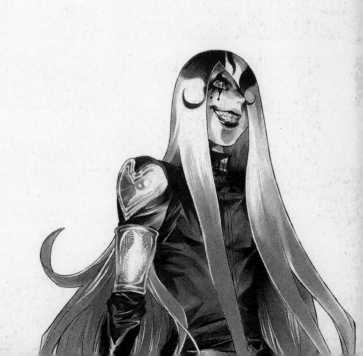

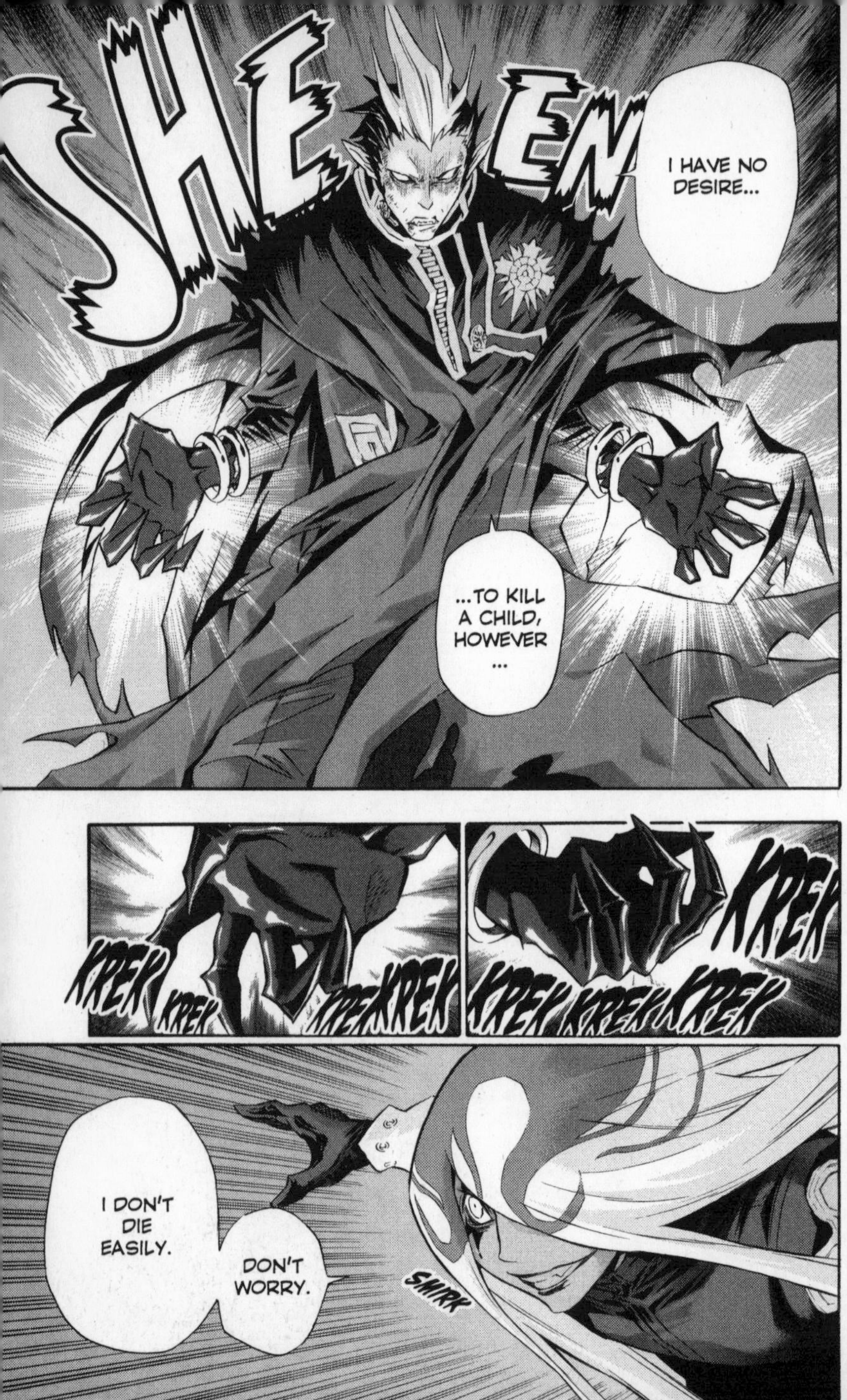
SHEEN
I HAVE NO DESIRE...
...TO KILL A CHILD, HOWEVER ...
KREK KREK KREK KREK
KREK KREK KREK KREK
SMIRK
DON'T WORRY.
I DON'T DIE EASILY.

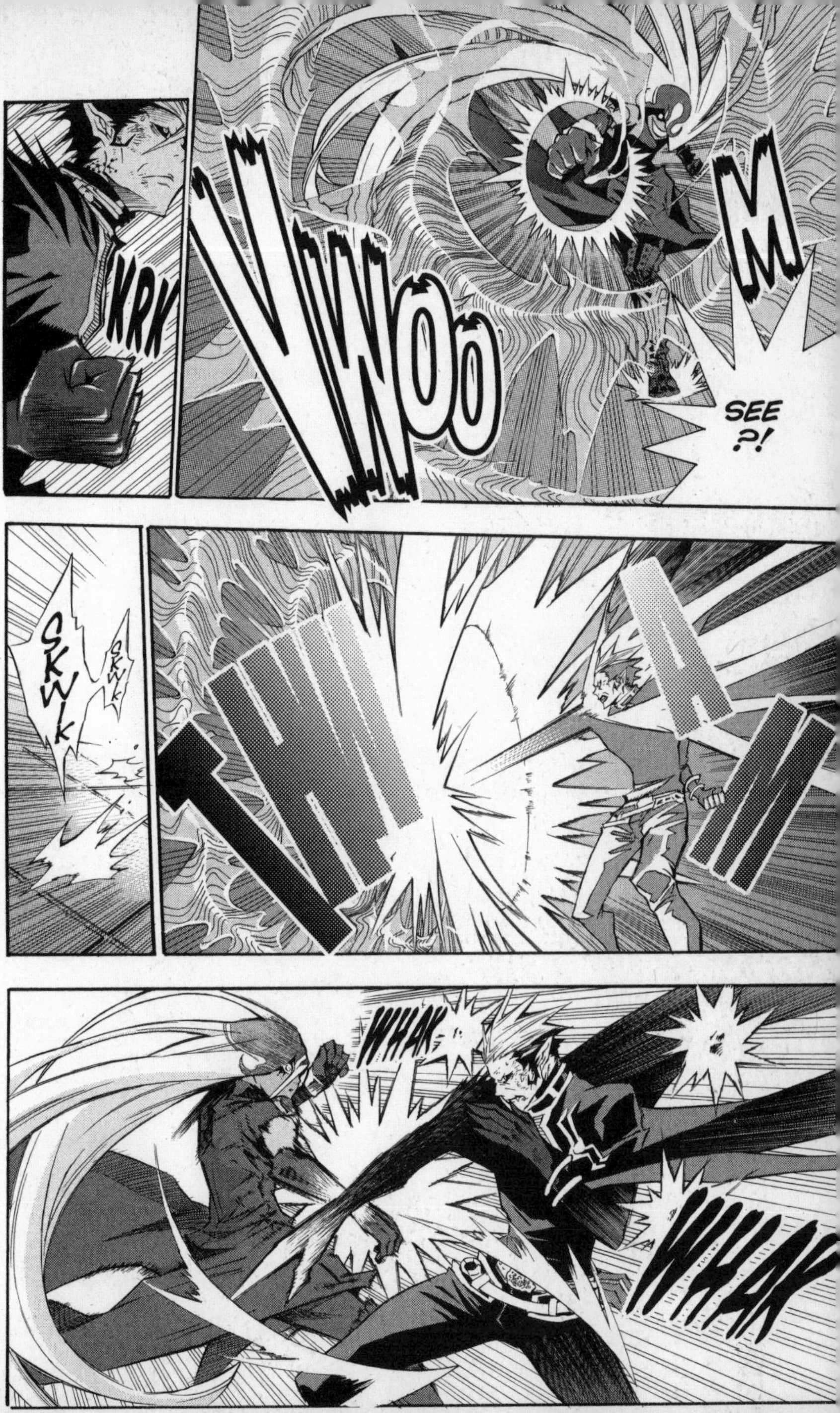
VWOOOM
SEE ?!
KRK
THWAM
SKWIK
SKWIK
WHAK
WHAK

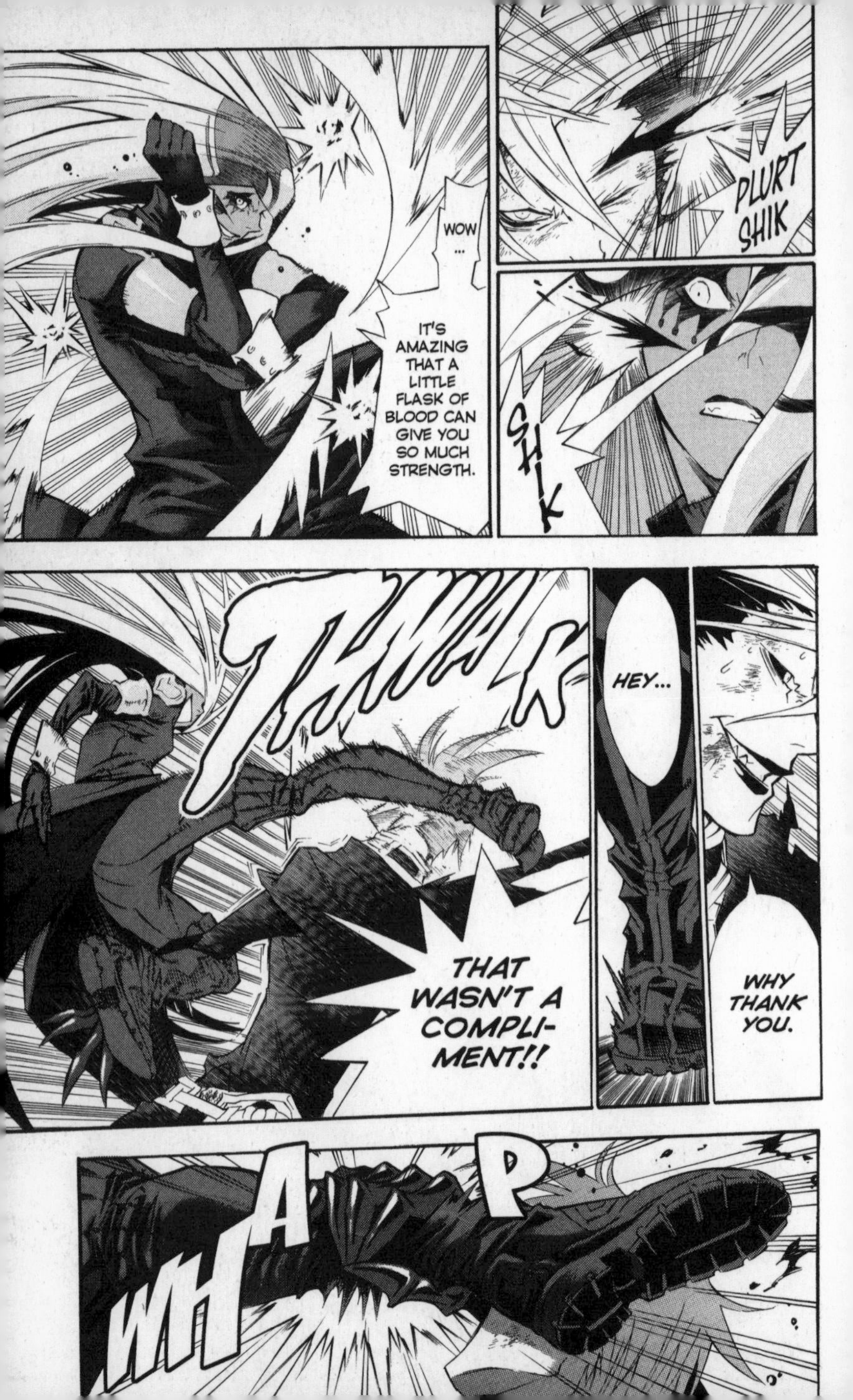
PLURT
SHIK
SHIK
WOW ...
IT'S AMAZING THAT A LITTLE FLASK OF BLOOD CAN GIVE YOU SO MUCH STRENGTH.
WHY THANK YOU.
HEY...
THWAK
THAT WASN'T A COMPLI-MENT!!
WHAP

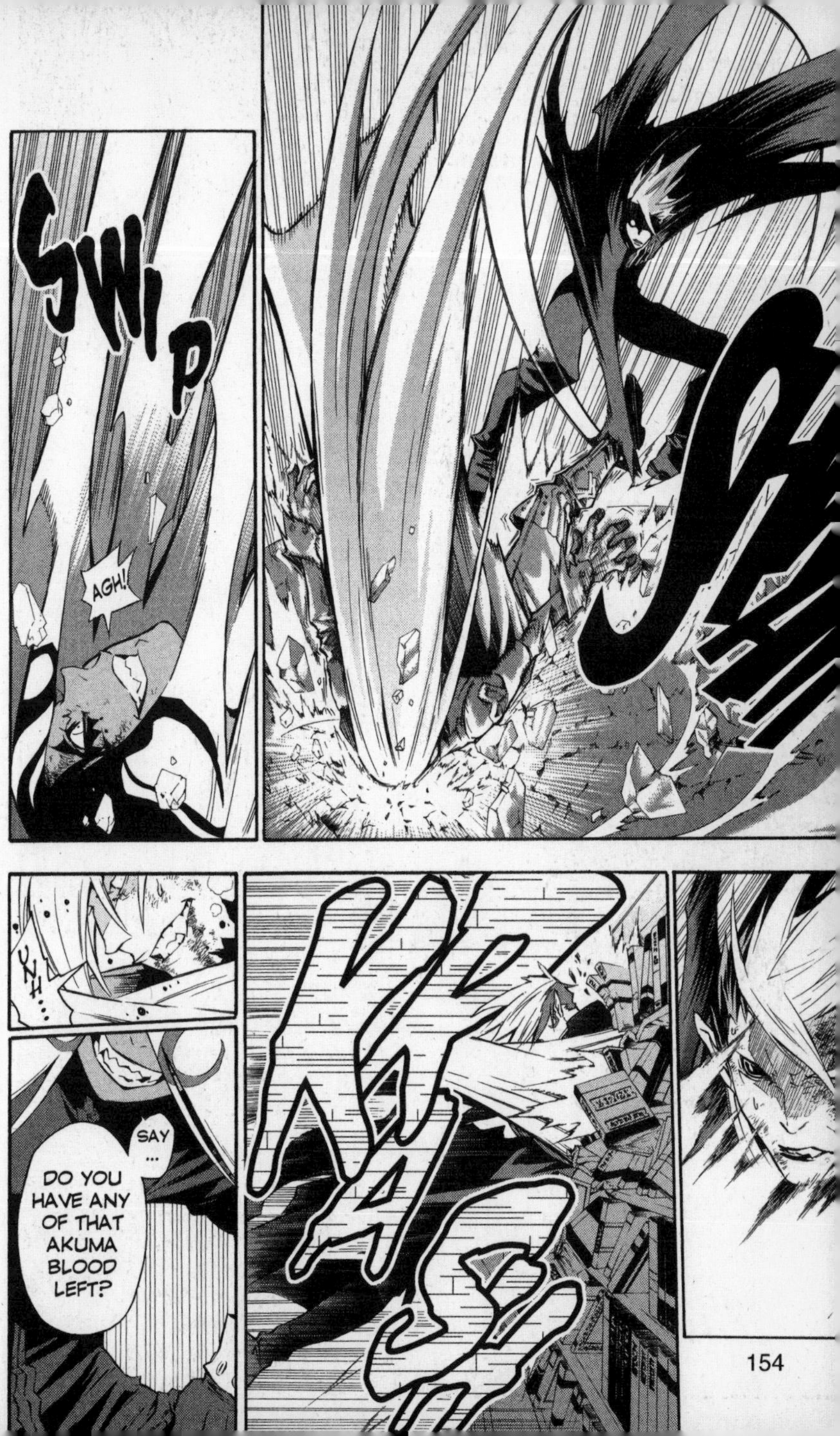
SWIP
AGH!
UNH...
SAY ...
DO YOU HAVE ANY OF THAT AKUMA BLOOD LEFT?

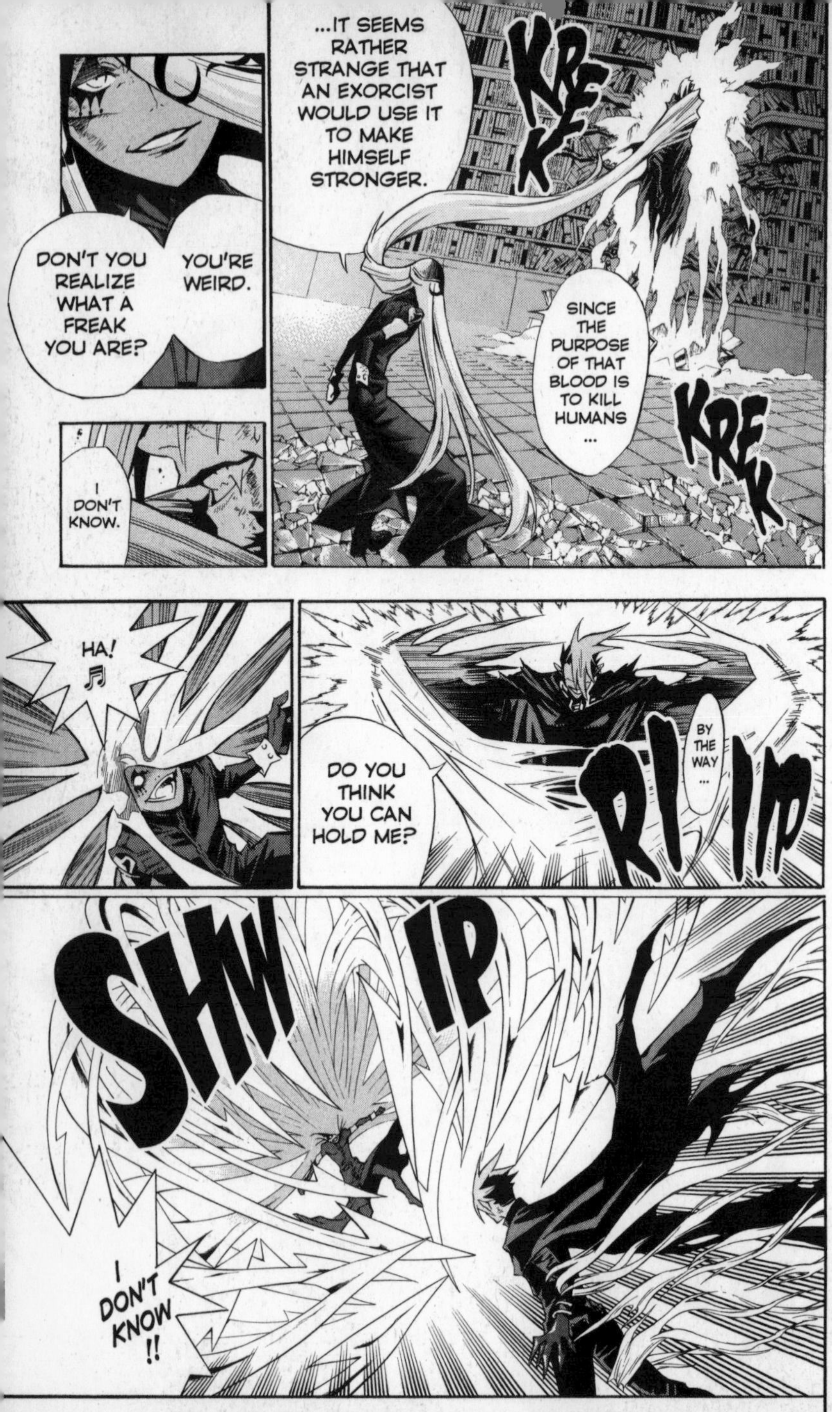
KREK
SINCE THE PURPOSE OF THAT BLOOD IS TO KILL HUMANS ...
...IT SEEMS RATHER STRANGE THAT AN EXORCIST WOULD USE IT TO MAKE HIMSELF STRONGER.
KREK
YOU'RE WEIRD.
DON'T YOU REALIZE WHAT A FREAK YOU ARE?
I DON'T KNOW.
BY THE WAY ...
RIIIP
DO YOU THINK YOU CAN HOLD ME?
HA! ♫
SHWIP
I DON'T KNOW !!

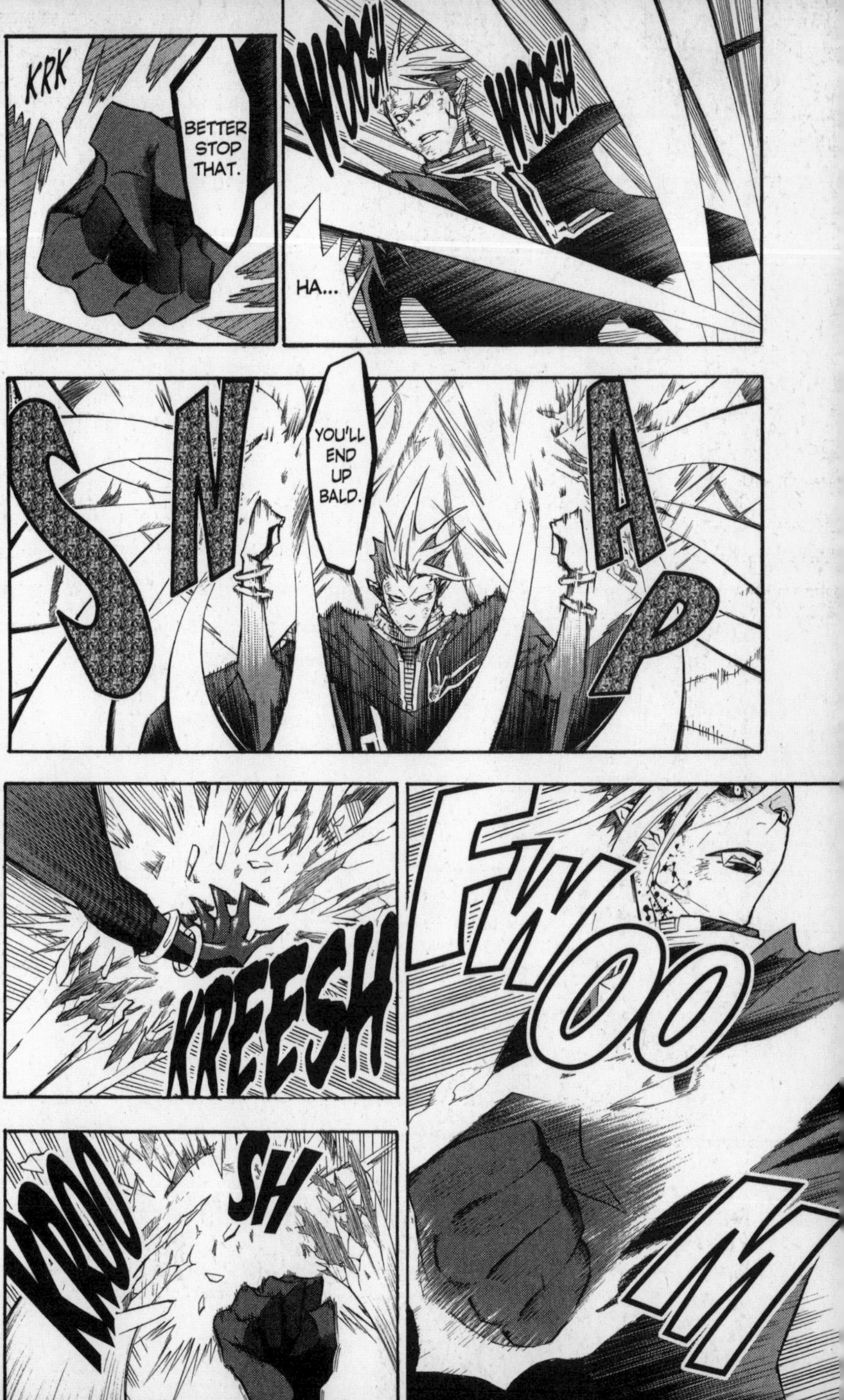
WOOSH
WOOSH
HA...
KRK
BETTER STOP THAT.
SNAP
YOU'LL END UP BALD.
FWOOOM
KREESH
WOOSH

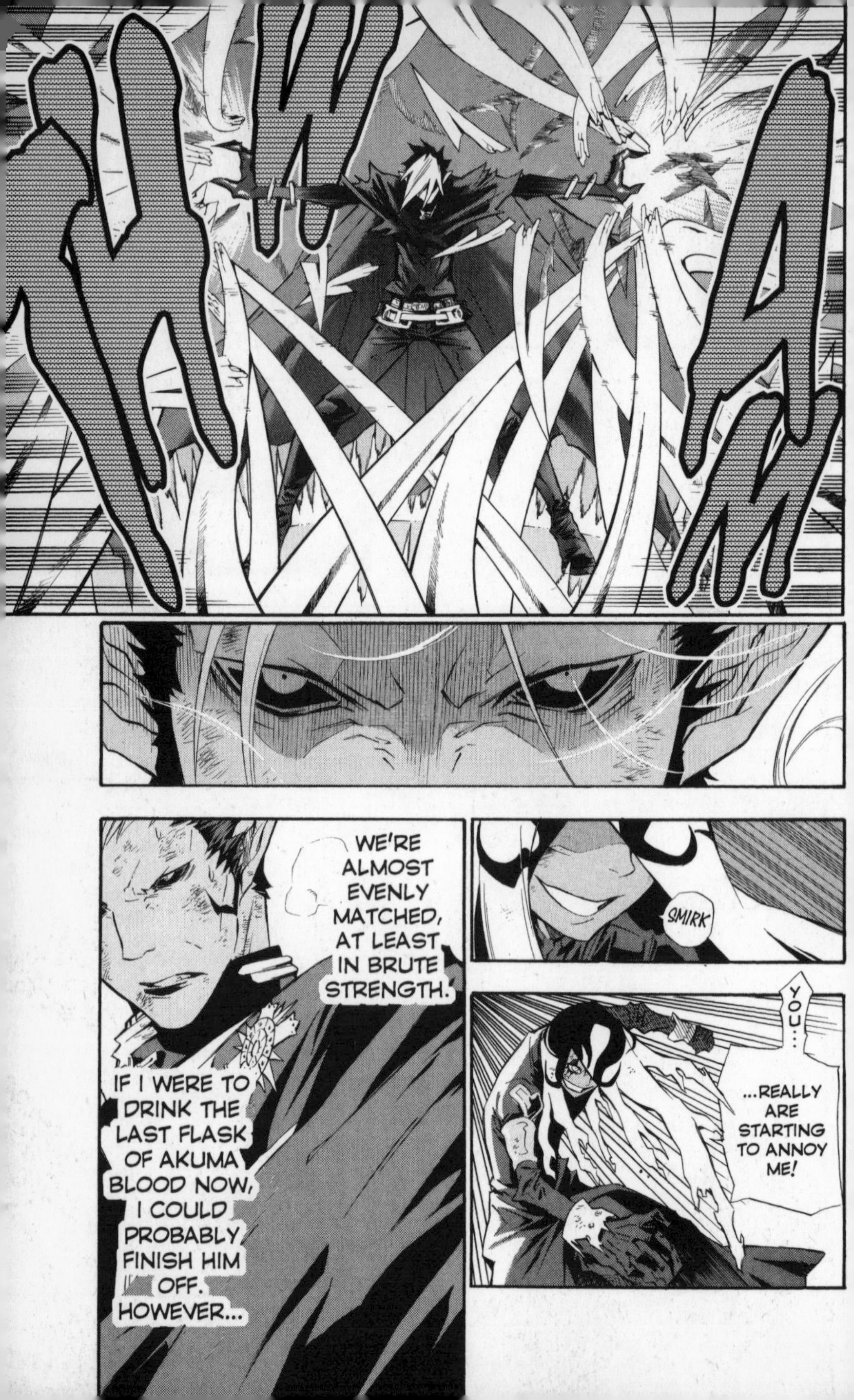
SMIRK
YOU...
...REALLY ARE STARTING TO ANNOY ME!
WE'RE ALMOST EVENLY MATCHED, AT LEAST IN BRUTE STRENGTH.
IF I WERE TO DRINK THE LAST FLASK OF AKUMA BLOOD NOW, I COULD PROBABLY FINISH HIM OFF. HOWEVER...

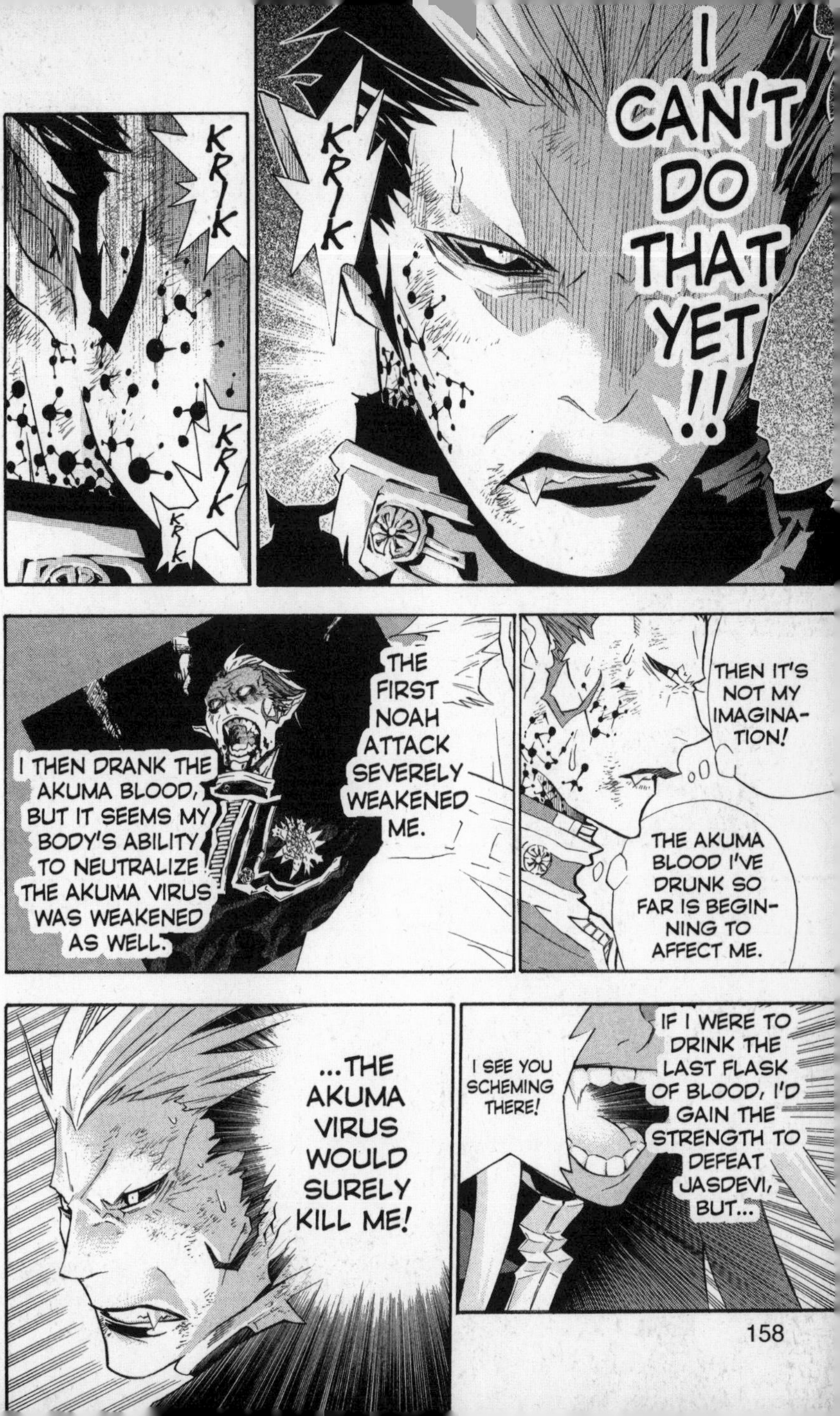
KRIK
I CAN'T DO THAT YET!!
KRIK
KRIK
KRIK
THEN IT'S NOT MY IMAGINATION!
THE AKUMA BLOOD I'VE DRUNK SO FAR IS BEGINNING TO AFFECT ME.
THE FIRST NOAH ATTACK SEVERELY WEAKENED ME.
I THEN DRANK THE AKUMA BLOOD, BUT IT SEEMS MY BODY'S ABILITY TO NEUTRALIZE THE AKUMA VIRUS WAS WEAKENED AS WELL.
IF I WERE TO DRINK THE LAST FLASK OF BLOOD, I'D GAIN THE STRENGTH TO DEFEAT JASDEVI, BUT...
I SEE YOU SCHEMING THERE!
...THE AKUMA VIRUS WOULD SURELY KILL ME!

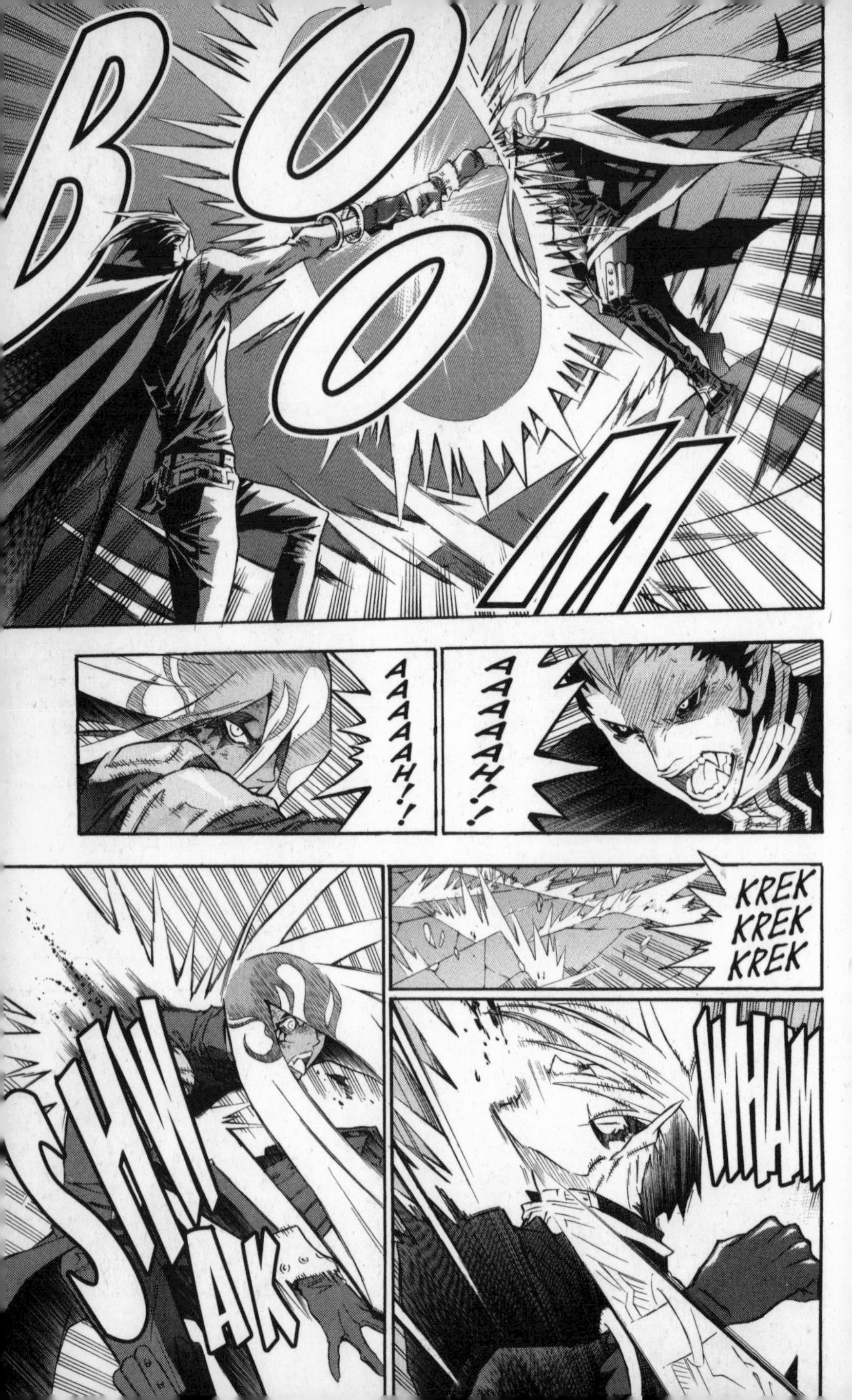
BOOM
AAAAAAH!!
AAAAAAH!!
KREK
KREK
KREK
WHAM
SHWAK

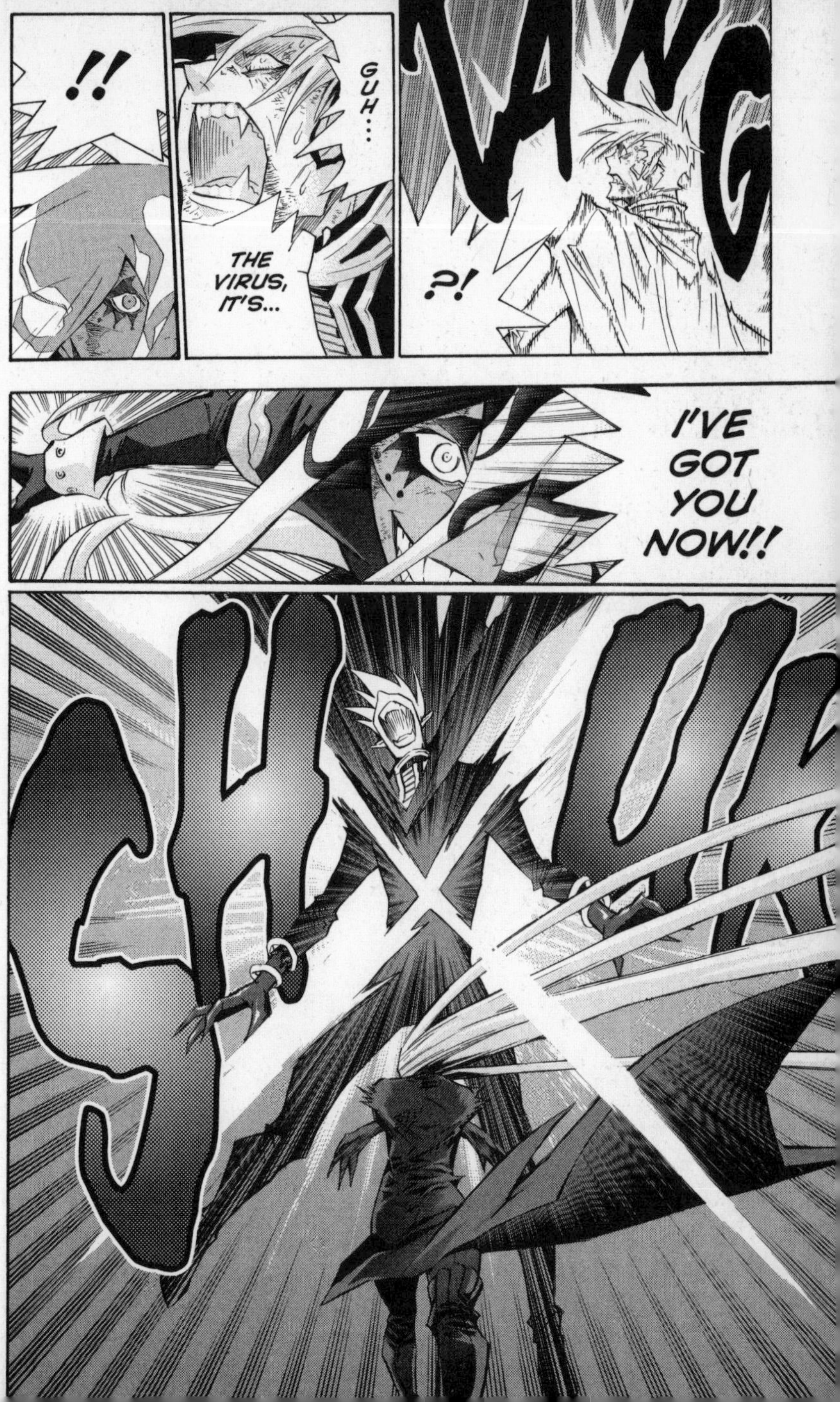
VANG
?!
GUH...
THE VIRUS, IT'S...
!!
I'VE GOT YOU NOW!!

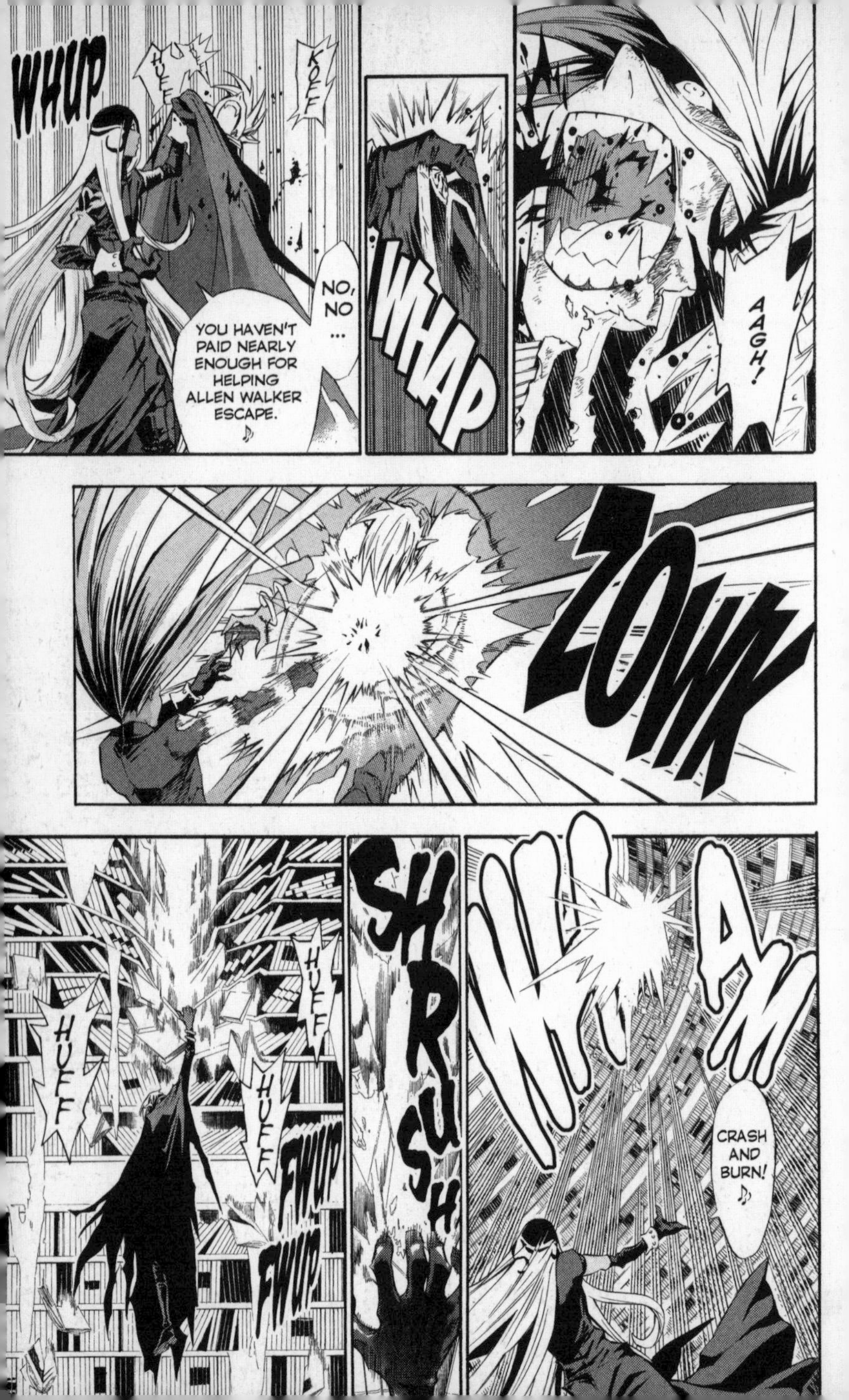
AAGH!
WHAP
KOFF
HUFF
WHUP
NO, NO ...
YOU HAVEN'T PAID NEARLY ENOUGH FOR HELPING ALLEN WALKER ESCAPE. ♪
ZOWM
CRASH AND BURN! ♪
SHRUSH
HUFF
HUFF
HUFF
FWUP
FWUP

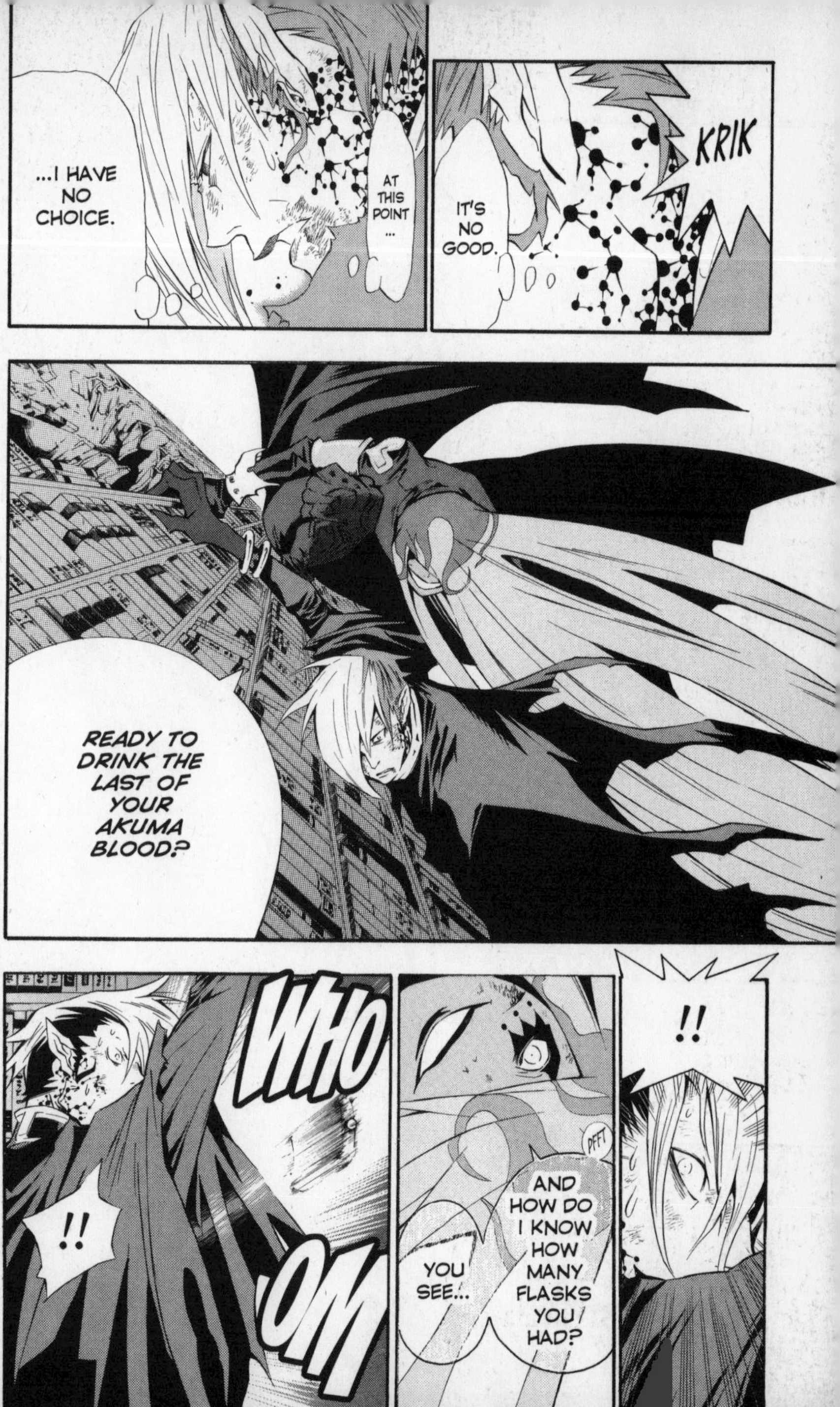
KRIK
IT'S NO GOOD.
AT THIS POINT...
...I HAVE NO CHOICE.
READY TO DRINK THE LAST OF YOUR AKUMA BLOOD?
!!
PFFT
AND HOW DO I KNOW HOW MANY FLASKS YOU HAD?
YOU SEE...
WHO
OM
!!

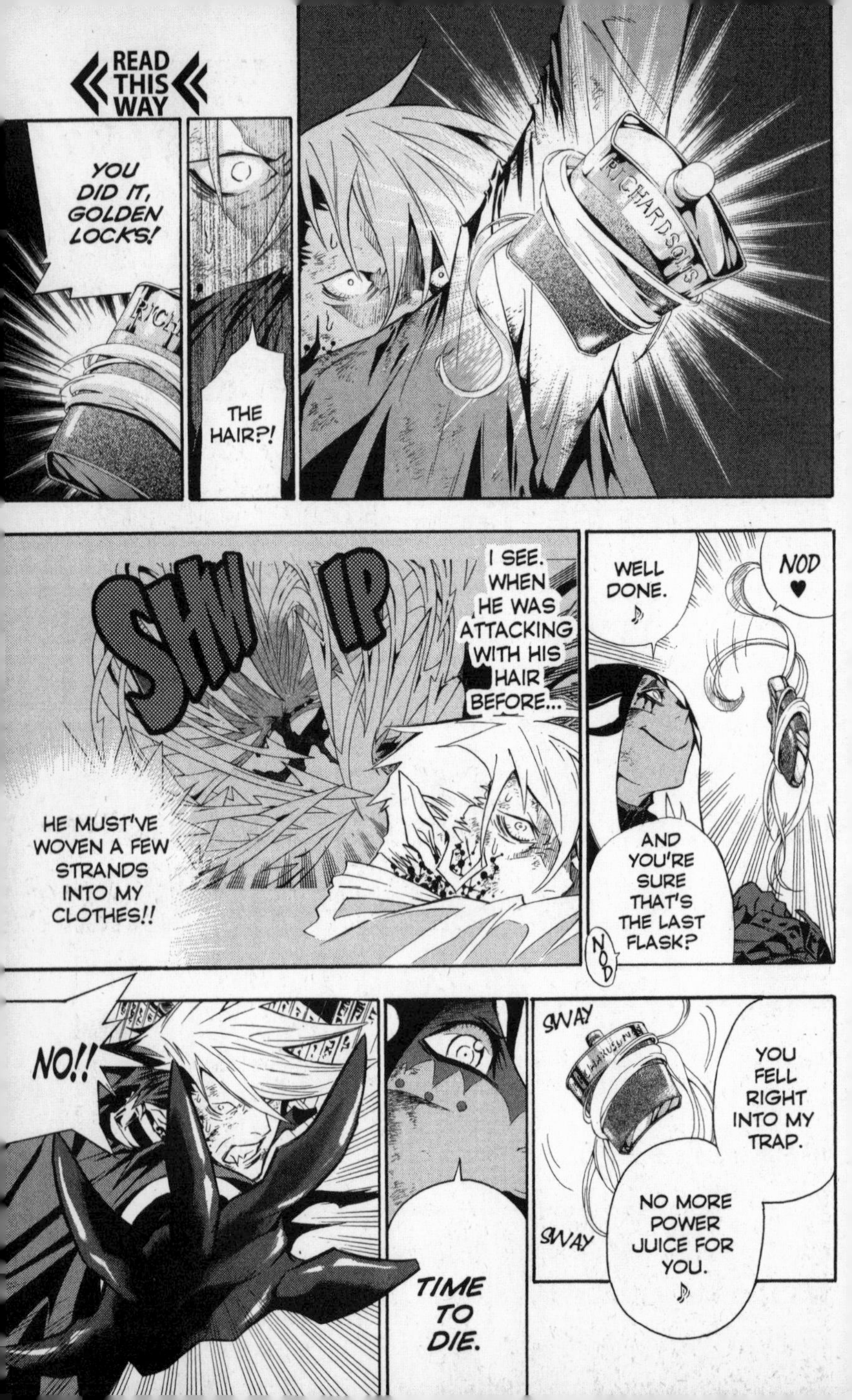
READ THIS WAY
THE HAIR?!
YOU DID IT, GOLDEN LOCKS!
NOD ♥
WELL DONE. ♪
AND YOU'RE SURE THAT'S THE LAST FLASK?
NOD
I SEE. WHEN HE WAS ATTACKING WITH HIS HAIR BEFORE...
SHWIP
HE MUST'VE WOVEN A FEW STRANDS INTO MY CLOTHES!!
SWAY
YOU FELL RIGHT INTO MY TRAP.
NO MORE POWER JUICE FOR YOU. ♪
SWAY
TIME TO DIE.
NO!!

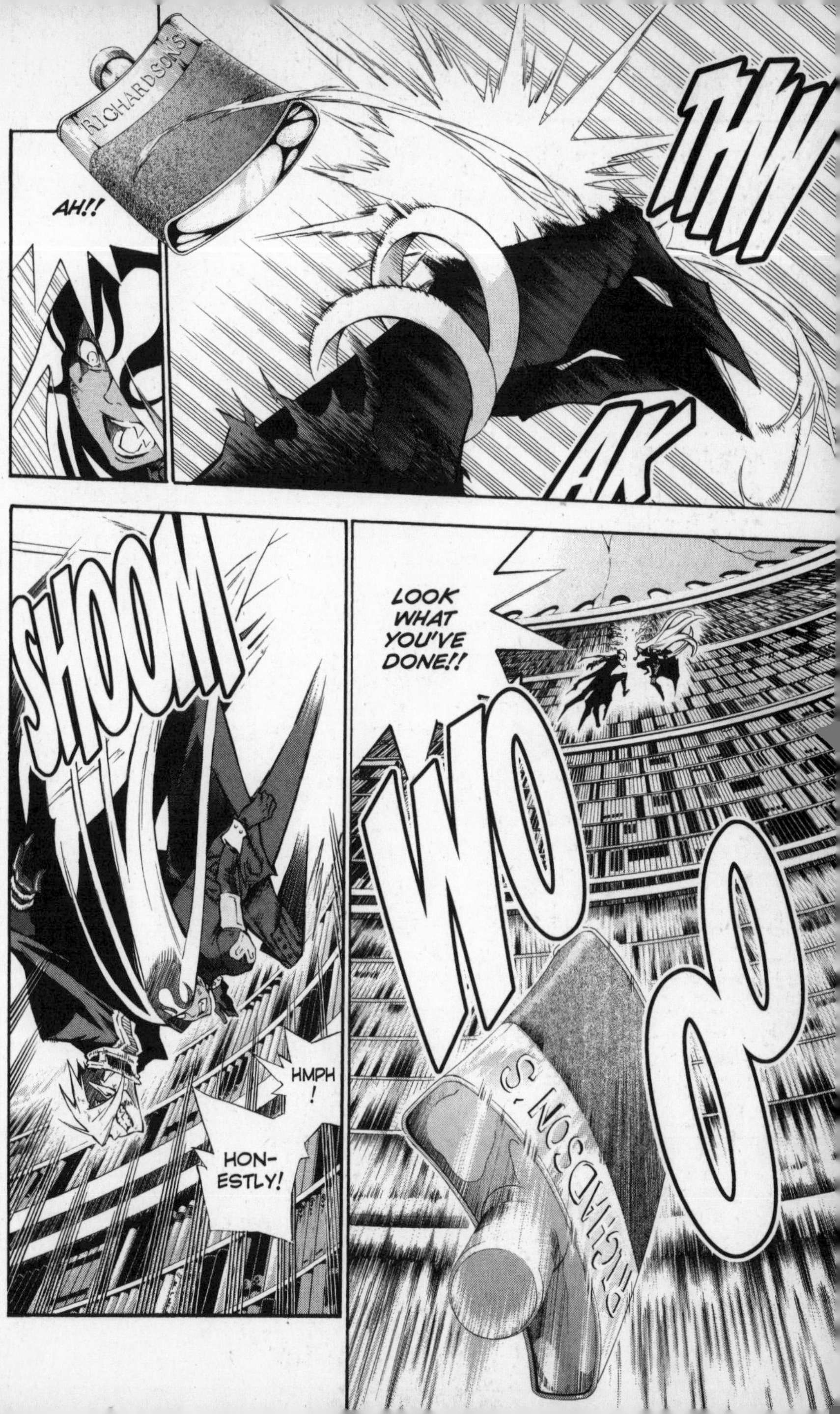

RICHARDSON'S
THWAK
AH!!
LOOK WHAT YOU'VE DONE!!
RICHARDSON'S
SHOOM
HMPH!
HON-ESTLY!

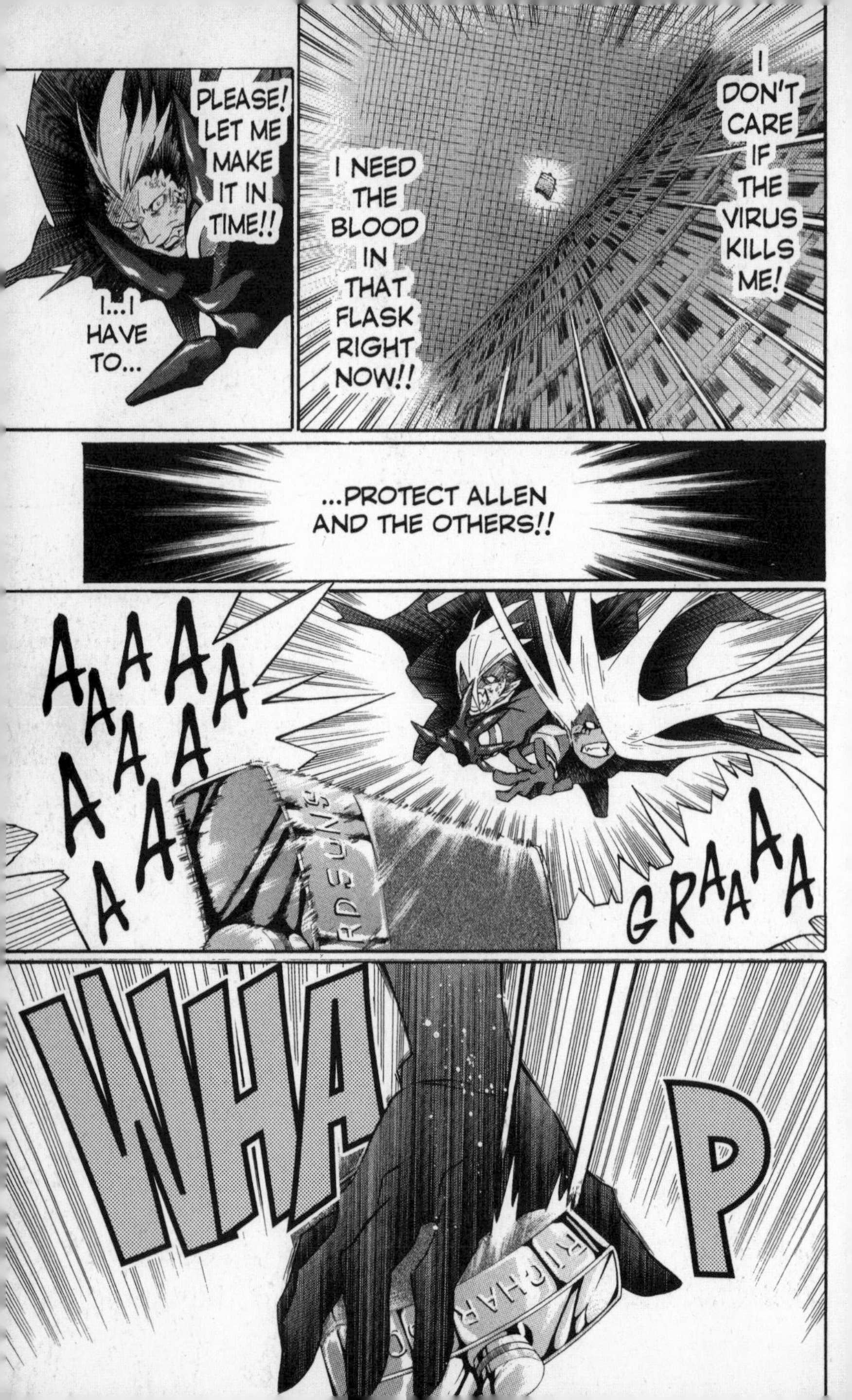

I DON'T CARE IF THE VIRUS KILLS ME!
I NEED THE BLOOD IN THAT FLASK RIGHT NOW!!
PLEASE! LET ME MAKE IT IN TIME!!
I...I HAVE TO...
...PROTECT ALLEN AND THE OTHERS!!
AAAAAAAAAA
GRAAAA
WHAP

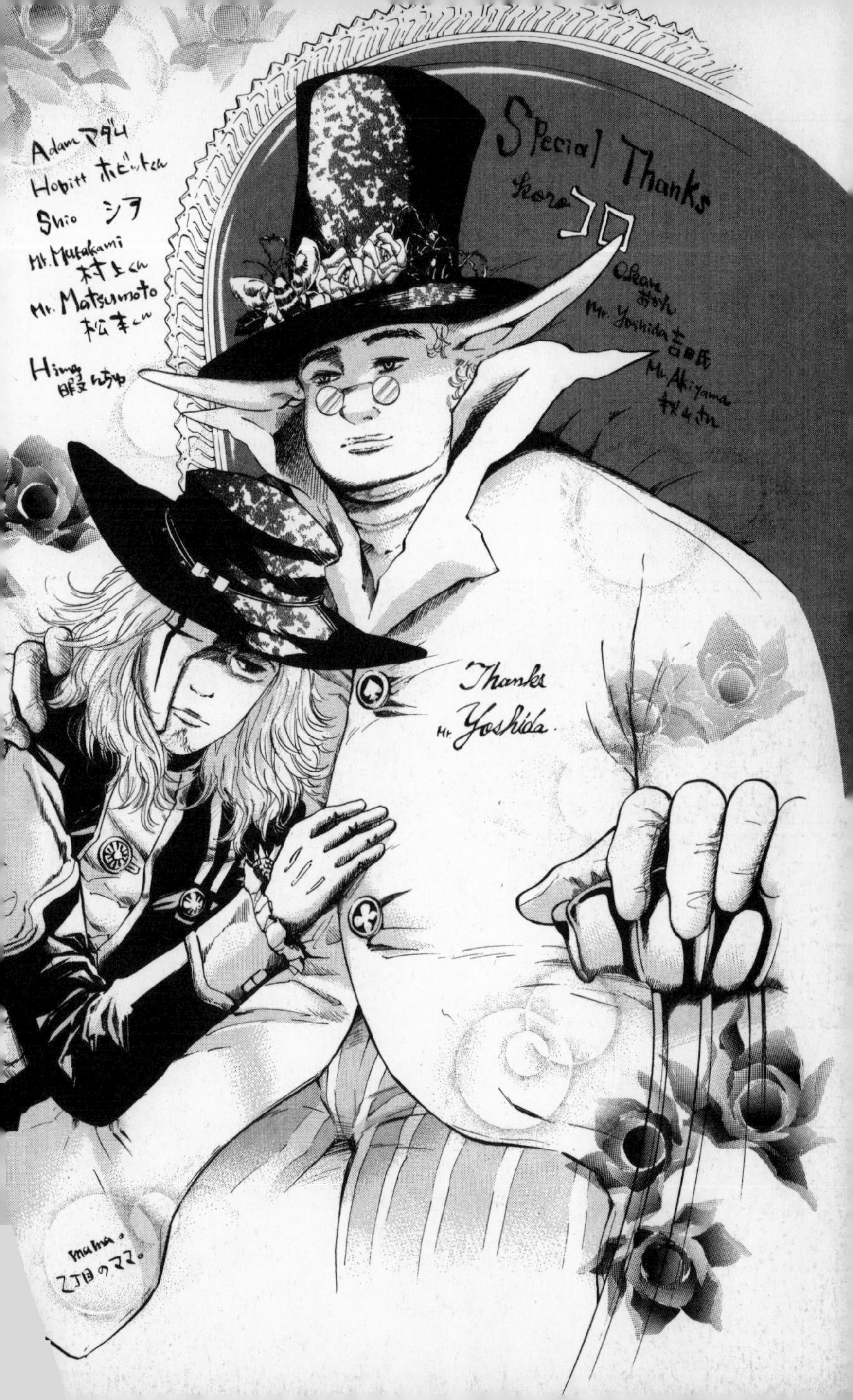
Special Thanks
Koro コロ
Okane おかん
Mr. Yoshida 吉田氏
Mr. Akiyama 秋山さん
Adam アダム
Hobitt ホビットくん
Shio シヲ
Mr. Murakami 村上くん
Mr. Matsumoto 松本くん
Hima 暇んちゃ
Thanks Mr. Yoshida.
mama. 2丁目のママ。

THE 107TH NIGHT: WHAT FLOWS OUT OF THE COFFIN...

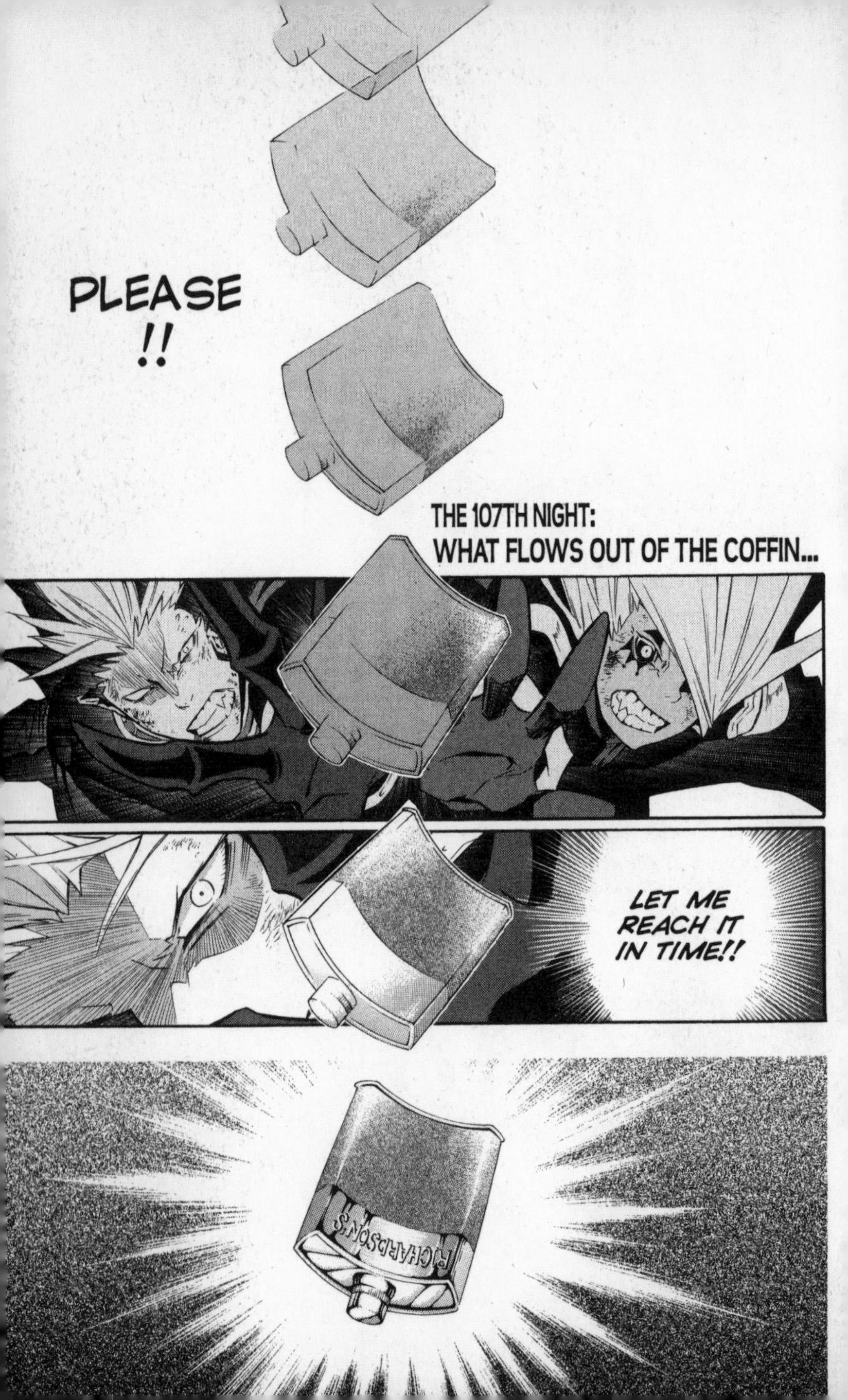
PLEASE !!
LET ME REACH IT IN TIME!!
RICHARDSON'S

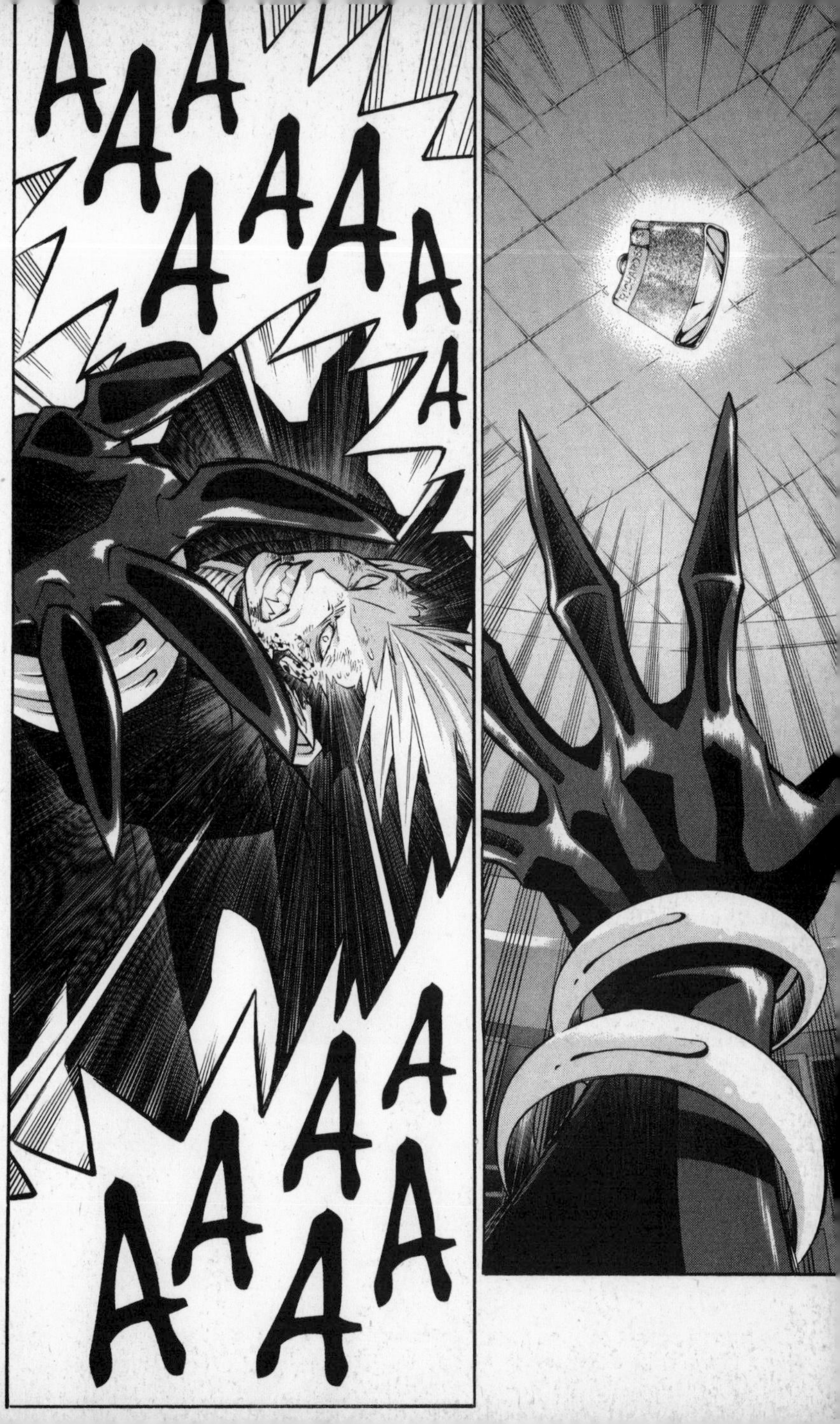
AAAAAAAAA
AAAAAAA

THE 107TH NIGHT: WHAT FLOWS OUT OF THE COFFIN...

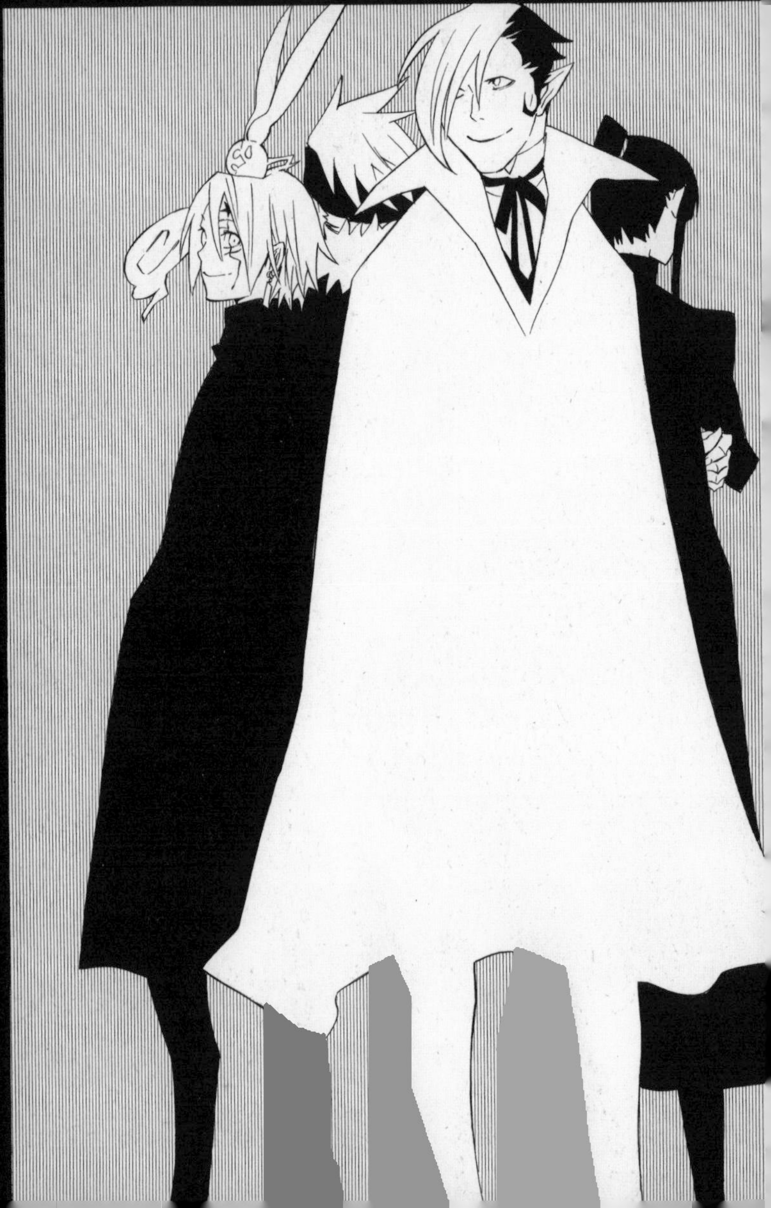

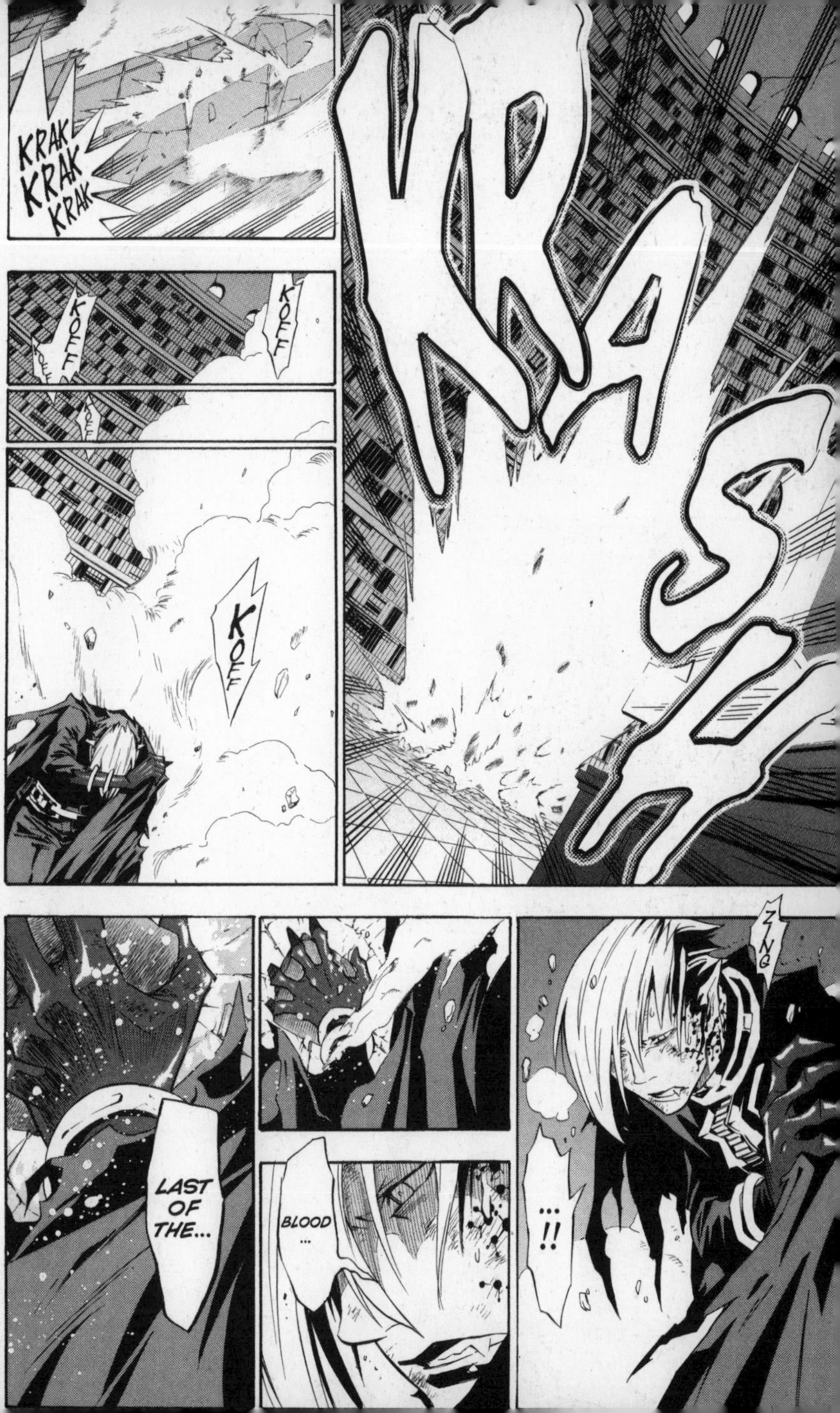

KRAK
KRAK
KRAK
KOFF
KOFF
KOFF
KOFF
KOFF
ZING
...!!
BLOOD...
LAST OF THE...

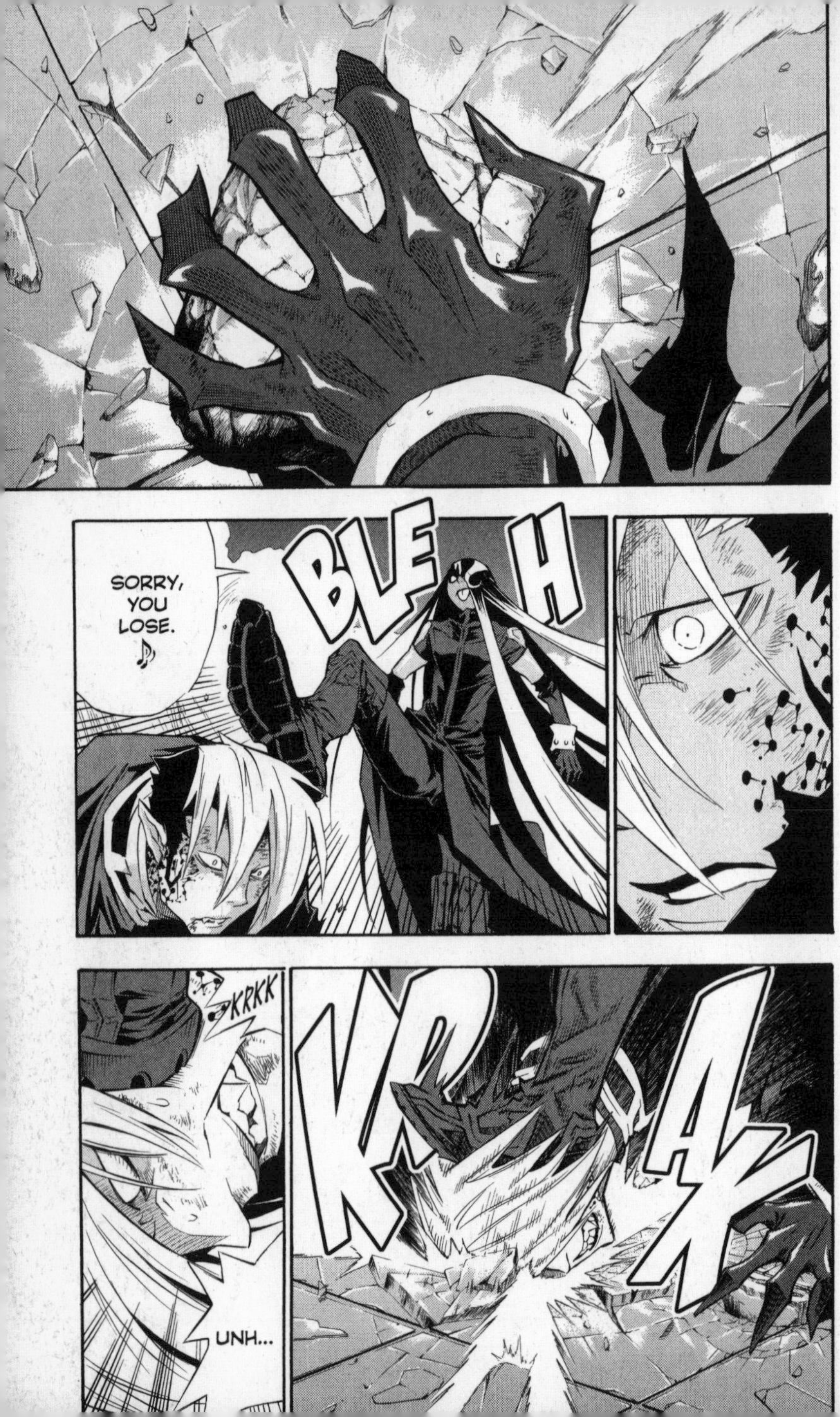

BLEH
SORRY, YOU LOSE. ♪
KRAK
KRKK
UNH...

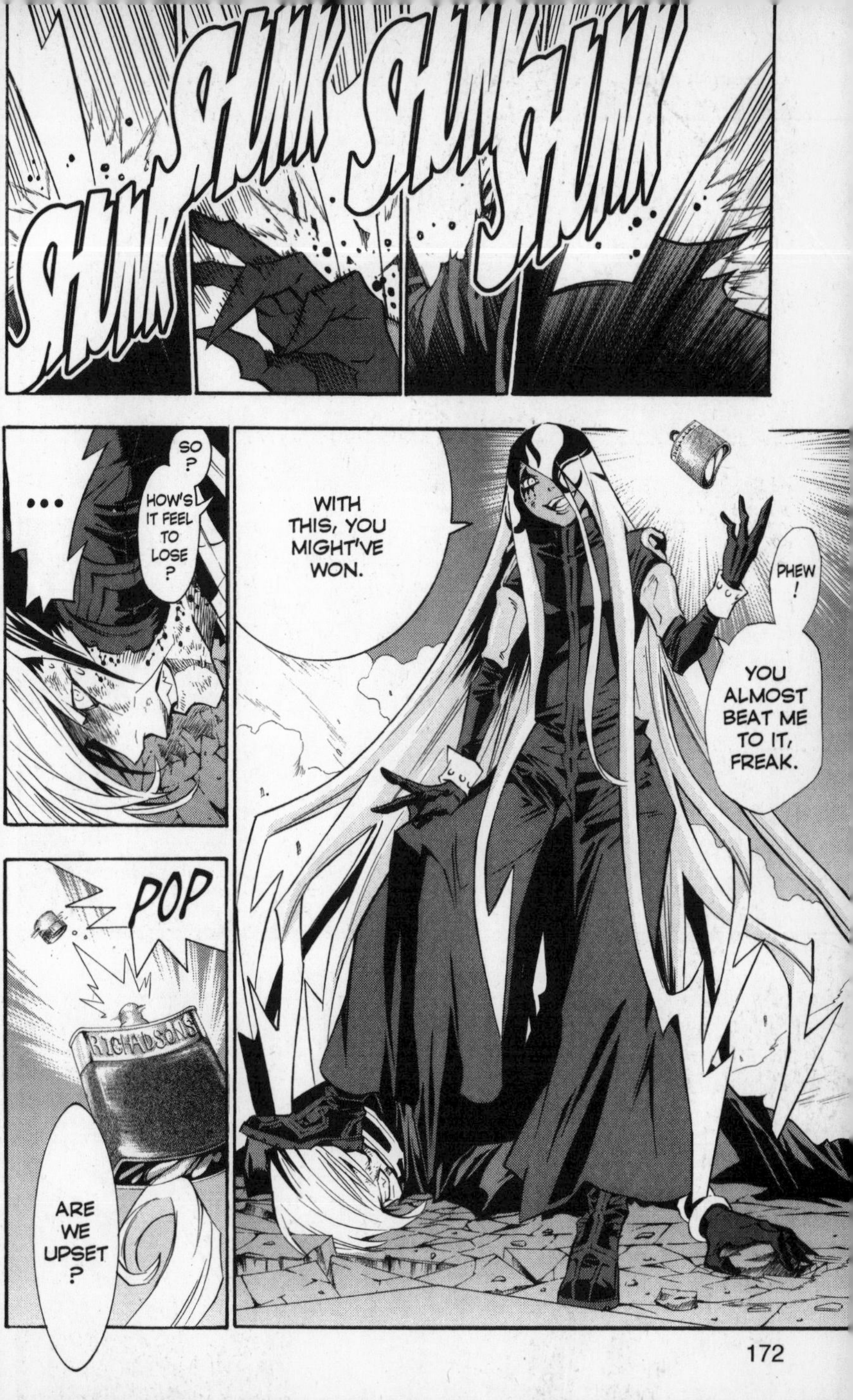
SHUNK SHUNK SHUNK SHUNK
PHEW!
YOU ALMOST BEAT ME TO IT, FREAK.
WITH THIS, YOU MIGHT'VE WON.
SO? HOW'S IT FEEL TO LOSE?
...
POP
RICHADSONS
ARE WE UPSET?

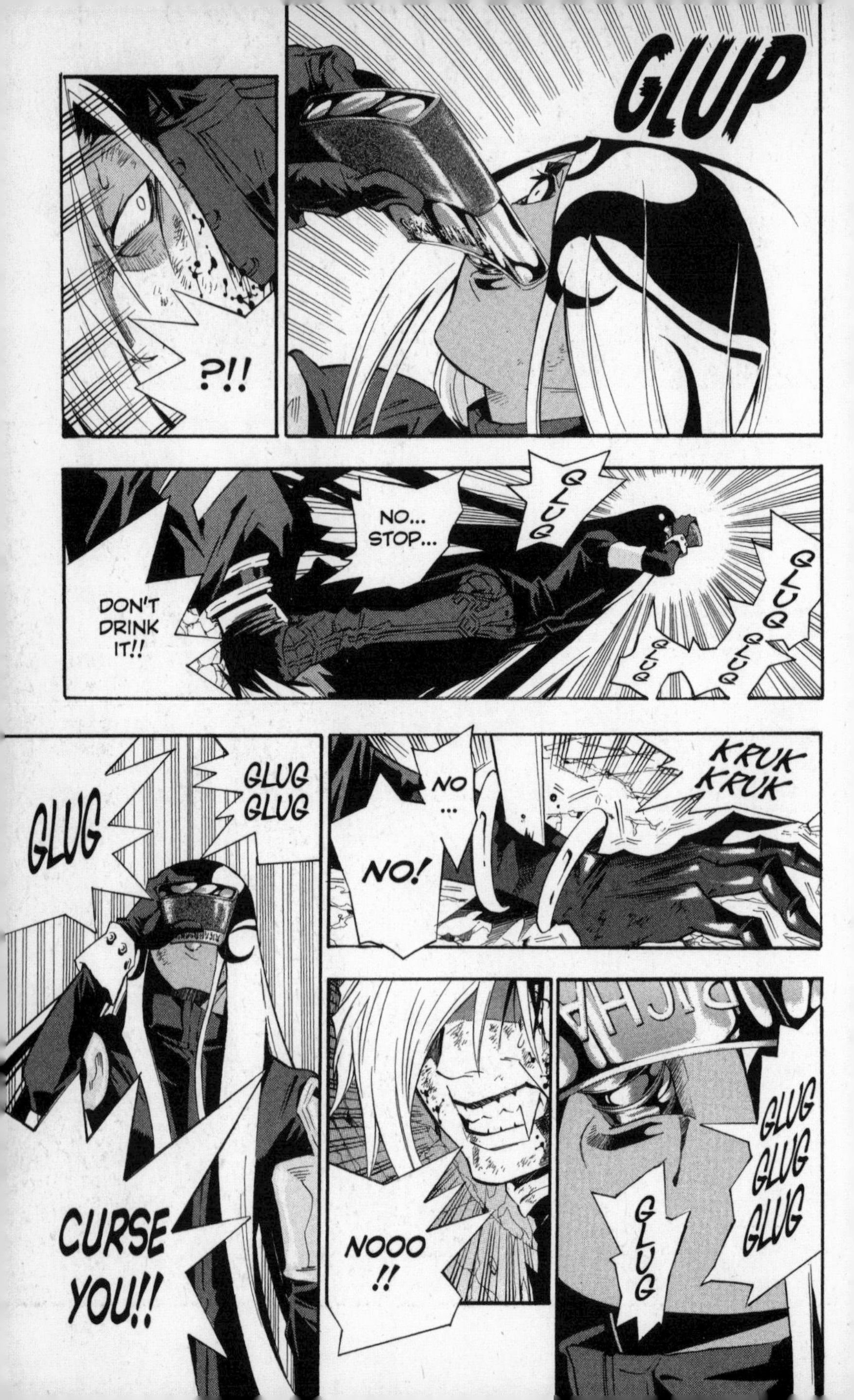
GLUP
?!!
GLUG
GLUG
GLUG
GLUG
NO... STOP...
DON'T DRINK IT!!
KRUK KRUK
NO ...
NO!
GLUG GLUG GLUG
GLUG
NOOO !!
GLUG GLUG
GLUG
CURSE YOU!!

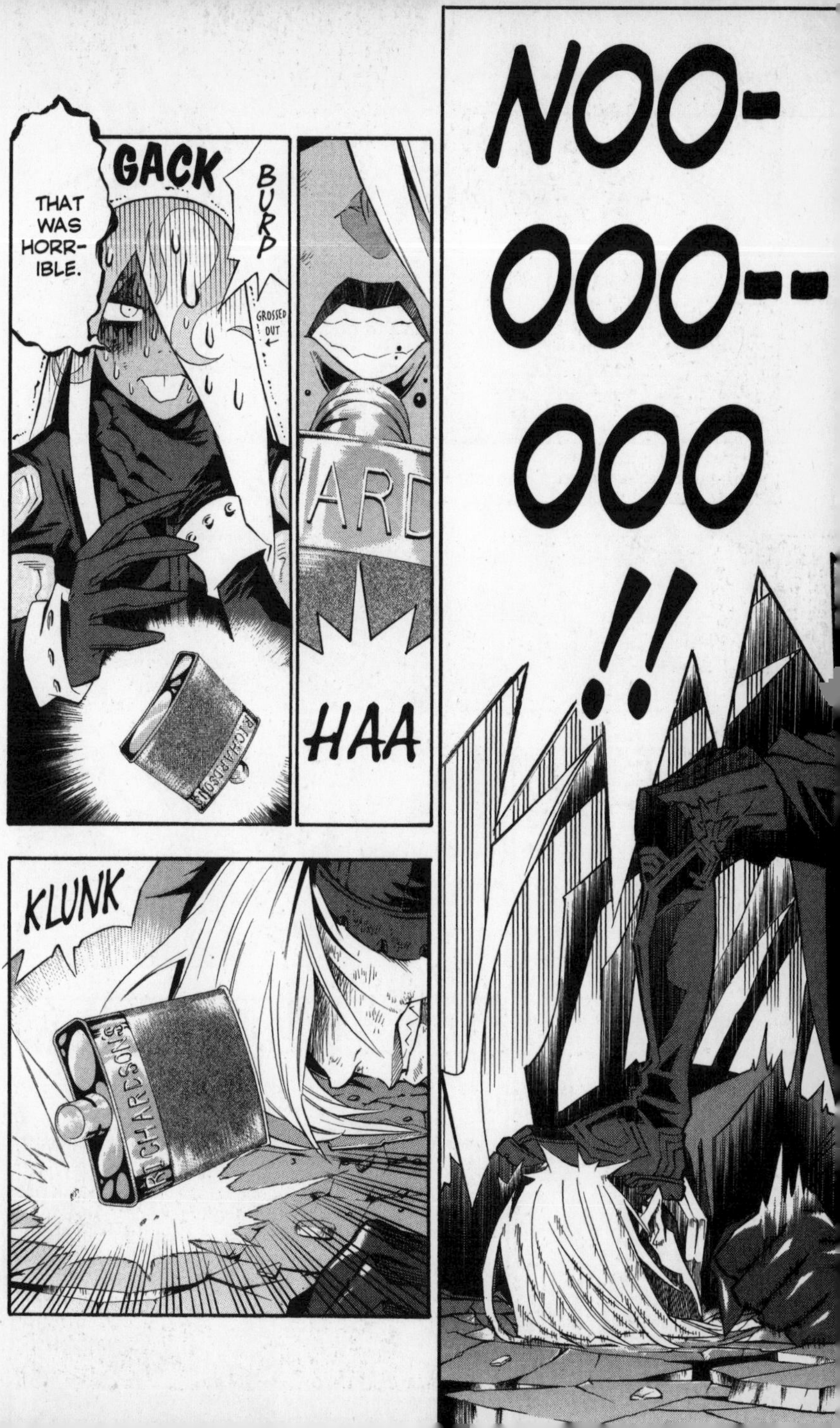
NOO-OOO--OOO!!
HAA
BURP
GACK
THAT WAS HORRIBLE.
GROSSED OUT
RICHARDSONS
KLUNK
RICHARDSONS

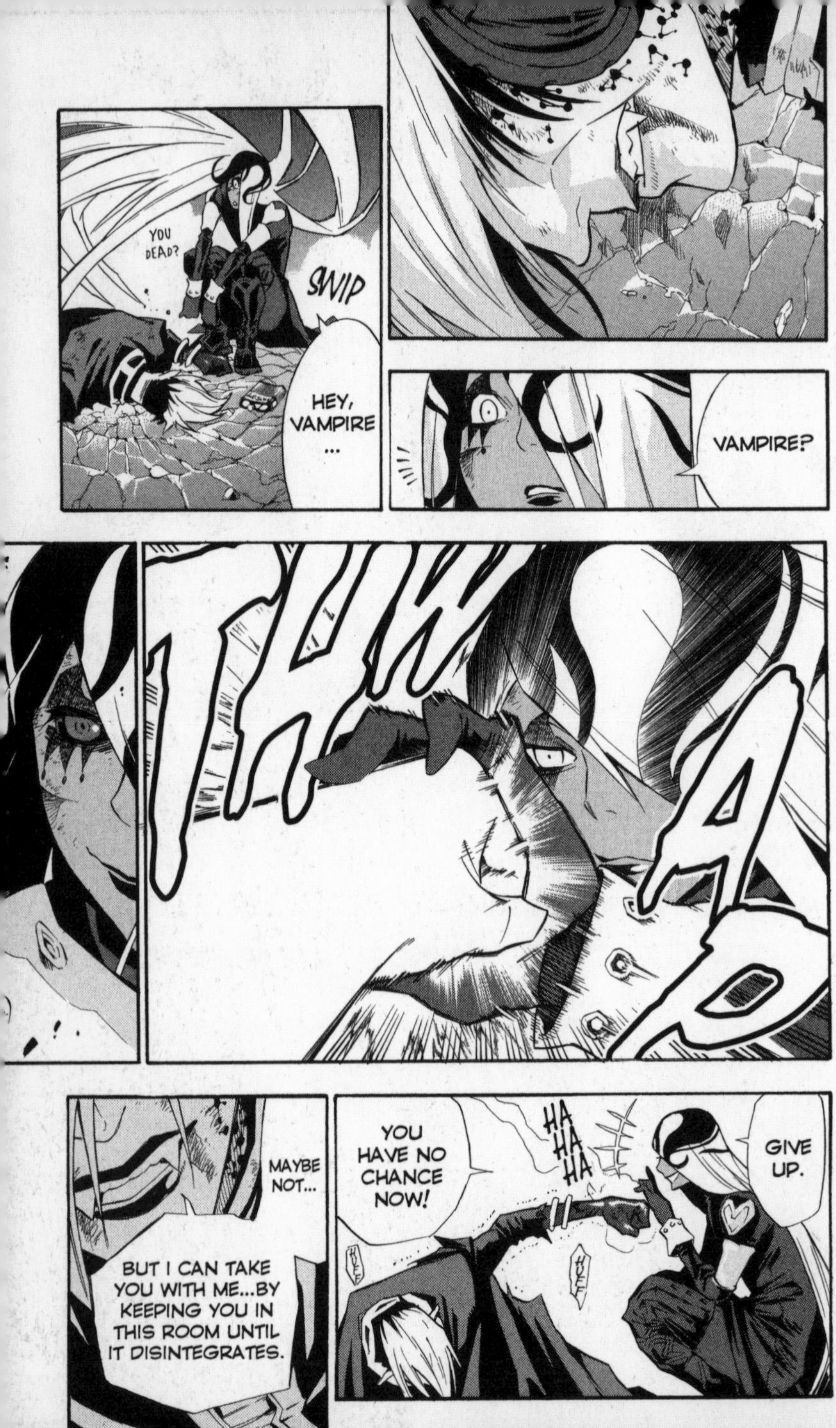
VAMPIRE?
YOU DEAD?
SWIP
HEY, VAMPIRE ...
THWAP
GIVE UP.
HA HA HA
YOU HAVE NO CHANCE NOW!
HUFF
HUFF
MAYBE NOT...
BUT I CAN TAKE YOU WITH ME...BY KEEPING YOU IN THIS ROOM UNTIL IT DISINTEGRATES.

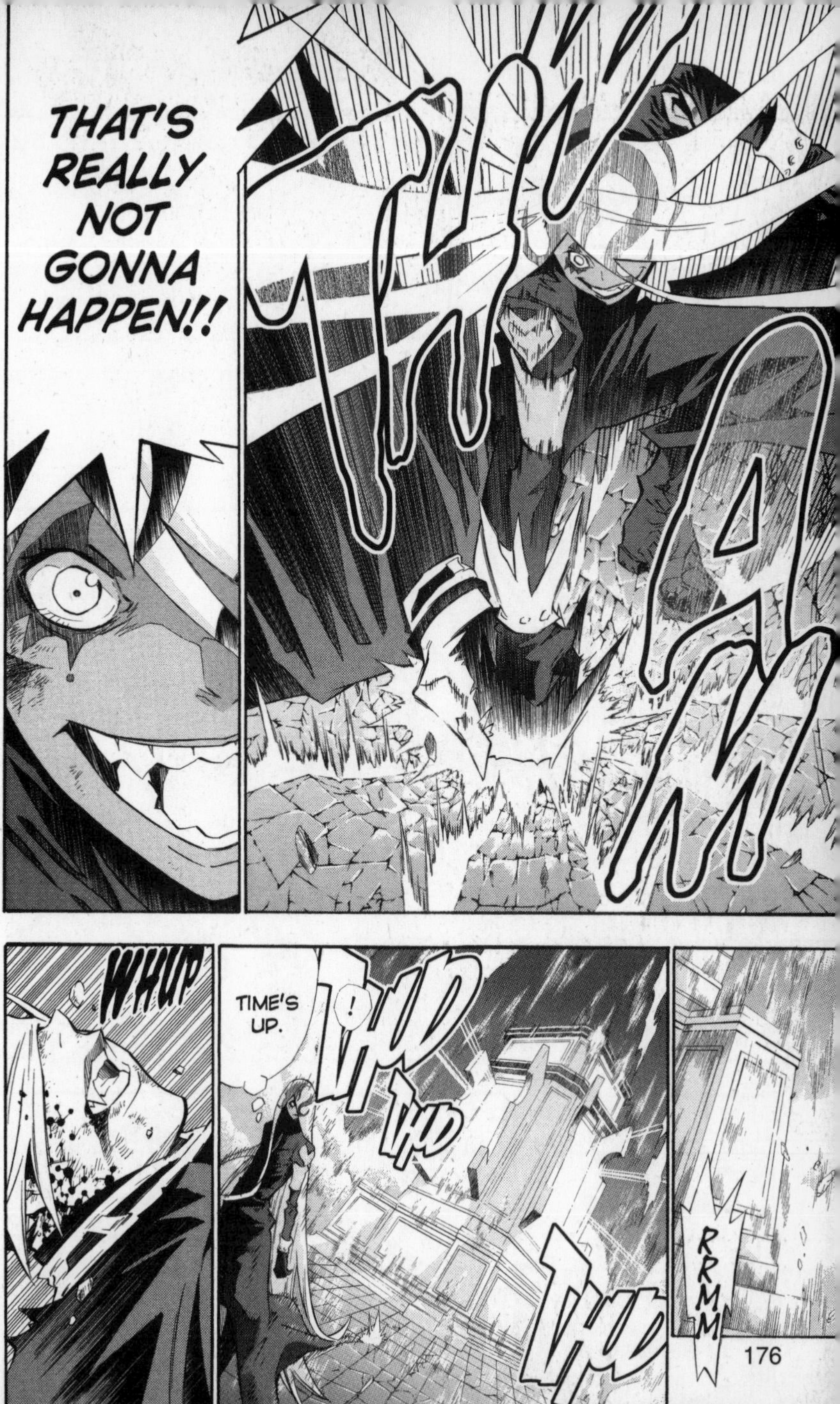
THAT'S REALLY NOT GONNA HAPPEN!!
RRMM
!
TIME'S UP.
THUD
THUD
THUD
WHUP

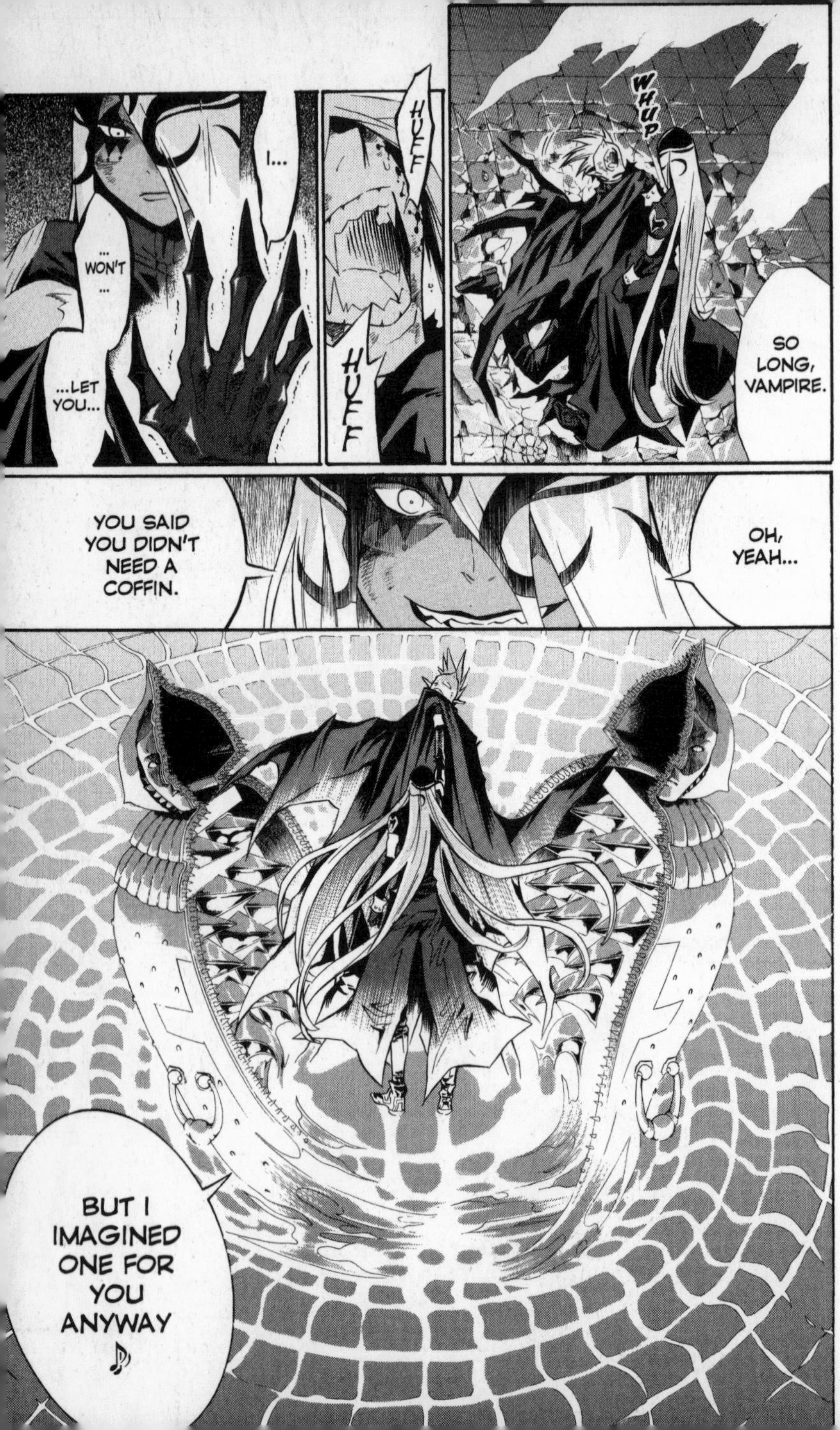
WHUP
SO LONG, VAMPIRE.
HUFF
HUFF
I...
...WON'T...
...LET YOU...
OH, YEAH...
YOU SAID YOU DIDN'T NEED A COFFIN.
BUT I IMAGINED ONE FOR YOU ANYWAY ♪

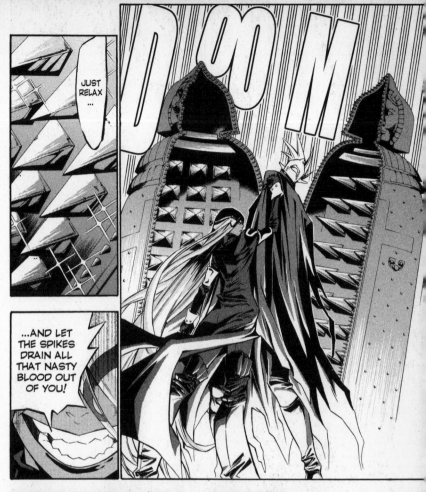

DOOM

JUST RELAX ...

...AND LET THE SPIKES DRAIN ALL THAT NASTY BLOOD OUT OF YOU!

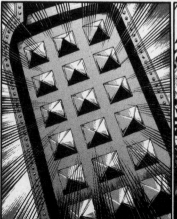

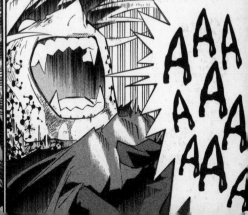

AAA
A
A
AAA

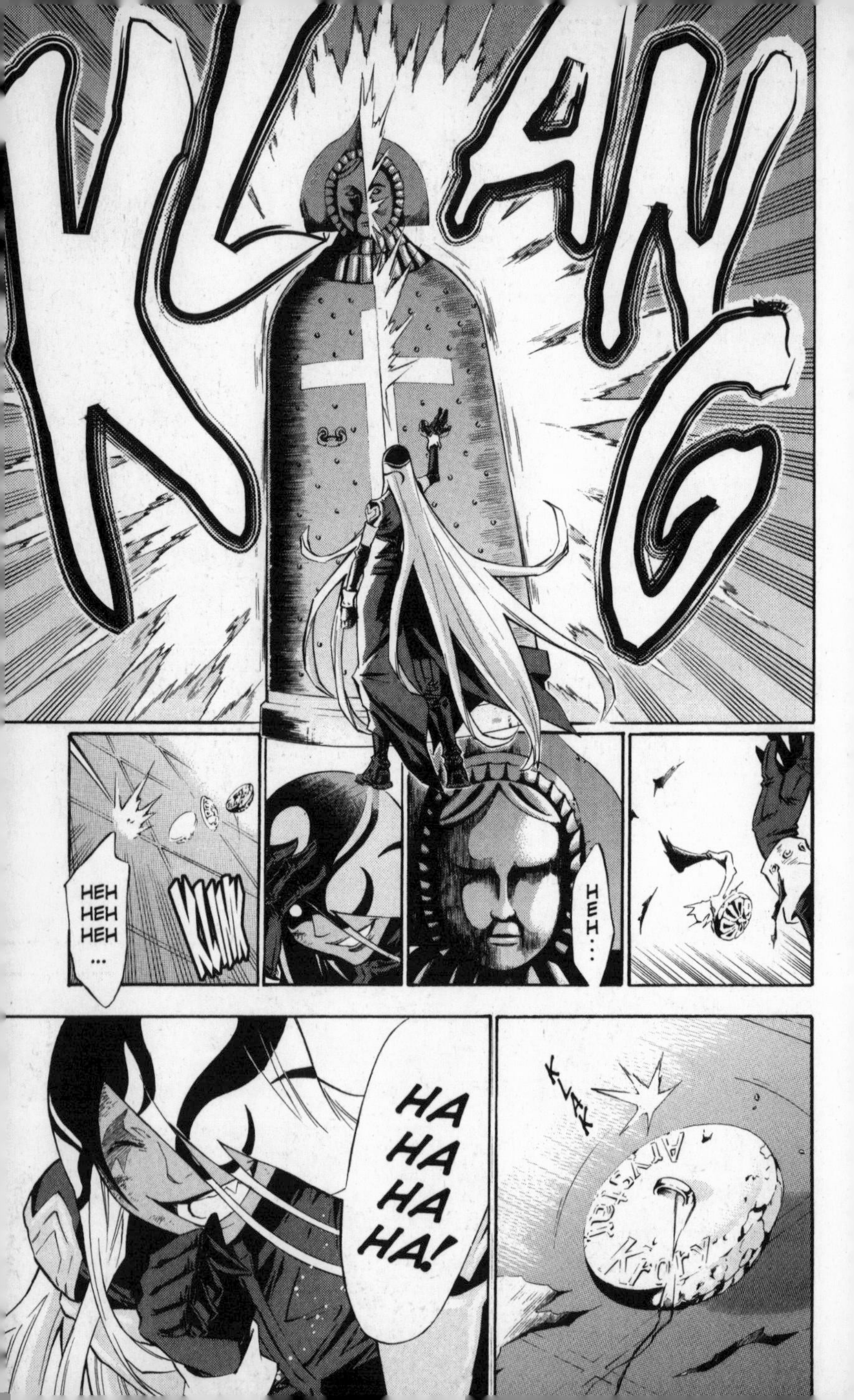
KLANG
HEH...
KLINK
HEH HEH HEH ...
K-VAK
HA HA HA HA HA!

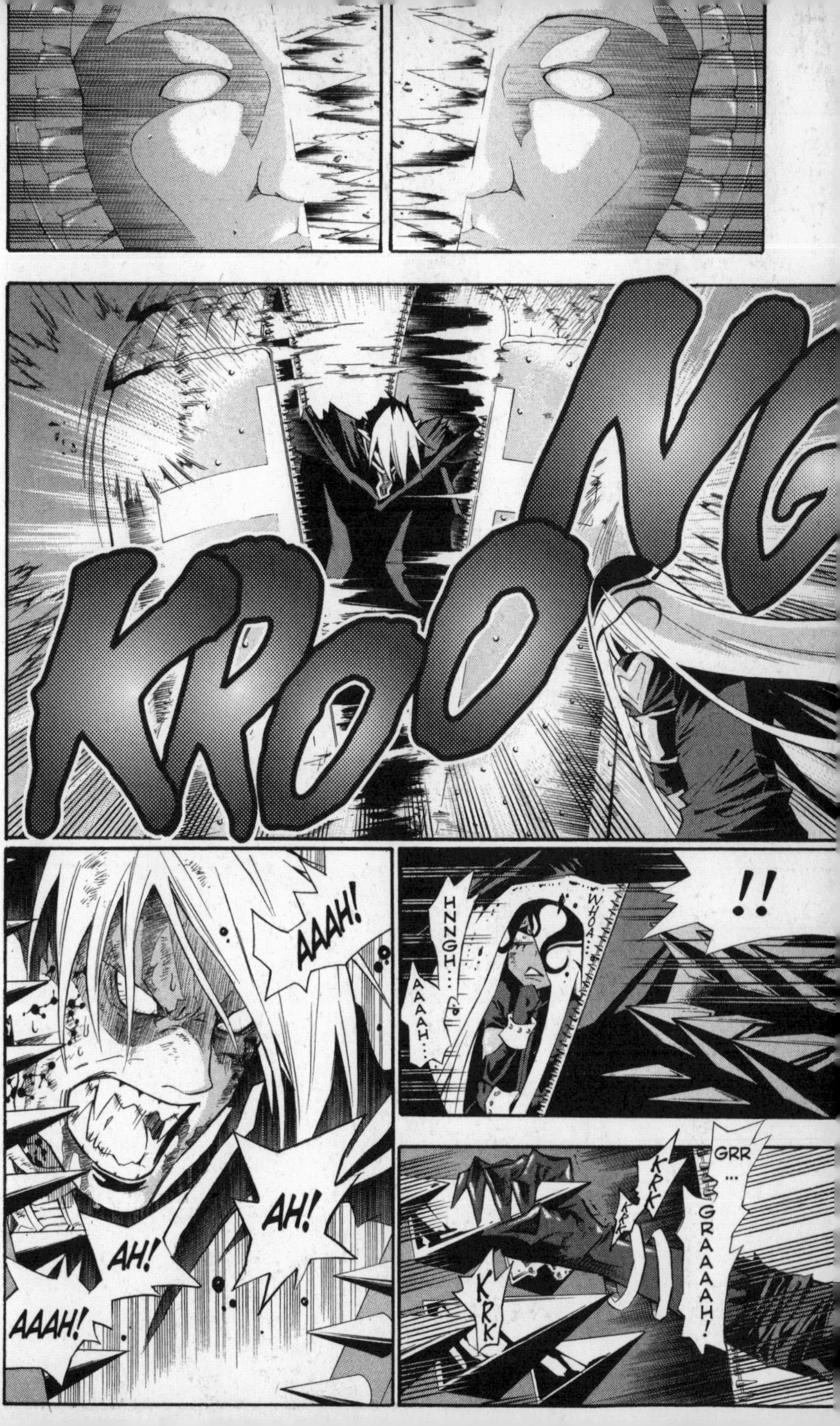
KROONG
!!
WHOA...
HNNGH...
AAAAH...
GRR ...
GRAAAAAH!
KRK
KRK
KRK
AAAH!
AH!
AH!
AAAH!

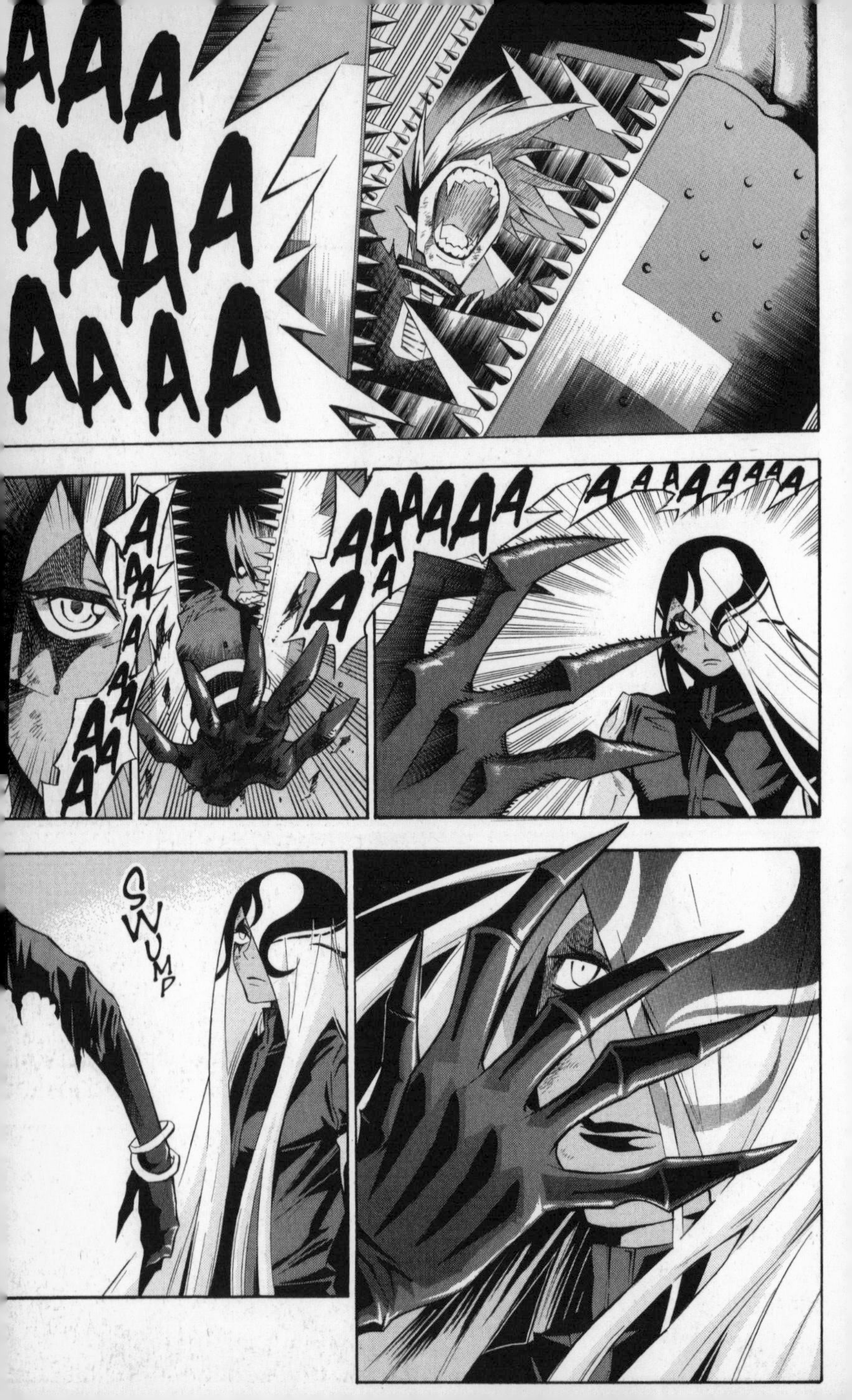
AAAAAAAAAAAAA
AAAAAAAAAAAAAAAAAA
AAAAAAAAAAAA
SWUMP

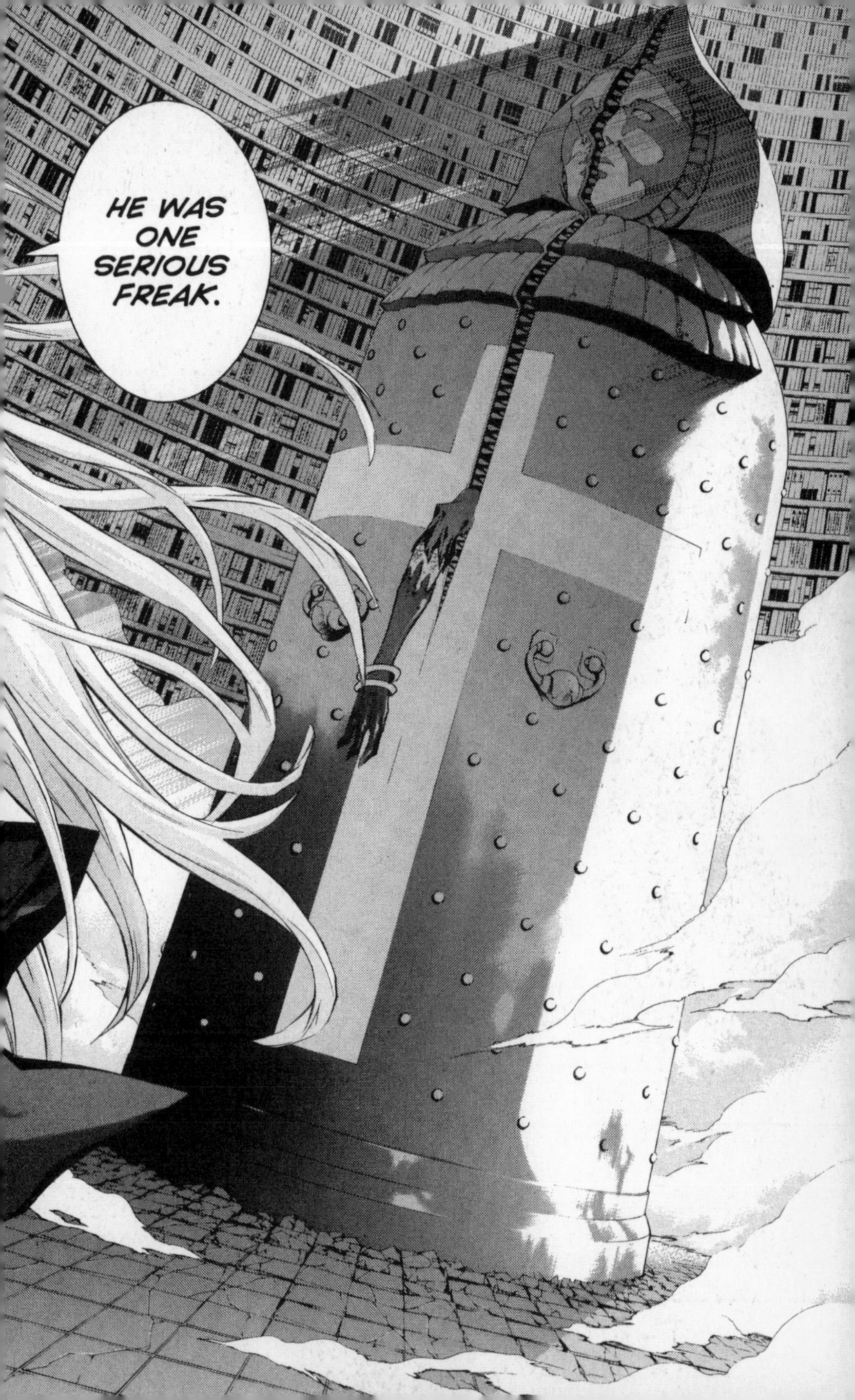
HE WAS ONE SERIOUS FREAK.

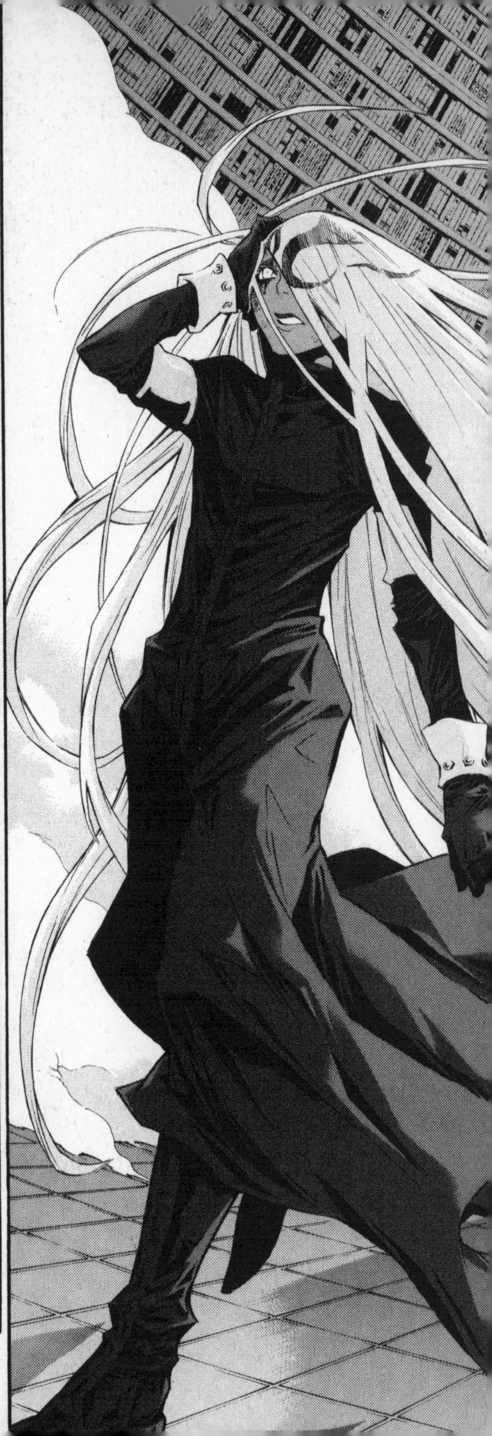

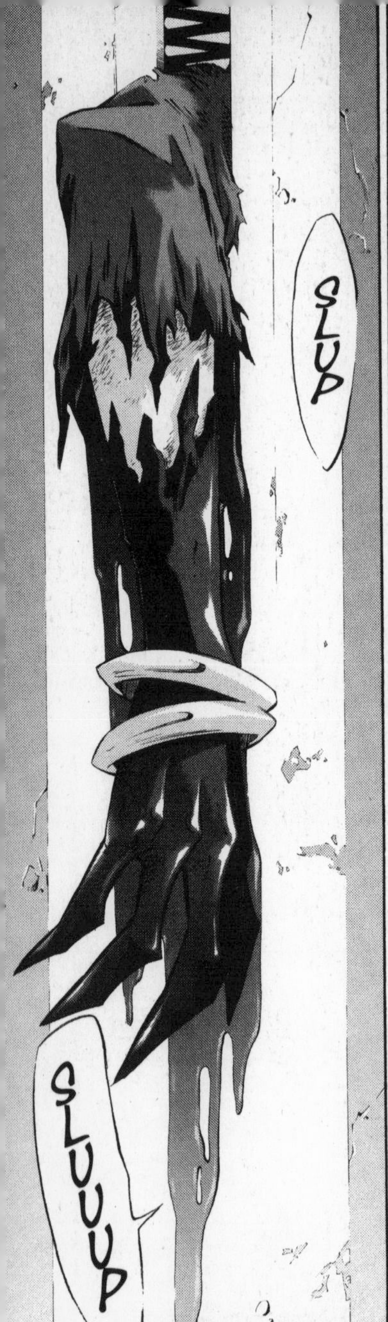
SLUP
SLUUUP

VOL. 11 FIGHT TO THE DEBT (END)

D.GRAY THEATER

THE HOSHINO FAMILY, PART 2
ART BY SOME ASSISTANT

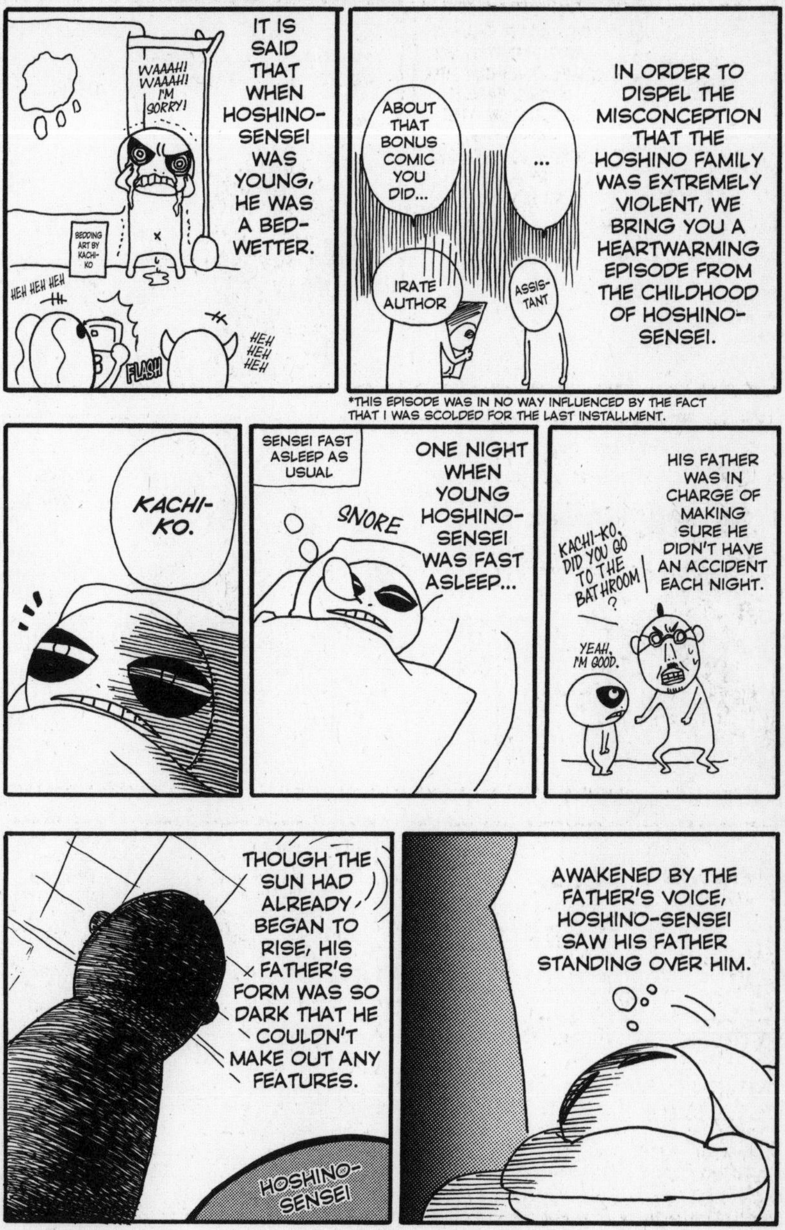

IN ORDER TO DISPEL THE MISCONCEPTION THAT THE HOSHINO FAMILY WAS EXTREMELY VIOLENT, WE BRING YOU A HEARTWARMING EPISODE FROM THE CHILDHOOD OF HOSHINO-SENSEI.
...
ABOUT THAT BONUS COMIC YOU DID...
ASSIS-TANT
IRATE AUTHOR
IT IS SAID THAT WHEN HOSHINO-SENSEI WAS YOUNG, HE WAS A BED-WETTER.
WAAAH! WAAAH! I'M SORRY!
BEDDING ART BY KACHI-KO
HEH HEH HEH
HEH HEH HEH
FLASH
*THIS EPISODE WAS IN NO WAY INFLUENCED BY THE FACT THAT I WAS SCOLDED FOR THE LAST INSTALLMENT.
HIS FATHER WAS IN CHARGE OF MAKING SURE HE DIDN'T HAVE AN ACCIDENT EACH NIGHT.
KACHI-KO, DID YOU GO TO THE BATHROOM?
YEAH, I'M GOOD.
ONE NIGHT WHEN YOUNG HOSHINO-SENSEI WAS FAST ASLEEP...
SENSEI FAST ASLEEP AS USUAL
SNORE
KACHI-KO.
AWAKENED BY THE FATHER'S VOICE, HOSHINO-SENSEI SAW HIS FATHER STANDING OVER HIM.
THOUGH THE SUN HAD ALREADY BEGAN TO RISE, HIS FATHER'S FORM WAS SO DARK THAT HE COULDN'T MAKE OUT ANY FEATURES.
HOSHINO-SENSEI

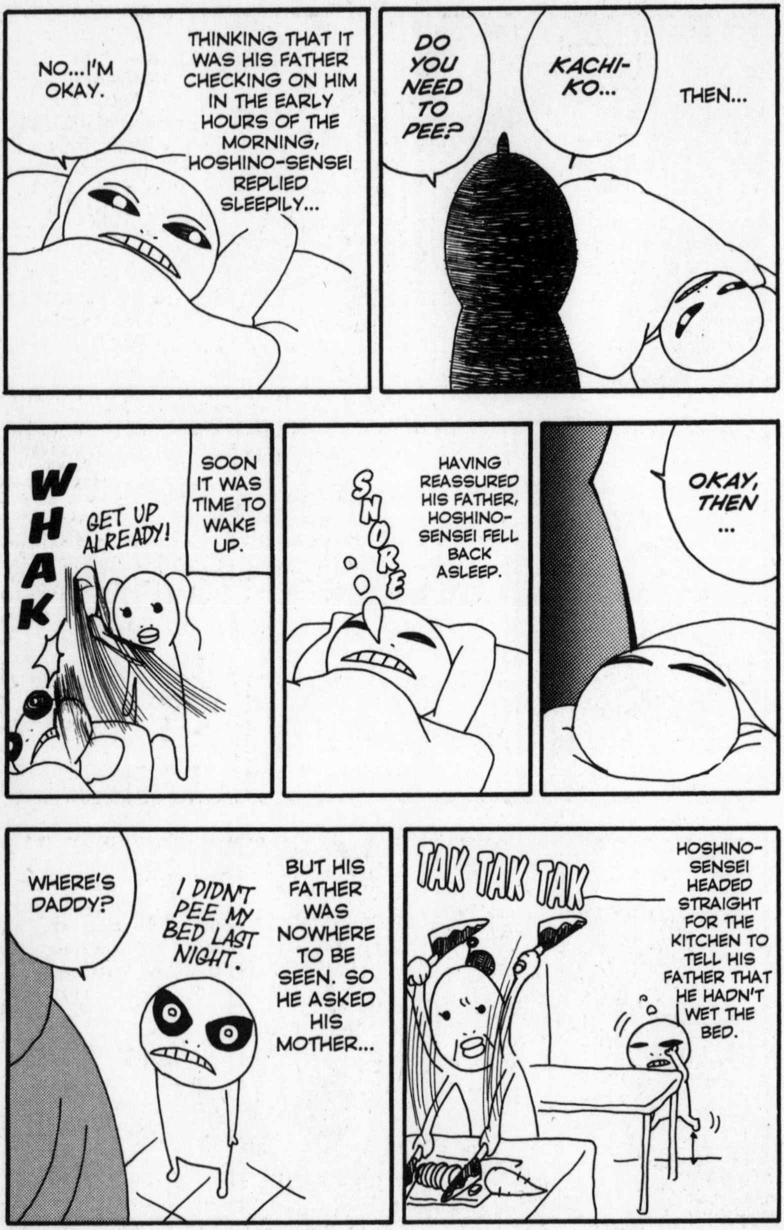
THEN...
KACHIKO...
DO YOU NEED TO PEE?
THINKING THAT IT WAS HIS FATHER CHECKING ON HIM IN THE EARLY HOURS OF THE MORNING, HOSHINO-SENSEI REPLIED SLEEPILY...
NO...I'M OKAY.
OKAY, THEN...
HAVING REASSURED HIS FATHER, HOSHINO-SENSEI FELL BACK ASLEEP.
SNORE
SOON IT WAS TIME TO WAKE UP.
GET UP ALREADY!
WHAK
HOSHINO-SENSEI HEADED STRAIGHT FOR THE KITCHEN TO TELL HIS FATHER THAT HE HADN'T WET THE BED.
TAK TAK TAK
BUT HIS FATHER WAS NOWHERE TO BE SEEN. SO HE ASKED HIS MOTHER...
I DIDN'T PEE MY BED LAST NIGHT.
WHERE'S DADDY?

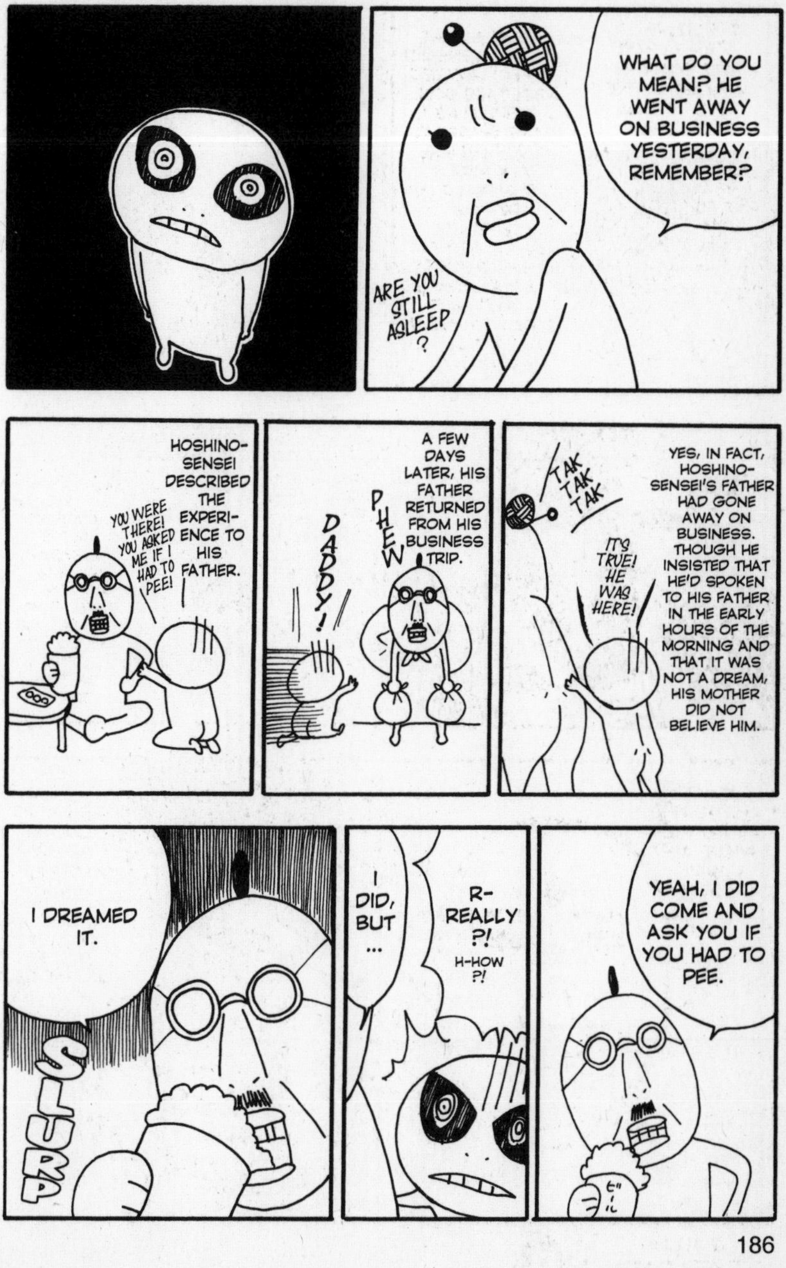
WHAT DO YOU MEAN? HE WENT AWAY ON BUSINESS YESTERDAY, REMEMBER?
ARE YOU STILL ASLEEP?
YES, IN FACT, HOSHINO-SENSEI'S FATHER HAD GONE AWAY ON BUSINESS. THOUGH HE INSISTED THAT HE'D SPOKEN TO HIS FATHER IN THE EARLY HOURS OF THE MORNING AND THAT IT WAS NOT A DREAM, HIS MOTHER DID NOT BELIEVE HIM.
TAK TAK TAK
IT'S TRUE! HE WAS HERE!
A FEW DAYS LATER, HIS FATHER RETURNED FROM HIS BUSINESS TRIP.
PHEW
DADDY!
HOSHINO-SENSEI DESCRIBED THE EXPERIENCE TO HIS FATHER.
YOU WERE THERE! YOU ASKED ME IF I HAD TO PEE!
YEAH, I DID COME AND ASK YOU IF YOU HAD TO PEE.
R-REALLY?!
H-HOW?!
I DID, BUT...
I DREAMED IT.
SLURP

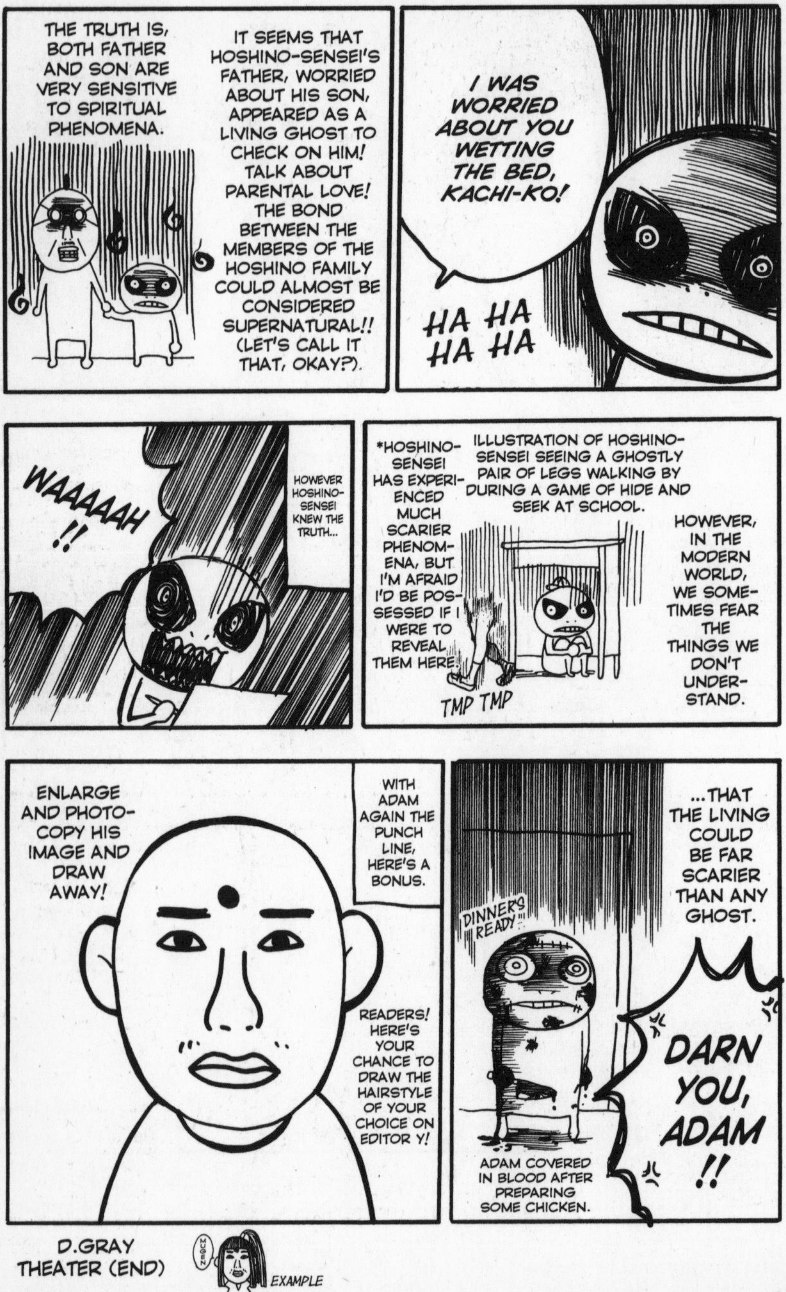
I WAS WORRIED ABOUT YOU WETTING THE BED, KACHI-KO!
HA HA HA HA
IT SEEMS THAT HOSHINO-SENSEI'S FATHER, WORRIED ABOUT HIS SON, APPEARED AS A LIVING GHOST TO CHECK ON HIM! TALK ABOUT PARENTAL LOVE! THE BOND BETWEEN THE MEMBERS OF THE HOSHINO FAMILY COULD ALMOST BE CONSIDERED SUPERNATURAL!! (LET'S CALL IT THAT, OKAY?).
THE TRUTH IS, BOTH FATHER AND SON ARE VERY SENSITIVE TO SPIRITUAL PHENOMENA.
ILLUSTRATION OF HOSHINO-SENSEI SEEING A GHOSTLY PAIR OF LEGS WALKING BY DURING A GAME OF HIDE AND SEEK AT SCHOOL.
*HOSHINO-SENSEI HAS EXPERIENCED MUCH SCARIER PHENOMENA, BUT I'M AFRAID I'D BE POSSESSED IF I WERE TO REVEAL THEM HERE.
HOWEVER, IN THE MODERN WORLD, WE SOMETIMES FEAR THE THINGS WE DON'T UNDERSTAND.
TMP TMP
HOWEVER HOSHINO-SENSEI KNEW THE TRUTH...
WAAAAAH!!
...THAT THE LIVING COULD BE FAR SCARIER THAN ANY GHOST.
DINNER'S READY!!
DARN YOU, ADAM!!
ADAM COVERED IN BLOOD AFTER PREPARING SOME CHICKEN.
WITH ADAM AGAIN THE PUNCH LINE, HERE'S A BONUS.
ENLARGE AND PHOTOCOPY HIS IMAGE AND DRAW AWAY!
READERS! HERE'S YOUR CHANCE TO DRAW THE HAIRSTYLE OF YOUR CHOICE ON EDITOR Y!
D.GRAY THEATER (END)
MUGEN
EXAMPLE

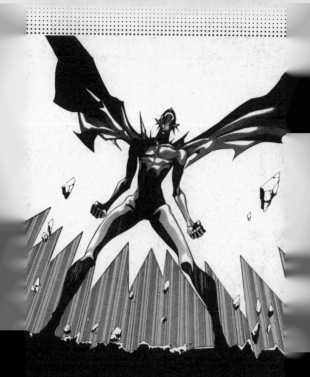

XT VOLUME...

s been bested in his battle with the newly fused and far more
i. Trapped, with seemingly no hope of escape, he receives a m
ation! His fellow exorcists, meanwhile, continue their struggle t
g Ark, unaware that one of them is coming to a new understa
why does Tyki Mikk want a nice, quiet chat with Allen?

ruary 2009!

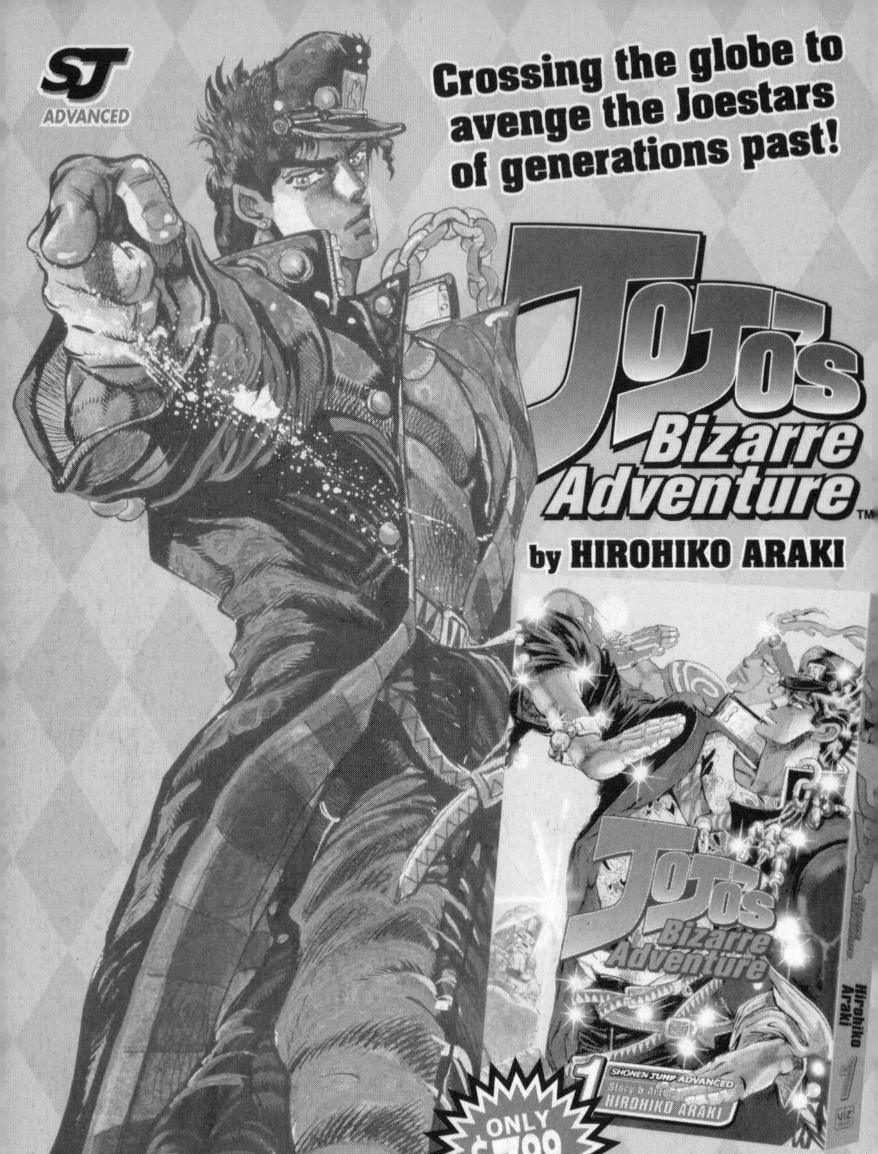
SJ ADVANCED
Crossing the globe to avenge the Joestars of generations past!
JoJo's Bizarre Adventure™
by HIROHIKO ARAKI
JoJo's Bizarre Adventure
1
SHONEN JUMP ADVANCED
HIROHIKO ARAKI
Hirohiko Araki
ONLY $7.99
Manga series on sale now

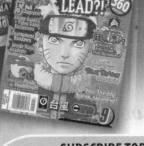
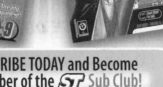

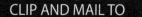